Nov 12, 2003

To Sue,
   I hope that you enjoy reading
this true blue Duke story,
       Leonard Rogoff
       Adjunct Professor of
       Southern Jewish History
       Duke University

Homelands

Judaic Studies Series

Leon J. Weinberger

General Editor

Homelands

Southern Jewish Identity in
Durham and Chapel Hill, North Carolina

❧ Leonard Rogoff

The University of Alabama Press
Tuscaloosa and London

9 8 7 6 5 4 3 2 1
09 08 07 06 05 04 03 02 01

Text design by Yuko Tanaka
Typeface is Bembo

∞
The paper on which this book is printed meets
the minimum requirements of American National
Standard for Information Science–Permanence of
Paper for Printed Library Materials, ANSI Z39.48-1984.

Library of Congress Cataloging-in-Publication Data

Rogoff, Leonard.
   Homelands : southern Jewish identity in Durham and Chapel Hill,
North Carolina / Leonard Rogoff.
      p.   cm. — (Judaic studies series)
Includes bibliographical references and index.
   ISBN 0-8173-1055-X (alk. paper)
   1. Jews—North carolina—Durham Metropolitan Area—History.
2. Jews—North carolina—Durham Metropolitan Area—Identity.
3. Durham Metropolitan Area (N.C.)—Ethnic relations.   I. Title.
II. Judaic studies series (Unnumbered)
   F264.D9 R66 2001
   975.6′563004924—dc21
                       00-012598

British Library Cataloguing-in-Publication Data available

Contents

Tables

Acknowledgments

Homelands: Southern Jewish Identity in Durham and Chapel Hill, North Carolina was originally commissioned by a Centennial Publications Committee as part of a program to celebrate the one-hundredth anniversary of the Durham–Chapel Hill Jewish community. The first intention had been to publish a commemorative history, memorializing and honoring those who had built the Jewish community. As the project evolved, the decision was made to publish an interpretive social history. In refining our purpose, and to promote readability, we edited many names. Those interested in genealogy or family history may wish to consult the Rare Book, Manuscript, and Special Collections Library at Perkins Library at Duke University, which holds taped interviews and documentary material that served as the basis for this book. To reduce the bulk of the endnotes, references to the interviews are cited in the text and listed in the bibliography rather than placed in the footnotes.

Many volunteers contributed to the oral histories that formed this text. I thank them as well as those who consented to be interviewed. Their names are recorded in the bibliography, and I apologize to any who have been overlooked. I also owe profound thanks to the staffs of the North Carolina State Archives in Raleigh, the Duke Archives and the Manuscript Room at the Perkins Library at Duke University, the North Carolina Collection at Durham County Library, and the Southern Historical Collection and the North Carolina Collection at the Wilson Library at the University of North Carolina. I am grateful for their help and interest, and their cordiality added to the pleasure of my research.

I am indebted to several others who prepared the ground for this history. First, I thank Dr. Sheldon Hanft of Appalachian State University, who was instrumental in organizing this project and establishing the research and interview procedures. Sydney Nathans guided the oral history and prepared the questionnaire. Sigmund Meyer, who lived in Durham for three quarters of a century, compiled a Jewish community history in 1951 that proved invaluable. Nathan Summerfield, grandson of a community founder, patiently responded to my many inquiries and took a deep personal interest in the project. Leon Dworsky, who seems to forget nothing, was an invaluable resource. Robin Gruber, a Duke University undergraduate, wrote a 1986 thesis, "From Pine Street to Watts Street: An Oral History of the Jews of Durham, North Carolina." She kindly granted permission to listen to her oral history tapes. I have benefited very greatly from Mark Bauman's critical readings of this manuscript. I thank the Johns Hopkins University Press for permission to cite from "Jewish Proletarians in the New South: The Durham Cigarette Rollers," *American Jewish History Journal* 82, nos. 1–4 (1994):141–58, © American Jewish Historical Society; the University of Alabama Press for "Divided Together: Jewish and African-American Relations in Durham, North Carolina," in *Quiet Voices: Southern Rabbis and Black Civil Rights,* edited by Mark Bauman and Berkley Kalin, Tuscaloosa: University of Alabama Press, 1997; the Southern Jewish Historical Society for "Synagogue and Jewish Church: A Congregational History of North Carolina," *Southern Jewish History* 1 (1998):43–82; and for citations from the R. G. Dun & Co. ledgers, Dun & Bradstreet and the Historical Collections Department of Baker Library, Harvard Business School.

The members of the Centennial Publications Committee—Eric Meyers, Sydney Nathans, Albert Heyman, Judith Ruderman, Herb Posner, and Steve Schewel—have been most patient. I especially wish to thank Steve Schewel for the thankless task of managing this enterprise and for his patience in seeing it to fruition. I wish to remember Elise Light, Gibby Katz, and Art Shain, who did so much to create the community documented in these pages. *Homelands* was supported with generous assistance from the Sara and E. J. Evans Family Foundation, the Blumenthal Foundation, Beth El Congregation, and the Durham–Chapel Hill Jewish Federation and Community Council. I also thank the Rosenzweig Museum and Jewish Heritage Foundation of North Carolina for a grant that assisted publication. And most of all, I thank my wife, Joan Lenowitz, for her love, help, and patience and my children, Lilah and Aaron, for suffering through this enterprise. I dedicate this book in loving memory of my parents, Nathan Rogoff and Selma Drexler Rogoff.

I Introduction
More or Less Southern

*The more Southern the person is, the less Jewish; the more Jewish the
person is, the less Southern.*
—Carolyn Walker-Lipson, *Shalom Y'All: The Folklore and Culture of Southern Jews*

*By being more "Southern"—that is, by participating in organized
religious activities—Southern Jews are at the same time more "Jewish."*
—John Shelton Reed, *One South: An Ethnic Approach to Regional Culture*

The South is no one place, and there are many ways to be a Jew. The
Jewish experience in the South evokes such terms as *ambivalence,
paradox,* and *contradiction.* "Who is a southerner?" and "who is a
Jew?" are sufficiently complex questions without the added complication
of asking "who is a southern Jew?" Southerners and Jews are Americans,
too, although both peoples have often found themselves outside the national mainstream.

Describing identity is an especially unstable process for southern Jews,
who are highly mobile and multinational in origin. Across the four centuries of Jewish settlement in North Carolina, Jews have constantly renegotiated and reinvented identities for themselves. Identity is not a fixed,
unchanging essence but is created and re-created in response to new circumstances. Given the length and variety of Jewish experience, historians
now question whether a normative Judaism can be described or whether
a monolithic Jewish essence can be defined. Nor is the South easy to place.
From the contours of its geography to the ethnicity of its people the
South has eluded easy definition. Neither is the American aspect of their
identities a fixed commodity. To be an American requires not membership
in a race or an ethnic group but allegiance to a democratic creed. Yet, in
contrast to this Enlightenment ideal, to be an American for much of this
country's history meant assimilation into white, Anglo-Saxon, Protestant
culture. Jews, however, resisted a total blending even as they melted in the
American pot. Jews have been exemplary multiculturalists.

Did local Jews identify themselves as southerners? If so, at what histori-cal point did this happen? In response to what circumstances did this oc-cur? Did they blend their southern experience into their collective Jewish memory? Were they different from other American Jews and non-Jewish southerners?

The Durham–Chapel Hill Jewish community formed in the 1880s and 1890s when the South, emerging from Reconstruction, and Jewry, under-going a massive immigration, were both reordering their societies. Jews wrote themselves into the southern narrative even as the South was re-writing its own past. Some Jews assimilated through intermarriage and conversion and became wholly southern, just as some native southern Christians joined the Jewish people, but the trajectory of the community as a whole was toward integration, not assimilation. A double-structured model of identity emphasizes the "interplay" between the newcomers and the host society; the immigrant group retains its ethnic difference but constantly renegotiates its relations with the larger society as it blends old and new.[1] In building a synagogue, for example, Jews created a place to preserve their traditions and collective identity, but the synagogue also served as a "Jewish church" that established the Jews' place as small-town southerners. Jews lived comfortably with the contradictions of being both provincial southerners who were citizens and neighbors in their home-town and cosmopolitans who were members of a global Jewish commu-nity. Indeed, identity is more than double. "Home" meant Durham or Chapel Hill, but it could also mean Baltimore, Vilna, and Jerusalem.

Mark Bauman, in *The Southern as American: Jewish Style* argues that the regional culture affected Jews in only a "relatively marginal fashion." The southern Jewish story, he observes, is more similar to the narrative of American Jewry than to the history of white southern Protestants. Behind Bauman's question is the contentious issue of southern identity itself. Is the South merely a "regional variant" of America, distinctive only in climate and weather? Or is the South—with its history of slavery and secession, its racial codes, its languid accents, and its rich folk life—distinct among American regions?[2] Historians and sociologists who insist on southern ex-ceptionalism have been disputatious as they attempt to inventory the at-tributes that distinguish the region and its people from the American mainstream.

Jews, as a mercantile, mythically wandering people, offer a counterhis-tory to the southern narrative of a rooted, agrarian people. In the Jewish narrative their southern sojourn was but one scene in a long drama of migration that opened in ancient Palestine and was last set, for most, in central and eastern Europe. Despite their geographical dispersion Jews over the course of four millennia maintained rituals, language, and communal bonds that kept their ancient past ever present. Nevertheless, Jewry was undergoing a political emancipation and acculturation in the nineteenth century that was challenging its peoplehood and religious traditionalism.

In the South Jews resided among another ethnic group, white southerners, whose principal attributes, orthodox Christianity and Anglo-Saxon heritage, seemingly precluded them from membership. Southern codes of hospitality graciously welcomed Jews, but the South, as Leo Frank tragically learned, was also the most violent of America's regions. Regional types include both the courtly southern gentleman and the night-riding Klansman. Entering a bipolar racial society, Jews found themselves straddling the color line in the southern hierarchy of place. Jews were an urban and commercial people, whereas southerners, even as they embraced industrialization, held nostalgically to the romantic mythology of the plantation ideal. Jews wandered in search of opportunity while southerners defined themselves locally in terms of soil and kinship. The southerners' "regional patriotism"—with their own flag, anthem, heroes, and holidays —was outside the historical experience of most local Jews, who were first- or second-generation immigrants.[3]

Historiography has tended to focus on the Germans as representative figures of southern Jewry. These nineteenth-century pioneers rapidly acculturated as southerners, and the region became a bastion of a distinctly American Reform Judaism. Indeed, Classical Reform is usually taken as the normative religion of the southern Jew. As historian Lee Shai Weissbach notes, however, communities that survived into the twentieth century were mostly east European.[4]

The question of southern-Jewish identity, Bauman notes, depends ultimately on a comparison of "sub-regional subtleties."[5] Durham–Chapel Hill is a prototype of the east European settlements that emerged across the region with the rise of the industrial New South. Migrations constantly reconstituted the community and reconstructed its identity. In the way of context this study begins with a precommunity history that traces the isolated, transient individuals of Sephardic and German origin who came to the agrarian Old South. The Polish, Russian, and Ukrainian immigrants who came in the late-nineteenth and early-twentieth centuries held on to their *Yiddishkeit* (ethnic Jewishness) and their links to an international Jewry even as they established homes in the North Carolina

Piedmont. Baltimore, Richmond, and New York became surrogate homelands that supplied the Durham–Chapel Hill colony with credit, merchandise, rabbis, spouses, and kosher food. Establishing a niche as mercantile
middlemen, Jews integrated economically before gaining social and civic
acceptance. The children of these east European immigrants who persisted
in the South began constructing an identity as southern Jews.

In the past thirty years the Sunbelt has drawn southward unprecedentedly large numbers of Jews among other migrants. If Jews had once been
reluctant to settle in the benighted South of racism, poverty, illiteracy,
and disease, they flocked to a mythic, superior Sunbelt, the economically
ascendant region with an enviable quality of life.[6] Jews have been in
the vanguard of an emerging multiethnic South. With the Sunbelt migration, southern culture is attenuating as the region becomes more like the
nation.

If *southern* and *Jew* are unstable terms, so, too, is *small town*. Nearly one-
quarter of the turn-of-the-century Jewish immigrants to America settled
outside metropolitan areas. Much of local Jewry's identity can be explained through the small-town rather than the regional factor. The Union
of American Hebrew Congregations defines small-town Jewry as having
one temple and less than 150 families. A recent anthology, *Jews in Small
Towns: Legends and Legacies,* uses a general population of twenty-five thousand as a criterion.[7] Durham–Chapel Hill's small-town character thus
needs qualification. By the 1920s Durham's population exceeded twenty-
five thousand, and in 1961 a second congregation formed. The small town
yielded to a mid-sized city and then to a Sunbelt metropolitan area. The
Jewish community, which had numbered less than four hundred from
1890 to 1950, totaled more than thirty-three hundred in 1990. Durham
and Chapel Hill are now two points of the Research Triangle metropolitan area of one million people. The area is highly representative of the
changing Jewish demography as Jews move southward from the north and
midwest.

Although Jewish numbers and percentages of the Durham–Chapel Hill
population seem small at any moment, the number of Jews who claim
southern-Jewish experience is far greater because of constant population
turnover. Moreover, the combined Jewish student bodies of Duke University and the University of North Carolina often equaled the population of
the established community. Added to these were soldiers who were stationed at nearby military facilities.

Durham, the New South industrial city, and Chapel Hill, the picturesque college town, differ in character and politics, but local Jewry, united by its synagogues and organizations, has always considered itself a single community. Historically, Durham Jewry is larger and older, dating to the 1870s when tobacco manufacturing turned the hamlet into a city. Chapel Hill's Jewish population did not become significant in number until after World War II. Suburban sprawl has virtually erased town borders, which were once eight miles apart.

2 The North Carolina Background, 1585 to 1870s

Jews who settled in colonial North Carolina abandoned Jewish community for a frontier. They were exiles not only from their European homelands but also from the American Jewish communities where they had first settled. Their cosmopolitan origins and mobility crossed national borders and boundaries of identity. They were a mix of Germans and Spanish-Portuguese with recent histories in England, Holland, and the Caribbean. From the port cities of Savannah, Charleston, Newport, and New York they moved on to the frontier. Living on the margins, they maintained Jewish identity through family, mercantile, and religious links to these distant communities. Few and transient, beyond the controls of rabbis and community, they rarely persisted in North Carolina as Jews beyond a generation.

Neither for Jew nor for Gentile was colonial North Carolina a land of opportunity. With a shallow, swampy coast, the colony did not develop the mercantile port—the Savannah, Charleston, or Richmond—to draw immigrants. North Carolina was a wilderness with few navigable rivers or passable roads. The political and economic climate was no more inviting than the geographical one. Frontier anarchy prevailed. Lord proprietors left their land titles in the hands of speculators and unscrupulous agents. Pirates raided the coast. The thickly wooded backcountry was the preserve of Native Americans. The Indian Trading Path brought a few Europeans down from Virginia into the Piedmont (where Durham and Chapel Hill are located), but colonization was slow and late. North Carolina's Jewish communal history does not truly begin until an urban commercial economy developed in the mid-nineteenth century.[1]

Although lacking community, Jews were present from the colony's founding. In 1585 North Carolina became home for the first Jewish settler in a British colony in the New World when Joachim Gans, a native of Prague, arrived on Sir Walter Raleigh's second expedition to Roanoke Island. A metallurgist, Gans had revolutionized England's copper industry. Returning to England, Gans in 1589 was taken to court after he declared before a clergyman—in both Hebrew and English—that he denied the divinity of Jesus. Gans was a prototype of Jewish settlers for nearly four centuries in his economic mobility, his cosmopolitan origins, and his outsider status as a Jew.[2]

North Carolina welcomed Jews ambivalently as the colony, and later the state, wrestled with the contradictions of being a society founded on both republican and Christian principles. When John Locke composed the "Fundamental Constitutions for the Government of Carolina" in 1669, he had expressly opened the colony to "Jews, heathens, and other dissenters." Nonetheless, Locke's constitution, which was never enacted, welcomed nonbelievers with the expectation that they would find Christ's truth. Protestantism was upheld as the religion best suited for a free people. Although the royal charter enfranchised the Church of England, dissenters flourished. Quakers dominated politics in the late-seventeenth century, but in the eighteenth century the migration of Scotch Highlanders, Scotch-Irish, and Germans from Virginia and Pennsylvania brought a swelter of Protestant sects to North Carolina. German Lutherans and Scotch-Irish Presbyterians spread across the Piedmont. Methodist circuit preachers conducted revivals. By 1775 the Baptists emerged as the largest denomination. With its sectarianism North Carolina remained inhospitable to non-Protestants. The state's 1776 constitution granted liberty of worship, but a religious test limited office to Protestants. Virginia, Georgia, and South Carolina offered more tolerant havens.

For Jews the deterrents of religious prejudice and political disqualification were less significant than the pull of economic opportunity. Over the eighteenth and nineteenth centuries Jews were commonly identified as a class with commerce, and Jews and Christians alike justified the Jews' emancipation for their "economic utility" to the state. In 1750 Lord Cuming proposed a bizarre scheme to settle three hundred thousand Jews in the North Carolina mountains in the hope that they would generate enough trade for the Crown to repay the national debt. Colonial records suggest a far humbler migration.[3]

North Carolina's early Jews were emissaries from distant commercial centers and were not distinctly regional. Jewish merchants in such port cities as Edenton, New Bern, and Wilmington were part of a coastal network that extended from Newport to Savannah to the West Indies. Their names—Gomez, Lopez, Rivera, Levy—were prominent in colonial commerce. This network, secured by family ties, was a colonial extension of the Jewish communities of Amsterdam and London. North Carolina's contribution to the transatlantic trade consisted of lumber, tobacco, rum, whale oil, and slaves. The well-known Newport merchant Aaron Lopez launched some thirty-seven ships to North Carolina between 1761 and 1775 and maintained agents and partners along the coast. As was typical of Jews nationally in the colonial and early Republic eras, Lopez's network involved Jews and non-Jews alike. Although Jews did not establish themselves as planters, as they did in Georgia, Louisiana, and South Carolina, some North Carolina Jews speculated in timber lands. Jews owned and traded slaves.[4]

North Carolina's early Jews did not have a specifically southern regional identity, and their civic status reflected the European situation. Economic integration was a first step in emancipating and secularizing Jews. Early North Carolina records suggest that Jews aspired to exercise their rights as citizens. In the eighteenth century occasional Jewish-sounding names, an unreliable indicator of Jewish origin, appeared in court records, militia musters, Masonic rolls, and land grants. A 1702 petitioner protested against illegal ballots from blacks, sailors, servants, strangers, and Jews. In 1740 Aaron Moses witnessed a will in coastal Perquimans County. Joseph Laney, identified as a Jew, was listed on documents from 1759 until after the Revolution. The notorious Tory David Fanning wrote that two Jewish rebels, Silvedoor and Rapely, challenged him when he attempted to rally North Carolinians to the British cause.[5]

Several Jewish mercantile families settled in coastal Wilmington in the late 1730s, but this community did not endure. As Wilmington grew into a seaport by the 1790s, more families arrived. They included Sephardic mercantile agents from Newport, New York, and Charleston and a few poorer artisans and petty tradesmen, some of German origin. A "Jewish rabbi," the Reverend Jacob Abroo, was reported to have died in New Bern in 1790. The 1790 federal census counted less than one hundred Jews in the state. In 1826 Isaac Harby, the Charleston author, estimated that four hundred Jews resided in North Carolina, but this figure has no factual basis.[6] North Carolina Jewry was too small and transient to constitute a community.

Maintaining family, trade, and religious links to urban commercial centers, North Carolina's Jews were typical of Jews on the frontier in their mobility and the impermanence of their settlement. This pattern was not exclusively southern. North Carolina's Jewish development, for example, parallels that of Connecticut, which had a brief, sparse colonial mercantile settlement linked to Newport and New York. As Jacob Marcus observes of Connecticut Jewry, Jews in a "monolithic" Christian religious and social milieu had "no future." Jewish settlements expired, sometimes reviving with new migrations, only to die again. The choice was to remain in the hinterlands and assimilate or return to an urban Jewish center.[7]

Orange County, which then encompassed Durham and Chapel Hill, offered little economic incentive to draw Jewish settlers. Chapel Hill remained a quiet "academical village" since the University of North Carolina opened its doors in 1795, and Durham was an unincorporated farming neighborhood. Hillsborough, the county seat and former state capital, was the commercial center. It supported a prosperous class of planters and lawyers. Colonial records mention a William Levy of Orange County who filed a petition to the governor in 1768, but nothing suggests Jewish origins except his name. The first record of an identifiable Jew was a marriage bond for a Christian couple posted by Isaac Mordecai in Hillsborough in 1802.[8]

The few Jews who made forays into the colony chose a place where they could not fulfill the commandments of communal prayer, obtain kosher provisions, or maintain Jewish family life. In antebellum North Carolina, Jews lacked numbers to sustain Jewish identities even when they resisted assimilation. Jacob Mordecai, who moved to Warrenton in 1792, was an observant Jew and biblical scholar who had written a Jewish apologia to refute Christian missionaries. Yet, in the next generation the family's Jewish aspect faded. Only three of his thirteen children married Jews (and four never married). Conversion, intermarriage, spinsterhood, and bachelorhood were common among the Mordecais, and birth rates were very low. Throughout the nineteenth century North Carolina Jews would lament the lack of suitable Jewish spouses. Those Jews who wished to persist as Jews mostly abandoned the state, often in search of Jewish spouses. The

North Carolina situation contrasts with national estimates that only 16 percent of pre-1840 marriages by Jews were with Christians. By 1840 Wilmington Jewry was "depleted."[9]

Jews found social acceptance, which hastened their assimilation. When Jacob Mordecai failed as a tobacco speculator in 1808, his neighbors prevailed upon the scholarly Jew to open an academy to educate their daughters. The Mordecais identified with Anglo-Protestant social elites and intermarried into leading families. Like Jews in Newport, New York, and Charleston, some Wilmington Jews who held membership in the Charleston synagogue also subscribed to pews in the local Episcopal church, where they were socially, if not religiously, active. Sephardim also had Marrano family histories that created a precedent for a double identity as private Jew and public Christian.[10]

Southerners typically demonstrated hospitality toward their Jewish neighbors even as they expressed suspicion of the alien, mythic Jew. Jews were welcomed as individuals and feared as a class. Southern codes of hospitality countered anti-Semitic beliefs and ideologies. In 1808 Jacob Henry was elected to the state legislature as a Federalist from coastal Carteret County, but a year later, Hugh Mills, a Republican opponent, challenged his right to hold office as a non-Protestant. Mills claimed that Henry "denies the divine authority of the New Testament and refused to take the oath prescribed by law." Son of a German immigrant, Henry defended the "natural and unalienable right" of religious liberty as a citizen and a Jew. On the house floor he asserted the civic virtue of his religion, proclaiming proudly that it accorded with the American creed in upholding "just, honorable, and beneficent maxims." In his eloquent oration Henry never mentioned Judaism by name and justified prophetic religion by quoting the New Testament. He defended a rational, moral, civil religion, not the traditional Judaism of revelation. Henry retained his seat on the technicality that the religious test applied to the executive, not to the legislature. The constitutional rights of the Jew as citizen were the subject of repeated constitutional debates, but it was sustained again in 1835 when "Christian" replaced "Protestant." Adherents of a Christian America, concerned with liberty of conscience for Protestants, overcame the Jeffersonians, who upheld Enlightenment ideals on the rights of man.[11] Henry's defense makes no specific regional reference—the constitutions of Connecticut, Massachusetts, Maryland, and New Hampshire also had religious tests—and the debate parallels arguments on Jewish emancipation made in England, France, and Germany. Henry echoes Moses Mendelssohn of Berlin in appealing to liberty of conscience and arguing for Judaism's compatibility with the interests of the state.

Jews avoided North Carolina, in contrast to Virginia, South Carolina, and Georgia, where commercial prospects were more inviting. In 1820 Richmond claimed two hundred Jews, and Savannah claimed one hundred. The Charleston community of seven hundred was the largest in America. Antebellum North Carolina remained backward and undeveloped, and it was aptly nicknamed the Rip Van Winkle State. Poor roads hindered the growth of markets. Slaveholding absorbed capital that might have been invested more profitably in commerce and industry. Between 1815 and 1850 one-third of its population, more than four hundred thousand people, left the state, often heading west. Farms were abandoned and towns emptied. From 1820 to 1840 the proportion of the state's urban population declined.[12]

The German Jewish Migration

Two historical forces converged to inspire a small but persistent Jewish immigration: the state's commercial economy began to expand as German Jews were arriving in America. Although this "second wave" migration is commonly labeled German in contrast to the Sephardic "first wave," it in fact consisted of Jews from diverse European regions and subcultures. European Jewry was migratory, and its national identities were fluid. During the nineteenth century Jews flowed from east to west and moved from the countryside into the cities. The divisions of Poland by Prussia, Russia, and Austro-Hungary further obfuscated Jewish national origins. Whatever their roots, Jews adapted German language and culture as the vehicle to enter modernity and European society.

Jews left the Germanic states to escape political and economic disabilities. The Industrial Revolution was especially hard on Jews who traditionally worked as artisans and petty merchants. Bavarian Jews also suffered from residency quotas, which restricted their ability to marry. In several principalities German nationalists provoked anti-Semitic rioting. In the 1830s Jews joined the German exodus from the villages of the Rhineland and southern provinces for America. After the failed revolution of 1848, with hopes for a more tolerant, democratic Germany crushed, Prussian Jews began emigrating in greater numbers. From 1840 to 1860 America's Jewish population grew tenfold, from 15,000 to 150,000. In Baltimore the number of Jews jumped from one thousand to eight thousand, and the city became a center of Jewish mercantile and religious activity. Richmond's

Jewish numbers burgeoned to more than one thousand. The ships that brought Virginia tobacco from Richmond to Bremen returned with German immigrants, including young Bavarian Jews.[13] These Jews, short of cash and marketable skills, fanned southward. As they had in the old country, they became petty traders to rural people. German Jewish peddlers were familiar figures across the rural South.

The peddlers trudged country roads, knocking on farmhouse doors. With luck they worked up to a horse and then a wagon. A peddler might find a crossroads or small town propitious for a general store. This store served as a way station where other peddlers could stockpile goods and perhaps spend a Sabbath. One former peddler, Lazarus Fels, operated a general store from 1855 to 1866 in Yanceyville, thirty-five miles northwest of Durham. Fels, a Confederate postmaster, expanded the store into a distillery and cotton mill, but the enterprise failed, and he moved to Baltimore.[14]

Awakening from its doldrums, North Carolina began reversing its decline. After reforming its constitution in 1835, the state embarked on a program of internal improvements. Better roads led to the development of market towns. In 1856 the North Carolina Railroad was completed, linking Charlotte to Goldsboro. The urban population started to expand as commercial networks developed, and the population center began shifting from the coast to the Piedmont. The railroad brought new opportunities of mobility.[15]

In the late antebellum years small numbers of German Jews began settling in North Carolina's market towns along rivers and rail lines. By 1850 nine families had settled in Charlotte. Isaac Wallace, a German immigrant from South Carolina, moved to Statesville in 1859 and opened a general store that formed the nucleus of a small community. Michael Grausman, a Bavarian Jew, who had tailored uniforms for the Confederate army, moved from Warrenton to Raleigh in 1862.[16]

North Carolina's Jewish communities tended to be colonial outposts of Charleston, Richmond, Baltimore, or Philadelphia, the places of first settlement. These urban centers were not just wholesale and distribution centers for rural merchants; they also served as Jewish homelands where they found a rabbi, a spouse, and a place to bury their dead. Goldsboro Jews retained family and commercial ties to Baltimore. In 1858 one merchant hired Herman Weil, a newly arrived German immigrant from Baltimore, to clerk in his store. The Weil family, over generations, took the lead in organizing North Carolina Jewry. Wilmington's Jewish community, a colony of Charleston, revived when a steamship line, the railroad, and a new road system improved the city's commercial prospects. By 1850 twenty-six Jewish merchants resided there. Richmond Jewish families settled in Tarboro, which had a "yidisha" (Jewish) street of eleven stores in the 1870s.[17]

Although welcome for their trade, Jews confronted sporadic anti-Semitic outbursts. Such episodes neither reflected popular feelings nor dissuaded Jews from settling in the South. In Goldsboro in 1857 Dr. John Davis, a prominent citizen, and Falk Odenheimer, an immigrant storekeeper, exchanged blows and pistol shots after a quarrel. At the trial an anti-Semitic lynch mob gathered, and Jews fled town. When tempers cooled, Jews returned without incident. The following year new Jewish immigrant families settled in town.[18]

Jewish growth in the Piedmont, perhaps the state's poorest region, was late and slow. Farming was still conducted on a subsistence level, although a few plantations raised cotton and tobacco for market. The character of the area was set by self-sustaining rural communities. These neighborhoods consisted of extended families, anchored by a church and a general store. The farm families, descendants of eighteenth-century German and Scotch-Irish settlers, remained stable over generations. Orange County society was insular, its people loyal to kin and land. In 1835, when the state constitutional convention considered removing the religious test, the Orange County delegate, James Smith, protested that he "was not willing . . . to let in Turks, Hindoos, and Jews." Smith did not care that people "might call him a bigot" and asked, "Must we swear a Turk on the Koran? Must we separate the Holy Scriptures that we must swear the Jew on the Old Testament?" The anti-immigrant Know-Nothing party made "respectable" showings in Orange County elections in the 1850s, and neighborhood caucuses passed resolutions calling for "native born" leadership and a twenty-year residency for naturalization.[19] The Know-Nothings were not pointedly anti-Semitic, but an immigrant bore the mark of an outsider.

In the absence of commerce there was little in the area to attract Jewish settlers. In 1860 Durham was a hamlet of one hundred people. It included one church, two barrooms, three stores, and thirty homes. It was not chartered as a city until 1869. Chapel Hill contained a boarding house, a few restaurants, a florist, and a bookseller to serve its 250 residents and 460 university students. In the antebellum years several Jews attended the University of North Carolina. The first was Marx Lazarus, who enrolled in

1837. He was the son of Wilmington merchant Aaron Lazarus and grand-son of Jacob Mordecai. Judah Benjamin, the Louisiana senator who be-came a Confederate statesman, sent his brother, Joseph Benjamin, and his nephew, Lionel Levy, to the university, both of whom were graduated in 1847. Two sons of Benjamin's sister followed. Henry Sessions was gradu-ated in 1856, and his brother Coleman Sessions was graduated in 1857.[20] With twice-daily chapel services the university, founded in part to train clergy, could not have been congenial to any Jew who observed his faith.

The November 15, 1851, *Hillsborough Recorder* advertised that Profes-sor Seixas, formerly of Harvard, would teach Hebrew to ministers at South Lowell Academy, a Methodist prepatory school. The professor was likely James (born Joshua) Seixas, son of Revolutionary War patriot-rabbi Gershom Seixas. James Seixas was the author of Semitic grammars and professor of Hebrew at Andover.[21] A Christian convert, he earned his liv-ing as an itinerant Hebrew instructor to clergymen. Whatever Jewishness he retained likely owed to family ties in Richmond and Charleston.

As the county's market center, Hillsborough offered the most promise for enterprising Jews. In the 1840s Aaron Lazarus of Wilmington traveled to Hillsborough in connection with his railroad investments. In the 1850s the railroad arrived, opening the area to northern markets. By 1860 Or-ange County contained a cotton mill, a woolen mill, two tobacco facto-ries, and several dozen flour and meal mills. In June 1860, Hammersplay and Mendels, "a branch of German Jew house in Salisbury" (Hammers-lough brothers), opened a Hillsborough store. The store failed after eight months.[22]

Until the advent of war, the question of southern identity had not im-posed itself on North Carolina's Jews, who were historically few and mo-bile. Southerners, factious and conflicted, had traditionally asserted their state loyalties, but their historical writings showed little consciousness of the South as a distinct entity. Historian John Hope Franklin observes that in the late 1840s and 1850s, as white Southerners defended themselves from national and international condemnation of slavery, they "began to think of themselves as having a set of common values, common problems, common dangers, and common aspirations that set them apart from other Americans." A distinctly southern identity emerged that asserted the re-gion's superiority to the North.[23]

Although the state's Jews consisted mostly of recent immigrants, they rallied to the Confederate cause. What compelled them? After the repres-sions of Germany, they were grateful for the political liberty and economic opportunity open to them in the South. They were doubtlessly swept by the war fever, the promise of adventure for an enterprise that promised to be short and glorious. For the poor, enlistment offered a bounty. Herman Weil, a German immigrant who spoke halting English after three years in America, was among the first in Goldsboro to enlist. Whiteville's citizens elected Jacob Bamberger, a recent German immigrant, as sergeant of a local regiment. War fever swept Leopold Oettinger into the Wilson Light Infantry six days after the first shot was fired at Fort Sumter. The twenty-one-year-old German immigrant fell at Seven Pines a year later. Charlotte's Jewish ladies donated $150 to the local Confederate volunteers, and its nine Jewish families contributed eleven soldiers. Altogether some seventy Jews served in North Carolina forces. Alfred Mordecai, the first Jewish graduate of West Point, resigned his U.S. army commission in 1861, but he sat out the war, not wanting to "forge arms" against "his aged mother, brothers and sisters in the south."[24]

Albert Moses Luria, a student at Hillsboro Military Academy from 1858 to 1860, was an acculturated Jewish southerner who became a Confederate hero. He was the son of the Georgia planter and lawyer Raphael Moses, who was both a proud Jew and an ardent Confederate. (Luria had adopted his mother's name in pride of her Sephardic lineage.) In 1861 Luria was appointed sergeant in the Twenty-third Light Regiment of North Carolina. Called "the bravest of the brave," Luria once grabbed a live shell and smothered it, then declined a promotion for heroism, saying he wanted only to prove himself in battle. A year later he, too, was fatally wounded at Seven Pines while brandishing a Confederate standard to rally his troops.[25]

A story passed down in the community tells of local Jews who celebrated Passover with soldiers at the Civil War's end. No evidence has been found to document such a legend—no local Jewish community existed then—but the story is plausible. During the war local homes and boardinghouses were filled with refugees from Richmond, Charleston, and Wilmington, all of which had Jewish communities. The Union army occupied Durham and Chapel Hill in April 1865, during the Passover season. The midwestern regiments stationed there included dozens of Jewish soldiers.[26]

As wartime inflation and food shortages inflamed tensions, Jews, many of whom were newly arrived foreigners, were accused of speculation and profiteering. In Richmond and Wilmington anti-Semitism grew vitriolic. Such charges were commonplace in the North as well as the South, and

Jews and their Christian defenders pointedly refuted them. North Carolina's "Israelites" and their Christian defenders protested the constitutional religious test for political office—a legislative committee condemned it as "a relic of bigotry and intolerance"—but as Jews fought and sometimes died for the Confederacy the legislature reaffirmed it in 1861 and 1865.[27]

Federal troops seized northeastern North Carolina in 1862; the Piedmont and mountains saw only sporadic military activity. Sherman's army arrived in North Carolina in 1865, accepting the surrender of Johnston's rebel army outside Durham without having to engage it in a major battle. No North Carolina town suffered the destruction of an Atlanta, Columbia, or Richmond.

Reconstruction found Orange County short of food, cash, and labor. The University of North Carolina, which had remained open during the war, closed from 1870 to 1875. Plantations were broken into small farms. Emancipated slaves became farm laborers—a few were tenants or landowners—though many abandoned their former masters altogether for the towns. The traditional pattern of small farms and rural communities reasserted itself.[28]

The uncertain politics and economic chaos of Reconstruction would have given an immigrant Jew reasons to hesitate settling in North Carolina. On the one hand, military rule and black-Republican government improved education and extended democracy. A constitutional convention in 1868 finally removed the Jewish officeholding disability. With blacks and then Jews granted full rights as citizens, however, white nativist fears were aroused. Resentments were directed against outsiders, northern carpetbaggers especially. From 1868 to 1870 Ku Klux Klan murder and terror struck the countryside. Yet the havoc of Reconstruction did little to change the prewar pattern of a small, but increasing Jewish migration. Economic opportunity proved a stronger motive than the disincentives of political turmoil or religious bias.

As defeated, impoverished southerners sought to rebuild their economy and reorganize their society, they extended a conflicted welcome toward the Jewish newcomers, desiring their capital and business acumen but distrusting their practices. The identification of the Jew with commerce had both salutary and prejudicial aspects. The *Richmond Whig* declared in 1866, "Where there are no Jews, there is no money to be made. . . . We hail their presence in the Southern States as an auspicious sign." In Goldsboro the newspaper lauded such people as the Weil brothers as men of "high character and personal integrity" who were very much "wanted . . . to help get the economy moving again" in the "bleak aftermath of a ruinous war."[29]

Yet Jews, who were economically mobile, also aroused suspicions. A bifurcated attitude toward the Jew is reflected in the R. G. Dun & Co. Credit Reports. The reports, written by local lawyers, merchants, or bank cashiers, were compiled nationally on businessmen who applied for credit. The usual practice when a Jew applied was to identify him as such. The term *Jew* implied economic speculation as in the case of a Tarboro merchant who was "of good character for a Jew." The reports drew lines between the "Jewish gentleman" who stood "high" in a community and the "doubtful floating kind" who moved constantly, often lasting in a place only months. Failing to establish themselves, storekeepers headed to new territories; some, like the Bloomingdale brothers, who had stores near Wilson in the 1840s and 1850s, returned to New York.[30]

Because Jewish merchants had difficulty obtaining credit through conventional channels, they created their own ethnic economy through family and landsmen networks that linked them to Jewish importers, manufacturers, and wholesalers in Philadelphia, New York, and Baltimore. In 1871 the Wallace brothers of Statesville established a herb trade that employed mountaineer pickers and country storekeepers in a network that extended to Baltimore and Europe. This pattern of urban homeland and country colonies was not distinctly southern but was typical of Jewish enterprise nationally. Distribution networks followed roads, rivers, and railroads. Cincinnati served as the center for smaller communities in Illinois, Indiana, Kentucky, Tennessee, and Missouri. San Francisco served a similar role in the Far West. Such cities as Richmond, Mobile, Memphis, St. Louis, and New Orleans, linked to New York markets, became regional wholesaling and manufacturing centers that supplied local retail merchants in the countryside. Peddlers fanned out from these small-town stores and suppliers. This credit and distributional network was secured by family and *landsleit* (homeland folk) ties. Immigrants climbed the "economic and status hierarchy" from peddler to storekeeper to wholesaler to importer or manufacturer. By 1878 sixteen North Carolina towns reported some Jewish population.[31]

Across the postwar South, Jewish merchants often played pivotal roles in developing rural economies. With the demise of slavery, planters divided their land into tenant farms to be worked by freed slaves and landless whites. The antebellum pattern of subsistence farming and rural self-sufficiency yielded to cash-crop farming and a market economy. Fields of corn and wheat were planted with cotton and tobacco. The storekeeper became the primary trader in the commodity market system. To obtain supplies—or simply to feed their families—cash-poor farmers borrowed from neighborhood stores using their future harvests as collateral. To obtain credit, farmers pledged crops to the merchant, who sometimes charged exorbitant interest rates. Fluctuating prices and high interest rates victimized the farmer and jeopardized the merchant. State lien laws passed in the 1870s required tenants to pay landowners their share of crops before satisfying other creditors. The sons of planters owned most local country stores. The landless Jew would have been at a disadvantage. These problems grew severe after the Panic of 1873. In the 1890s agrarian mobs burned Jewish stores in Louisiana and Mississippi.

Economic distress intensified suspicions about Jews. Allegations of profiteering that had afflicted Jews in Richmond and Wilmington during and after the Civil War were repeated in the countryside, where few or no Jews lived. Morris Cohen, a veteran of the Richmond Zouaves, opened a variety store at C. M. Latimer's Old Stand in Hillsborough in 1866. He employed two Gentile clerks, which likely gave him liberty to peddle. In the November 3, 1866, *Hillsborough Recorder* Cohen printed a charming, if not exactly polished, "Cheap Store" poem that advertised merchandise for cash or barter, including "CALICOS of every Style, HOOP SKIRTS there are pile on pile." The poem concluded

> In fifty lines I cannot tell
> Of all he has, and how he'll sell,
> But this I know, *he's selling cheap,*
> *and profits large he doesn't reap.*
> He'll take just what you bring to sell,
> And *though called* 'Jew' will treat you well.

Cohen's apology assumed that local folks held prejudices against Jewish traders, though no other Jew is known to have lived in the county. Their only acquaintance was likely with peddlers.[32]

Rural families needed Cohen's merchandise of dyes, sugar, spice, crockery, and hardware, especially by barter, but he also appealed to fashionable, well-to-do town dwellers, judging by his advertisements for velvet caps, English princess skirts, and "the latest style of Bonnets." The general store brought a taste of the cosmopolitan world into the provinces, a role well suited for the European-born Jew. Hillsborough, however, was insufficiently urban to support him. Business was also hurt by poor harvests in 1866 and 1867, which aggravated a generally depressed postwar economy. Cohen's store lasted until January 1868. A year later it was reported that Cohen, bankrupt, had returned to Germany. Another merchant, Julius Israel, set up shop in Hillsborough in 1868. R. G. Dun reported that Israel "conducts himself well, don't know nothing of his means." The store failed after seven months.[33]

A Jewish merchant, as a social outsider, would have economic disadvantages. Local families typically operated the rural general stores, which served as neighborhood social centers where kin and friends gathered around the stove to talk, smoke, and play cards. An immigrant "new man" of whom "nothing is known," as the Dun credit reports described Cohen, had difficulty establishing himself in a closely knit community. To the landed families, Jews had no rootedness but their portable stock. Violence, often directed against freedmen and white northerners, wracked postwar Orange County. The Ku Klux Klan killed five blacks and once assaulted residents of the poorhouse. A local newspaper warned that Klan violence would "prevent Northern men coming here and settling."[34]

Religious History
Few and mobile, southern Jews were slow to institutionalize their Judaism. In 1861 there were only twenty-one congregations in the South, and North Carolina had none. Only Baltimore had a rabbi whose credentials could be verified. Early American congregations were all Orthodox, but in larger cities they divided along national lines. Richmond, the first American home of most early Durham Jews, offered a paradigm: The Sephardic-rite Beth Shalome was founded in 1789 followed by the Bavarians' Beth Ahabah in 1841, the Prussians' Polish-rite Kenesseth Israel in 1856, and the Russians' Sir Moses Montefiore in 1880. Ethnic lines were not sharply drawn. Beth Shalome's membership consisted mostly of Germans, who appreciated its socially decorous ritual. Over time Prussians gravitated from Orthodoxy toward Beth Ahabah, which evolved toward Reform.[35]

Paralleling their family and commercial networks, North Carolina's Jews retained religious links to congregations in Richmond, Charleston, Norfolk, and Baltimore. Until the arrival of east European Jews at the end of the nineteenth century, North Carolina Jewry was too small to factionalize into national congregations. Smaller communities tended to be ethnically and religiously diverse. The twenty-four Jews in Tarboro, for example, included Jews of English, Polish, Prussian, Alsatian, and Bavarian origin. The need to accommodate dictated religious compromise. This tolerance was typical of small-town Jewries regardless of region.

The German legacy shaped North Carolina Jewry as it did southern Jewry generally. Of 300 Jews listed in the state's 1870 census, 210 were born in Germany, Bavaria, or Prussia. Only twenty-six were American born.[36] Over the course of nineteenth century, as German Jews entered the national economy and gained political rights, they abandoned Yiddish for German, modernized their religious Orthodoxy, and, as Germany urbanized, entered the bourgeoisie. Even before their departure from Europe, Jews in Bavaria and southwestern Germany had felt the emancipating influences of the Enlightenment and Napoleonic conquest. Forces of *haskalah* (Jewish enlightenment), acculturation, and religious reform gradually and unevenly were working their way eastward through Jewish communities across Europe. This movement followed the Jews' tentative adoption of German culture. Those who emigrated tended to be poorer, more religiously devout village Jews less affected by these urban, liberalizing currents. When German immigrants first organized congregations in North Carolina, they reestablished traditional modes of worship and community. Historical trends worked to mitigate their Orthodoxy. In America they found an open, voluntaristic society that encouraged assimilation.

Transatlantic religious developments, the trends of modernization, flowed from Germany to America's urban centers and then into the countryside. The processes of Reform worked unevenly within and across communities in North Carolina as they did the country. The Hamburg temple shaped the ritual of Baltimore's Oheb Sholom, which, in turn, influenced the practice of North Carolina's immigrants. New Bern's Jews worshipped with hymnals from New York's Temple Emanuel, whose ritual included prayers in German, English, and transliterated Hebrew.

North Carolina, too, was a contending ground between the Reverend Isaac Leeser, the tireless advocate of traditional Judaism in America, and Rabbi Isaac Mayer Wise, the organizer of a moderately reformist American Judaism. When North Carolina's Jewish communities institutionalized, they followed the classic pattern: a burial or benevolent society formed, then a congregation was established, and finally a synagogue was built. Under the personal prodding of the Reverend Leeser, the spiritual leader of Philadelphia's Mikveh Israel, Wilmington Jewry founded a burial society in 1852 and advertised in New York for a hazan, *schochet* (ritual slaughterer), and *mohel* (ritual circumciser) in 1860. Seven years later, Wilmington's Jews founded an Orthodox congregation. It soon failed, and Rabbi Wise announced that Wilmington would have a *Minhag America* temple.[37]

The forming of cemeteries and congregations was a sign that the state's Jews, historically few and transient, now were sufficiently prosperous and numerous to envision themselves as a permanent community with a future as both Jews and southerners. In the colonial and antebellum eras Jews were identified with commerce and welcomed for their economic utility. Intermarriage with elite families points to social acceptance. Nevertheless, the Jews' religious difference disqualified them as full-fledged citizens politically. Demanding their rights, such Jews as Jacob Henry became southerners by rationalizing Jewish difference. The immigrant German Jews who came at mid century arrived when southerners were asserting their separate, regional identity, which manifested itself in secession. Despite their outsider immigrant status, Jews demonstrated their southern nationalism by their ardor for the Confederacy. Through their family, business, and congregational networks, the immigrants remained linked to Jewish urban centers and to fellow immigrants across the state. They maintained their collective identity as Jews while asserting their southern loyalties.

North Carolina's commercial economy was too underdeveloped to attract large numbers of Jews. The pace of Jewish migration quickened with the advent of industrialization, which redrew the state's economic map. As North Carolina embraced the New South creed of industrial progress, furniture, textile, and tobacco factories expanded. For a Jewish community to endure, Durham would need to make the transition from an agricultural market to an industrial center.

In Orange County Hillsborough was soon to be eclipsed as the area's commercial center. Dr. Bartlett Durham donated several acres to build a railroad depot at his general store. A new community formed around Durham Station, and at war's end it boasted a population of two hundred. A tobacco factory located there in 1858. Hillsborough remained a small mill and market town, but Durham emerged as a New South industrial center.

If the railroad created the market town, tobacco built the industrial city. After the war soldiers foraged the countryside, helping themselves to the local leaf. Northern soldiers sacked John Green's tobacco factory. When the veterans depleted their supplies, Green was swamped with orders for more "Durham Bull" leaf. The word spread. In 1869 after Green died, his factory, which employed less than a dozen workers, was bought by W. T.

Blackwell. His partner, Julian Carr of Chapel Hill, launched an advertising campaign that plastered the Durham Bull across continents. Within a decade the Blackwell factory employed nearly one thousand workers.[38]

No longer a whistle-stop, Durham was now a budding industrial center with rail access to northern markets. That lone Durham tobacco factory of 1858 grew to a dozen by 1872. In 1871 a tobacco auction market opened, drawing farmers to town. From 1866 to 1880 the number of businesses in Durham exploded from five to one hundred. A young Jewish immigrant would have found Durham an inviting place when he chose to set out on his own. Fortunes were being made there. The streets were leafed with gold.[39]

3 A German Jewish Colony, 1870s to 1880s

Durham was the New South and proclaimed its creed of industrial progress. "The word 'Durham' is synonymous with 'business,'" the *Durham Tobacco Plant* exulted. The prevailing morality was the work ethic, and only the obligation to do Christian charity restrained the pursuit of wealth. The Durham philosophy was "live and let live." Durham was highly representative of the changes wrought across the southern landscape as mill and market towns in the thousands sprouted around railroad depots. For thirty years after 1880, the southern village and town population grew by five million. Jewish mobility and enterprise very much fit the spirit of an emergent New South. An 1878 survey listed 290 towns in the South with Jewish population. Nearly 20 percent of America's 130,185 Jews lived in the region.[1]

From 1870 to 1910, North Carolina towns numbering one thousand grew from seventeen to more than fifty, and the percentage of urban dwellers leaped from 3.4 to 14.4 percent of the population. Jewish population growth correlated with urban trends. Raleigh's Jewish population jumped from one to ten families. In Wilmington, its mercantile importance having grown during the Civil War blockade, Jewish population doubled to two hundred. In 1878 Goldsboro and Charlotte each held more than one hundred Jews, and Elizabeth City, Fayetteville, New Bern, Tarboro, Wilson, and Winston-Salem all counted Jews in double digits. From 1878 to 1905 the state's Jewish population rose from an estimated 820 to 6,000.[2]

Stepping from a train at Durham station in the late 1870s, a young Jew saw opportunity beckoning. Durham was a boom town. Storefronts stretched down Main Street. Tobacco factories and warehouses lined the railroad tracks. City dwellers would need shoes and clothing. These could be purchased in Baltimore or New York and shipped by rail to Durham. Farmers in town for market day could barter eggs or bacon for some fabric. The produce could then be resold to the workers.

Durham began to compete with the Virginia cities of Danville, Petersburg, and even Richmond as a tobacco center. The town's population grew from 256 in 1870 to 2,041 in 1880. Blacks and whites flocked to town. Durham's appeal was enhanced after the Panic of 1873. The depression lasted five years nationally but brought only a respite in Durham's boom. In February 1874, Durham factories reported that they were operating at full capacity.[3] A month later the first two Jewish merchants, Abe and Jacob Goldstein, opened a store. Four more Jewish merchants arrived within a year. By 1880 about ten had moved to town.

There was a restless movement of peoples across the South with the rise of new industries in textiles, furniture, and tobacco. The genteel plantation ideal yielded to the new-money Gilded Age. The young Jewish merchant arriving from Baltimore or Richmond had his counterpart in the planter's son heading from country to town to open a store or start a factory. "The rapidly growing ranks of commerce . . . claimed the majority of white men," Edward Ayers writes in *The Promise of the New South*. Ambition and failure drove Jew and Gentile southerner alike.[4] As a merchant and town dweller, the Jew was a representative New Southerner.

Native southerners, not northerners, built the New South. Virtually all of Durham's industrial leaders arose from the planter classes that had dominated the local economy in antebellum days. The agrarians of the Old South became the capitalists of the New. W. T. Blackwell, who owned the Bull Durham factory, came from nearby Person County, and his partner, Julian S. Carr, was the son of a wealthy Chapel Hill merchant and landowner. Washington Duke's family ranked among Orange County's largest landholders. The economic upheaval of the war had reduced Duke to peddling tobacco from a wagon, but in 1874 he moved to Durham to join his son Brodie, who had begun to manufacture tobacco in his home.[5]

Although early Durham Jews differed from native southerners in that perhaps half were foreign born, none was a recent immigrant. The Jewish merchants were typical of those flocking to Durham in being drawn largely from the region. The early Jewish settlement was largely a colony of Richmond Jewry. Joseph Kempner, who opened a store in 1875, had been a Richmond clothier. Augustus Mohsberg, a Union army veteran from Maryland, was the son-in-law of a Richmond wholesaler. The Goldsmith brothers were sons of a prominent Richmond merchant. Myer Summerfield had emigrated from Germany to the United States shortly after the Civil War. He had peddled through Tennessee, Kentucky, and Ohio before settling in 1872 in Danville, Virginia, a mill and market town seventy miles north of Durham. Polish-born Jacob and Fannie Goldstein arrived from Wilson, North Carolina, where they had lived at least since 1860.[6]

"Strangers locating here every day," the *Durham Herald* announced. "Come On, we have room for all who come." The traditional southern wariness of the stranger, the carpetbagging northerner, yielded to a warmer hospitality for those who could bring capital and profit. Durham newspapers wrote fondly of Jewish merchants as "our Hebrew friends." Yet, "Jew," as Hillsborough merchant Morris Cohen acknowledged, still implied a sharper who may *not* "treat you well."[7]

Ambivalent Relations

As the South rebuilt its economy with the end of federal occupation in 1876, it was also renegotiating its social and racial relations. With the Democratic overthrow of black-Republican government, society reorganized along a color line. Not only were the Jews religiously different, but in the lexicon of the times they were a separate race. They were white, but not Anglo-Saxon. Jews, identified as a class with commerce, were both admired and resented for their business abilities. Venerated as Children of Abraham, Jews were damned as Christ killers. Raised on the Bible and Sir Walter Scott, southerners subscribed to a romantic philo-Semitism. They espoused a race pride that exalted blood and heritage. In the prevailing spirit of racial romanticism, southerners extolled the Jews for their alleged racial purity, their unbroken lineage from antiquity, but they also suspected Jews for their racial otherness. Former governor and U.S. senator Zebulon Vance, the state's most venerated statesman, in the 1870s began delivering and publishing his celebrated philo-Semitic speech, "The Scattered Nation" from lecterns across the South. "The Jew," Vance declared, "is beyond doubt the most remarkable man of the world—past or present." He called Jews "our wondrous kinsmen." Vance wanted to refute popular "objections to a Jew as a citizen."[8] Yet, his profusive and prolific defense would not have been necessary if there were not an underlying popular uncertainty about the Jew's racial qualifications.

Durham's German Jews were identified as white. During an era when anti-Jewish racial discrimination was making itself felt nationally—climaxed by the infamous rejection of banker Joseph Seligman at a Saratoga hotel in 1877—Durham Jews seemed not to have been seen as different. In urban Atlanta, Mobile, and Richmond, where Jews had once participated in elite societies, doors began closing in the late 1880s as the South succumbed to a racial extremism that discomfited the Jew as it delegitimatized the African American. North Carolina, where Jews were few and well integrated socially, did not feel such urban anti-Semitic tremors.

Open for Business

The R. G. Dun & Co. Credit Reports suggest that Durhamites were not sharply reactive toward Jews. Of the eight Durham Jewish merchants listed, only four were labeled specifically as Jews. In three cases "Jew" implied warnings about the allegedly unscrupulous practices of bankrupt merchants who "behaved badly, not to be relied upon." In another case the reporter testified to the worthiness of the "Jew." Joseph Kempner, who opened a store in 1875, was rated as a "steady and good businessman, . . . worthy of credit" until he went bankrupt; then he was repeatedly described as a "Jew," "not reliable," and "doubtful." That the reporters did not label the other four merchants as Jews suggests that local businessmen saw Jews individually and not categorically. One reporter was tobacco magnate William Blackwell, who as a banker was so personally generous with credit that he soon went bankrupt. Young, native-born southern Jews, such as the Goldsmith brothers from Richmond, no longer fit the stereotype of the Jew as a heavily accented foreigner. They were not specifically identified as Jews, although they also went bankrupt. Contrarily, the Goldstein brothers, who were Yiddish-speaking, Polish immigrants, were invariably labeled as Jews.[9]

The Dun reporter expressed ignorance, and often suspicion, about the sources of Jewish capital. "Jew—cannot tell what his worth," a report noted of Jacob Goldstein. The Dun reporters had problems establishing the reliability of "strangers" who had "no property except stock." Most early city merchants—Mangum, Markham, or Freeland—were related to rooted farm families who owned land and country stores. Established local families, too, controlled the tobacco trade and industry. In the 1880s the Jewish-owned Richmond tobacco firm of Strause and Raab maintained an agent in Durham, and two Russian immigrant brothers, the Siegels, started a cigarette factory. These enterprises were short lived. Jews were limited to their ethnic, mercantile niche.[10]

Jews resumed their European role as economic middlemen who mediated between city and country. Durham was both a mill and market town. Town limits faded into fields. When tobacco markets opened, farmers flocked to town for overnight stays. One Jewish merchant advertised that "I will take your eggs, butter, chicken in trade."[11] He was bartering the products of family farms, which he resold to town dwellers, not speculating in crops. What attracted Jews to Durham was the growth of an urban clientele created by the tobacco industry. "Cheap stores" catered to factory workers. Industrial growth also spawned a class of owners and managers who could afford fashionable, factory-made clothes and haberdashery. In the 1880s the general store, with its miscellany of groceries and dry goods, began yielding to the specialty shop. Durham merchants Summerfield, Lehman, Nachman, and Levy were all men's specialty clothiers.

Jews replicated their European pattern of maintaining a separate ethnic economy within a larger national economy. As was typical of Jews, the store was a family enterprise. Samuel Lehman brought his brother Nathan and niece Esther from Germany to clerk in his store. Summerfield employed his sons and daughters as well as other Jews as salespersons. Carrie Levy was a buyer at her husband's dry-goods store.

The family credit system was especially important in Durham because the first bank did not open until 1879. With the country on the gold standard and the issuance of currency linked to the national debt, cash was at a premium. Jewish merchants would have to establish their own commercial networks. Most frequently, Durham merchants were financed by their parents or in-laws in Richmond. Clara Mohsberg's brother, Simeon Fleishman of the Richmond firm of Heller and Fleishman, paid a call to Durham in 1877. No doubt he supplied his kinsmen's store with his firm's shoes, trunks, and satchels. Soon thereafter, he became the store's bookkeeper. When Samuel Lehman and Louis Nachman opened the Durham Clothing Store as a branch of their Richmond business in 1878, Nachman's mother financed the venture.[12]

Supported by family credit, Jews were economically resilient and independent. The Goldsmith brothers, who opened a store in a rented house in 1875, were "single men of no tangible means." Raphael Goldsmith was "steady in his habits," the Dun agent noted, but his brother was a "little wild and careless." The store failed after three months. Their father, a wealthy Richmond merchant, paid their debts, saving the family from embarrassment. When Joseph Kempner's store failed, his brother-in-law, Isaac Levy, a merchant from Enfield, went to Baltimore to compromise his debts with his suppliers. In 1877 he was again selling groceries, boots, and shoes. In "The Scattered Nation" Vance observed, "If a Jew is broken down in business, the others set him up again."[13] The Jews' independent financial networks differentiated them from other southerners.

Despite Durham's relative prosperity, national economic conditions remained unstable after the Panic of 1873. Three of the six Jewish stores founded in Durham in 1874 and 1875 went bankrupt before 1880. From 1875 to 1877 no new Jews settled in Durham. All but one of the Jewish merchants experienced some failure, although the local tobacco economy remained relatively strong. The Jews' high incidence of bankruptcy was typical of New South enterprise. Their failure certainly was due to the national depression, but it also had roots in their large ambitions. When Abe and Jacob Goldstein returned from a buying trip to New York in 1877, local businessmen were astounded at the size of their inventory and questioned whether the market justified it. The Goldsteins aspired to be wholesalers for peddlers. They soon went bankrupt, reporting liabilities of $10,000. To protect themselves, the brothers put their stores in their wives' names, listing them as "free traders." Abe's wife, Esther, opened a general store, advertising in 1878 that "she will purchase this fall the largest stock of goods ever seen in Durham."[14]

Jewish merchants moved from store to store and frequently from town to town. Aaron and Myer Summerfield had drawn each other to promising territories, and the brothers loaned money back and forth. Myer had moved to Danville, Virginia, to join his brother's wholesaling business. After a bankruptcy, Myer relocated to Durham, opening a clothing store in 1882. Aaron later joined him, starting "the only liquor house in Durham, said to be the largest in the State."[15] Isaac Newman had been a partner of his brother in Whittakers and Littleton. When the Goldsmith brothers went bankrupt, they, like many North Carolinians, headed west toward Louisiana and Texas.

By the late 1870s German Jewish merchants were well established in the town's central business district, which extended four blocks from Main and Mangum Streets. Of the thirty-four stores in Durham, Jews operated a half dozen, including five dry-goods stores. In the 1880s Isaac Newman, Marx Bernstein, David Kaufman, and S. Schlomberg opened dry-goods stores on Main Street. Unconstrained by kosher laws, Fred and Julius Schwartz operated butcher stalls at the city market, where they slaughtered cattle and sold pork, mutton, and sausage. At his oyster bar Solomon Kaufman satisfied the southerners' taste for seafood. Although no Jews worked in non-Jewish firms, Summerfield and Jacob Levy also employed non-Jewish clerks. In 1879 Nachman and Lehman advertised that "Green A. Reams, salesman, would be pleased to see his many friends." A clerk from a native family brought the intangible of goodwill that would be especially important for "new" men in a small town.[16]

Jewish entrepreneurial energy very much fit the spirit of New South enterprise with its relentless boosterism. Jewish clothiers promised newly citified Durhamites the latest Richmond and New York styles. "Kempner's Corner" was a popular gathering place, and the ambitious merchant placed fashionably dressed advertising dummies on the sidewalk. Ads from Jewish stores dominated the newspapers. Mohsberg boasted of enormous stocks of boots, shoes, and Christmas toys. One ad promised, "Quick sales and small prophets [sic]." In 1881 the Levys advertised the town's first low-priced clothing house: "New Store. Immense Rush."[17]

Tax records document Durham's economic boom. In 1883 the total aggregate value of real and personal property of nine identifiable Jewish merchants was $26,431; a year later these same merchants reported property worth $36,605. At a time when a person worth $10,000 was considered wealthy, Levy and Summerfield prospered. Levy in 1886 held property worth $30,000. In newspaper ads, Levy boasted stocks of eight thousand shoes. By 1884 Summerfield had four employees and advertised an inventory of one thousand men's suits. He later started a pants factory on Carr Street. Lehman and Nachman and the Goldsteins had firms in the $5,000 to $10,000 range, which would suggest at least modest success.[18]

Residential patterns suggest that the Jews divided by both class and ethnicity. In a small town that stretched only five or six city blocks along a railroad, the Jews did not concentrate in a neighborhood. In the 1880s the Summerfields, who would raise seven children in Durham, resided in a large house on Pettigrew Street near their pants factory and across from a Duke mansion. The Levys lived on Dillard Street, where Durham's prosperous Christian citizens built fine homes, and they kept a "colored" servant. Their four children were driven to school by a pair of "aristocratic white horses," and they were bathed in one of the town's first ceramic bathtubs. Other merchants, such as the Mohsbergs and Lehmans, who also had smaller families, lived downtown above their stores. The Goldsteins, the town's only Polish Jews, remained on Pine Street in the Bottoms, a roughneck neighborhood inhabited by poor whites and blacks, many of whom worked in the nearby factories. Purchasing cottages as rental properties, the Goldsteins became catalysts for an east European ghetto.[19]

Economics alone does not explain the push, pull, or persistence of Jews to and from Durham. Despite the favorable business climate, Jews, like other potential settlers, had ample reasons to avoid Durham. In the 1880s a resident recalled that though Durham was an "incredibly good place to establish a business," it remained "a crude town, raw and alien." Six of the eight Jewish households established in Durham before 1881 consisted of families, not the single men typical of pioneers. Durham was not healthy or congenial for a family with children. Factory workers attracted brothels and saloons. Even as the Dukes and Carrs built elaborate mansions, the unpaved streets were quagmires of mud and garbage. Tobacco dust thickened the air. Shallow wells and stagnant ponds bred a typhoid known as "Durham fever." In 1887 a doctor observed, "Durham smelled to high heaven." The Mohsbergs, financially prosperous, left Durham for reasons of "health." After losing two infants in childbirth in Durham, Carrie Summerfield traveled to Virginia and Pennsylvania to deliver her children. A hospital did not open until 1895. City elders were slow in making civic improvements. A public school was not established until 1882, and it remained precarious as the public resisted school taxes. The People of the Book found themselves in America's most illiterate state. Jews looked elsewhere to raise families.[20]

The German Jewish merchants who persisted in town quickly integrated into the city's social and economic life as white southerners. The native North Carolinians, who brokered and manufactured tobacco products, and the Jewish "strangers," who owned a few retail stores, had complementary, rather than competitive, business interests. Jewish capital and mercantile services were welcome. Their numbers were too small to be threatening. Unlike carpetbaggers, local Jews showed no political ambitions, although Jews commonly won local elective office across the South. In North Carolina, Jews served on the Wilson town council in 1867, as sheriff in New Bern in the 1880s, and as mayors of Tarboro and Wilmington before 1900.

The Jews found social place. The compactness of Durham fostered intimacy among the citizenry and its leadership. Durham's industrialists, who lived near their workers and factories, were the Jews' customers, neighbors, and friends. As was typical for American Jewish men, Masonry was one avenue of acceptance. Lehman was elected a deacon and Mohsberg a steward of Lodge 352. The lodge included almost every member of the Durham Board of Trade, which controlled the town's politics and economy.

At the card tables Myer Summerfield joined regularly with Washington Duke, and Jacob Levy played in a circle that included W. T. Blackwell. Carrie Levy enjoyed sociable carriage rides with the Duke family. The *Durham Daily Globe* described the Mohsbergs in 1885 as "so long and so favorably known in the community."[21] (The merchants' heavy advertising no doubt encouraged the newspapers' solicitude.)

At a time when Jews were experiencing social discrimination nationally, North Carolina welcomed Jews. The 1886 graduation at the University of North Carolina featured Zebulon Vance delivering "The Scattered Nation." In 1883 the university awarded an honorary doctor of laws degree to Rabbi Samuel Mendelsohn of Wilmington, author of a text on Talmudic jurisprudence. His congregant, Solomon Cohen Weill, became the first Jew to teach at UNC when he served as acting professor of classical languages in 1884 while earning his bachelor of arts and bachelor of laws degrees. Weill also served as a university trustee from 1887 to 1895. A few youths from the state's established German families began attending Chapel Hill.[22]

Southerners drew the lines between Americanized Jews and east European immigrants. Vance in his "far-famed lecture" had contrasted racially the "most intelligent and civilized" central and western European Jews, who resembled their "Gentile neighbors," to the east Europeans. Unlike the acculturated Germans, many of whom were second-generation Americans, the Polish-born Goldsteins—Yiddish-speaking immigrants who signed their papers with X's—bore the label of Jew. They also lived on the fringe of the African American Hayti neighborhood. Jews were often disparaged for soliciting black trade, as in the case of a Wilson Jew who was reported to do a "mongrel trade with negroes & the lowest characters." In contrast to the Germans, the Goldsteins advertised as a "Jew store." The Jew store, with its miscellany of goods for barter or at "cheap" prices, must have been familiar to southerners. The *Durham Morning Herald* in 1876 reported an altercation when "two gentlemen of the Jewish persuasion"—likely peddlers—visited the Goldsteins. The men left their horse unattended, and an officer took the animal into custody. They paid a $2.50 fine, but the Goldsteins "took exceptions to the course of officer Herndon and for a time the quiet streets of Durham presented a lively scene." Reference to "gentlemen of the Jewish persuasion," rather than the more polite "Hebrew," suggests distaste. For the next thirty years newspapers commented sardonically about Abe Goldstein's volubility.[23]

The Jewish Church

To be respectable in the South meant joining a church. When Jews organized a synagogue, they were not only affirming their faith and peoplehood, their resistance to assimilation and their desire to preserve their
collective identity, but also establishing their place as church-going southerners. As the New South was rebuilding itself racially, socially, and economically, so, too, it was reorganizing itself religiously. Southern Christians spoke respectfully of the synagogue as the "Jewish church." Jews
organized themselves at the very time when Christian revivalism was
sweeping the South. In the 1880s and 1890s, as villages grew into towns,
the South experienced a frenzy of church building. Jewish communal activity in Durham commenced precisely when the town's Christians, too,
were undergoing a rush of congregation forming and church building.
From 1875 to 1890 Durham's Baptists, Methodists, Episcopalians, and Presbyterians all built new edifices. In the 1890s Roman Catholics, another
outsider group, formed a congregation and met, like the Jews, in a second-
floor hall before building a church.[24]

Stirrings of organized Jewish life in North Carolina intensified in the
1870s as southern hamlets began evolving into towns and as Jewish numbers achieved the critical mass to sustain community. In 1870 a Cemetery
Society formed in nearby Raleigh. Four years later the tailor Michael
Grausman, who had some rabbinic training, converted a room in his home
for religious use. In 1876 Wilmington's Jews erected a synagogue, the
state's first. In 1885 Raleigh's Jews organized a congregation. Other societies or congregations formed in Tarboro in 1875, Goldsboro in 1880, New
Bern in 1881, Statesville in 1883, Asheville in 1891, and Charlotte in 1893.
By 1895 North Carolina claimed ten congregations.[25]

North Carolina's early Jewish communities were satellites of congregations in Richmond, Baltimore, and Philadelphia, and rabbis from these cities traveled the state to lead services, perform marriages, and start religious
schools. Tarboro Jewry was a "colony" of Richmond's Orthodox Kenesseth Israel. Goldsboro's Jews adopted the name and constitution of the
Reform-oriented Oheb Shalom of Baltimore. Leading figures of American Judaism—Marcus Jastrow, Isaac Leeser, Solomon Schecter, Benjamin
Szold—all visited North Carolina communities to organize congregations
or dedicate synagogues. The most active was Rabbi Edward Calisch of
Beth Ahabah in Richmond. Calisch, a Classical Reform advocate, headed
a national circuit riding committee, and he saw himself as a missionary to
North Carolina's "country" Jews.[26]

Despite its few numbers and peripheral location, North Carolina Jewry responded to national religious movements. When Rabbi Isaac Mayer Wise sought to unify a factionalized Jewry by convening a Union of American Hebrew Congregations (UAHC) in 1873, nearly half the delegates were southern, and representatives of Reform congregations dominated. The UAHC, although lacking an ideology at its founding, evolved into the governing body of the Reform movement. In 1885 radical Reform Jews promulgated the Pittsburgh Platform, which called for a rational, American Judaism. Jews constituted a religious community, the platform stated, not a nation; it rejected Zionist nostalgia and messianic expectation. Dismissing Orthodoxy as "primitive," the Reformers advocated an ethical, universalistic civil religion that befit a modern people. Reform Judaism found fertile ground in America even as it slowed and backtracked in Germany, the land of its birth. It especially blossomed in the South, and by 1907, 41 percent of the UAHC congregational members were in the South even though the region accounted for only 14 percent of America's congregations.[27]

However traditional the immigrants' religious belief and behavior, they entered an open American society that encouraged assimilation according to Protestant models. As Jews acculturated, they created an American Judaism that mitigated their religious difference with their Christian neighbors. Reform Jews shortened the services; included more English; and introduced family pews, organs, and choirs. Observance of dietary laws eroded. In 1872 Wilmington Jews summoned Rabbi Marcus Jastrow of Rodeph Sholom in Philadelphia, a conservative, to advise them on the "gradual modification of the old Orthodox ritual." In 1882 Tarboro's Prussian Orthodox Jews appointed a committee "to see what could be done to adopt a reform service" and solicited advice from Rabbi Wise in Cincinnati. In "The Scattered Nation" Vance distinguished between Americanized Jews who "have become simply Unitarians or Deists" and the "Talmudical" east Europeans. Prussian Jews, who emigrated from German lands ceded from Poland, tended to remain loyal to Orthodoxy. They maintained regimens of daily prayer, Sabbath observance, and kashruth.[28]

Disputes over the length of services, mixed-gender family pews, and English prayers rended southern congregations no less than those of the North. A Jewish newspaper in 1877 reported that in Wilmington "dissensions" were "disturbing seriously the attendance at services." Synagogue minutes in Goldsboro and Statesville record debates on whether male worshippers could remove hats. Family pews, rather than gender-segregated seating, was commonplace. The sectarian labels of Reform, Conservative, and Orthodox do not demark the variety of religious practice that might be found within a nineteenth-century synagogue.[29]

The first mention of Jewish religious life in Durham was a report in July 1878 about the visit of an itinerant Hebrew teacher, Benjamin Miller. In October 1878 the *Durham Tobacco Plant* noted that the "Hebrews in Durham all faithfully observed the festival of 'Rosh Hashana' Saturday. At sunset Friday all places of business were closed, work of all kinds religiously abstained from." Such notices became nearly annual features thereafter. The character of religious observance in the early community is unknown, but it was likely a pragmatic blend of tradition and accommodation. In Durham, like most small southern towns, Jews lacked numbers to factionalize along either national or religious lines as they did in urban communities.[30]

The Durham settlers of the 1880s were a national and religious mix. Prussian-born Joseph Kempner had been a member of the Orthodox Kenesseth Israel in Richmond. The Levys, of Bavarian and southwest German origin, had family ties to Beth Ahabah in Richmond and identified themselves as Reform. The Mohsbergs were also a Beth Ahabah family. The Polish-born Goldsteins were east European Orthodox. German-born Myer Summerfield was Orthodox, but his American-born wife, Carrie Bowers Summerfield, and children were Reform. Religiously observant, Myer Summerfield took the lead in organizing the Jewish community.

Durham's Jews maintained their Jewish identity through the intertwining social, familial, and commercial ties that kept them networked to other Jewish communities in Virginia and North Carolina. Newspaper columns reported frequent visits of Levys, Mohsbergs, and Summerfields to German Jewish families in Raleigh, Goldsboro, and Richmond. Such Jewish associations served as a counterforce to assimilation.

As might be expected, several early Jewish settlers assimilated into the Christian community. Lila (or Delilah) Walters Durham, wife of the Reverend Columbus Durham, who served the First Baptist Church from 1876 to 1887, claimed to have been of Jewish birth although she observed her husband's faith. Isaac Wissburg was a German-born tailor who immigrated to Durham after the Civil War. Wissburg became "identified with the Episcopal Church." He was remembered as a learned man, a "Hebrew scholar," and kept some Jewish communal ties, witnessing the naturalizations of immigrants. Jews recalled him as a strange man who was the butt of children's pranks.[31]

Myer Summerfield founded the Cemetery Society in 1884 and several years later served as first synagogue president. The Prussian-born Summerfield, an Orthodox Jew, and his American-born wife, Carrie Bowers Summerfield, a Reform Jew, exemplify the religious diversity of the small, early Durham community. (Courtesy of Carol McCaskill)

Beginning in the mid-1880s the newspapers began reporting local Jewish ceremonies and visits of rabbis, mostly from Richmond. The articles featured wealthy Jews only, not peddlers or workers, and they suggest southern acculturation as Jewish rites became public, socially decorous events. In 1885, the Reverend D. Rosenthal officiated at the marriage of Fannie Siegel, daughter of tobacco manufacturer David Siegel. Seventy-five guests "partook of the beautiful repast." In 1886, the *Durham Tobacco Plant* described "The Celebration of an Ancient Custom," an "elegant repast" for the circumcision of Max Siegel's son Abraham. "Rabbi Ph. Hirshberg," president of Richmond's Polish Orthodox congregation, performed the ceremony. In 1887 the *Durham Tobacco Plant* described Purim festivities that culminated with a "supper ball," a popular American domestication of a traditionally boisterous religious holiday. Although men controlled worship and the cemetery society, this social gala was a woman's event. Among the ladies chaperoning the gala were the Summerfields, Newmans, Levys, Bears, Mohsbergs, Meaneys, and Schlombergs. This decorous, "uptown" German affair was fit material for the society pages.[32]

The first formal act of Jewish communal organization occurred in 1884 when Durham Jews purchased a corner parcel of the town cemetery. Jacob Levy, Samuel Lehman, Myer Summerfield, and August Mohsberg paid $90 for the plot. Levy's seven-year-old daughter, Ida, was the first to be buried there. When final payment for five hundred square feet of property on Morehead Road was made in 1886, records listed Abe Goldstein, P. Ahler(?), and Myer Summerfield as trustees of the Hebrew Burial Association. By 1889 the Jewish Cemetery Society held monthly meetings at Summerfield's store under the auspices of C. [sic] Summerfield, president; Julius Witcover, secretary; and Abe Goldstein, treasurer.[33] The officers were German, Dutch, Polish, and American born, and they were a mix of Reform and Orthodox.

The Cemetery Society, typically called a Benevolent Society, was a Chevra Kadisha (Holy Brotherhood). A traditional institution transplanted from Europe, the society ensured that the dead were buried in a ritually prescribed manner—the body washed, attended, and shrouded—and paid the expenses of the poor. Because Jews were not dying in sufficient numbers in Durham to justify monthly meetings, the society likely took responsibility for religious services and social welfare. In 1886 or 1887 Jews formed the Durham Hebrew Congregation, holding services in rented halls, with Myer Summerfield as president. Like those in most small-town congregations, services were lay led, with N. Newman, a merchant from Philadelphia, serving as prayer leader. Durham's Jews gave their congregation a distinctly American title, attaching their city's name to the dignified "Hebrew."

The synagogue was a sign that Jews intended to take full roles in civil society without sacrificing their collective identity. Indeed, as their elegant balls and repast suggest, these early settlers, mostly Jews of German background, were blending their Judaism with southern mores without assimilating into Christian society. They sought and won social recognition as Jews. Southerners, as a church-going people, respected the Jews' religiosity, and they certainly appreciated the Jews' economic utility as they worked to rebuild their economy. Jews found a welcome social place at the card tables and, as was common across the South, in Masonic halls.

The early German Jewish settlers differed from other Durhamites in lacking a southern agrarian heritage. Jews could not be found among the ranks of those who plowed the soil, bagged tobacco, or laid railroad track. If the German Jews were not proletarians, neither did they enter the capitalist elite. They created a niche as middlemen, primarily as sellers of dry goods. Their cosmopolitan origins contrasted with that of native southerners, who held nostalgically to Anglo-Saxon blood and heritage after the racial dislocations and political disorder of war and reconstruction. Without a local kinship network, Jews established their own social and economic ties with Jews across the region. From Richmond came rabbis and ritual circumcisers. Durham's early German Jewish settlers maintained a double identity as Jews and southerners.

Durham's German Jewish settlement responded to the town's economic cycles. In the late 1870s and into the late 1880s Durham rapidly urbanized. The *Durham Tobacco Plant* observed that a new house had risen monthly in 1876, then weekly in 1878, but daily in 1880. A disastrous 1880 fire, which destroyed some twenty buildings, hardly impeded this progress. Yet, by the end of the decade, economic depressions ended the German Jewish community's viability. The 1888 collapse of Blackwell's Bank of Durham, a victim of easy credit, brought sixteen merchants down with it. Within days D. L. Kaufman declared bankruptcy. Three weeks later Isaac Newman "quit business" at his Globe Clothing Store. Marx Bernstein—listing $3,000 in debt and $1,000 in assets—turned over his inventory and home furnishings to his son-in-law, the butcher Julius Schwartz. Only a few German families, primarily the Levys and Summerfields, persisted in Durham into the second generation. They were joined in 1899 by the extended family of Benjamin Kronheimer, whose parents had emigrated from Bavaria to Virginia in the 1840s. Kronheimer opened a department store that grew into the town's largest. Several American-born Jewish men of German origin remained after marrying the daughters of local east European immigrants.[34]

If a Jewish community were to survive, the town would need to draw Russian immigrants. Those southern small towns that did not draw an east European migration, historian Lee Shai Weissbach notes, saw their Jewish communities wither and often die. With their net worth secured only by inventory, Jews tended to move on. A study of Louisiana mercantile Jews, for example, observed that they differed from non-Jews in their mobility and lack of attachment to land both materially and culturally. German Jewish communities in such towns as Eufaula, Alabama; Port Gibson, Mississippi; and Owensboro, Kentucky, which had at least one hundred Jews in the late 1870s, nearly or completely disappeared.[35] Again, this situation was not uniquely southern, and small towns in the Midwest experienced similar decline or stagnation. To draw immigrants, the local economy had to create more opportunity than the limited prospects of an agrarian market town. In Durham the German Jewish merchants were soon overwhelmed by the arrival of hundreds of east European proletarians drawn to Durham by a new industrial product, cigarettes.

4 Russian Tobacco Workers
A Proletarian Interlude, 1880s

Faced with Blackwell's popular Bull Durham tobaccos, W. Duke and Sons took a gamble. "My company is up against a stone wall," James Buchanan "Buck" Duke realized. "It cannot compete with the Bull. I am going into the cigarette business."[1]

Producing pipe tobaccos had required only unskilled labor to sort, pack, and bag the leaf, and the industrialists had a ready pool of cheap labor in the young African Americans who had been drawn to town from the countryside. Duke needed skilled workers to roll cigarettes, but, like other southern industrialists, he wanted to maintain the racial division of labor. With the abolition of slavery, southern capitalists looked to immigration to revive the region's languishing farms and to serve its budding industry. Rapid expansion of the railroads aggravated the labor shortage. Like other southern states, North Carolina appointed a Board of Immigration with an agent in New York, but these efforts met with little success. The great European immigration after 1881 largely bypassed the South. From 1880 to 1890 the portion of foreign born in North Carolina dropped from 0.27 percent to 0.23 percent while nationally the portion in the nation rose from 13.3 percent to 14.6 percent. Despite small numbers, colonies of immigrant workers, recruited by labor contractors, sprouted across the South. Poles and Germans worked in the steel mills of Greenville, South Carolina; Hungarians tended Louisiana gardens; Japanese labored in Texas and Florida fields; and Russians laid track in North Carolina.[2]

In 1881 Buck Duke headed north, intending to hire immigrant Jewish workers. They not only would produce cigarettes but also would train local rollers. The cigarette fad had first struck Europe in the 1830s. East European aristocrats trained peasants, Jews among them, to roll cigarettes. The fad spread to America, and in 1864 tobacco factories began opening in New York. Jewish immigrants were a source of cheap, skilled labor. Some had learned the craft in the old country. For the unskilled, cigarette rolling required only a one-month apprenticeship.

On a New York dock Duke met Moses Gladstein, a Ukrainian immigrant who had learned the trade from Russian nobility. Gladstein had lost his job at the Goodwin Tobacco Factory for leading a strike. Duke hired him to organize some strikers to work in his factory, offering to pay their train fare to Durham.

On the basis of his experience with southern workers, Duke felt confident of his ability to control the New Yorkers. North Carolina labor laws were written to serve the capitalists' interests. Native workers were notably compliant. Isolated by religion, culture, and language, immigrant Jews would not have the communal support in Durham to sustain a labor movement. The strikers were poor, likely agreeable to whatever terms Duke offered. Duke, who desperately needed skilled labor, would be acquiring trained workers from a competitor. The risks were manageable.

Not to be outdone, Blackwell added cigarettes to its product line and began hiring Jewish rollers. The number of workers swelled to more than one hundred. They were mostly young, some in their early teens, and newly arrived from Poland and Russia. Gladstein, who was only nineteen, had been in America for a year. After settling in Durham, he sent for his wife and infant son.[3]

To supervise the workers, Duke hired a Jewish manager, Joseph M. Siegel, a native of Kovno, Lithuania. Siegel had learned the trade in St. Petersburg and London, where he had managed tobacco factories. In New York Siegel had worked for the Goodwin Company, the firm that had employed Gladstein and his strikers. W. T. Blackwell responded by engaging Joseph's brother David, a supervisor with Kinney Brothers in New York, as a manager at the Bull factory. The brothers were paid a weekly salary of $45 to $50, five times a roller's pay.[4]

One roller, Bernhard Goldgar, wrote a memoir, which gives insight into the workers' culture. (Unfortunately, it ends with his arrival in Durham.) Goldgar described his shtetl of Kodna, Poland, as a "mudhole" whose people were "steeped in ignorance and superstition." After fires twice dev-

W. Duke and Sons employed Russian Jewish cigarette rollers in this wooden factory in the early 1880s. (Courtesy of the North Carolina Division of Archives and History, Raleigh)

astated his home, his family moved into a wood-paneled dugout. Hunger pangs and numbing regimens of religious study marked his childhood. A precocious cheder student, Goldgar was hired as a children's tutor by wealthy urban Jews and became acquainted with novels and newspapers, the world beyond the shtetl. In 1879, frustrated by his inability to afford a university education, the teenager left for Hamburg, where he boarded a steamer to Glasgow and then to New York. He arrived with his prayer book, phylacteries, and eighty cents. He knew four languages but no English and did not have a friend or relative in America. He peddled door to door and slept on the floor of a tenement basement. Eager to advance himself, he coauthored a Yiddish-English grammar for new immigrants. He convinced the philanthropist Jacob Schiff to publish the book, but it failed to secure his fortune. He learned to roll cigarettes. "Misery and despair" shattered his dreams, but the oratory of "revolutionary socialists" revived his spirits. Meditating in a forest in a soulful mood that has resonances of Tolstoy, Goldgar experienced a spiritual rebirth: "As I sat there deep in thought, a new light lighting up my sorrowful past appeared before me and I became a son no longer of Israel alone; the great world became my country and the whole human race my people. Were not the masses, like myself suffering from the same causes, was not their cry for freedom my own? I embraced socialism right then and there in that dark woods of New Jersey. I suddenly found an aim in life." Shortly before departing for Durham, Goldgar went to hear a "famous social-anarchist" newly arrived in America after twenty years in German and English prisons for the "brave advocacy of his ideas." Goldgar met his future wife, Annie, at the lecture. He was saddened to learn that she did not share his revolutionary ideals. Nonetheless, they married, and a few months later he departed for Durham with a group of twenty men. He soon sent for his wife, and they moved into a cottage.[5]

The cigarette workers settled on Pine Street near Duke's factory. "Yiddisha Streetal" was in the Bottoms, a neighborhood of shacks, pens, and warehouses. A cottage could be leased for three dollars a week. Many workers rented rooms or found boarding houses. Their workday extended from early morning to ten o'clock at night, six days a week. The New Yorkers were paid a rate of seventy cents per one thousand cigarettes for rolling premium brands, a higher wage than that of the native workers. Because a skilled worker could roll about twenty-five hundred cigarettes a day, he could expect to earn eight to ten dollars a week. Brodie Duke remarked to the rollers that he wished that he could make money as fast as they could.[6]

The Duke factory was a two-story wooden building. Six rollers worked at a long table behind four-foot partitions. Black workers hauled boxes of tobacco from a nearby log cabin and placed them on the tables. The roller took paper and shredded leaf (the "makin's" or a "monkey"), wet and matted it, and then rolled it on a marble or pasteboard slab (a "kleunky"). The paper was pasted into tubes with a flour and water mix. Some New Yorkers used another technique, forming the paper around a stick and then packing it. Taking four or five tubes in hand, the roller cut them into cigarette lengths with a sharp blade. Mishandled shears cost the rollers time and money.[7]

However skilled the immigrant rollers, they could not produce a sufficient number of cigarettes or train local workers fast enough to satisfy the demand created by Duke's aggressive marketing. In 1883 Duke was producing 250,000 cigarettes daily. Eager to gain an edge on the competition, Duke committed himself to James Bonsack's cigarette rolling and cutting machine. The machine was installed on April 30, 1884. The New Yorkers reacted by threatening to destroy it. Bonsack's mechanic, William O'Brien, received anonymous letters menacing his life.[8]

A Labor Movement

The manufacturers, the Dukes especially, were hostile to all attempts at labor organization. In 1875, when black tobacco workers had struck the Bull Durham factory for higher wages, Blackwell simply fired them and then replaced them. Under state law, labor had the status of "chattel," complained Morris Bernstein, a Duke roller, claiming that North Carolina's courts gave "advantage to the employers greater than those offered in almost any other state." A job applicant was required to produce a written permit from his former employer or risk a $50 fine.[9]

The Jews, with their experience in labor and socialist movements, were less pliable than the natives, who were former tenant farmers and rural laborers recently settled in town. Largely uneducated, the native southerners were accustomed to hard work at long hours, and tenancy had habituated them to obedience to their bosses. Many were children. In 1882 Duke had advertised for "twenty-five white girls to make cigarettes." Laura Cox, a country girl trained by Jews, was eight when she started in Duke's factory.[10]

In July 1884, three months after the Bonsack machines were installed, the New Yorkers, allied with white southerners, organized Local Chapter 27 of the Cigarmaker's Progressive Union (CMPU), "the first of its kind in the State of North Carolina," William Blumberg reported to the union journal, *Progress*. The chapter began with fourteen members; seven of its nine officers were Jews, including Bernhard Goldgar. Within months it grew to seventy members, "the greater proportion" of whom were New Yorkers.[11]

Fortunately for the rollers, the Bonsack machine was prone to breakdowns, and their skills were still needed to maintain production levels. As Bonsack and his mechanics worked over the next fourteen months to improve the equipment, the machine's capacity increased to 250,000 cigarettes a day, and Duke installed a second machine. After meeting with the CMPU national executive board in New York, Duke announced that he was reducing each roller's daily quota to one thousand cigarettes and cut the workers' wages two-thirds, to around three dollars weekly. Nonunion hands were permitted higher quotas.[12]

Duke intended to dismiss the Jews gradually "to avoid all possible danger of doing injustice . . . and all risk of collision with labor organizations." He anticipated that "many may leave." With "the leading New York hands" gone, *Progress* reported, the others would be "unable to support a

Union themselves." The Jews protested against Duke's "scheme," but their situation was desperate. "We would soon be compelled through starvation to submit to any terms he offered no matter how enslaving," a worker wrote *Progress*. Duke imposed "tyrannous shop rules," inflicting "fines and charges until they took the greater part of our hard earned wages." The rollers were required to contribute one thousand to four thousand cigarettes a week for a "missionary box" to cover the factory's "slack." Junius Strickland, a native southerner who served as union secretary, urged the workers to arm themselves for the coming revolution.[13]

Increasingly the work was turned over to native laborers trained by the New Yorkers. In 1886 Duke offered "inducements" for five hundred local boys and girls to learn the cigarette trade. Duke "knows that the Durham or native hands would never rebel or attempt to belong to a union," a roller reported. "They not only remain outside the union but oppose it and try to prevent its progress in every way they can conceive, also acting very unkindly to all union hands, thinking it is a sin to disobey the boss." Already in conflict with their bosses and coworkers, the Jews were further hurt when the CMPU nationally changed from a tobacco to a cigarmaker's union. The Durham chapter folded.[14]

As the Bonsack machine was achieving peak efficiency, some former CMPU members started a local assembly of the Knights of Labor, the biracial international workers brotherhood. Altogether seven Knights of Labor assemblies organized in Durham; two were composed of cigarette makers and one of tobacco workers. The Knights, federated with the white Farmers Alliance, presented a political as well as an economic challenge to Durham's capitalists. In the 1886 elections Raleigh Knights succeeded in electing a workman to the U.S. Congress.[15]

Duke's factory foremen threatened to dismiss any Knights in their employ. A letter to a Knights newspaper in 1888 signed "Durhamite" spoke of the "New Yorkers" who resisted the wage cuts but ultimately gave way to the machines and unorganized workers. The letter denounced machinery as the "curse of labor" and condemned the manufacturers. Although the Knights never formally went on strike, they engaged in work stoppages.[16]

White native southerners and immigrant Jews formed a labor alliance. In his 1884 *History of the Town of Durham, North Carolina*, the Reverend Hiram Paul, a Baptist minister who published the Knights of Labor's *Workmen*, idealized the cigarette rollers in a paean of fustian prose: the "wandering Jew—the illustrious cosmopolite, whose ancient prestige and glory, richly embellishing the ethical and aesthetic pages of history, though buried beneath the hoary locks of time, yet wield a salutary influence upon the morals of the world."[17] Paul did not see the Jews as economic refugees from eastern Europe but as a biblical people come to life. A southern progressive, he espoused the brotherhood of the social gospel.

Typically in the South, which lacked an established proletariat, local Knight leadership came from sympathetic merchants, editors, and professionals. The recording secretary of Local Assembly 7539 was D. L. Kaufman, a merchant who boarded with Abe Goldstein on Pine Street. Kaufman had emigrated from Germany to America in 1866. In 1884 he had taken the job of bookkeeper in Goldstein's store, and a year later he took over Esther Goldstein's Main Street stand, selling shoes and dry goods. The *Durham Tobacco Plant* described Kaufman as "a young man clever in business," and he was sufficiently sociable to be elected an officer in the local International Order of Odd Fellows.[18]

Kaufman, who lived among the workers in the Pine Street ghetto, was motivated by principle rather than by self-interest. In 1887 he was elected state inside esquire of the Knights of Labor. In that year he wrote a letter on his store's stationery to Terence Powderly, the international Knights of Labor master workman, protesting the repeated whipping of (non-Jewish) child laborers at the Duke factory. In 1888, after a buying trip to the North, Kaufman "made a regrettable assignment to W. M. Morgan." Two months later Kaufman sold his inventory and left town. By then, the last skilled cigarette rollers had been removed from Duke's factory. The Knights of Labor faded as white racists scorned it as a "Nigger" organization and as farmers and industrial workers came into conflict over the issue of rural labor.[19]

Durham workers were "pitiably disorganized," *Progress* reported in 1885. "We cigarette makers here have been leading a most imbittered life, tyrannized and imposed on shamefully by our bosses," a roller wrote. The power of Duke, his machinery, and his "native" labor overwhelmed and fragmented the workers. The Jews were sucked into "the great whirlpool of destruction which the capitalist have prepared for us," a worker wrote. In 1888 a brick mason reported to the state labor board that in Durham "the laboring people are at war with each other." Age, color, and gender divided the workers. In 1890 41.6 percent of Duke's cigarette and smoking tobacco workforce were women, and 13.2 percent were children.[20]

In the April 5, 1896, *Raleigh News and Observer*, Washington Duke reflected on his employee relations:

When we began to employ a large number of people, we organized a Sunday school in one room of our factory, and out of that Sunday school grew Main Street Methodist church. We try to carry the religious idea all the way through. We worship with those we employ. We like them and we believe they like us.

We never had any trouble in the help except when 125 Polish Jews were hired to come down to Durham to work in the factory. They gave us no end of trouble. We worked out of that, and we now employ our own people. There have been 800 or 900 young men and women working together in our factory here. We encourage them to be self respecting, and to be religious. There has never been a breath of scandal here. People want emigration. If good citizens come, well and good, but there are plenty of North Carolinians here who are glad to work.[21]

The distinction between the "Polish Jews" and "our own people" defined the conflict. The Jews, unwilling to accept their place, challenged Duke's self-regard as benefactor and guardian. Corporate paternalism, couched in a high Christian tone, subjected the workers to ruthless social and economic control. Duke, Carr, and Blackwell were all Sunday school teachers. Their preaching and church building were intended to create a loyal, sober, and chaste work force. Junius Strickland, the southern labor radical, was later converted in the Duke factory church room and became a loyal employee and Sunday school teacher. In the absence of a living wage, Duke promised the Jews salvation neither in Durham nor in the world to come.

By the 1890s, as Duke stated, the South was less receptive to immigrant labor as home workers demanded jobs. As outsiders, Durham Jews failed to sustain proletarian solidarity with ethnic white southerners, and the town did not have populations of other outsider immigrant groups with whom to ally. By contrast, in Tampa, where the tobacco industry growth roughly paralleled that of Durham, Cuban, Italian, and Spanish cigar makers melded into a labor alliance that began in the 1880s and persisted into the 1930s. Engaged in sometimes violent confrontations— among their targets was the militantly antilabor Duke tobacco trust—the Tampa workers won little more than symbolic victories. New York Jewish union activity in the 1880s was unstable and often improvisational. An 1883 strike of mostly Jewish workers at Kinney Brothers tobacco factory dissipated after weeks. American labor unions, especially in the skilled trades, saw the immigrants as a threat and did not welcome the newcomers.[22]

The Jews' labor activism was motivated not just by class solidarity, with roots in European socialist movements, but also by their aspiring Americanism. They sought to find a fraternal place in a South rampant with Granges, Farmers Alliances, and Democratic machines. They rallied to the rhetoric not of Jewish unity or historic grievance nor of international socialist solidarity, but of American republicanism, railing against tyranny and insisting on civil justice. But the ethnic conflict transcended the political and economic struggle. However much the Jews sought to achieve proletarian brotherhood with native southerners, however much they insisted on their rights, ethnicity and dramatically different historical experiences isolated and divided them.[23]

The Jewish workers gradually left Durham. In September 1886 the *Durham Tobacco Plant* reported that "all the Hebrew cigarette workers . . . returned to New York, excepting two." Most workers did head north, fortified by twenty-five dollars in severance pay, but directories in 1887 still listed a half-dozen Jews in the tobacco industry. Several workers remained in town but turned to retail trades. In 1889, when Duke decided to manufacture cigars, he hired Isaac Seligson, the superintendent of a New York cigarette factory, to come to Durham to train workers.[24]

A roller who left, Bernard Harris, recalled that the workers returned to New York because they preferred city life to country living. "The climate here does not agree with them; quite a number of them were confined to their rooms for weeks," Morris Bernstein observed of his coworkers. Complaints about Durham fever recurred in the *Progress,* and the union served as a benevolence society, collecting funds for the sick and homebound.[25]

The workers must have found Durham to be lonely and disheartening —especially because many of the men were young and single. Some workers who returned to New York resumed their employment at the Goodwin Company, only to be discharged six months later when the "busy season" ended. In 1887 a former roller, Sam Edelsohn, was killed by a locomotive in Jersey City, an apparent suicide. After leaving Durham, he peddled matches for a living. "Distressingly poor," he had in his pocket a worthless check for $20,000. Bernard Harris was more fortunate. He liked North Carolina and returned in 1890, settling in Raleigh.[26]

The few Jewish workers who remained quickly turned from proletarians to petite bourgeoisie. The Jews' ambition was to rise out of the working class, not with it. Bernhard Goldgar's youthful, revolutionary ardor cooled as he confronted economic realities at home. He had children to support. His wife did not share his socialist views. Goldgar opened a grocery store. In 1887 this socialist who had come to America with eighty cents advertised that he had "started with hardly anything in this city three years ago," but now owned "three stores . . . all prosperous . . . in addition about one thousand dollars in Real Estate." Duke paid labor contractor Moses Gladstein $1,000, which financed a dry-goods store. Former roller Joe Smolensky married a local Jewish woman and opened a store before moving to Henderson. After his one-year contract expired, cigar maker Isaac Seligson settled in Raleigh, where he founded Ike's Bargain Store and hired Bernard Harris as a clerk. Roller "Joe Jew" Cuddle, "a lazy and indolent fellow," became an early town "sport." Small towns did not sustain a Jewish proletarian culture.[27]

Documentary evidence on the Jewish workers is scarce. The newspapers were quiet on labor activities. (Few newspapers or factory records survived major fires in 1880 and 1886.) The *Durham Tobacco Plant* in its boosterism identified the interests of the capitalists with the welfare of the entire city. An 1884 Durham history rhapsodized on the Blackwell factory: "Here all classes of honest and industrious mechanics and laborers find profitable employment, kind friends. . . . Here the song of human industry and progress floats upon the balmy bosom of every zephyr, . . . inspiring new hope and energy in the dreamy soul of the humble laborer. Durham today is an asylum for the poor, a place where the 'wandering Jew' . . . finds a peaceful and profitable retreat."[28]

The New South propagandists promulgated a myth of the harmony of labor and capital. William Boyd wrote in *The Story of Durham: City of the New South* that "the interest of the capitalists of Durham in the welfare of their employees has made the city notable for its lack of industrial conflicts"; the unions were "ephemeral." Duke himself blamed his labor troubles on outside agitators, Polish Jews.[29]

Jewish Capitalists

While the workers and Duke battled, the Siegel brothers started their own tobacco factory in 1883. They occupied a small building on Poplar Street and began producing five thousand hand-rolled cigarettes a day under the trademark of Cablegram, named for the trans-Atlantic telegraph. That level of production was about the daily quota of two skilled hand rollers. Effective merchandising rapidly increased demand—within a year the tax value of the firm rose from $1,000 to $6,000—but in 1884 a fire "burned out" their business. In 1885 they reestablished themselves in a house with "quite a number of hands employed." They increased production to more

than 570,000 cigarettes a month, enough for ten rollers. It is likely that
some of the workers were Jews who had left Duke's employ. In 1886 the
Siegels boarded two rollers—Jacob Ettelson and Jacob Berger—in their
home. As the Siegels prepared for greater success, a fire swept the factory
in 1887. The Siegel brothers left town.[30]

The Siegel fire aroused suspicions among the Jews. Competition in the
tobacco industry had provoked sporadic acts of industrial sabotage. Carr
had compared Duke and Blackwell to bulls goring each other in an open
pasture. Rival factory squads waged pitched battles over laying railroad
track. Through mechanization and aggressive marketing Duke was able to
force Blackwell out of the cigarette business in 1887. Yet, factory fires occurred frequently, and the industrialists maintained fire squads to deal with
spontaneous outbursts in the dust-filled, wood-framed buildings. Despite
increased use of brick, Durham had three major fires in the five years preceding the Siegel conflagration. Whatever the cause of the fires, the rumors
of arson reflected the distrust that the Jews harbored against Duke.[31]

Legacy of the Cigarette Rollers

The immigrants had come from pre-industrial societies, and machine-age
America no longer needed their skills. Two of Duke's Bonsack machines
turned out the total monthly production of Siegel's hand rollers in a little
more than a day. Ultimately, the Jews aspired to accumulate sufficient capital to open a store, to move on. Jews integrated into Durham not through
the corporate economy but by establishing an independent ethnic, mercantile niche.

While Jewish workers struggled, Jewish merchants prospered. It was a
typically Jewish predicament to find themselves both allied with and organized against the town powers. Class lines formed in the small Jewish
community between the wealthier, established German Jewish merchants
uptown on Main Street and the poorer, newly arrived Russian Jewish
workers downtown in the Bottoms. The militant greenhorns may have
embarrassed the acculturated, socially conservative German Jews. While
the workers organized, the merchants joined Duke for card games. The
workers never participated in the city's civic life or formed a congregation.
The cigarette rollers "came here to earn a livelihood and were interested
in practically nothing but their work," observed a Durham Jewish community history.[32]

Although the Orthodox Jewish community for the next century would
trace its origins to Duke's tobacco workers, no evidence survives of their

religious life. The Cigar Makers Progressive Union, meeting on Saturday nights, served as a "benevolent and protective association" that raised funds for the indigent and cared for the sick.[33] Jewish labor militants were sometimes indifferent—if not hostile—to Orthodoxy, which was regarded as too passive, an Old World anachronism, though Jewish unionism was imbued with Yiddishkeit. With their poverty and twelve-hour workday, the workers would have been hard-pressed to organize a congregation. Religiously educated workers, such as Bernhard Goldgar or Moses Gladstein, would not have needed the formal apparatus of a state-chartered congregation to convene a prayer quorum of ten men. Founding a "church" was a civic gesture, a commitment to the future, but the workers remained outsiders for whom Durham was only an interlude. Jewish merchants organized a formal congregation soon after the labor militants left in 1886 or 1887. Perhaps they wanted to impress upon their neighbors that they were a conservative, religiously dutiful people.

Community divisions were not categorically rich against poor, German against Russian, or acculturated against immigrant. D. L. Kaufman, a German-born merchant, led the Knights and lived in the Pine Street ghetto. The founder of the Orthodox synagogue, which became an east European shul, was a German-born merchant, Myer Summerfield. In its early years the Jewish community was too small to institutionalize its differences.

The New York workers became the stuff of folklore, and a century later academic historians, the popular media, and local citizens, both Jewish and Gentile, pointed to them as the founders of the Durham Jewish community. Two novels written in the twentieth century evoked their world. Romance aside, the novels were thinly veiled descriptions of Durham.

Ernest Seeman's *American Gold* described how the New Yorkers brought the Lower East Side down south with them to Turpentine (Pine) Street. His novel romanticized the Jewish ghetto with a stereotypical cast of fire-eyed, rabbinical graybeards and wizened old women in shawls. Flashy city slickers paraded up Main Street, tobacco dust on their derbies, trying to impress the jezebels in their tight skirts. The neighborhood air smelled thickly of garlic and herring. To light their Sabbath stoves, the Jews hired "fire-goys," ex-slaves or white country women. In the mornings they gathered early for prayer in a room over the store of Moisheh Solomon (Myer Summerfield?). For upper-class Gentiles, Seeman contended, the immigrants became a butt of jokes and anti-Semitic barbs.[34]

Foster Fitz-Simons in *Bright Leaf* turned the Jews into Ukrainians. The worker Jascha Lipik, never seen without a hat, bought a house on Maple (Pine) Street near the black area of Jamaica (Hayti). The Ukrainians had a passion for buying property, and a ghetto of cottages sprouted amid dumps and tobacco factories. The women took in boarders to augment their husbands' meager incomes. Fitz-Simons's novel focused on the love of a tobacco magnate, modeled on Buck Duke, for a beautiful young Ukrainian worker, Sophie Lipik.[35] For Gentile Durham, Jews were The Other, objects of fiction and fantasy, of sexual lust.

Jewish community folklore over the years exaggerated the cigarette rollers' numbers and importance. A 1921 report referred to Duke's three hundred Jewish workers. A 1944 community history extravagantly claimed that Washington Duke "owes his title of Tobacco King to a group of Ukrainian Jews whom he brought to America in the 1880's." These "masters of the ancient art of tobacco blending and the making of cigarettes taught Washington Duke the art which he industrialized and through which he amassed a fortune." The labor antagonisms and Siegel fires were forgotten. More recently, Eli Evans in *The Provincials: A Personal History of Jews in the South* recounted the oral history that he heard in his Durham childhood, of how the "roots of the Durham Jewish community reached directly into Mr. Duke's cigarette-rolling rooms." Unlike authors of earlier accounts, Evans acknowledged the labor strife between the Jews and Duke, but the bitterness had long since dissipated. Evans observed that Jews "could identify" with the Dukes as people who had worked "their way from poverty to riches in one generation." The Dukes were "builders of a manufacturing empire," not "plantation-bound and honey-dipped . . . landed aristocracy," Evans explained.[36]

If Jews could not be Old South romantics, they became New South sentimentalists. The rollers' sojourn in Durham was brief and marked by class and ethnic conflict. They were alienated from native southerners. Durham Jews, however, were selective in their remembering and forgetting. The narrative that persisted in their collective memory represented the tobacco rollers as pioneering southerners, forefathers of the enduring community. The story of the tobacco workers as an invented tradition offered the Jewish community a unifying creation myth, a single dramatic narrative, that gave it southern origins. The story has touches of folktale, a Duke anointing a pauper, and of biblical fable, a Moses leading Israelites to a new land. The story appealed to both Jews and southerners, for the South is, as Evans observed, "a storytelling place."[37] Jews, as they had in

Europe, sought the protection of a nobleman, or as the tobacco magnate once signed himself: Washington, Duke of Durham. The folklore of the cigarette rollers aligned the Jews with the city's social and economic elite, minimalized their difference, and demonstrated how integral they were to Durham's creation and growth.

The Jews' identification with the town's origins enhanced the civic comfort and integration of Jews who arrived later. Ironically, rather than demonstrate the integral character of Durham Jewry as southern, the experience of Duke's Jewish workers demonstrated the failure of southern industrial and immigration policy as nativist, antilabor, antiradical biases prevailed over economic self-interest. By 1900 only 6 percent of the nation's foreign-born population lived in the South.[38] Although Durham's industrial economy was rapidly expanding, almost no Jews chose to work in its tobacco or textile factories. Durham's Jewish artisans and shopkeepers identified with the capitalists. They showed scant interest in working-class nostalgia, and they did not establish the proletarian institutions to preserve Jewish socialist culture. The Arbeiter Ring (Workmen's Circle), a secular Yiddish, self-help society that organized nationally in 1900, did not form locally, although chapters arose in Macon, Nashville, Savannah, and Richmond.

The Jewish proletarian interlude in Durham lasted less than a decade. The community that persisted was mercantile. What the workers contributed to the development of Durham Jewry was to create a critical mass that drew other immigrants. Several families that established themselves for generations were pointed to Durham by relatives who had rolled cigarettes. In the 1880s and 1890s east European immigrants who came to peddle and open stores created an enduring Durham Jewish community.

5 East European Immigration

From Old World to New South, 1886 to 1900

Apermanent Jewish community formed in Durham from the 1880s to 1920, the era of mass east European immigration to America. The identity of Durham Jewry changed. In the late 1880s it became overwhelmingly Russian. The Jewish population increased from 40 in 1880 to about 200 in 1900 and then rose to 350 in the World War I era, where it remained for decades. Meanwhile, the number of German Jews declined to less than twenty. Durham was highly representative of the population changes that the east European migration wrought on the "vast majority" of southern Jewish communities.[1]

Cycles of growth and decline changed the composition of the Jewish community. In the 1880s merchants prospered, but the local bank collapse of 1888 undermined the town's economy. Virtually all of the German Jews abandoned Durham. Bernhard Goldgar relocated to Macon, Georgia. Durham barely recovered before the Panic of 1893 hit the nation. Two Jewish-owned stores in Chapel Hill, Levy and Rosenburg's Racket Stores, both failed. The local real estate market collapsed. Of the thirty-five Jews listed in the 1887 Durham city business directory, only five still remained in 1902.[2] Yet, despite widespread failures across the South in the 1880s and 1890s, east European immigrants arrived in increasing numbers.

For generations Durham's east European Jews referred to themselves nostalgically as "50 families." The stability of this number is misleading because it conceals considerable internal dynamism. By 1938 only five of the fifty families had local roots that extended before 1900. Few families remained beyond a second generation, but new arrivals replaced the departures. Such mobility was typical of small-town Jewish communities regardless of region. A study of Jews in three Kentucky towns revealed "fluidity and motion," which led to continual "population turnover." The "most striking quality" of the Jewish community in Muncie, Indiana, was its "restlessness as individuals moved in and out of town."[3]

Nor was this mobility an exclusively Jewish dynamic in the South, and it must be seen in the context of larger migrations wrought by the changing New South economic landscape. The rise of new industries—lumber, mining, textiles, tobacco, furniture—led to population shifts. Lithuanian immigrants looking for a place to peddle or to open a store shared railroad cars with sharecroppers heading to lumber camps and planters' sons canvassing new territories as salesmen. Nor were Jews unique in departing from a benighted South, which, despite its embrace of industrial progress, was still diseased, impoverished, and ill educated. From 1880 to 1910, 537,000 blacks and 1,243,000 whites left the South as it lost population to every region of the country. Mobile Jews did not remain long enough to acculturate as southerners.[4]

The presence of east European immigrant Jews in noticeable numbers in Durham was but one sign that the South was becoming more American in its ethnic composition. The defeated, secessionist South had been a land apart among America's regions. As a New South integrated into the nation economically and politically, however—especially after Grover Cleveland's Democratic victory in 1884 and the patriotic paroxysms of the Spanish-American War—the South reentered the national mainstream.

The east European Jews arrived in Durham at the moment when anti-immigrant nativism was rising in the South. With few Jews and a small foreign population, the South historically had not felt national anti-immigrant passions. At first southerners welcomed immigration in the hope that it might resolve the region's labor shortages and racial imbalance. In the 1890s southerners began voicing anti-immigration sentiments. Washington Duke's complaint in 1896 about "trouble" with his "Polish Jews" reflected a growing disillusionment.[5]

As the South urbanized and commercialized, anti-Semitism came down the rail lines with the immigrants. In the 1890s Jews in such cities as Mobile, Atlanta, New Orleans, and Richmond found themselves excluded from societies that they had once helped found. Jewish religious and economic stereotypes were increasingly expressed in terms of race. Acculturated southern Jews of German origin, who worshiped in Reform temples, now found themselves cast with impoverished, Yiddish-speaking green-horns from Poland and Lithuania, a seemingly unassimilable people who practiced a "primitive" religion.[6]

The Jew's racial status was uncertain. Although Durham's Jews lacked a slaveholding past, they were beneficiaries of prevailing racial customs and attitudes. In the tobacco mills Jews had held privileged skilled positions while blacks were relegated to hauling tobacco. Yet Jews also resided near African Americans, and white southerners disdained Jewish peddlers and storekeepers who catered to black trade.

In the South antiblack racism provided a model for anti-immigrant rhetoric. As white redemption overthrew the racial progress of Recon-struction, customs of African American segregation were codified into Jim Crow laws, most notably in the voting booths in 1900. White supremacy was a rallying call to stifle black assertion and to revenge black political domination. In 1898 a bloody race riot left ten dead in Wilmington. In the political campaign of that year racist Red Shirts rode the countryside.

The roots of this racialism were both folkloric and ideological. South-erners imbued with a romantic sensibility exalted blood and heritage. Cults of the Anglo-Saxon spread across the region. A eugenics movement warned about the degenerate stock of newly arrived eastern and southern Europeans, reinforcing folk biases against allegedly dark, inferior peoples. Durham was the site of Confederate reunions, which glorified southern heritage and underscored the outsider status of recently arrived east Euro-pean immigrants.

Southerners perceived Jews through the lens of myth. With their ro-mantic religiosity southerners saw Jews not as an ethnically European people encountering modernity but as a Biblical people come to life. Southerners knew the matriarchs and patriarchs intimately. Once on his pastoral rounds in Durham the Reverend Kolman Heillig met a trolley conductor who took a fancy to his daughter Rachel. "If the Rachel of the Bible was as pretty as this here girl," he remarked to the rabbi, "no wonder Jacob waited seven years to marry her." According to a famous apologia attributed variously to Benjamin Disraeli and Judah Benjamin, the ances-tors of the Jews were priests in the Temple of Solomon when those of the Anglo-Saxons were barbarians in the caves of Gaul. In 1885 a Durham newspaper quoted this defense in a lavish encomium on the glory of the Jews. Religious anti-Semitism was heard mostly on the playgrounds rather than in polite, adult company. Young Roy Levy was confronted by a schoolyard bully who wanted to know why he killed Christ. "I didn't do it," Roy answered innocently. "My brother Dave did it."[7]

Despite the immigrants' obvious poverty, southerners continued to associate Jews with commerce. The disparagement of Jews as financial parasites coexisted with a countermyth that extolled Jews as archcapitalists. Gilded Age Durham saw virtue in people who could bring a profit. "What a wonderful race of people is this Jewish race," the *Durham Tobacco Plant* editorialized in 1888. "Well may they be proud of their race." The industry of the Jews was cited as a model for other races. "Everywhere there are men of the highest culture and attainments," the *Durham Tobacco Plant* rhapsodized in 1896. Jews were the "money kings" of Paris, London, Vienna, Frankfort, and New York. Yet, in defending Jews, even Zeb Vance conceded that Jews were not invariably honest or had less compunctions about cheating Gentiles. (These traits he attributed to Christian persecution, not to Judaism.) Beside religious bias there was the more modern anti-Semitism that saw Jews as a cog of an international financial conspiracy. North Carolina governor Elias Carr, who served from 1893 to 1897, charged that "our Negro brethren, too, are being held in bondage by Rothschild." Carr, a "dirt farmer," was tapping an anti-Semitic vein in populism that blamed Jewish capitalism for the South's agrarian ills. Durham's Jewish peddlers and grocers, struggling to rise from poverty, could not have much resembled a cabal of international financiers. The rampant racism of North Carolina's politics in the late 1890s with its white supremacists and night-riding Red Shirts—a black was lynched on the Durham–Chapel Hill road—seemed not to have touched Durham Jews.[8]

East European Immigration

The reasons for Durham's increasing Jewish population had as much to do with upheavals in eastern Europe as with economic developments in the growing city. From the 1880s to the 1920s more than two million Jews immigrated to the United States, transforming American Jewry, which had numbered two hundred thousand in 1870. The flow of emigration reflected cycles of repression. The assassination of reform-minded Czar Alexander II in 1881 provoked a round of anti-Semitic legislation, the May Laws of 1882, and, even worse, unleashed a bloody wave of pogroms. Rioting mobs, augmented by police, swept through more than one hundred Russian cities. Residency and occupational restrictions were imposed, and a *numerus clausus* (closed number) denied secular education to all but a few. Jews as young as eight years of age were pressed into military ser-

vice for terms that extended to twenty-five years. After the expulsion of
Jews from Moscow, emigration reached record levels in 1891 and 1892 and
then peaked again from 1903 to 1909 after a new round of pogroms.[9]

Although persecution drove Jews from Russian lands, the push to emi-
grate was largely economic. In 1900 nearly seven million Jews still lived
in eastern Europe, compressed in urban ghettos and rural shtetls. High
birth rates added to the economic problems created by the czarist policy
of confining and pauperizing the Jews. Furthermore, the increasing availability of manufactured goods threatened the livelihood of Jews who
were traditionally artisans or petty traders.

At first the immigrants crowded into the ghettos of New York, Philadelphia, Baltimore, and Chicago, but nearly one-quarter of the immigrant Jews, pushed by urban poverty, moved to small towns of heartland
America (see table 5.1). Although only about 7 percent of Jewish immigrants settled in southern states, they constituted a disproportionate 15
percent of all immigrants to the region. East European Jews flowed into
Durham and by 1900 constituted 3.1 percent of the town's population,
compared to 1.2 percent of the nation's population. From 1882 to 1887
thirty-one Jewish men applied for naturalization in Durham County.
(Only men were processed, their wives and children qualifying with
them.) Twenty-eight were from Russia, and only three were from Germany. The Jews applied in groups, witnessing for each other. The peak year
was 1886, when seventeen filed. In the 1890s forty-three Jews filed, all
but one having emigrated from Russian domains. From 1900 to 1920
more than forty Jews filed final petitions; all were Russians excepting one
Austro-Hungarian. Most Durham immigrants had departed from Ant-
werp, Bremen, or Liverpool and arrived in New York, though a smaller
number entered through Chicago, Baltimore, or Philadelphia.[10]

Naturalization papers filed in Durham County draw a profile of the
east European Jewish community. The residency requirement was five
years in the United States and one in North Carolina. In 1900 the Durham
east European immigrant averaged ten years in America, and the median
year of immigration was 1889. Some Durham Jews had lived in America
more than a decade before applying for citizenship. On the basis of their
experiences in Russia, Jews were distrustful of government and reluctant
to register with authorities. Nevertheless, Jews had a powerful incentive to
naturalize: some states required proof of citizenship to obtain peddling or
retailing licenses.

In contrast to the Germans, who arrived as individuals or nuclear fami-

TABLE 5.1. Last Place of Residence, 1885–1910

	Number	Percentage
Southern states	23	46.9
Arkansas	1	
District of Columbia	1	
Georgia	1	
Kentucky	1	
Maryland	5	
North Carolina	4	
South Carolina	2	
Tennessee	1	
Virginia	7	
Northern states	26	53.1
Maine	1	
Michigan	1	
New Jersey	1	
New York	16	
Pennsylvania	7	

Sources: Alien Naturalization and Citizenship Records, 1882–1904, Durham County, North Carolina, North Carolina State Archives, Raleigh; Naturalization Petition and Record, 1908–1922, Durham County Superior Court; Durham County Tax Rolls, 1874–1910, North Carolina State Archives, Raleigh; Durham County, North Carolina, Enumerated District Lists, Twelfth Census of the United States, 1900, North Carolina State Archives, Raleigh; Durham County, North Carolina Enumerated District Lists, Thirteenth Census of the United States, 1910, North Carolina State Archives, Raleigh; reports in newspapers and oral histories.

lies, the Durham east European Jewish migration fits the pattern of "small family-based migration chains." This pattern is also seen among Italians, Mexicans, Slovaks, and Russians. A pioneering settler drew other kinsmen until an entire village might follow. Naturalization documents confirm that Durham's Jews arrived in family and landsleit groups. Although some Durham Jews came from Galicia, Romania, Slovakia, Hungary, and Poland, most Jews can be traced largely to two places of origin. A small, early migration was from Kiev, Ukraine (Gladstein, Primakoff, and Hock-field), but the larger number emigrated from Latvia and Lithuania in the Pale of Settlement, the zone prescribed by the czars for Jewish residence: from Lithuanian shtetls of Vidzh (Kaplan, Murnick, Scher, and Freedman); Zager (Brown and Debrowne); and Akmian (Swartz, Abelkopf, Bane, and Kropman). Others were from the Jewish urban centers of Vilna, Lithuania (Berman, Rosenberg, and Berlin) and Dvinsk, Latvia (Apter, Margolis, and Zuckerman). Most of the town's Jews had common origins in a compact area of the Pale. Vidzh is located between Vilna and Dvinsk. Akmian and Zager are nearby towns. Some Durham Jews from Lithuanian shtetls de-scribed themselves as Vilna Jews. In eastern Europe, too, Jews had been migratory. Philip Dave was a native of Minsk who had moved to Kovno where he met his wife, a native of Vilna. Like their southern neighbors recently removed from farm to city, Jews brought their kinship and com-munal ties with them.[11]

Kinship ties and intramarriages strengthened the sense of the small Jewish community as an extended family. Even before their arrival in Durham, the Margolis and Zuckerman families had been linked by mar-riage in their native Dvinsk. The Primakoffs and Hockfields, both from Kiev, were in-laws. The Gladsteins were related to the Enochs, Levys, and Smolenskys, and the Levins were related to the Silvers, Blooms, and Blankfields. This kinship pattern was typical of small-town Jewish com-munities.

As soon as the immigrants established themselves, they brought family members. Shoemaker Philip Kaplan came to Durham alone, but he soon sent for his wife and four children in Lithuania. Several bachelors made their way to Durham and then summoned their fiancées. The Bane family illustrated the intricacies of the family web. A. Bane, who was pointed to Durham by an uncle who had rolled cigarettes, was joined by Morris Bane from West Virginia, followed by their cousin Solomon from Montreal, who then sent for his wife and children and his nephew Max, who was listed on Solomon's passport as his son. Max in turn brought to Durham two brothers, two sisters, and a cousin.[12]

Most Russians were drawn south by family and landsleit, though such groups as the Industrial Removal Office (IRO), the refugee resettlement agency, also organized efforts to disperse Jews from the unhealthy north-ern ghettos. Of the 73,960 individuals the IRO dispersed from New York from 1901 to 1917, 113 were sent to North Carolina. In 1915 Dr. Rosenson, southern representative of the Hebrew Emigrant Society, visited Durham

As a young family, Moses and Bessie Gladstein and their three sons were typical of early east European Jewish immigrants. Gladstein was the labor contractor who led the cigarette rollers to Durham in the early 1880s. (Courtesy of the Rare Book, Manuscript, and Special Collections Library, Duke University)

to investigate the town's suitability for receiving immigrants. Local Jews contributed "liberally."[13]

The story of one new arrival in Durham vividly illustrates the travails of emigration. With Sam Rapport, a local optician, translating from Yiddish, Isra (Isidor) Eisenberg told a *Durham Daily Sun* reporter the harrowing story of his escape from Russia. Eisenberg's brother Morris, who worked for the Summerfield Pants Company, had sent money to his home in Rowna, Russia, to pay for his brother's voyage. In 1904 Russian officers had come to his school to pull out "recruits" to fight the Japanese. Eisenberg joined a band of forty deserters who headed for the German frontier. They confronted robbers and evaded czarist police, who would shoot them on capture. The group bribed the border guards, but the police grabbed Eisenberg. He was questioned closely but managed to escape and rejoin his party. They crossed Germany to Rotterdam, where they embarked to Liverpool. Some sailed to South America, but Eisenberg headed to New York. At the Castle Garden immigration center he was detained four days until his brother sent him money for a train ticket to Durham. When he arrived in Durham, Eisenberg was thirteen years old.[14]

A few immigrants such as Eisenberg came directly to Durham, but most first resided in northern cities or wandered the South. Louis Stadiem's family emigrated from Poland to New York in 1881, moved to Richmond in 1886, to Danville in 1889, then to Rocky Mount, and then to Greensboro. The Swartzes, judging by the birth records of their children, had been in Kentucky, Arkansas, and Tennessee before moving to North Carolina (see tables 5.1 and 5.2).

Durham supports the generalization that the east European Jewish migration was a "young family migration" (see table 5.3). The immigrants who came to Durham show a similar pattern of self-selection. Twenty-two of the thirty-two Jewish households of 1900 consisted of nuclear families, a figure that rose to forty-eight of fifty-three in 1910. Of the 201 Jews who listed an age in 1900, 94 were fourteen years of age or younger. With high birth rates the median age of east European Jews in 1900 was seventeen for men and thirteen for women. In 1910 the average household had 3.6 children. The immigrants often arrived with two or three children in hand and then had several more in Durham. Harris Abelkopf had three children born in Russia, two in New York, and one in Durham. When the Freedmans were naturalized, they had seven children, and the Kadis, Dave, and Swartz families each had six. Others listed four or five. By 1900 more than 55 percent of Durham's Jews were American born, and of these 114 individuals, 93 were born in southern states—including 71 North Carolinians—whereas only 20 were born in northern states.[15] These Jews were becoming a southern people.

An Ethnic Economy

The concentration of Jews in trade and commerce differentiates east European immigrants in the South and in small towns, regardless of region, from those in urban centers. In 1900 83.6 percent of Durham's Jews were

TABLE 5.2. Places of Birth of Durham Jews, 1900

	Number	Percentage
Foreign born	91	44.4
American born	114	55.6
Southern States		45.4
District of Columbia	1	
Maryland	10	
North Carolina	71	34.6
Tennessee	1	
Virginia	10	
Northern states		9.7
Maine	4	
Michigan	1	
New York	12	
Pennsylvania	3	
Western states		.5
Colorado	1	

Source: Durham County, North Carolina, Enumerated District Lists, Twelfth Census of the United States, 1900, North Carolina State Archives, Raleigh.

TABLE 5.3. Age Distribution of Durham Jews, 1900 and 1910[a]

	1900		1910	
	Eastern European	German	Eastern European	German
Median age—Male	17 (87)	19.5 (9)	14 (130)	26.5 (6)
Median age—Female	13 (97)	30.0 (7)	13 (159)	28.5 (10)
Average age—Male	19.3	26.5	21.3	20.6
Average age—Female	16.6	33.5	17.7	29.0
Children per household	3.3 (36)		3.6 (53)	

Sources: Durham County, North Carolina, Enumerated District Lists, Twelfth Census of the United States, 1900, North Carolina State Archives, Raleigh; Durham County, North Carolina Enumerated District Lists, Thirteenth Census of the United States, 1910, North Carolina State Archives, Raleigh.
[a] Figures in parentheses are actual numbers.

employed in trade and commerce and only 14.5 percent in manufacturing. A turn-of-the-century survey revealed that 70 percent of employed Jews in towns under one hundred thousand population worked in trades and services in contrast to cities such as New York, where 60 percent of employed Jews worked in manufacturing. For impoverished immigrants in an urban sweatshop the pull of Durham was the opportunity to be self-employed. One family came to Durham when a letter from a relative made the classic appeal, "Come south. The streets are paved with gold."[16]

The tobacco and textile industries fueled the town's growth as Durham's population rose from 2,041 in 1880 to 18,241 in 1910. James "Buck" Duke, headquartered in New York, organized the American Tobacco Company and rapidly monopolized the industry. In 1884 Julian Carr opened the town's first textile mill to supply bags for the tobacco industry. Eight years later the Dukes, with William Erwin of nearby Alamance County, began opening mills. German Jews, who had made the climb from peddler to merchant or broker, joined the textile investors. In 1897 Gustave Rosenthal, a Raleigh merchant, served as president of Durham's Commonwealth Cotton Mills. Jews, too, owned mills in nearby Roxboro and Burlington. In 1895 Caesar and Moses Cone built the South's largest textile mill in Greensboro.

Corporate paternalism governed the city's social as well as economic life. Duke, Carr, and George Watts, a banker and Duke partner, underwrote churches and promulgated the gospel in their factories. In the 1890s they built mill villages in Edgemont, East Durham, and West Durham. Entire families, newly urbanized from the countryside, labored in the factories. In the black community no less than in the white, class lines divided the merchants and capitalists from the mass of the city's working poor. In the city, workers replicated their country pattern of kinship and neighborhood, anchored by a mill-built school and church.

Although the Jewish immigrants shared poverty with Durham's proletarians, they aspired to join the bourgeoisie. In contrast to the 57 percent of Durham's households that had members employed in the textile and tobacco mills, 83.6 percent of Durham Jews worked trade and commerce. In 1900, 29 percent of women worked in the factories, and another 21.4 percent were employed in domestic service. No Jewish women were so employed, and no Jewish children worked in the mills.[17]

Like the Germans before them, east European Jews maintained a separate ethnic economy where they financed and employed each other. In Durham east European Jews occupied a racial, economic, and geographic niche. Jews began opening groceries that positioned them as a petite bourgeoisie between the workers and the elite capitalists. Three Jewish grocery stores of 1887 jumped to thirteen in 1900. The stores circled the Main Street business district, near the factories and mill villages. A cluster of Jewish-owned groceries surrounded Liggett and Myers. Durham was a hard-drinking town, and Jewish merchants satisfied the workers' passion for liquor. Simon Haskell operated a saloon on Peabody in a working-class district. Jews were occasionally arrested for selling wine without a license or beer on Sunday. Even after Durham went dry some continued to retail whiskey or huckleberry cider. They paid small fines and promised to desist. With Prohibition Haskell closed shop and left town.[18]

Opening a grocery was the first step of upward mobility for clerks and peddlers. The scale of trade was often only slightly improved from ped-dling. Harry and Rosa Levin, who came to Durham in 1889, opened a small grocery and fruit stand on Corcoran Street across from the train sta-tion. When the train pulled in, Rosa sold fruit and sandwiches to the pas-sengers. Max Bane, who started as a scavenger of junk, became a grocer and then a meat wholesaler. No Jewish merchant captured Durham's capi-talist spirit more than Adolph Max, a Russian immigrant. In 1895, a news-paper identified him as "one of the largest merchants in Durham County." After a fire destroyed his store, he opened a department store and then added a wholesale grocery. In 1904 "Col. A. Max, our bustling Hebrew merchant," as the *Durham Sun* described him, retired from retail business to open a brick factory with D. Z. O'Briant, advertising one million bricks for sale.[19] Jewish mercantilism harmonized with the New South entrepre-neurial culture.

Black and white neighborhoods alternated across Durham, and Jewish merchants served a mixed clientele. Jewish grocers moved into black areas as early as the mid-1880s when Esther and Michael Gumpel opened a store on Fayetteville Street in Hayti. By the 1890s three more Jews opened groceries there, and a decade later this number would double. Jewish stores were also located in the black Crest and Pettigrew neighborhoods. In this latter area, nicknamed "Mexico," Jewish stores interspersed with Greek restaurants and confectioneries. Jews avoided the isolated country store. In 1887 only one of the county's sixty-six country stores was owned by a Jew, H. Goldscheider, and he located there only after his downtown auc-tion house failed. He soon returned to Baltimore.

Unlike the German Jews who lived above their downtown stores or in elite Gentile neighborhoods, the east Europeans concentrated in an ethnic enclave. In the early 1880s a ghetto formed on Pine Street. In Durham, with its hills and gullies, wealthy families lived on high ground. Pine Street lay in The Bottoms amid shacks, saloons, dumps, and animal pens. It bordered the African American neighborhood of Hayti and a red-light district that served factory workers. The first Jews to settle there, the Polish-born Goldsteins, purchased nearly a dozen properties that they rented to new immigrants. Jews supplemented their incomes by offering room and board to transient peddlers and salesmen. Pine Street was just several blocks from the tobacco factories and the downtown business district.

The desire of Jews to concentrate in a ghetto was in measure a matter of choice. Certainly they sought the comfort of Yiddish-speaking landsleit, and poverty limited options. Nevertheless, several other Jews were scattered in boarding houses across town or lived behind or above their stores. Jewish grocers were the only whites to reside in Hayti. A similar residential pattern prevailed in Atlanta, where Russian Jews at first settled on the fringes of a black district; some grocers lived in the black neighborhood.[20]

The east Europeans' residential position between black and white was symbolic of their social status. The newly arrived immigrants remained outside civic and political life. The 1880s and 1890s were times of political turmoil. The end of Reconstruction saw Democratic Redeemers, fearful of the return of black-Republican rule, establish white supremacy as a governing principle. Excepting 1896, when a fusion of Populists and Republicans won the governorship, a conservative Democratic machine, beholden to industrial and railroad interests, dominated local and state politics.

As greenhorns, the east European immigrants remained apolitical. In 1900 the foreign born constituted 44.4 percent of Durham's Jews but only 1.3 percent of the general population. Jew meant alien. The immigrants were culturally distant from southern politics and too bound by poverty to enter arenas beyond the store. Wealthy, acculturated German Jews were the first to participate as citizens. Early juror rolls listed Levy, Summerfield, and Kronheimer, but never the recently naturalized Russians. Durham's east Europeans neither had nor sought political power, and they did not attempt to integrate socially; their primary concern was economic security, which meant long hours in the family store.

Durham Jewry was, as the newspapers described it, a "Hebrew Colony" that drew sustenance from the Jewish world beyond its borders. Family, business, and religious ties meant a constant flow of Jews through town. Despite its isolation Durham was located on a main railway line that kept local Jews well connected to Richmond, Norfolk, and Baltimore, where they found rabbis, spouses, and kosher supplies. Many immigrants sub- scribed to Yiddish newspapers published in New York. Jewish visitors from rabbis to vaudeville entertainers streamed through town. Fields's minstrels and H. R. Cohen's theatricals played the Durham Opera House before the turn of the century. As a colony, Durham Jewry remained linked to urban Jewish communities, which served as surrogate homelands.[21]

Congregating Jews

Although German Jews had conducted services, purchased a cemetery, and formed a benevolence society, they did not persist in Durham as they did in Raleigh, Greensboro, or Wilmington. By the 1880s the Reform move- ment was ascendant among America's 277 synagogues. By the turn of the century, 73 percent of the South's Jewish communities had Reform congregations.[22] Demographics led Durham to become east European Orthodox when most southern communities were turning Reform. The Ukrainian, Polish, Galician, Latvian, and Lithuanian immigrants who came after 1881 appropriated the German's cemetery society and then founded a congregation. They were traditional Jews, who were nominally Orthodox. As they Americanized, their ritual observance and communal bonds loosened, but they remained traditionalist. The immigrants felt con- tradictory impulses as they held to the traditions of a world that they had abandoned.

Leading Orthodox rabbis in eastern Europe, such as the Chofetz Chaim, warned Jews not to immigrate to an America that they regarded as a *treyf* (unkosher) land. The migration from the Old World to the New was the first break from a traditional community; the departure from the Jewish centers of Baltimore or New York to the hinterland of North Carolina represented another. Recognizing the difficulties of Jewish observance outside urban areas, the Industrial Removal Office screened Jews about their observance of kosher and Sabbath laws before sending them into the small-town South.[23]

Bernhard Goldgar's memoir traces a common religious genesis. He had become "enlightened" before his departure from Europe, and his ambi- tion was to enter a university. He recalled his rabbinic instructors as ty- rants and lamented how religion kept the masses enthralled in superstition. Nonetheless, when Goldgar traveled to America on steerage, he brought his phylacteries and chose to go hungry rather than eat nonkosher meat. Before his arrival in Durham Goldgar became a socialist, wanting to be not just a "Son of Israel" but a "Citizen of the World." But skepticism did not dispel the habits of traditional religious behavior.[24] Religiously educated Jews such as Goldgar and Moses Gladstein did not need a state-chartered synagogue to be observant. In later years each would serve as president of an Orthodox synagogue (although Goldgar was criticized for not keeping kosher).

In small-town North Carolina ritual modernizing was gradual and inconsistent. Wilmington and Statesville had committed to Reform by the 1880s, whereas Asheville, Goldsboro, and Raleigh did not join the Union of American Hebrew Congregations or adopt the Union Prayerbook (1894) until the early 1900s. Most North Carolina congregations were too small to be sectarian, and their religious programs were pragmatic and inclusionary. The tendency was toward conservatism, and most North Carolina congregations employed Benjamin Szold's moderately traditional prayer book with English emendations by Marcus Jastrow. In Raleigh, Greensboro, and Asheville, Reform and Orthodox, German and east European, at first worshipped together. In Durham the Reform Jews, who had helped found the cemetery society, were too few and mobile to act as a counterbalance to the Orthodox or to sustain a congregation of their own. They were effectively disenfranchised as the congregation evolved into an east European shul. The Germans became outsiders among Durham Jews even as they gained acceptance in town society.[25]

The east European migration transformed North Carolina's congregational history as it did the nation's. As North Carolina urbanized and new immigrants arrived, the number of congregations increased from one in 1870 to fourteen in 1910 to twenty-two in 1927. These statistics reflected national trends. From the 1880s to the 1890s the number of American synagogues nearly doubled, and most were now Orthodox. East European immigrants founded congregations in Winston-Salem in 1888, Charlotte in 1895, and Gastonia and Wilmington in 1906. In 1888 the Association of the American Orthodox Congregations issued a call in English and Yiddish for all Orthodox congregations to join together, but it failed in establishing Old World rabbinic authority among the Americanizing immigrants. In 1898 fifty congregations, a fusion of older central European and more recent east European congregations, formed the Union of Orthodox Jewish Congregations of America. Concerned with adopting Orthodoxy to modernity, these rabbis acted to resist the inroads of the Reform movement and to ensure the immigrant's continued affiliation. In 1902 east European traditionalists founded the Union of Orthodox Rabbis, which was

Likely taken at the Academy of Music in 1896 when the Durham Jews dedicated a Torah, this photograph illustrates the youth of the community and its religious diversity, from the bearded, black-hatted men in the rear to the southern boys and girls in the front. (Courtesy of the Rare Book, Manuscript, and Special Collections Library, Duke University)

even more steadfastly resistant to Americanizing trends. The east European Orthodox shul served as a counterweight to the prevailing force of secularization.[26]

In 1886 or 1887 the Durham Hebrew Congregation Company was organized as the east European immigrants were superseding the small community of German Jews. The congregation's first president was Myer Summerfield, a German-born Orthodox Jew and Jewish Cemetery Society leader. For the next twenty years the congregation met in a *shtibel,* a rented room or store. The first home was a third-floor hall at 102½ Main Street. For holidays the congregation rented the Opera House or Academy of Music. In 1892 the Durham Hebrew Congregation formally reorganized as Orthodox with a state charter. The east European Jews now achieved hegemony. Abe Goldstein, the town's senior Polish Jew, became president. The congregants also summoned from Montreal the Reverend Kolman Heillig, a Lithuanian landsman, to serve as their first spiritual leader. As early as 1897 Morris Enoch, a merchant's father, began tutoring boys for the Bar Mitzvah in a cheder, which met in a livery stable on Pine Street. The sessions, conducted in Yiddish, met after public school. Despite its Americanized name, the Durham Hebrew Congregation took the form of a *chevra,* a society or "fellowship of cronies" thickly imbued with the Yiddishkeit of the immigrants' east European homelands.[27]

A photograph of the Durham Hebrew Congregation—likely taken in 1896 to celebrate the arrival of a new Torah—shows a composite of the community. Intended to commemorate the community's unity, the photograph documents its diversity. About sixty people posed in a large hall. Bearded men in bowlers and black suits, the uniform of the immigrant Orthodox Jew, stood against the rear wall distant from the women. One thickly bearded man, perhaps the rabbi, held the Torah scroll open. Before these greenhorns stood about twenty clean-shaven or mustached men, fashionably attired southerners in sporty peaked caps and straw hats. The women sat in the foreground around a long banquet table. The younger women, too, were stylishly dressed and coiffed. None appeared to have the wigs or scarves of Orthodox women. Small children—boys, barefoot and in short pants, and girls in white lace dresses—sat up front. Younger Jews clearly were lessening their aesthetic difference with small-town southerners.

In the late 1880s the identity of the Durham Jewish community was changing. Unlike the acculturated, more prosperous Germans who integrated into the town's social life as individuals, the impoverished east European immigrants were largely ghettoized as outsiders in their Pine Street ethnic enclave on the city's margins. Yiddish accents and language differentiated them from their native southern neighbors. Family and landsleit ties, which survived migration, tightened communal bonds. Racially, they were situated between white and black Durham. Typical of small-town Jews, they maintained an ethnic mercantile niche as middlemen. Their concern was to provide economic security for their growing families. Their mobility suggests their lack of local heritage and loyalty. The migrants were a self-selected group of young families intent on establishing themselves as independent trade people. Without civic affiliations, their one institutional membership was the synagogue, a reconstruction from the Old World. Their traditional Judaism differentiated them from southern Christians and, in measure, from native southern Jews. Over time they were adopting modes of dress and language that made them less different from native southerners. With high birth rates they were increasingly a southern people.

6 Creating an American Jewish Community, 1900 to 1917

In the decades before World War I, the Durham Jewish community was building the institutions to create a permanent community while contending with the conflicts of immigrants aspiring to become Americans. For southern Jews, being Jewish and American was more complex and multifarious than a double identity. They had to accommodate to a society that in terms of its demographics and culture still differed from the nation, especially in regard to race and immigration. As the Jews negotiated their new identity in the small-town South, their communal life was marked by family, clan, class, and religious conflicts. They created institutions to unify themselves and sustain a community even as they continued to be highly mobile and wracked by internal dissent and factionalism. Through religious and institutional networks they affirmed their Jewish peoplehood both locally and globally while expressing their civic and patriotic loyalties as citizens of Durham. Their Jewish ethnicity was also blending into the local culture as they adapted small-town mores.

Most important in southern society was to have *place,* and Jews fit comfortably in the southern social hierarchy. As business people, they aspired to earn public trust. Durhamites saw southern virtues in the Jews: they were a religious, family oriented, hardworking, law-abiding people. If, as C. Vann Woodward suggests in *The Burden of Southern History,* the southerners are distinctive in having a "collective history" as a "People of Poverty" in a land of plenty, then the impoverished immigrant Jews, however different their personal histories, knew well the southern condition. Jews arrived in Durham as an urban people with commercial skills, the very direction the South was heading. Jews and Christians cited their common values in explaining the acceptance of Jews in the South. They shared tragic pasts as defeated peoples; their codes demanded family loyalty, religious devotion, and reverence for ancestry. The immigrants were eager to assimilate, to conform. Those Jews who refused to accept their place, such as the labor militants of the 1880s, were soon driven from town.[1]

Jewish numbers were too small to present a cultural or political threat to the established order. In 1900, 0.3 percent of North Carolina's population was foreign born, the lowest percentage in the country, compared with a national percentage of 13.7. In 1910, 603 North Carolinians listed Yiddish as their mother tongue; that figure rose to 935 two years later. Given their tendency to open stores in downtown business districts, the Jews were the most visible element of Durham's immigrant population, which included Greeks, Italians, and Germans. Of the 258 foreign-born residents in 1910, nearly half were Russian Jews. Each group carved its own economic niche. At the turn of the century the town supported two Italian restaurants and a Chinese laundry. The Greeks opened restaurants, soda fountains, and candy stores. The Jews favored groceries and dry goods. The presence of Jewish merchants, with their links to Baltimore and New York wholesalers, was another sign of the New South's integration into the national economy.

Durham made room for new people and new money. It proclaimed itself the "City of Opportunity" or "The Foremost City of the New South." Financiers from Raleigh, Greensboro, and Baltimore capitalized its banks and industry. When Sam Wittkowsky, "the wonderful Hebrew builder of Charlotte," spoke before the Durham Building and Investment Association in 1909, the *Durham Morning Herald* welcomed the prospect that "one of Charlotte's richest men, a near millionaire," would consider investing in the town.[2] From 1900 to 1920 the city's population leaped from 6,679 to 21,719.

Race relations were thought to be good, and—with the financial support of Julian Carr and the Dukes—a black middle class developed. In 1898 African American businessmen had founded the North Carolina Mutual Life Insurance Company, which spawned the Mechanics and Farmers Bank ten years later. In 1912 Dr. James Shepard founded the National Training School, which evolved into state-supported North Carolina College. The college spawned an educated, entrepreneurial elite. Both

Booker T. Washington and W. E. B. Du Bois praised Durham's "hands off" attitude toward black aspirations, and the town became famous as the "Negro Wall Street."[3]

An Ethnic Economy

After 1900 Durham was completing its transition from an agricultural to an industrial economy. Although the Supreme Court dissolved Duke's tobacco trust in 1911, its successors, American Tobacco Company and Liggett and Myers, dominated the market and accounted for nearly two-thirds of the nation's cigarette sales. The textile industry continued its growth, and by 1917 Durham supported nine mills.[4] With its rapid industrialization Durham suffered recurrent labor troubles. A 1900 strike at Erwin mills was crushed when the protestors were summarily dismissed. World War I labor shortages provoked more unrest, and strikes hit the mills in 1918 and 1919.

In contrast to Durham's workers, with whom they shared poverty, Jews avoided corporate employment and chose to be self-employed. After the departure of the cigarette rollers, only two Jews listed employment as laborers in Durham's tobacco or textile factories, and they were second-generation Jews who soon left town. Small-town immigrant Jews, regardless of region, contrasted with urban immigrant Jews in their concentration in trade and commerce (see table 6.1). The larger the city, the more likely an immigrant Jew worked in industrial labor; the smaller the city, the more likely the immigrant was in trade. In 1910, 73 percent of New York Jewish immigrants were "occupied in manufacturing industries" compared with 55 percent in Detroit; 23.7 percent in Providence, Rhode Island; 4 percent in Johnstown, Pennsylvania; and none in Durham. The numbers nearly reverse for "self-employed in trade": 16 percent in New York; 34 percent in Detroit; 65.3 percent in Providence; 83 percent in Johnstown; and 77.4 percent in Durham (see table 6.2).[5] The figures suggest a process of self-selection as entrepreneurial Jews, seeking personal autonomy and economic independence, broke from the urban centers.

As storekeepers, Jews depended on the workers for their livelihood. Their stores, located near the factories, supplied uniforms and boots for factory workers, both black and white. Although the immigrants' poverty had much in common with that of the workers, the Jews had ambitions of rising in class. Jewish youth excelled in the public schools whereas the workers' children commonly dropped out. The millworkers, exhausted by

Carol A. Kolmerten, Ph.D., is Director of Major Gifts and Planned Giving Assistant Officer and Director of the Honors Program at Hood College in Frederick, Maryland. She came to admire Ernestine Rose, a Jewish woman who fled her Eastern European Orthodox roots, to seek a better life in America. A life she dedicated to social justice and equality.

Leonard W. Rogoff, Ph.D., is research historian of the Jewish Heritage Foundation of North Carolina. Mark K. Bauman, Editor of SOUTHERN JEWISH HISTORY, published by the Southern Jewish Historical Society, wrote in a review of HOMELANDS that "it ranks amongst the very best studies of a southern Jewish community".

Recommended Reading

MORDECAI: AN EARLY AMERICAN FAMILY   by Emily Bingham
MY FATHER'S PEOPLE: A FAMILY OF SOUTHERN JEWS by Louis D. Rubin
AGAINST THE TIDE:ONE WOMAN'S POLITICAL STRUGGLE   by Harriet Keyesering

For Middle Readers by Norman Finkelstein

FORGED IN FREEDOM: SHAPING THE AMERICAN JEWISH EXPERIENCE
HEEDING THE CALL: JEWISH VOICES IN AMERICA'S CIVIL RIGHTS STRUGGLE

****

Learn more about the Southern Jewish Experience
Join the Southern Jewish Historical Society
General Membership Dues for 2003-04 are $ 35
Mail checks, payable to SJHS, to SJHS Box 5024 Atlanta, GA 30302-5024

PENINSULA JEWISH HISTORICAL SOCIETY
Founded 1986

HAMPTON ROAD SECTION, NATIONAL COUNCIL OF JEWISH WOMEN
Founded 1921

BOOK AND AUTHOR LUNCHEON
Wednesday, November 12, 2003
11:00 A.M.
Temple Sinai Social Hall
Newport News

Panelists

Samuel Althaus, "WHERE IS GOD: Auschwitz-Birkenau to Dachau 1942-1945

Carol A. Kolmerten, : THE AMERICAN LIFE OF ERNESTINE L. ROSE

Leonard W. Rogoff, HOMELANDS: Southern Jewish Identity in Durham and Chapel
Hill, North Carolina

*Samuel Althaus, Holocaust survivor and successful businessman, has resided in
Newport News over fifty years. His book tells of his*

TABLE 6.1. Occupational Distribution of Russian Jews, Comparative Data, 1900–1902

Occupation area	Fifteen cities[a]	Durham (1902)	Atlanta
Manufacturing and mechanical	57.1	14.5	18.0
Trade and commerce	23.3	83.6	78.7
Domestic and personal service	7.0	0.0	1.6
Clerical	6.8	—	—
Professions	2.9	0.4	.8
Agriculture, fish, forestry, mining	0.5	0.0	—
Public service	0.4	0.0	—
Numbers	720,052	55	122

Sources: Data from Atlanta and fifteen cities cited from Steven Hertzberg, *Strangers within the Gate City: The Jews of Atlanta, 1845–1915* (Philadelphia: Jewish Publication Society, 1978), 248; Durham data from *Directory of Greater Durham, 1902* (Durham: Samuel Adams, 1902).
[a] The data of the fifteen metropolitan cities include some non-Jewish Russians, but they were mostly Yiddish speakers.

low wages and long hours, lacked economic or occupational mobility. Most Jews, in contrast, left poverty behind in a decade or two.

For Jews the family store was a way of life. Youngsters spent after-school hours sweeping floors or replacing stock. Three generations worked at Adolph Max's store. His children, Ralph and Muchie, clerked while his sixty-five-year-old, Russian-born father, Jacob, manned the grocery department. This pattern of family enterprise was typical for both poor and wealthy, Russians and Germans.

"The women were the breadwinners," Hazel Gladstein Wishnov recalled of her immigrant mother. In the groceries their hours extended into late nights and early mornings "as long as customers came in." Some men left the stores in their wives' hands while they played cards or speculated in real estate. Widows became independent merchants. The newspaper praised Carrie Levy, who owned a notions store, as a woman of "fine taste

TABLE 6.2. Occupational Distribution of Durham Jews, Comparative Data, 1910[a]

Occupation	Durham immigrant	Durham second generation	Johnstown, Penn., immigrant	Johnstown, Penn., second generation	Providence R.I., immigrant (1915)[b]	New York immigrant	Philadelphia immigrant	Detroit immigrant
Self-employed in trade	77.4	6.6	83.0	4	65.3	16	18	34
Store owner	(61.2)	(6.6)	(33)	(4)	(23.2)			
Self-employed artisan	(11.2)		(23)		(19.8)			
Peddler	(4.8)		(27)		(22.3)			
Commercial employee	17.7	66.6	12	93	7.1	9	10	15
Professional	4.8	13.3	1		3.2	2	1	1
Occupied manufacturing		13.3	4	3	23.7	73	71	55
Manager			(1)		.5	(9)	(10)	(8)
Employee		13.3	(3)	(3)	23.2	(64)	(61)	(42)

Sources: Durham data derived from *Hill's Durham, North Carolina, Directory, 1909–10* (Richmond: Hill Directory Co., 1909); Johnstown, New York, and Philadelphia data derived from Ewa Morawska, *Insecure Prosperity: Small-Town Jews in Industrial America, 1890–1940* (Princeton University Press, 1996), 41; Providence data from Joel Perlmann, "Beyond New York: The Occupations of the Russian Jewish Immigrants and Providence, R.I., and Other Small Jewish Communities, 1900–1915," *American Jewish History* 72 (March 1983): 369–94; for Detroit, see Jacob Lestschinsky, "The Economic Development of the Jews in the United States," in *The Jewish People: Past and Present*, vol. 1 (New York: Jewish Encyclopedia Handbooks, 1946).

[a] Numbers in parentheses are percentages by subcategory.

and an expert buyer."[6] Carrie Kronheimer and Birdie Lehman, American-born descendants of antebellum German immigrants, served as buyers and managers at their brother's department store.

Typically, immigrants owned stores, and the second generation worked as clerks or salespersons. In 1910, 77.4 percent of the Durham immigrants were self-employed, and only 17.7 percent were commercial employees. By contrast, only 6.6 percent of the second generation worked on their "own account," whereas 66.6 percent were clerks or salespersons. Again, this situation was typical of small-town Jews. The study of Johnstown, Pennsylvania, reveals a similar employment pattern in 1910: 12 percent of the immigrants were commercial employees, and 93 percent of the second generation held such positions.[7] Small-town Jews had little occupational mobility other than the store.

Stores opened and closed, moved from town to town, and spawned branches. In 1914 Sam and Mary Berman, Lithuanian immigrants, oper-ated stores in both Durham and Chapel Hill, commuting by wagon be-tween them. Two years later they moved to Chapel Hill, becoming that town's first permanent Jewish residents. Morris Eisenberg started with a store in Hillsborough and then moved to Burlington, to Carrboro, to Dur-ham, and to Winston-Salem. He returned to Durham in 1925 to open a clothing store. Adolph Max operated store branches in Rose Hill, North Carolina, and Florence, South Carolina. The Summerfields had a second store in Roxboro, as did Max Shevel in Cary. The sense of Jewish mobility was reinforced by traveling salesmen, agents for wholesalers and manufac-turers, who constantly flowed in and out of town. Herman Citrenbaum took two-month tours north and south as a salesman for the Summerfield Pants Company. Max and Artie Summerfield had routes that took them across the southeast.

Jewish mercantilism very much fit the pattern of New South enter-prise. Clerks, storekeepers, and salesmen were among the most mobile of southerners. Clerking was a first step to store ownership, and family net-working provided a job and financing. Jew and Gentile alike opened racket stores, so named because they sold cheaply for cash. The typical business leader of a New South town was a young man who had recently arrived in a city to clerk in a store. After a year or so, most were prepared to climb the ladder to greater success. That was the pattern of business elites in Roanoke, Greensboro, and Nashville, among other towns.

Many North Carolina Jews got their start from Jacob Epstein and his Baltimore Bargain House. The Lithuanian-born Epstein, who rose from rags to riches, pointed immigrants to territories and extended credit and merchandise. A trusting, generous man, he was quick with credit or a loan through hard times. Epstein's jobbers, sample cases in hand, traveled the state, and local merchants made buying trips to his twelve-story warehouse.[8]

The ethnic adhesiveness that governed business was not exclusively Jewish. One Gentile merchant, William Belk of Charlotte, began with a New York racket store. Jewish merchants, too, frequently incorporated "New York" in their store names, which suggests that southerners were more impressed with big city tastes and prices than biased against "damn Yankees." Like the Jews, Belk also brought his family into the business as he opened stores across the region, including Durham and Chapel Hill.[9] Southern Jews, such as the Riches of Atlanta or Thalhimers of Richmond, followed similar routes, as did small-town North Carolinians, such as the Leder brothers in Whiteville and the Heilig and Meyers families in Goldsboro. Immigrant Jews and southern Gentiles shared the spirit of enterprise that created the New South.

Russian Jews, with little capital, tended to live on the economic margin as peddlers, scavengers, or grocers. In 1902 four Jews listed themselves as junk collectors. When Max Bane first arrived in Durham, he scoured town and countryside for scrap, bones, hides, and used bottles. Julius and Morris Katz, Yiddish-speaking immigrants, worked as laborers, but Morris soon bought a wagon to haul produce from farm to town, selling to Jewish grocers. He soon opened a grocery of his own. Two others were painters, and one was a truck driver. Within a few years these Jews either turned to peddling and shopkeeping or left town. Jewish culture traditionally disparaged manual labor. Myer Summerfield hired Russian immigrants as cutters and pressers in his factory, but, like the cigarette rollers, they preferred city life. Summerfield moved his factory to Baltimore in 1906.[10]

The 1907 depression sparked new failures and departures. A year later M. Bane's New York Stock Company closed with $24,000 worth of debts and $16,000 of inventory. Bane attributed the failure to "business depression and slow collections." A month later Philip Jaffe and Son closed with a debt of $6,000 and assets of only $2,500. Not all failures were due to the state of the economy. A. Tonkel, who opened his Durham Dry Goods Store in 1908, closed it in 1912, $5,000 in debt. Tonkel reopened months later, only to fail again, this time $10,000 in debt. Tonkel blamed his losses on his compulsive gambling and poor bookkeeping.[11] Tonkel's case was hardly unique, nor was it exclusively a Jewish problem. Durham merchants kept card tables in rooms behind or above their stores where immigrant and native cardsharps gambled.

Hard times after 1907 brought Jewish pawnbrokers to town. In 1910 Louis Stadiem, financed by his father, began the Union Loan and Pawn Company, the town's first. Stadiem's clientele included farmers and factory workers, both black and white. The shop was near a red-light district, and patrons would pawn cars, watches, or jewelry at 20 or 30 percent of value to finance their weekend gambling or drinking.

Following the crisis of 1907–1910, Durham rebounded. The ascent from poverty for most Jews was rapid. Peddlers opened stores, and clerks became merchants. In 1911 Benjamin Kronheimer bought a twenty-five-thou-sand-square-foot, three-story building—with elevator—on Main Street that may have been the largest department store in the state. Kronheimer's move was a risk, but the store's success drew the business district westward. Max Shevel built a four-story building on Main Street for his Model Fur-niture business. In 1910 he had eleven employees.[12] Wealthy Jewish mer-chants entered the town's business elite.

Town dwellers and farmers in town on market days saw a row of Jewish dry-goods stores on Main Street. These included Gladstein's "The Under-selling Store, Home of Bargains"; the Bane brothers' New York Stock Company at three locations; A. Tonkel's Durham Dry Goods Store; Carrie Levy's Enterprise Millinery; Arthur Greenberg's Three, Five, and Ten va-riety store; Harry Miller's Globe Department Store; and Frank Silver's general store. A. Saks, Mark Switzer, Sam Hockfield, Abe Wilson, Philip Jaffe, and Morris Haskell were all clothiers, a trade Jews dominated. In 1902 eight of the town's eleven dry-goods stores were Jewish owned. In 1907 Morris Haskell built a thirty-six-hundred-square-foot, two-story building on Main for his shoes and ready-to-wear clothing.

In the early 1900s nearly a dozen Jews listed their profession as peddlers. They included not only town canvassers, who stationed themselves by mills and warehouses, but also country salesmen, who traveled great dis-tances with backpacks or by horse and wagon. The newspaper described one wagon as a Hebrew "portable dry goods and notion store . . . on wheels." A monthly license for a "legal right to peddle" cost $12. Many "Hebrew peddlers" were itinerants, although Durham with its Jewish community would have been an appealing way station.[13]

A family store served as a headquarters for sons who peddled. Benjamin Morris worked a Durham grocery while his boys traveled. In 1901 the *Durham Sun* reported that one son was murdered on Whitetop Mountain in Ashe County. The body was buried on the mountain with $150 in a shoe, the newspaper claimed, and a riderless horse was found dragging a wagon. The victim's brother and J. Saks, a Durham grocer, took a train to Ashe County and hiked sixty miles to retrieve the body. "It was a rough trip," the newspaper reported. "They hope they will never have to take it again." Climbing a mountain road, they spotted young Morris riding toward them, unaware of his alleged demise. "Grief Is Turned to Joy," the headline proclaimed the next day. The story evokes the hardship that peddlers underwent in a state that lacked basic roads. Ashe County was almost two hundred miles from Morris's home. The report that a "Jew-peddler" hid $150 on his person may reflect some latent bias about the secret wealth of Jews because a peddler would need many months to earn that sum.[14]

Another peddler, Morris Eisenberg, had arrived in Durham in 1904 thinking that he would work in the tobacco industry. After a stint as a pants maker for Summerfield, he moved to Hillsborough and took to the road. The short, barrel-chested Eisenberg threw a pack on his back loaded with needles and thread. His eighty-mile route took him on foot from Hillsborough to Burlington to Chapel Hill and then back to Hillsborough. He found customers as they sat on porches or worked in barns. Morris Witcowsky, who peddled southern Virginia and northern North Carolina, carried a 120-pound pack on his back with a 40-pound "balancer" in front. Arriving at a farm house, often preceded by excited children, he would unroll his stock of ribbons, thread, buttons, needles, fabric, garters, socks, and stockings. He knew twenty peddlers who worked his territory, each clearing about $8.40 a week.[15]

Jews worked their way out of such a backbreaking profession. From 1902 to 1911 the number of Durham Jews still listed as peddlers declined from twelve to two. Several peddlers—Jacob Blankfield, Daniel Freedman, Elias Tabatchnick, Harry Bloom, Benjamin Abelkopf—became grocers. Bloom had peddled for six years before opening a store in 1904. The Zuckerman brothers had hawked newspapers on the street until they opened a stand.[16]

Poorer Jews opened groceries, which tended to be home businesses. The thirteen Jewish grocers of 1887 increased to twenty-one in 1911. The small grocers struggled against poverty. The Abraham Cohen family lived in two rear rooms of their store. Mrs. Cohen spent nights in the kitchen preparing food for sale. Morris Katz, a Hayti grocer, was so poor that he could not afford boots and wrapped his feet in burlap bags. The Katzes' home had but one fireplace, and their children awoke at night in bone-chilling cold to drag their quilts to the fire. Yet the pennies multiplied, and the widowed Lena Katz was able to finance college educations for her children from the store. Sara Zuckerman's grocery helped send four sons to college.[17]

At the turn of the century only a few Jewish skilled craftsmen worked in Durham, but after 1910 their numbers rapidly grew. In eastern Europe the growing availability of manufactured goods threatened the liveli-hoods of Jewish artisans, and subsequent migrations brought Jewish tailors and shoemakers to America. In 1903 only one Jewish shoemaker worked in Durham, but from 1911 to 1916 seven more arrived. The same pattern held for tailors. There was but one in 1887 and four in 1911. Custom tai-lors, several of whom were refugees from New York's Lower East Side, proffered Fifth Avenue fashions to small-town southerners.

Real Estate

The store is enshrined in Jewish folklore as the stepping stone of upward mobility. Certainly it anchored family life and provided financial security. Socially and economically, it also served as the principal agency in inte-grating the immigrants into town society. Nevertheless, for many Durham Jews the store was only a means to provide capital for real estate invest-ment. Jews had a passion for buying property, a right largely denied them in Europe. Nominally shopkeepers, the men left a clerk or a wife at the store while they busied themselves with their investments. "Real estate, they all did that," Abe Stadiem recalled, noting that his father began buy-ing properties soon after opening his pawnshop. In 1897, 44 percent of local Jewish households owned real estate; by 1910 that figure had risen to 52.7 percent, and by 1925 it was 63.5 percent.[18]

First the merchants would purchase their store building and their home and then expand their holdings. In 1900 one Jew owned a home and twenty-three rented; by 1910 twenty-two owned homes and thirty-one rented. Abe Goldstein, the town's senior Jewish resident, closed his store and listed his occupation as "landlord" or "real estate." When he left town in 1905, he owned eleven parcels. Urban land prices soared as the city's population grew tenfold from 1890 to 1930. In 1899 Henry Brady bought a lot for $140. Two years later he purchased another lot for $2,200 and a year later a brick house for $700. From 1908 to 1922 Brady purchased fourteen more properties. Business directories listed Max Shevel as a furniture dealer, but at his death in 1917 he left his widow, Sarah, three houses, two downtown buildings, and sixty lots in the Geerwood section, in addition to other real estate worth $30,000 (see table 6.3).[19]

Real estate gave the Jews a high degree of public visibility. Adolph Max bought a former public school for $1,000 and then purchased an old beer house. The *Durham Sun* found one venture especially ironic: "A. Max, who buys anything from a goose to a church, has invested in one of the latter. He has purchased the Presbyterian Mission Church. Anyone wanting to rent a consecrated Christian house can apply to Col. Max, who will dish them out any denominational room they wish." Max converted the chapel into a house.[20]

The merchant's investments were also directed toward rental properties in the African American community "because that's where you get your best rent from," Stadiem recalled. Contrarily, a white working-class neighborhood such as Edgemont "wasn't no good," Stadiem remembered, even though houses could be purchased as cheaply as $500.

Jews received ready credit from downtown banks, and others turned to the black-owned Mechanics and Farmers. Jews were no longer exclusively dependent on their ethnic credit system because their real estate investments brought them into the town's corporate economy. Ben Kronheimer and Nathan Rosenstein were both directors and stockholders of Carr's First National Bank. In Rosenstein a Jew had a willing advocate for a loan. Rosenstein himself made some forty-three land purchases from 1911 to 1935. At his death in 1938 Kronheimer owned Durham property valued at more than $102,000.[21] The willingness of bankers to lend to Jews was another sign of Durham's tolerance, especially where mutual profit was concerned.

Economic Integration

Real estate investment was but one barometer that indicated that the Jews were breaking from the ethnic economy and integrating into the general economy. Some Jews held managerial positions in non-Jewish firms. Zeke Guggenheim, a Tennessean of German origin, managed the Swift and Company plant from 1903 to 1904 before opening his own slaughterhouse. By 1907, with four cutters and salesmen, he was the city's largest butcher. In 1914 Charles Zuckerman, from an east European family, was working for the Home Insurance Agency, a field not usually receptive to Jews, where he became an officer. Mary and Esther Cohen, grocers' daughters

TABLE 6.3. Aggregate Value of Real Estate and Personal Property, 1883–1910

Amount ($)	1883		1884		1897		1910	
	German	Eastern European	German	Eastern European	German	Eastern European	German	Eastern European
0–100						3	1	4
100–500		1				7	2	17
500–1,000					1	4		5
1,000–								
3,000		1				2		6
3,000–								
5,000	4		2		1	1		3
5,000–								
10,000		1	3	2	1	1		5
10,000–								
15,000							2	1

Sources: Durham County Tax Rolls, 1883, 1884, 1897, 1910, North Carolina State Archives, Raleigh.

who had attended business school, were employed as bookkeepers in Gentile firms.

Several Jews broke the boundaries of the ethnic economy. Adolph Max in his brick factory, Ike Zuckerman in his pharmacy, and Michael Margolis in his wholesale grocery all formed business partnerships with non-Jews. This Jewish-Gentile cooperation was exceptional, and it was not seen in such cities as Atlanta. In the 1907 panic Ben Duke found his bank short of cash. He turned to the clothier Abe Wilson whom he heard kept a hidden stash. Wilson brought Duke $10,000 in a shoe box, and the two men came to terms on a loan over a handshake, eschewing any bond but their words as southern gentlemen.[22]

Business, the desire for profit, drew Jews into civic life. The charter members of the Chamber of Commerce and Industry formed in 1902 included not only A. Summerfield and B. F. Kronheimer but also the Russians B. Enoch, M. Gladstein, and S. Rapport. Jews employed Gentiles as clerks in their stores. For an immigrant storekeeper, who may have spoken English poorly, the Gentile clerk brought the intangible of goodwill so necessary in a small town. In 1904 Moses Gladstein helped lead a petition drive among his fellow merchants in support of the demands of the clerks' union for reduced store hours, thus averting a strike. (Gladstein himself had led a cigarette rollers' strike twenty years earlier.) In gratitude the clerks held a barbecue for the merchants, including several Jews. Immigrant Jews began joining Progressive Era campaigns for civic reform and betterment. In 1907, when the town fathers conducted a drive to build a new Watts Hospital, a synagogue committee organized to raise funds. Jews were welcomed into civic and economic circles before they found social acceptance.[23]

Several second-generation youth rose from grocery or dry-goods stores to become professionals. The presence of local universities created opportunities for advancement generally lacking in small towns. Ike Zuckerman studied pharmacy at the University of North Carolina, and in 1910 he opened a drug store of his own. The *Durham Morning Herald* noted, "He is one of the number here going from soda fountain clerk to higher position."[24] David Gladstone and Benjamin Lovenstein were both young men who had failed as dry-goods merchants, but they became attorneys after taking law courses at the University of North Carolina. Like many Jewish merchants, Lovenstein served a mostly black clientele. Optician Sam Rapport, who arrived in 1897, and optometrist Nathan Rosenstein, who came in 1905, traveled a local route, taking orders at drugstores in country towns one week and returning the next to fill the prescriptions. Both men held office in the Optical Society of North Carolina, with Rosenstein serving as state president. As a doctor and graduate of an optometrical college, Rosenstein was respected as a professional and was the acknowledged Jewish spokesman to Gentile Durham.

College Town

Durham and Chapel Hill appealed to Jews as college towns. The academic communities made the area more cosmopolitan than was typical of the small-town South. For the new generation a college diploma was the passport to America. The local universities allowed financially strapped youth to realize that typically Jewish passion for education while living at home and helping in the family store. College offered a route from the store into the professions. Jews found greater acceptance on the campuses than they did in the community at large. The University of North Carolina was a vanguard institution of the progressive South. Methodists imbued with the social gospel endowed Trinity College and its successor, Duke University. The campuses, however, were certainly not free of discrimination, and the label of "Jew" was inescapable. Yet, relative to society at large, the campuses were tolerant. They served as primary agencies of Jewish acculturation and upward mobility.

After 1900 the second generation of east European Jews began to enroll at Trinity and UNC. In 1912 there were sixteen Jewish students at UNC. Five years later only eight of the 1,158 students were Jews. At this time, too, a smattering of Jewish students came down from the North, a few from the Bronx or Brooklyn, several of whom were Russian born. For some immigrant families, such as the Bradys, Rosensteins, and Greenbergs, college was an expectation for both sons and daughters. As a condition of an 1896 endowment, Washington Duke had required Trinity College to admit women on equal standing with men, a policy that was carried forward to Duke University. UNC did not admit women until their junior years. Women who did not attend college often went to business school to become stenographers or bookkeepers.[25]

Despite their isolation, Jews participated in campus life and retained warm memories of college days. They were accepted into academic if not social elites. In 1900 a Harvard graduate, Jacob Warshaw, was appointed instructor in modern languages at UNC while earning his master of arts degree, becoming the second Jew to teach there. Fanny Gladstein graduated magna cum laude from Trinity in 1911, and a year later Bessie and

Yeddie Greenberg won honors in French and philosophy. Louis Jaffe, who also graduated magna cum laude from Trinity in 1911, was editor of the campus newspaper, the *Chronicle*. Abraham Rosenstein as president of the Chemistry Club turned "Crowell Science Hall into a synagogue," the yearbook noted with a complimentary stereotype: "He is a true Israelite, and has a great share of his race's talent for music." His sister Eva, a classmate, was a star athlete.[26]

The campus environment was both progressive and Christian. Secular studies—learning science, literature, or new languages—acculturated children of Yiddish-speaking immigrants into modern society. Joe Dave, who entered Trinity in 1916, "welcomed" compulsory Bible classes and daily chapel for the "opportunity to learn something" of his classmates' religion. Samuel Newman, UNC class of 1915, recalled that the university made adjusting to America "easy": "I was readily drawn into the currents of university life and experienced the refreshing influence of the famous exponents of liberalism and the New South. . . . The prevailing religious atmosphere at the University of North Carolina was that of liberal Protestantism, with a strong emphasis on the social message of Christianity. To me it was an aspect of prophetic Judaism in its noblest expression. It was natural for me to participate in the YMCA activities and I was encouraged to enter literary contests." Newman won several gold medals for his efforts.[27]

In 1912 Newman formed the Hebrew Culture Society at UNC, the first such organization at a southern university. Fourteen of the sixteen Jewish students joined. A year later Harry Hurwitz, a Harvard undergraduate who had founded the Intercollegiate Menorah Association, visited UNC and enlisted the group as an affiliate. Hurwitz, who founded Menorah Society offices on some eighty campuses, was dedicated to humanistic Judaism, "the study and advancement of Jewish culture and ideals." It was this liberal, "prophetic Judaism," as described by Newman, rather than immigrant orthodoxy, that appealed to an assimilating college youth. Frank Graham, secretary of the YMCA, offered a room in the campus Y building for Menorah Society offices, but an official at the YMCA national headquarters objected. Graham conceded that it was "quite unorthodox," but he stood his ground.[28]

Certainly the most colorful figure at Trinity College was the first dean of the Law School, Samuel Fox Mordecai, who arrived in 1904. A great-grandson of Jacob Mordecai, the dean had been raised as a Christian, but he nonetheless enjoyed calling himself "Mordecai the Jew" or a "Methodist, Episcopal, Baptist Jew" in honor of his collegiate affiliations and religious ancestry. The eccentric Mordecai, still remembered for his sharp wit, multicolored coat, and omnipresent dog, delighted in signing his personal checks in Hebrew. After he was mentioned as a candidate for college president, he penned a satirical verse, "Trinity's Jewish President." When Mordecai died in 1927, a colleague eulogized, "In religion he was Christian, but how he did love the sound of his Hebraic name and the tingle of his portion of Patriarchal blood!" Mordecai exulted in that antiquarian philo-Semitism that was a legacy of the Victorian southerner.[29]

Southern Civic Life

Across America in the early 1900s, nativist feelings intensified as immigration grew into the millions. Fears were expressed nationally for the survival of American civilization. Northern racial thinkers, eugenicists, and Social Darwinists inveighed against aliens who were allegedly polluting the national bloodstream and undermining the republic with their radicalism. White southerners, having put African Americans in their place with Jim Crow laws, expressed anxiety over new, dark, alien *races* such as Italians and Jews. Southern folkloric prejudices found sanction in the ideology of a cosmopolitan racial science. In *The Jew A Negro* (1910) the Reverend Arthur Abernethy, a rustic journalist in the North Carolina mountains, argued by anthropology and scripture that Jews ought to be disenfranchised by virtue of their drop of African blood. In 1907 Senator Furnifold Simmons, leader of North Carolina's Democratic machine, declared his "opposition and that of the people of my state to unrestricted immigration," especially from "Southern and Eastern Europe." Simmons —whom W. J. Cash called the Senate's "stateliest Neanderthaler"—saw in "the degenerate progeny of the Asiatic hoards [*sic*]" a threat to "Anglo-Saxon blood." Even the philo-Semitic Zebulon Vance warned of a "pell-mell influx" that would "diminish our society." When the state recruited immigrants in the early 1900s, it directed its efforts to people of "Teutonic, Celtic or Saxon origin."[30]

Whatever their suspicions of political radicalism or fears of racial contamination, Durhamites were rarely overt in their anti-Semitic prejudices, nor were they given to the paroxysms of violence that wracked the South. Codes of hospitality and Christian charity countered group prejudices. Strains of anti- and philo-Semitism coexisted. Although Cash in *The Mind of the South* labeled the Jew the "eternal Alien," he saw in southern Christianity a spirit that was "essentially Hebraic." Jews often told stories of devout southerners who would sit with them for hours talking religion. The peddler Morris Witcowsky recalled how his customers would insist "that I stay overnight and discuss the Bible with them." Harry Richter, a peddler from Mount Gilead, recalled a poor farm family named Haywood who turned their home into a boarding house for Jewish peddlers. They reminded the Jews of their religious duties, loved to hear Yiddish spoken, and carefully separated pork from the eggs that they fed them. "In the South," Richter reflected, "the orthodox Protestants granted us dignity; they were the first to make us feel that we really belonged." In his Durham pawnshop Solomon Dworsky spent hours discussing the Bible with customers.[31]

The southerner, according to Cash, worshipped the "Jehovah of the Old Testament" and held to a Christian rectitude that was "Mosaic in its sternness." In 1909 "two long-haired, Israelitish looking preachers" visited Durham seeking "converts." They preached that "good deeds" and "rigorous adherence to the law" would redeem from "bodily death." These sectarians, who provoked debates in the streets, adhered to a Hebraic Christianity. Southern gentlemen commonly invoked the Gospels, Scott, or Shakespeare when discussing the Hebrews, alluding to Jesus' Jewish origins. "For good or ill, being a Southerner is like being a Jew," claimed Raleigh editor Jonathan Daniels, citing their heritages as defeated and despised minorities.[32]

Southerners saw in the Jew the exemplary American. The Jew was Horatio Alger, the self-made man who picked himself up by the proverbial bootstraps. The Durham newspapers wrote admiringly of the Jews' "perseverance" and trumpeted on the front page the glowing story of how J. W. Jacobson had risen from a Durham store clerk to a Chicago mining broker. According to a local joke, "Two merchants with large stores on opposite corners had big sales—over their entrances they put up signs reading 'Big Sale.' A little Jew who had a small store between the two painted and hung up a sign reading 'Entrance Here.'"[33]

The image of the weak, unmanly "little Jew" who compensates for his vulnerability with guile is an anti-Semitic stereotype, but the tone here is gentle and admiring. Durham thought well of a man who knew how to make a profit. "Fortunately" for Durham, Southgate Jones, a prominent businessman wrote in a memoir, some Jewish tobacco workers remained in town after the industry mechanized. They "made fine, substantial citizens," Jones asserted, "and their descendants occupy respected places in the community today."[34] Americans liked rags-to-riches stories that confirmed their belief that they lived in a land of unlimited opportunity.

Although suspicious of aliens, southerners were hospitable to strangers. In the early 1900s Durham newspapers reported on an "object of pity" or a "Jewish tramp" who arrived in town "ragged, cold and almost starved." The refugee was given a warm bed in the police station, and a Jew was called to translate. One such barefooted "tramp" claimed that he had not eaten in three days. The Russian was treated to a restaurant meal before being sent on a train to New York.[35] If a Jew were short of cash a town benefactor such as Julian Carr reached into his pocket for a personal loan.

In the countryside, too, immigrants found hospitality. A farm family at the end of the rail line in nearby Caswell County welcomed Jewish travelers who knocked at their door. They wanted the Jews "as strangers on the road to come in and have a meal with them." The hungry, kosher Jews, however, asked only to dig vegetables in the garden. The family gladly obliged, but they thought the Jews "a little strange" for preferring to eat bread and onions outside rather than partake of home hospitality.[36]

Durham newspapers told touching stories of Jewish women who emigrated from Russia to be reunited with their beaux. In 1901 the *Durham Sun* proclaimed in a front-page headline, "Bride Came All the Way from Russia to Durham to Join Her Intended Husband." Annie Wolck suffered the "vicissitudes" of "true love" to join A. Wolff. "Strong and enduring must be such love as that," the *Sun* rhapsodized.[37] These stories, which the newspapers turned into melodrama, appealed to the sentimental tastes of the age.

The public schools welcomed immigrant children. "I made friends very quickly with my non-Jewish classmates," recalled Joe Dave, who emigrated as a child from Kovno. "The city school system at that time was very liberal in their thinking—the superintendents, the principals, as well as the teachers, were very courteous and helpful to all students who came from Europe." Lithuanian-born Henry Bane recalled that as a child who learned English at an early age he had fewer problems than his heavily accented older brother. Bane's progress was so swift that he was promoted from third to fourth grade in a week. When a classmate died, a teacher asked him to recite William Cullen Bryant's "Thanatopsis" to the school assembly. From the first, public schools listed Jewish children on honor rolls, and they excelled in the declamation contests so popular among southerners. In 1914 David Brady and Henry Clay Greenberg, sons of

Yiddish-speaking immigrants, were champion debaters at Durham High School and went to the state finals. Brady was praised for his "clear cut speech and brilliant rejoinder." A year later Isaac Kadis won a prize as Durham's best high-school debater.[38]

"Most of the Gentile fellows treated me real nice," Sam Margolis recalled, except for a group who lived near the working-class neighborhood of Edgemont. The rich kids egged the Edgemont boys to pick on Jews. "I got beaten up three times a day . . . just because I was a little waif of a Jewboy," Gibby Katz remembered. Once a group decided to de-pants the Jewish boys, and the fights caused several anti-Semitic children to be suspended from school. After he had reported them, Margolis was threatened in the school yard by the boys, but a huge football player named Taylor Cheek stepped forward, telling the bullies that they would have to fight him before he would let them touch Margolis. At Fuller School children were occasionally beaten or chased home. After three boys jumped Joe Hockfield, he waylaid them one at a time. A Christian playmate invited Henry Bane home for a drink, but the boy's mother refused to let a "dirty Jew" share a glass with his friend.

A strain in Protestant Christianity depicted the Jews as unsaved and worked for their conversion. Few Jews recalled any personal attempts to convert them, but circuit-riding "converted Jewish" preachers appeared in local churches. In 1904 Mark Levy, general secretary of the Society for the Propagation of the Gospel among Jews, spoke in a half-dozen Durham churches. "All are welcome," the newspaper stated, "but Levy especially invites Jews." Two years later Simon Lubracki, a native of Warsaw, preached at the Gospel Tabernacle on the "Messianic Reign." A. Lichenstein, superintendent of the Jewish Christian Mission of St. Louis, spoke from three Durham pulpits on "the return of the Jews to Jerusalem in connection with the second coming of the messiah." The last was the Rev. J. H. Rosenberg, a graduate of Southwestern Presbyterian University, who declared that his mission was "to brush away the prejudice he says some Christians feel toward the Jew" as well as to bring word of the messiah to Jews.[39] These speakers confirmed Christians in their faith rather than converted local Jews.

The Jews suffered little worse than stereotypes. "Jew" meant commerce. When Harry Miller achieved "remarkable" business success, the newspaper praised him for having the "characteristic push of his race." The Reverend Beaman of the Anti-Saloon League noted economic competition:

"The Jew was afraid that if he closed before the Gentile did, the latter would get a quarter he ought to have, while the Gentile thought that the Jew would get a quarter if he (the Gentile) closed first." Chapel Hill dramatist Paul Green, a lifelong student of southern folk culture, collected in his *Wordbook* several references that reflected popular prejudices. "Jew" or "jew down" meant "to cheat, to persuade a lowering of prices." A "jew price" was "a reduced price from a usually over-high price to start with and never on the even dollar, most often like $4.99 or $4.98."[40] Jewish businesses were "Jew stores."

The encounter of immigrant Jew and native southerner sparked cultural dissonance. In a society so uniformly Anglo-Saxon the Jews' odd names and language perplexed southerners. Rabbi Rabinowitz's name was hardly ever spelled twice the same way and was once rendered Rabbi Robin Novitz. Mayerberg became Meyerberry. Max Siegel was christened Mark Seagull. Native Durhamites found comedy in immigrant Yinglish, the immigrants' hybrid Yiddish-English dialect. When Max Bane sued the railroad in 1915, the newspaper reported that "his testimony furnished fun for the jury and the court. Bane did not intend to be funny but at times his broken English and enthusiasm for his case produced some curious results in the spoken language." A country woman, hearing the cry "drunk man," grabbed a gun, not realizing it was an immigrant shouting "junkman." When Simon Levy told how two fighting boys collapsed the roof of his chicken coop, he "entertained the crowd." A Jewish woman, exasperated at a lawyer's question, responded, "What I done I dels you I done, and what I didn't do you makes me tink I done."[41]

Yet Jews aspired to be Americans, and when they naturalized, the immigrants Anglicized their names. Leib became Louis, Chazkel became Charles, and Katzergersky became Katz. Lipe Tevio was reborn as Philip Dave. Jews adopted American family names such as Allen, Brady, and Wilson. Joseph Branson took the name of a prominent local family. Second-generation names such as Abraham Lincoln Wissburg, Benjamin Franklin Kronheimer, or Henry Clay Greenberg expressed patriotism.

Although Durham had the reputation as a gambling, hard-drinking town, it aspired to a high Christian tone. In 1911 two Jewish salesmen from Philadelphia, R. J. Levins and J. Bell, fell afoul of the city's blue laws. Engaged in a game of pinochle on the Murray Hotel porch one rainy Sunday, they were arrested for card playing. Judge Sykes did not understand pinochle, could not even spell it, but given that Sunday was not the Hebrew Sabbath, he fined them only court costs, which they "gladly paid." [42]

The newspapers did not specifically report anti-Semitic incidents, but several episodes suggest malice. J. Saks's Pearl Mill grocery was torched in 1901, and "he expressed himself as believing that the building was fired by some enemy." Some boys lit a bag of kindling under the bedrooms of Abraham Cohen's home and grocery. In 1909 Joe Keffler, a Jewish "boy," was put on a chain gang in New Hill, south of Durham, for violating an ordinance he did not understand. Local Jews were disturbed, and attorney Benjamin Lovenstein appealed to Governor Kitchin, who pardoned Keffler so that he could join the community for Rosh Hashanah. In 1910 Jews were "stirred up" by several charges of usury; one was against the pawnbroker Reuben Roth for supposedly collecting $1.60 on a $5.00 loan. They disputed the facts and claimed that a lawyer was spitefully pursuing a case in which he had no interest. [43]

The 1907 depression exacerbated social tensions and tested the community's tolerance. Durham witnessed several well-publicized indictments of Jews on arson charges. Since the nineteenth century the fire insurance industry had discriminated against Jews. After Harry Bloom's soap factory burned in 1909 while he was in Norfolk, the insurance company refused to pay the $3,000 Bloom demanded. The "Hebrew gentleman," as the newspaper called him, was accused of arson. Although a candle and coal oil were found in the debris, no evidence linked Bloom to the crime, and both Jews and Christians testified in his defense. He was acquitted and settled with the insurance company for $275. [44]

In 1910 Arthur Greenberg's variety store burned soon after he had increased insurance for his Christmas inventory. He, too, was arrested. His business—with a net worth between $3,500 to $6,500—had been "tottering" near bankruptcy. The defense lawyer, Percy Reade, a Trinity College professor, alleged that anti-Semitism lay behind the arrest, calling it not a "prosecution" but a "persecution." The firemen, who suspected arson, "were uniformly considerate of the young Hebrew." The prosecutor declared that he "shall not fall into the mistake of calling him a Jew and a Hebrew." The delicacy with which all parties treated the defendant's Jewishness, the assumption that "Jew" or "Hebrew" implied shady dealings, suggests an undercurrent of anti-Semitism. Greenberg was acquitted. "There was one irresistible fact of a Jew and a fire, but that was all," the newspaper concluded. [45]

The fires provoked jokes in Durham. After the Fire Insurance Company refused to settle with Adolph Max, he hired Judge R. W. Winston, who succeeded in winning payment. As Winston counted his share and passed the remainder to Max, the merchant grimaced, "Look here, Mr. Winston, who had this fire, you or me?" Another local joke concerned two Jewish businessmen who "decided" to have a fire. One went to New York, where he was to receive a telegram on Tuesday informing him of the fire. When it arrived on Wednesday, he exclaimed, "Look, here's a telegram I just received when I should have got it yesterday!"[46] Despite the jokes and suspicions no Jew was convicted locally of arson.

There were several accounts of fights between Jews and non-Jews. Harry Kahn, who bought the Biltmore Hotel in 1907, got into a name-calling brawl with his steward, R. B. Faucett, and soon left town. A waiter at the Corcoran Hotel insulted New York "travelling man" B. H. Kamen after he returned an order of bananas and cream, and fists flew. Max Shevel, a "prominent citizen," was involved in several fisticuffs.[47]

The major case of anti-Semitism that rocked the South hardly caused a ripple in Durham. Newspapers reported the trial, conviction, and lynching of Leo Frank in Georgia for allegedly having murdered a girl in his pencil factory. In 1913 on the day the *Durham Morning Herald* reported Frank's conviction, its lead story described a local synagogue banquet under the headline "The Hebrews Celebrated." After Frank was lynched in 1915, local newspapers reprinted editorials condemning the act but did not comment. Boycotts and mob violence threatened Atlanta's Jews, but Durham felt no repercussions. Frank's body passed through Durham on a train taking it to New York for burial.[48] The local reaction suggests that the Frank case was an anomaly in southern-Jewish relations.

Nothing so marked Jewish southern acculturation as participation in sports. In the 1890s sports fever had swept the South, as it had the nation. Sports embodied the Progressive Era virtues of health and manliness. The first Jews to prove themselves were the sons of the early German Jewish settlers who, as Durham boys born and bred, were more familiar with the rituals of boxing and baseball than were their coreligionists lately removed from the cheder and yeshiva of the Pale. Roy Levy and Artie and Max Summerfield were members of the town's "sporting fraternity." Summerfield, son of a synagogue president, was perhaps Durham's best boxer, and fifty years after the event stories were still being told about his 1901 prizefight against Charley Clark. Boxing, with its heavy betting, violated city codes, but the law did not stop one hundred fans from gathering in an upstairs hall on Main Street. Young Summerfield was holding his own in the eighth round until a voice in the back yelled, "Police!" Summerfield turned his head as Clark launched an uppercut that knocked him cold. The joint was raided. Summerfield continued his fighting career and later turned promoter, once sparring with Jack Dempsey in Durham.[49]

Children of east European immigrants sought to prove their mettle as Americans, yet they were segregated as Jews. In 1911 a "Hebrew" baseball team competed in Durham's neighborhood leagues. The First Baptist Church Sunday School defeated the Hebrews 10-1 in an early battle. By 1913, however, behind the pitching of Zuckerman the Hebrews vanquished Fuller School, 5-2. When the Hebrews fell a week later to Duke Street, 19-8, the *Durham Morning Herald* reported, "At no stage of the game did the non-pork-eaters have a chance," though Brady "gladdened the hearts of his tribe by jumping on the horsehide for 3/4s of a home run."[50]

In its early days basketball, a northern city game, was a Jewish sport. In 1913 a "Hebrew Quintet" whipped the Boy Scouts 35-7 at the YMCA. "The Scouts played a good game," the newspaper conceded, "but they were simply outclassed by the Jews." Leo Stein of Wilmington played on UNC's first basketball team in 1911, and a year later Joe Brady of Durham captained the Trinity College squad.[51]

"Jews Dominate Checkers," the *Durham Morning Herald* headlined, as Julius Enoch, Louis Stadiem, and Julius Haskell won city championships at the YMCA from 1911 to 1913.[52] However much Jewish sportsmen adapted southern ways, though, they retained their distinction as "Hebrews," and the newspaper often looked bemusedly, and sometimes condescendingly, at their endeavors.

Overt anti-Semitism was not respectable in Gentile Durham. All local Jews remembered childhood taunting, yet none recalled anything more than social discrimination or an isolated incident in their adult years. Jews had Christian "acquaintances," but few friends, Fanny Gladstein reflected. "They were very nice, but there's always something you feel you're not wanted." Southern-born, acculturated German Jews, such as Ben Kronheimer, or wealthy East European Jews, such as Dr. Rosenstein, integrated more successfully into Durham society. Rosenstein, though Russian born, spoke English without an accent. As a professional man, he had higher status than the shopkeepers.

Durham Jewry, like American Jewry generally, did bifurcate socially along ethnic lines. The German families, who were mostly native born, integrated more rapidly and successfully into Gentile society than did the east Europeans. The Kronheimer women were alumnae of the Oxford Female Seminary, and Ben penned satirical verse for the newspapers. The Kronheimers' social circle was Episcopalian. In 1902 Rosa Summerfield won twenty-one votes as Queen of the Carnival, and her brother Max traveled the state competing in firemen's tournaments as a member of Hose Company Number 2.

James Leyburn, son of a Presbyterian minister, in his memoir of Durham life from 1900 to 1920, observed "two very different groups" of Jews: "A small number of substantial families who from the outset became identified with the leading elements of the city; and a somewhat larger number of people who had only recently arrived in this country from eastern Europe." Among the first Leyburn included the Kronheimers, Rosensteins, and "several increasingly prosperous merchants." Those in the second category ran small stores and junk yards. Leyburn claimed, "Most responsible citizens would have been shocked by any display of religious prejudice." Yet he noticed that the "awareness of Jews as 'different' led to certain reticences on the part of Gentiles and certain inhibitions on the part of Jews."[53]

Leyburn, who wrote his memoir from his perspective as professor of ethnography and minority problems at Johns Hopkins University, saw the Durham Jews as clannish, preferring "privacy to public attention." That inclination, he believed, explained why they remained civically uninvolved. Leyburn's father spent long hours talking to Dr. Rosenstein in his office, and the optometrist gave matzoh to the minister every Passover. Young Leyburn, a pianist, was a "good friend" of Abe Rosenstein, a violinist. Although the Rosensteins were considered "among our favorite friends," the Leyburns were "never in their home nor they in ours." Leyburn recalled, "An invisible wall seemed to keep Jewish and Gentile social relationships in very constricted limits."[54]

Leyburn shed light on Gentile attitudes to Jews both in his insights and misconceptions. Leyburn denied that "taunting language" was ever heard in the schools, although Jewish children recalled fights and shouts of "Christkiller." He affirmed differences of class and acculturation among Jews but did not recognize the ethnic and religious lines between Germans and east Europeans, Reform and Orthodox. Leyburn denied that anti-Semitism existed in the South before the arrival of east European Jews. He described anti-Semitism as a northern vice, a fear that Jews brought with them. This assertion of Christian goodwill to Jews was repeated among Durham's "respectable citizens." Yet, Leyburn conceded, "To be respectable meant being a member of a Protestant church."[55]

As Jews ascended the ladder of class, they also abandoned their cottages in the Pine Street Bottoms for houses up the hill and across the railroad tracks on North Roxboro near Holloway and Cleveland Streets. The change in residence followed a national pattern of Jewish upward mobility. This second settlement paralleled the move of New York Jews from the Lower East Side ghetto to better neighborhoods in the Bronx and Brooklyn. Roxboro Street served as the Jewish neighborhood for four decades. The magnet was the Fuller School, which had been built in 1897, and a synagogue, which opened on Liberty Street in 1904. After the depression of 1907–1910, real estate investors began demolishing cottages in the area and building rental properties. Many Jews found homes in these two-story, two-family box houses with their large, neighborly porches. The merchants were now two or three blocks from the synagogue and their downtown stores. Some thirty to thirty-five families, about two-thirds of the Jewish community, clustered in the six-block area. Jewish homes were interspersed with those of non-Jews. Greek immigrant and wealthy white Christian families lived nearby.

Although non-Jewish Durhamites did not perceive Roxboro Street to be a Jewish neighborhood, Jews recalled it affectionately as a "ghetto without walls." Yiddish was spoken in the street. Front doors were left open to welcome cousins. Roxboro Street remained a little Jewish world with a kosher bakery, delicatessen, tailors, and shoemakers. Louis Jaffe's bakery served as the social center. Jaffe, who had arrived from Pinsk in 1912, reconstructed a Russian-style brick oven in his backyard. Customers who wanted bread entered Jaffe's house—with or without a knock. By horse and wagon he delivered his challah, rye, white, and pumpernickel breads across the city, from the Kronheimers in Trinity Park to the grocers in Hayti.[56]

The decision to live in a Jewish neighborhood was a matter of choice. German Jews remained outside this community in affluent neighborhoods. The Summerfields resided in a large house on Pettigrew Street near the Duke mansion. In 1904 the Kronheimers, Durham's wealthiest Jews, moved into a $7,000 home with a garden and hen house on Queen Street. A butler, cook, chauffeur, and yardman served them.[57]

Jews and African Americans

The east European Jews as an intermediary ethnic group occupied, socially and geographically, a middle ground between white and black Durham. From the first, black domestics worked in Jewish homes. One Jew-

ish family who had arrived in the 1890s hired a houseworker, a man
the children knew by the slave term of "uncle," who slept under the
porch with the cow. Newspapers reported minor scraps between Jews and
blacks. In the early 1900s several Jews were charged with receiving stolen
goods from blacks or overcharging black customers. L. Dwartz got into a
fight over a watermelon with one John Jones, who "cursed the Hebrew";
Dwartz was accused of drawing a gun, but the case was dismissed. Other
accounts mention Jewish merchants in Hayti who kept guns, so they must
have felt some apprehension. Jews were occasionally robbed or beaten, and
the assailant, in the practice of the time, was identified as black. These incidents increased early in the century when a cocaine epidemic sparked a
crime wave.[58]

The peddler Morris Witcowsky, who worked northern North Carolina,
claimed that the Jewish peddlers "were probably the first white people in
the South who paid the Negro people any respect at all." He addressed his
black customers as "Mr." and "Mrs.," never as "uncle" and "aunt." For
blacks who bought on credit the peddlers kept "a book on the *shvartzers*
[blacks]," but Witcowsky insisted that the term implied no insult, and he
always found their credit to be good. Economic relations flowed two ways.
Black farmers sold produce to Jewish grocers. As early as 1887, Julius
Schwartz listed his boarding place as William Overby's restaurant, a "colored" business.[59]

Pauli Murray—the black writer, lawyer, and Anglican priest—recalled
that in the Durham of her pre–World War I childhood, blacks and whites
"lived close together, and, within the limits of the strict racial code, considerable familiarity existed in their dealings with one another." Murray
named Dora and Moses Greenberg among the white individuals whose
"humanity" overcame the "walls of segregation." Her Aunt Sallie, who
shopped at the Greenberg grocery store on Proctor Street up the hill from
her home, always found them "very friendly." The Greenbergs boasted
about their son Henry, who won the high-school Shakespeare contest, and
her aunt praised her niece Pauli, who had earned a prize for reading the
most books in the "colored" library. (Years later, attorney Murray argued
a case before the New York State Supreme Court with Justice Henry
Greenberg presiding.) Murray's memoir also validated a local legend about
a black man who walked into the synagogue and read the Torah in Hebrew. Her uncle, Reverend Small, knew Hebrew, "which made a bond between him and the Jewish family."[60]

The attorney Benjamin Lovenstein, the Greenbergs' son-in-law, became a favorite in the black community, where he was known as "Mr. Holstein" or "the Hebrew lawyer." He gained notoriety for his spirited defense of a black man named Major Guthrie, who was convicted of murder. Lovenstein threw himself into a "moneyless job" to have Guthrie pardoned. He organized a statewide petition drive that led the governor to commute Guthrie's sentence. Lovenstein was once held in contempt of court when he resisted a judge's order to sit while defending a black man on trial for the "usual colored infirmities." The *Durham Morning Herald,* which had at first hailed Lovenstein as "one of Durham's young legal lights," took an increasingly dim view of his activities. After the fourth of Lovenstein's black clients escaped from jail, it noted disapprovingly that the attorney was "delighted."[61]

Lovenstein defended blacks largely because he was too poor to choose his clients. In this regard he was like the Jewish grocers in Hayti. When an African American asked Lovenstein to assist in his defense, Lovenstein refused when he learned the man had also hired a black lawyer. The newspaper noted that even Lovenstein "drew a color line." Lovenstein, driven by a sense of his own "humble origins,"[62] was committed to civil justice, if not social equality, for African Americans.

Booker T. Washington had urged blacks to "imitate the Jew," but in Durham, Jews borrowed the theme of uplift from blacks. Two years after Dr. James Shepard founded the National Religious Training School and Chautauqua for the Colored Race, the Durham Hebrew Congregation appointed a committee "to make arrangements for a Jewish training school in this city."[63] The project was never launched, but it was likely inspired by Rabbi Abram Simon, a Reform rabbi from Washington, who served on the board of trustees for Shepard's institution. When the rabbi visited Durham, he spoke in both the synagogue and the black church. These were the nascent years of a national black-Jewish alliance when Jews joined blacks to form the National Association for the Advancement of Colored People.

Tennessee born and college educated, Rabbi Simon appealed to congregational modernists. Rabbi Simon had similar messages for both Jewish and black audiences. In 1909, he spoke at the synagogue on "the duty of the Jew in the small community," calling for strong leaders who could promote Jewish education. His talk was so well received that the Jews followed him to the black White Rock Baptist Church. There Dr. Shepard introduced Simon as "the foremost rabbi in the Jewish church in America." Simon's speech had a touch of both Du Bois and Washington; he called on blacks not only to pursue industrial education but also to aspire to the genius of Plato, Darwin, or Shakespeare. He endorsed Shepard's call for an educated black clergy as the vanguard of racial progress. In 1911 Simon returned to Durham, and once again Jews crowded into the church's front rows, which had been reserved for white people. In his address Rabbi Simon quoted Jesus and St. Paul. After the speech, he went to a B'nai B'rith dinner meeting and later spoke at the synagogue.[64]

Politics

Politics served as an index of the Jews' civic integration. Concerned primarily with their financial security, Jews remained outsiders by virtue of their immigrant culture, social isolation, and Yiddish language. Poll taxes and literacy tests, intended to disenfranchise blacks from politics, also discouraged poorer, uneducated whites from voting. The Democratic machine with its patronage remained a closed society. Cronyism dominated city hall. The Democratic party was subservient to business interests although the Dukes remained conspicuously progressive and Republican. Aldermen often showed more interest in enhancing their own finances and properties than in improving the city's welfare. Calls for reform became a regular feature of Durham politics until a new charter was finally enacted in 1921. The Jews' indifference to politics was a widespread southern condition. In the early 1900s only about one-third of all southerners voted.[65]

Jews, like other citizens, voted their economic interests and aligned themselves with either conservatives or progressives. In 1903 eight Jews, Germans and Russians, joined one hundred "prominent citizens" in signing nominating petitions for a board of aldermen. This group of "conservative" business leaders opposed the temperance platform of the Anti-Saloon ticket. They feared that skilled labor would not come to a dry town. Despite the opposition of the Baptist and Methodist churches, the "wets" prevailed in Durham city but not in the county. Four years later Jews supported the antimachine progressives who demanded reform of the city's health and educational systems. Sixteen Jews signed a petition for direct election of the city's aldermen, calling for an end to "politics" in city hall.[66] Such reform campaigns were common features of town politics across the South.

After 1900, immigrant Jews began demonstrating their Americanism. When a Polish-born anarchist assassinated President McKinley in 1901, Chevra B'nai Israel, a newly formed Orthodox congregation, held a public display of mourning in a rented hall. Frank Pruschankin "made a most touching tribute to his memory, which brought tears to many eyes." The Jewish memorial—duly noticed by the newspaper—was likely intended to assure southerners that their immigrant Jews were no foreign radicals.[67]

The first Jew to seek public office was a self-proclaimed progressive. In 1908 Benjamin Lovenstein, an attorney with a predominantly black clientele, ran for a seat in the general assembly. Lovenstein had only recently moved to Durham from Philadelphia after marrying Rebecca Greenberg, the daughter of local east European immigrants. As an outsider, he ran for office in "the New York way," plastering the city with illustrated posters and circulars. His tactics were labeled "radical," and he adopted as a motto—with a flair for drama—a saying from the French philosopher Proudhon, "If I can't live a freeman, I'll die a warrior."[68]

That Lovenstein made a "special bid" for Durham's labor vote is significant. In the New South newly urbanized workers responded to populist anti-Semitic appeals, blaming the Jew for the industrialization that displaced them from the farm and impoverished them in the factory. During the Leo Frank trial Tom Watson's anti-Semitic rantings would strike a chord among working-class Georgians. In Durham the mills in fact were having persistent labor troubles as union agitation mounted in the early 1900s. Unlike those in Atlanta, Durham's Jews were not identified as manufacturers.

Lovenstein boldly challenged the local capitalists. "Let the Laboring Man Have at Least as Much to Say as the Man With a Million Dollars Behind HIS SIGNATURE," read one broadside. He attacked the corporations, demanded the creation of a recorder's court, and advocated a state reformatory "to protect our boys from disgrace!" He quoted "a few rods from E-pick-erus, a Grecian writer" on the perfectibility of mankind. Lovenstein's platform aligned him with Democratic party progressives who had split with the probusiness conservatives. At the top of the ballot in 1908 was reform gubernatorial candidate W. W. Kitchin, "the people's choice," who challenged the Democratic machine and attacked oil, tobacco, and railroad trusts.[69]

Like a populist on the stump, Lovenstein went to Stagville, Braggtown, and Pickett's Hill, where he delivered rousing speeches to a "good crowd" of workers and country folks. The Greenberg family "went out in style and gave the front portion of his audience a decidedly good appearance," the newspaper reported. The largely Republican crowd cheered on the "Israelite captain" with shouts of "Go it Lovey!" "The Hebrew lawyer," the *Durham Morning Herald* noted, "made a fearful assault on the county machinery." He attacked the practice of basing the income of the police and magistrates on the fines that they levied, a custom that he claimed led to corruption.[70]

Lovenstein sought office as an American; Durham saw him as a Jew. Anti-Semitism entered the campaign when one opponent, Arley Moore, stated that "he did not want to be crucified between a Jew and a Yankee." Lovenstein responded, "I charge that Arley Moore ought not to have tried to prejudice you against me because I am the son of Hebrew parents." Lovenstein retorted that if the "most infallible man in the world . . . Christ Jesus could be crucified for the world's sins, Arley Moore could be crucified for the good of Durham." The crowd roared. Lovenstein continued with a race-proud speech, pointing to the twenty-seven Jews in the United States Congress, Senators Simon Guggenheim and Isidor Raynor, and the statesman Oscar Straus. "I charge in conclusion that there are many Hebrew good citizens," Lovenstein thundered. The *Durham Morning Herald* observed that "Mr. Lovenstein speaks highly of his many opponents . . . whereas Mr. Moore thinks one of his negro clients has greater mentality than Lovenstein."[71]

Lovenstein ended his campaign on the courthouse steps before another "good crowd." He attacked Rockefeller and the oil trusts, announced that he would support his opponents if they won, though Moore only reluctantly. When Lovenstein finished, his old nemesis, Moses Levy, rose to attack. Levy claimed that he too wished to run for the legislature and read a prepared speech. He attacked Lovenstein's "graft and greed," calling for "men who hear above the clamor of mammon the clarion call of conscience." He then dropped his text and attacked Lovenstein for having defended a black man in court against him. He complained that Lovenstein had only whipped him in a recent fisticuffs because he had to fight the entire Greenberg family, too. The newspaper concluded with some humor: "Of course there was sympathy for the young Hebrew who assayed to whip too much population."[72]

Lovenstein lost, but his vote was "larger than those opposed to him expected it to be." Lovenstein attributed his defeat to insufficient ballots in his home district and to "the little peccadillos of politicians" who did not deliver promised support. The only precinct he won was the Mangum precinct near the Jewish neighborhood. Although the progressive Kitchin was elected governor, Lovenstein's antibusiness views were out of kilter with the capitalist spirit of Durham, home of Duke's tobacco trust. Reform suffered repeated setbacks in Durham elections. After the local

Democratic party split, a Republican claimed that Lovenstein "is with us now. He will control the Hebrew votes." The *Durham Morning Herald* observed that "that last sentence is a large mouthful though."[73] By 1908 the newspaper recognized community divisions.

Lovenstein, doubly marked as a Jew and a Yankee, sought to prove himself as an American and a fellow southerner. Yet southerners saw him not as a citizen asserting his rights but as a Hebrew, a representative of an interest group. He challenged the political hegemony of white, Anglo-Saxon Protestants even as he sought to join them. Racially and religiously disparaged, Lovenstein responded with a race-proud defense of Jews as American citizens. Jews were blood of the "infallible" Jesus. Like the merchants who sought wealth as the route to respectability, Lovenstein laid claim to property of a different sort, Epicurus and Proudhon, the heritage of western civilization. The "enlightened" Jew immersed in secular culture was a stock figure in Jewish society.

Although hardly revolutionary, Lovenstein's anti-establishment politics evoked the messianic zeal of the young east European Jews who flocked to the socialist parties. His politics were merely progressive, but the ardor with which he pursued his views aroused suspicions of Jewish radicalism in conservative North Carolina. Lovenstein, who owned a haberdashery, was a budding capitalist himself even as he championed the oppressed and excluded. Lovenstein did win the Jewish vote, but community traditionalists opposed him because his humanism challenged their Orthodoxy and because his progressive politics affronted their business interests. Jews, habitually insecure, admonished themselves not to be too visible, and Lovenstein's political courage was, for some Jews, unseemly hutzpah.

Lovenstein, after having failed at politics, soon failed in business. His problems became front-page news. Lovenstein's investments in a hat shop and tonsorial parlor had left him deeply in debt. His mother-in-law, Dora Greenberg, went to Julian Carr, the banker and tobacco magnate, who lent her $250 to help cover his debts. The attorney juggled his finances, one step ahead of his creditors. Finally, in July 1910, he was indicted for embezzling $75 from a black client when his check bounced. Lovenstein cited articles in the *Raleigh News and Observer,* the *Greensboro News,* the *Charlotte Observer,* and the Durham newspapers as evidence of a statewide conspiracy against him. The defense lawyer, Percy Reade, a Trinity College professor, argued against "this clamor for the crucifixion of a Jew." Lovenstein claimed, too, that the "Hebrews of the city were his enemies because of his heterodoxy." With all the public interest, the court venue had to be changed from Durham to Hillsborough. There a jury acquitted him in five minutes, unable to find any intent of fraud. Lovenstein published a memoir, *As I Saw It, or the Borrower Is Servant to the Lender,* dedicated to "the future welfare of man." Lovenstein left Durham for Richmond, where he and his wife established a successful law practice. Lovenstein's political career had no lasting impact; indeed, it was forgotten by the Jewish community.[74]

Jewish Communal Life

Durham Jewry remained a Hebrew colony, an outpost connected materially and spiritually to distant Jewish communities. Even as Jews aspired to become small-town southerners, they organized institutions to observe their religion, strengthen their ethnic association, and formalize their ties to world Jewry. Their primary community was not with their Christian neighbors but with a cosmopolitan Jewry. As a colony, Durham was an outpost, a way station for transients. Peddlers, salesmen, and hungry immigrants on the road headed to Durham for a kosher meal and a place to spend the night. In 1911, after being injured in a train accident near Henderson, the New York baker R. Group asked to be taken to Durham, the closest city with a Jewish community. Group died in Watts Hospital ten days later, but local Jews buried him and cared for his wife and child. A couple from Smithfield, unable to find a rabbi, traveled to Durham to be married. The community supplied witnesses and treated them to a party. Jewish musicians, including Arthur Rubinstein, appeared at local venues. In an age when the Chautauqua was popular entertainment Rabbi Joseph Kohn of Brooklyn captivated a crowded synagogue in 1907 with an oration on "The Gardener and his Flowers." To educate themselves, Durham Jews subscribed to the Jewish Publication Society (JPS). For Americanizing immigrants, the society offered the classics of Jewish literature, a biographical series for youngsters, and a new English translation of the Bible. Of the nine Durham subscribers in 1915, several were Hayti grocers with limited means and little formal education but great reading appetites. About 1 in 40 Durham Jews joined the JPS, compared with national statistics of 1 in 250.[75] Despite the isolation of Durham Jews, the cultural forces transforming American Jewry soon came down the line to them.

Durham Jews built social and religious institutions that would allow them to maintain their collective identity as traditional Jews even while they were culturally blending into the small-town South. The immigrants, having moved from preindustrial European countries to America, had to not only mediate the conflicts of tradition and modernity but also cope with the small-town South. This process of constant renegotiation created considerable unease and led to communal conflicts, which were carried into the synagogue. Where Christian Durham tended to see "the Jews" categorically, the Jews themselves fractured. Intimacy created tensions. The feuding, however, in no way severed the ethnic ties that bound the Jews.

Although Orthodoxy certainly attenuated, it continued in Durham more persistently than was typical of southern towns. Frequently in southern towns of less than one thousand Jews, Lee Shai Weissbach observes, Orthodox synagogues "died out within a few decades of their establishment." The Durham community was nearly homogeneously east European, bound by landsleit and kinship networks. The constant flow of new, unacculturated immigrants refreshed its Yiddishkeit. Moreover, the town lacked a Reform alternative. In urban areas *landsmanshaftn* (societies of countrymen) served as benevolence societies for self-help, burials, and ethnic bonding, but in small towns the congregation assumed this role. The Durham Hebrew Congregation evolved into a east European chevra. There Jews found a rabbi, kosher meat, and a prayer quorum. The Judaism practiced was traditionalist rather than scrupulously Orthodox. The chevra was not just a worship gathering but also the place where landsleit met to gossip and conduct business, where they found a Yiddish home. For women the Ladies Aid Society served as a chevra where they socialized and organized welfare. Several Durhamites described their parents as "Jews by nature," who went "through the motions" of prayer even as their "religiosity fell off." Although Henry Brady attended services regularly and served seven terms as president, he was a "freethinker," his son Lehman recalled.[76]

The congregational history was marked by repeated schisms, which were invariably followed by efforts to reconcile. The instability of the Durham congregation was reflected in its pulpit. Durham's early rabbis were "reverends" without *semicha* (rabbinic ordination). The reverend served as cantor, tutor, schochet, and mohel. As Gibby Katz put it, "He circumcised you, married you, buried you, and killed your chickens." A post in a small, poor congregation far from Jewish centers was not appealing, and finding a rabbi acceptable to both modernists and traditionalists was a perennial problem. Immigrant Jews regarded an English-speaking rabbi as a threat to the sanctity of their faith. Parents who were concerned about their

American-born children wanted a rabbi who spoke English well. None was "extremely Orthodox." They were accommodators who learned to compromise with their congregants, who were more lax religiously.[77]

Durham's difficulty in finding rabbis reflected the disorder of an Orthodoxy thrown into confusion by the massive east European migration. Kosher standards were unregulated, and self-proclaimed rabbis asserted authority. Orthodox Jews splintered into competing factions. In 1902 east Europeans established the Union of Orthodox Rabbis. This group succeeded in certifying kosher standards and rabbinic qualifications, but it was less effective outside metropolitan areas. The movement to develop a domestic Orthodox rabbinate began in New York with the founding of the Etz Chaim yeshiva in 1886 and the Rabbi Isaac Elchanan Theological Seminary in 1897. They merged into the Rabbinical College of America in 1915. Thirteen years later Yeshiva College was founded, combining secular and Judaic studies. Rabbis committed to a distinctly American Orthodoxy founded the Jewish Theological Seminary and the United Synagogue of America in 1913, preparing the ground for what would become Conservative Judaism. These developments trickled down to Durham as self-declared "reverends" yielded to ordained rabbis. The European-born products of Old World yeshivot were succeeded by American-born, university-trained professionals.

Conflicts in the pulpit were not an exclusively Jewish problem. Newly founded, financially strapped churches, both black and white, struggled to develop a professional clergy beyond part-time, self-anointed preachers. The evolution of Durham's rabbinate parallels developments in the town's Christian clergy. The African American White Rock Baptist Church splintered in 1898 as wealthier members pressed for a more educated clergyman and decorous services.[78] Increasingly, as the rabbi took his place among the town's clergy, many congregants wanted a man who appeared modern, American.

Durham resembled many small communities. Synagogue governance was in the hands of businessmen, and the president, rather than the rabbi, held power. Durham's first professional "rabbi," Kolman Heillig, a native of Kroz, was typical in being an unordained jack-of-all-trades who served as circumciser, slaughterer, and prayer leader. Perennial conflicts arose over the rabbi's salary, which was always low. Rabbis argued with congregants over ritual and allotments of kosher meat. Once a rabbi slaughtered a chicken for a congregant, but when the headless bird ran off, the rabbi declared it treyf. The impoverished congregant assaulted the rabbi.[79]

Durham's Jews, living in an open, democratic society, lacked the rabbinic authority that they had known in Europe. Yet, Durham Jews were strongly connected. In 1900, when Adolph Max was president, the congregation listed an income of $560 with thirty-one membership families. About thirty-seven Jewish families lived in Durham at the time, so the community had a high rate of affiliation. Three or four families were Reform. Their small-town Jewish allegiance contrasted to the nation, where after 1900 the percentage of affiliated Jews declined even as the number of synagogues proliferated. Isolated in a Protestant society and removed from their familiar Jewish worlds, Durham's Jews attached themselves to the synagogue more strongly than Jews in urban centers.[80]

Just before Rosh Hashanah 1901, the *Durham Sun* reported that "some of the best Hebrews in the city . . . split from the old church" and organized a "society to be known as 'Chebre Bnay Israel,'" holding services in the Redmen's Hall. Chevra B'nai Israel (Fellowship of the Sons of Israel) was led by Mr. Somers whom the *Sun* identified as "the new sheeka" (schochet). Disputes over kosher meat would arise for the next half century. The schochet was responsible not just for assuring the ritual purity of the meat but also, with the rabbi, for apportioning provisions to the community. Jealousies arose between poor and rich Jews, between synagogue members and officers, over the quantity and quality of the meat cuts that were allotted. "There was hardly a Jewish community in America where rabbis and schochets were not involved in community-rending disputes," historian Abraham Karp notes, because kashrut supervision was a prime source of a rabbi's income. The Raleigh Orthodox congregation was similarly riven, and in Charlotte seven of the nine synagogue bylaws governed kosher meat distribution.[81]

In the small immigrant community, personality, economics, and family loyalties underlay much of the religious contention. A month before the congregation splintered, the *Durham Morning Herald* ran the headline, "An Affray over a Bible. Two Hebrew Merchants in Court Yesterday Morning. One Wanted to Swop Wives." Frank Pruschankin had gone to the home of Adolph Max to retrieve his Torah, "a Bible—a very costly document written on parchment." The newspaper continued: "Severe words ensued, and finally Mr. Max told him that he would have his store closed but for the fact that he loved his (Pruschankin's) wife." Pruschankin advised Max to love his "own wife and not mine." A fight ensued. Max claimed in court—with Abe Goldstein translating—that it was Pruschankin who wanted to swap wives. The judge ruled in Max's favor and fined Pruschankin, admonishing them that Durham would not tolerate wife swap-ping.[82]

The story—with its mix of sex, money, and religion, all argued in Yid-dish—could easily have been set in Isaac Bashevis Singer's Poland. Lost in the marital squabble was the Torah, which was necessary for the survival of the second congregation. Max had been president of the Durham He-brew Congregation the year before the schism. Only months earlier, Pruschankin as a member of the Chevra Kadisha had served as a pall-bearer at the funeral of Max's father. The synagogue leaders were drawn from the town's wealthiest merchants, Max among them. Nevertheless, the businessmen met resistance as they sought to use their economic leverage to dominate community affairs. Max's prerogatives extended not only to the synagogue but also to women, who were pawns in this fray.

For the next decade Durham experienced rapid turnovers in the pulpit as disputes and schisms continued unabated. Shortly after the schism, the Reverend Heillig left town. A stern man, he was likely at the center of the controversy, especially because a schochet led the breakaway congregation. The Reverend Jacob Levinson arrived from New York in 1903 and re-turned there nine months later. The Reverend Jacob Kadishewitz (short-ened to Kadis) followed. He operated a general store on Cleveland Street. Because he, too, was not ordained, out-of-town rabbis were called to offi-ciate.

By the Jewish new year of 1902, Chevra B'nai Israel had faded. Shortly thereafter, the Durham Hebrew Congregation Company received a formal "Certificate of Incorporation" from the State of North Carolina. The charter was intended to regulate congregational affairs to prevent fu-ture ruptures. Neither Max nor Pruschankin signed it. Moses Greenberg, who led the Chevra Kadisha, headed the list. The others were E. Cohen, M. Haskell, B. Enoch, A. Land, S. Miller, and H. Brady. The signees in-cluded not only wealthy Main Street merchants but also Hayti grocers. Provisions were made to purchase land for a synagogue.[83]

Excluded from synagogue offices and ritual, women were rarely recog-nized publicly although they sustained the congregation through wel-fare and philanthropy. Although the Chevra Kadisha was a men's society, women prepared female corpses for ritual burial. Women organized and chaperoned social banquets, such as the 1887 Purim Ball. In 1904 Dora Greenberg collected funds to furnish several "Jewish rooms" on behalf of the congregation. The rooms likely included a hall for prayer and social meetings, classrooms, and perhaps a shelter for indigent Jews.[84] The first

The Reverend Kolman Heillig, a Lithuanian immigrant,
served the Durham Hebrew Congregation from 1892
to 1902. The Yiddish-speaking Heillig was typical of the
unordained "reverends" who served poor, immigrant
shuls. (Courtesy of Ruth Simand Malis)

formal Jewish women's organization was a traditional benevolence society, the Society for the Relief of Strangers, founded in 1905 by Nathan
Rosenstein. The Ladies Aid Society, as it was called, borrowed its name
from church groups. The Jewish women soliciting funds for social welfare,
synagogue upkeep, and European and Palestinian relief were the counter-
parts of church ladies raising money for their houses of worship and missionary societies. From 1915 to 1926 Sarah Chai Miller, a woman widely
recalled as a community matriarch, led the group. Its monthly meetings,
conducted in Yiddish, drew thirty-five to fifty members.

In 1905 the congregation purchased for $1,850 a church on Liberty

Street owned by the North Carolina and Virginia Christian Conference. The wooden building needed repairs, and the congregation was hard-pressed financially. The congregants had raised only $600, each member having been assessed $10. Synagogue officers Morris Bane and Max Shevel were brought to court for maintaining a public "nuisance." Two months later the newspapers reported "extensive improvements to the Christian church," which was now a "pretty place." The wooden synagogue was no larger than a cottage, with a balcony for women, but it was, as Fanny Gladstein recalled, "really the beginning of the Jewish community. . . . It brought all the Jewish people together, and not only for religious activities, but more like a big family."[85]

Although the newspaper in a spirit of civic boosterism reported that "the congregation is getting stronger each year," it in fact struggled. The synagogue "cost considerable money," a situation made worse by problems in collecting dues. It took ten years to pay off the $1,250 owed on the building. Dissenters also persisted, and the congregation drew articles for a new constitution in 1907. It was the second effort to establish bylaws in five years. The bylaws were a reproof to religious laxity. They were attempts to adjust to the American situation where synagogue support was voluntary, not obligatory as in the Old Country. Application for membership was five dollars, and anyone failing to pay dues for two months was suspended. Those who pledged money for "mitzvihs" but did not honor them were also suspended. Article 4 evoked the congregation's tenor: "The President shall . . . have full power to impose a fine upon members for disturbing the meeting and for not coming to order when instructed to do so. The fine shall not be less than twenty five cents nor more than one dollar." That synagogue affairs were disputatious was shown when Morris Haskell resigned as president in "disgust" after two days.[86]

In Durham, Jews lacked the institutions of self-government that sustained Jewish life in eastern Europe. This problem was illustrated by the second marriage of Abe Goldstein, Durham's senior Jewish resident. Goldstein's first wife, Esther, died in 1905 and left Abe a sizeable estate, $200 of which he donated to the synagogue. Abe placed an ad in a Jewish newspaper in Brooklyn, asking for a wife. A woman named Fannie answered and came to Durham, where she became the second Mrs. Goldstein.

One day Abe Goldstein appeared on the street with his face cut and bleeding. "'What's the matter? Has a cat attacked you?' asked a friend. 'No,' said Abe, 'it was an elephant.'" Abe swore out a warrant for assault and battery against Fannie. When the officer went to serve papers, Fannie had her face wrapped in a cloth, claiming that she been beaten. Abe was in the street, completely mystified, and the newspaper speculated he had been "whipped at his own game." The case went to court. M. Bane tried to translate from the Yiddish, but the newspaper commented that this case would require a "dozen expert interpreters." Abe was a garrulous sort, and the court could not quiet him. "If we have any further trouble," warned his lawyer, "we are going to sell our client to the highest bidder." Fannie pleaded guilty. Abe paid her fine and agreed to "do his part towards making the home life happy."[87]

Five months later Abe was hauled into court for nonsupport. Fannie admitted that she had a home and plenty to eat, but she showed the court her shoe, which had a hole in its sole. Abe denied that he knew the shoe's condition and claimed that he had bought her six pairs in less than a year. Fannie waved her *ketubah* (marriage contract) before the judge. The newspaper noted that she put "great store" in the contract, feeling that it would "make old man Abe do just as she wants." The court fined Fannie $9.20 in costs. Fannie argued "in broken English" that she had no money and no friends. She told the court, "Here I am, take me, and do what you please with me." She refused to pay the fine and demanded to be sent to the workhouse. Moses Gladstein stepped forward and posted bond, saying that "as long as he [was] in Durham" no Jewish woman would go to the workhouse. The next day Abe and Fannie took a train to Norfolk, where a rabbi granted them a *get* (divorce). It cost Abe $1,700, but he rejoiced in being a free man. Shortly thereafter "old man Goldstein" announced a "BIG SALE PROPERTY" and left town.[88]

The incident demonstrated the persistence of traditional Jewish behavior. Abe arranged a marriage, the conditions of which were sealed by a ketubah. He insisted on his patriarchal prerogatives. Fannie asserted women's rights under Jewish law, naively expecting a civil court to enforce her wedding contract. American Jewry was sharply divided, in fact, as to whether civil or religious law should hold precedence on questions of marriage and divorce.[89] The Goldsteins traveled hundreds of miles to have a *beth din* (rabbinic court) certify their divorce. Although the Goldsteins resided in Durham, Jewish community took them home to Norfolk and Brooklyn.

Southern ladies and gentlemen, bred on courtesy and decorum, did not understand these emotive, voluble Jews. The newspaper headlined the trial for days, and the case turned into a public spectacle. It described the affair as "laughable but at the same time pathetic," commenting that Goldstein "hurried to the courts to get revenge—this is one of the privileges that the average foreigner seems to think is his."[90] After thirty years in Durham, Goldstein was still a "foreigner."

Unlike Russia, where Jews lived in mortal fear of a legal summons, the Jews turned willingly toward American justice. Their litigious nature provoked sardonic comment, but Jews habitually looked for a legal formula to resolve their difficulties. American justice brought Fannie Goldstein humiliation—and Jewish law forbids the public shaming of a Jew, especially before the Gentiles. So Moses Gladstein stepped forward as a *mensch,* a morally responsible man, to protect the community's honor. However much Durham's Jews sought a place as southern citizens, they retained their traditional communal behavior as Jews.

Newspapers reported frequent clashes between Jews. Economics lay at the heart of most disputes, but they were carried into the home and synagogue. M. Kruger sued M. Haskell for slander after an argument over cash accounts in their Cary store. When Cora Morris and Rebecca Nurkin argued over a chicken, the indignant Nurkin and her "venerable Hebrew sister" went before a judge. Families were divided. A mother sued her son, demanding repayment of a $200 loan, and the son countersued to have her removed from his store. "He was the best boy I ever saw until lately," the mother lamented, as her tears moved the court. When Moses Levy was arrested for shooting craps, he had an altercation with Benjamin Lovenstein. Levy challenged the attorney to a fight in his offices, which were next door to those of Dr. Rosenstein. The optometrist covered the bets but asked the "featherweights" to take the fray to other quarters. Lovenstein gave Levy a whipping. Unfortunately, Lovenstein's mother-in-law, Dora Greenberg, threw a banana at Levy, and he promptly filed an indictment against her for assault. Every party in this case came from a family in the congregational leadership.[91]

Generational conflicts arose between an Americanized, college-educated youth and the older, traditional immigrants. In 1906, when the young lawyer Benjamin Lovenstein, a religious liberal, confronted in court the pawnbroker Reuben Roth, an Orthodox Jew, the case became a religious as well as a legal battle. Roth, a "large Hebrew," testified against a black client that Lovenstein was defending. "Lo and behold," Lovenstein scorned Roth, "we have a swell bellied, swell headed, swell faced Israelite from Jerusalem, so very conscientious that if he had come earlier, we could have used him to lead the Jews across the Red Sea. The moment he begins to speak his mental operations cease." Under this scathing assault, Roth—"a brother of the tribe of Judah"—withdrew. Lovenstein's attack against the "Israelite" as an unthinking devotee of Jewish law was a common criticism that enlightened Jews made against the Orthodox. That same year Lovenstein lectured on "The Jew in Modern Times" before a "large audience" at the synagogue. He was elected congregational secretary but served only one year. He claimed that local Jews opposed him because of his religious "heterodoxy."[92]

The congregation was the battleground over contentious issues of tradition and modernism. Younger, secularly educated men and women directed the education program, and ritually observant men maintained a hold on worship. Immigrant traditionalists such as Ezrael Cohen and Moses Greenberg also oversaw the Chevra Kadisha. With increasing Jewish numbers and growing prosperity, the congregation reached understandings that accommodated the contradictory interests of its members. Conflict did not inhibit institutional growth. By 1913, the synagogue sported a fresh coat of white paint, a red brick foundation, and a new shingle roof. It "will rival any church in the city built of timber," the newspaper exulted.[93]

The congregation compromised in the pulpit, too. Rabbi Herman Ben Mosche of Richmond, who was an ordained "Ruv, a big Rabbi," moved to town about 1907 and lasted for little more than a year. The Reverend R. N. Rosenberg, a "rabbi who handles well English, German [i.e., Yiddish], and Hebrew," served for three years. In 1912 Rabbi Abraham Rabinowitz (his name was spelled in various ways) arrived. An ordained rabbi, he was a traditionalist who never fully mastered English. The rabbi was admired for his cantorial talents and his ability to deliver a heartrending Yiddish sermon that reduced his congregants to tears.[94]

Conflict was perennial and persistent. "JEWS TO HAVE A NEW CHURCH, A SPLIT ON THE OLD CONGREGATION" read a front-page headline in the June 24, 1913, *Durham Morning Herald*. Chevra B'nai Jacob—Fellowship of the Sons of Jacob—began with a parade from the home of Samuel Swartz on Roxboro Street. The "line of carriages"—with both a Torah and an American flag at its lead—proceeded down Main Street to the Knights of Pythias Hall. There, a banquet featured a special Torah ceremony. Hebrew letters were outlined in a scroll, and congregants bid for the honor of filling them in. Each member thus fulfilled the commandment to inscribe a Torah. Afterward, at a business meeting, plans were made to construct a new synagogue. Sam Hockfield, an officer of the Durham Hebrew Congregation, was president, and Frank Silver served as cantor. Members included E. Cohen, A. Primakoff, J. Goldberg, P. Dave, A. Wilson, S. Swartz, M. Margolis, L. Rosenberg, H. Abelkop, and M. Zuckerman.[95]

The *Durham Morning Herald* described the reasons for the split as "complicated," citing "friction among the members." Stories passed down attributed the schism to a variety of causes. Some pointed to financial tensions after a rise in monthly dues from $1.50 to $2.00—not long after an increase from $.30 to $1.00. This was hard on all but the wealthy. B'nai Jacob members were mostly small tradesmen. Barney Enoch, a wealthy jeweller who served as president of the older congregation, demanded, "What I say has got to be," at which point Harris Abelkop led the walk-out for a new synagogue. Business, personal, and family disputes lay in the background. Abe Wilson and Max Shevel went their separate congregational ways. Several years earlier they had traded punches as they both sought to purchase stock at a Jewish merchant's bankruptcy sale. "They have not been the best of friends for many years," the newspaper noted.[96]

The complications may also refer to disputes over nuances of ritual and prayer. Some attributed the break to a quarrel over use of the *mikva* (ritual bath). Unlike urban areas, where Jews divided into landsleit congregations, small towns pressed together subethnic groups. Durham's "Russian" community consisted mostly of Litvaks (Latvians and Lithuanians), but there were also Poles, Galicians, and Ukranians. These groups often disputed questions of Jewish practice. Even their Yiddish accents differed. Abelkop, a Litvak, was especially observant. Disputes with the rabbi were commonplace in Orthodox shuls, and Rabbi Abraham Rabinowitz, who held the Durham pulpit, did not shun conflict.

Chevra B'nai Jacob eventually settled in an upstairs hall over Kaplan's shoe-repair shop on the corner of Morris and Chapel Hill Streets. As late as 1915 the newspaper reported that Yom Kippur services "will be held in the synagogues and also in some of the homes." Shortly thereafter Chevra B'nai Jacob faded. Home services may refer to Durham's Reform Jews or to Orthodox prayer groups that met informally outside the synagogue. Walking one day to Liberty Street, Sam Margolis passed the house of "Judge" Cohen, a Chevra B'nai Jacob member, where a separate minyan had gathered. "Everytime somebody got mad, they started their own synagogue," Melvin Gladstein recalled.[97]

Months after Chevra B'nai Jacob formed, the Durham Hebrew Congregation showed increased vitality. In August 1913, "The Hebrews Celebrated" as the Ladies Society presented the "church with the Talmut [*sic*]," according to a newspaper account. In the face of dissent the members may have wished to reassure Rabbi Rabinowitz with a display of loyalty. Three hundred gathered for a banquet in the synagogue hall, which was decorated with both American and Zionist flags. The newspaper noted admiringly that the "Jewish people . . . are always enthusiastic in the performance of their religious duties."[98]

Rabbi Rabinowitz left town in July 1914 to visit his father, a rabbi in Grodno, Poland. The Durham rabbi was trapped behind the lines when World War I erupted, and the *Durham Morning Herald* reported the dramatic story of his father's death. The elder Rabbi Moses Judah Rubinowitz [*sic*] had mounted the synagogue pulpit and prayed for God to take his life but to spare Grodno from the Germans. He instantly fell dead, and at that very moment the Germans retreated. The Durham newspaper described the elder Rubinovitz as a rabbi of the old school, one who never compromised with modernity.[99]

By 1910 five-sixths of the Durham Jewish community was American born, and the community created a double-structured education program as a compromise between old and new. The community supported both an Old World cheder and a typically American Sunday school. The cheder was unblended and anachronistic, whereas the Sunday school was intended to create a new generation of Jewish Americans. A more formal Talmud Torah or Hebrew school, which was more pedagogically modern, waxed and waned according to finances and leadership.

The cheder rebbe was an immigrant peddler or grocer who supplemented his income by giving lessons in his home or store. Rebbes Shapiro, Sobrowski, and Tabatchnick drilled the boys in the rote repetition of prayers, taught them to read Hebrew if not to understand it, and instructed them to chant their haftorahs. Rebbe Tabatchnik was a short, bearded man who held class in his delicatessen. The lessons were spiced with the air of the Rebbe's herring, which he parceled to a customer with one hand while he pointed to a Hebrew text with the other.[100]

A Sunday school was organized in the 1890s for both boys and girls. Attending Sunday school was a civic duty in the Protestant South, and the town fathers—Duke, Carr, Watts—personally taught classes. Early superintendents tended to be younger, college-educated men and women who used materials supplied by the rabbi. The lessons consisted mostly of Bible stories and explanations of Jewish customs and holidays. With its mixed-gender, English-language classes, it was the one Jewish institution that united Reform and Orthodox, Germans and east Europeans. One principal, Benjamin Lovenstein, described himself as religiously "heterodox," whereas another, Lily Kronheimer, was Reform. Unlike the rebbe who left indelible memories of pinched cheeks and pulled ears, Kronheimer was remembered as "gentle, kind . . . like an angel." The discipline lacked the rigor of cheder, and the boys were especially rambunctious. To ensure the children's attendance, Dr. Rosenstein as superintendent gave them a hay ride to Chapel Hill, where they feasted on watermelon. Boys and girls attended until they were thirteen years of age. In 1906, when the school met at Yearby's Hall, seventy children were registered. Thirteen years later it enrolled 105.[101]

With more than one hundred Jewish children in town, the congregation in 1910 organized a Talmud Torah, a more formal religious school. This too was an east European institution, but it tended to be a public, communal effort with higher educational standards than the private cheder. Congregational funds and appeals underwrote it. The teachers also tended to be better trained, more versed in American ways, and often ardently Zionist. The children were grouped in grades, and the curriculum encompassed not just rote competence in prayer and ritual but also the broader spectrum of Jewish history, customs, and literature.[102]

Life Cycle Events

The Jewish community was mostly young, as one would expect from those who had endured the rigors of emigration, and many were in their twenties when they arrived in Durham. Of the twenty Jewish marriages recorded in a county register from 1881 to 1906, the man's median age was twenty-six and the woman's was nineteen. Several men arrived alone to establish themselves in America before sending for their beaux. In 1905 Joseph Silver married his "childhood sweetheart," Minnie Tanchum, newly arrived from Russia. The bride spoke no English and had to be coached to say "I will." In Old World fashion Morris Katz's marriage to Lena Chesler in Norfolk was arranged by their parents, and the bride got her first glimpse of her future husband as she peeked from a second-floor window when he arrived at her home to take her hand.[103]

As was typical in small towns, several individuals found spouses within the community. The intramarriages reinforced Durham Jewry's sense of itself as an extended family. The Enochs married into the Gladstein, Haskell, and Smolensky families. The furniture dealer Max Shevel married Sarah Morris, the grocer's daughter. Frequently, Durhamites married southern Jews from such places as Asheville, Charlotte, Roanoke, and Norfolk. These marriages often involved business links among the families, and a son-in-law might clerk in the family store or open a place of his own. The biannual buying trips to northern markets presented occasions to socialize. When Morris Bane married Ray Hurwitz of Baltimore, the *Durham Morning Herald* noted, "Bane not only secured his spring and summer stock of goods but secured a wife."[104]

The son of one prominent Jewish family created a town scandal that drew headlines for weeks in 1913. The young fellow was a sporting type who raised dogs and prize chickens. During one sportsman's holiday to Virginia, he returned with a wife (apparently Jewish) whom he had met in a brothel. They were soon embroiled in a "sensational" front-page divorce; to the relief of many local citizens—including the new husband's neighbor, Brodie Duke—the wife agreed to leave Durham for Savannah.[105] The chastened young man then married a respectable Jewish woman from Baltimore and settled down. Marriages pulled Jews away from Durham more than they drew them, and daughters often left town to join husbands in Baltimore, Philadelphia, and New York.

Intermarriages with the Christian community were rare before World War I and often provoked a storm. In 1911 a Jewish girl ran away from Richmond with her Gentile boyfriend to be married furtively in the baggage room of the Durham railroad station. Durham's first intermarriages took place among the Reform German Jews. Zeke Guggenheim, a butcher, married Mary Campbell in a Christian ceremony in 1903, but he announced that he had "decided to be united by the Jewish rabbi," too. There is no record that such a ceremony was ever performed. Benjamin Kronheimer's sister Minnie wed William Frazier before two witnesses in a "quiet home affair" conducted by the Reverend S. Bost of St. Philip's Episcopal Church.[106]

When Kronheimer's niece Mattie Lehman married Julian Goldberg of Jacksonville, Florida, Kronheimer hosted a lavish affair, with guests arriving from great distances. Reform Jewish weddings were elaborate celebrations that drew Durham's elite—a sign of the family's integration into society. Mattie Lehman was a member of the Fun Lover's Club, the smartest of the city's "younger social set." Mildred Levy's wedding to Sidney Jacobs of Philadelphia was preceded by a "musical programme" that featured Edgar Cheek singing "In Loveland" and "The Song of the Soul." Jacob and Carrie Levy imported Reform rabbi Edward Calisch from Richmond to perform the rites for their two daughters.[107] Two American-born men from German families married the daughters of local east European immigrants.

The east European affairs also grew more elaborate as the immigrants increased their wealth and social status. First, the bride and groom had a civil wedding before a magistrate according to the "laws of the land." Several weeks later a Jewish ceremony was held at the synagogue, which was decorated with palms and cut flowers. The guests received engraved invitations in both English and Hebrew. The Durham rabbi usually officiated, sometimes assisted by an out-of-town rabbi. The Goldsboro rabbi married Sophie Fagan and Charles Zuckerman because they wanted a clergyman who could speak English. In the evening as many as three hundred—"practically every member" of the "Hebrew colony"—crowded into the armory or the Knights of Pythias Hall to celebrate. Relatives came from Danville, Norfolk, or Baltimore.[108]

In the early 1900s newspapers reported that "also the Gentiles" attended. "At a Hebrew wedding," the *Durham Sun* said of a 1901 gala, "true hospitality and sociability abounds." The newspapers described in fine detail the satin and crepe de chine of the wedding gown. Speeches were made and telegrams were read. A bridal chorus sang. The younger set, serenaded by a string orchestra, danced well past midnight. For their honeymoon, the couple visited relatives in the North or traveled to Niagara Falls or Atlantic City.[109]

Clearly, these elaborate affairs announced to Durham that the immigrants had socially—and economically—arrived. The embossed invitations, the elegant gowns, the lavish banquets, the honeymoons—all showed the Jews' eagerness to assimilate the mores of polite Gentile society. With the popular music and mixed dancing these celebrations did not follow Orthodox strictures. Affairs that were exclusively Orthodox—or those where the newlyweds were too poor to afford public festivities—were unlikely to make the social columns. For poor Jews a circumcision or a Bar Mitzvah was celebrated by drinks and cake in the back of the store.

If weddings were culturally blended Jewish-American events, funerals followed Orthodox scruples. Most ceremonies were performed in the home or the synagogue. The Chevra Kadisha, the burial society, consisted of ten men appointed annually. Women prepared the female dead. When sixty-eight-year-old Hannah Enoch died one morning in 1907, she was buried that very afternoon. After Abe Wilson died in 1914, the family held daily services at their store for the prescribed eleven months. They never had a problem obtaining a prayer quorum. Funerals divided Reform and Orthodox Jews. When Jacob Levy died in 1906, both Jews and Christians served as pallbearers. Although Levy had helped purchase the cemetery in

1884 to bury his daughter, with the Chevra Kadisha now in Orthodox hands he himself was interred in Richmond.[110]

Clubs and Societies

Community organizing affirmed both local allegiances as small-town southerners and cosmopolitan loyalties to international Jewry. As Durham grew from a town into a city, it was awash with social, commercial, and religious clubs. The economic changes wrought by the New South reordered society. Durham's fluidity was a microcosm of America as foreigners arrived, country folk urbanized, and the new rich climbed the social ladder. Across the country in the Gilded Age millions were joining some five hundred newly established clubs and orders.[111] These societies started in the 1880s and 1890s, when public betterment became a civic rallying cry, and continued through the Progressive Era. Durham's Lyceum, Up-To-Date Club, Academy of Music, and Chamber of Commerce and Industry promised cultural or economic uplift. Excepting the Chamber of Commerce, Jews, either because they were excluded or wished to preserve communal bonds, were outsiders. They created their own social place.

The local organizing also occurred as American Jews, in response to mass immigration, were building institutions and regulating their communal life. In 1893 the National Council of Jewish Women was formed and grew to fifty thousand members by 1925. The immigrant mother and homemaker, who often worked the family store, yielded to a new generation of college-educated, civic-minded women. In 1906 German Jews established the American Jewish Committee in response to czarist persecutions, and nine years later east European Jews organized an American Jewish Congress, which was ardently Zionist. When Jews were threatened in Russia or Palestine, relief committees formed in New York, and fundraising groups gathered in Durham.

Jews faced a crisis not only abroad but also at home. In cities the influx of immigrants created chaos. The ghettos were condemned as dens of crime and ignorance. The turn of the century brought discrimination in employment, housing, and university admissions. After the Leo Frank trial of 1913, B'nai B'rith formed its Anti-Defamation League.

At first Durham's Jews organized themselves along traditional lines. The Chevra Kadisha, Hachnoses Orchim (welcoming society), and chevra were societies Jews brought with them from the Old Country. As the immigrants integrated into civic Durham after 1900, they developed institutions that performed the old functions in new, Americanized forms. These

groups were of two types. The first were local clubs that were Jewish ver-
sions of local Gentile societies. The second were affiliates of national Jewish organizations. Both served social as well as charitable purposes. They
arose as Jews increased in numbers and prosperity. Frequently, a newcomer
was the catalyst in starting them. The groups were dynamic, and they faded
and arose depending on the leadership. These groups offered a means for
youth and women to achieve status apart from the synagogue, which businessmen dominated.

In 1907 American Jews were galvanized when the State Department
acceded to the czarist government by denying passports for American Jews
to travel to Russia. Jews protested, demanding that the United States
abrogate an 1832 trade treaty to punish the Russians. When President
William Howard Taft backtracked, the American Jewish Committee, supported by B'nai B'rith, mobilized public opinion to pressure Congress.
Lionel Weil of Goldsboro acted to unify North Carolina Jews. He wrote
to Henry Brady, a Durham merchant, asking him to organize a B'nai
B'rith Lodge. In 1910 Durham Lodge No. 664 of B'nai B'rith formed. It
was later renamed the Ticvat Lodge, with Nathan Rosenstein as president.
The lodge's first act was to pass a resolution calling on the United States
to abrogate the Russian treaty. B'nai B'rith did not firmly establish itself
in Durham, and its charter was revoked in 1912. After Congress voted to
cancel the trade treaty, Jewish passions cooled as the expected benefits of
the abrogation campaign—greater tolerance of Jews here and abroad—did
not materialize.[112] The community, too, may have been too insular in its
east European ethnicity to participate fully in a society with a German
legacy and leadership. The Durham situation, again, was atypical of the
South, where a network of B'nai B'rith lodges linked Jewish communities
and advocated for Jewish interests.

As was typical of east European Jews, Durham's Jews were ardently Zionist. Although the Jewish South is stereotyped as non- or anti–Zionist,
the east European migration saw the rise after 1900 of Zionist societies
in towns in Texas, Mississippi, Kentucky, Arkansas, and Virginia. In 1901
the Durham community under the Reverend Kolman Heillig purchased
shares in the Jewish Colonial Bank in Palestine. In 1905, after lurid newspaper accounts of Russian pogroms reached Durham, Jews gathered at the
synagogue to hold a memorial. The Reverend Laibel Swartz spoke, and
eight dollars was collected. Max Shevel led a drive that forwarded $102
more to New York. Swartz soon left Durham for Palestine. Zionism gained
legitimacy in America after Louis Brandeis assumed leadership in 1914 and

after the British announced the Balfour Declaration three years later. In 1916 Madame Pevsner, wife of a Russian Zionist, visited Durham, inspiring Fanny Gladstein to start a Pevsner Zionist Society. A year later, when the Zionist Organization of America was founded, Michael Margolis, William Bane, and Ethel Greenberg formed a local chapter.[113]

Local societies focused on assuring Jewish associations for youth. These civic clubs had a Progressive Era emphasis on sports, exercise, and education. In 1911 a Hebrew Boys' Club held a picnic for the young ladies' club at the pump station. The day-long affair featured games and rowing for the eleven boys and eleven girls, with older sisters serving as chaperones. In 1913 a Hebrew Social and Literary Society formed under the presidency of Louis Rosenberg, a tailor. "Composed of nearly all the younger members of the race in the city," the *Durham Morning Herald* observed, it included both Germans and east Europeans. Despite its elegant title the society was more dedicated to basketball than to literature. In 1915 the society, aptly renamed the Hebrew Social Club, opened clubrooms on Main Street. That year the Wide-Awake Circle was organized for young women as a reading and discussion group on public affairs. The circle organized a masquerade ball at the Durham Armory, which attracted two hundred young Jews. The costumed Fatimas and Chinamen paraded in a grand march, followed by dancing until midnight. The affair inspired demands for a second ball with profits to be donated to Polish relief.[114] The Jewish social clubs were in the town spirit. Such pretentious names as the Social and Literary Society suggest a reaching for respectability. Surely a Jewish masquerade could not have differed from a Gentile affair. The women's Wide-Awake Circle seemed more serious in its efforts to educate.

The Jewish variable in the Jewish-American equation did not remain distinct but was culturally blending. The synagogue, which was intended to preserve Jewish associations and traditions, accommodated to small-town southern life as the Jewish church. While working to maintain communal ethnic bonds, Durham's Jews eagerly represented themselves as Americans to their neighbors. Their first step in integrating was economic, not just through their stores but more so through their extensive real estate investments. Jews still adhered to their ethnic mercantile niche —maintaining family credit networks, purchasing each other's stocks and stores—but Jews as individuals also financed with local banks and formed business partnerships with non-Jews. Relative both to urban Jews and to their non-Jewish neighbors, Durham Jews were exceptional in the extent to which they were self-employed in trade and commerce. They also differed from the mass of the city's working classes, with whom they shared poverty, in their pursuit of education. The public schools and universities acculturated Jews and provided routes of upward mobility. After 1900 the east European Jews began involving themselves in civic affairs, including the sporting fields, and one took the bold step of running for public office. Yet Jews still resided in an ethnic enclave, and they maintained the Yiddish language, which was a portable homeland. However much the Jews identified themselves as civic boosters and loyal citizens, however much they accommodated to America, the larger community, both black and white, saw them as "the Jews." They were outsiders socially and politically. There was a "structural separation" between Jewish and Gentile Durham, which limited personal, intimate contacts while civic and economic exchanges abounded.[115]

The Jews retained their collective identity, but they divided internally. Personal, family, and generational conflicts rended the community. Intent on "making it" in America, individual Jews no longer relied on traditional communal structures. A few Jews, such as Lovenstein, crossed the boundaries of their ethnic community and aspired to join the civic elites. As Eli Lederhendler notes, Jewish communities can succeed while at the same time suffer from discord and mobility. Even as individuals integrate and assimilate, the group preserves its integrity and remains marginal to mainstream society.[116]

Durham's Jews both resisted and accommodated southern society. They created both hybrid and traditional institutions to preserve their unity. Multiple forms of Jewish association allowed Jews to encompass multiple forms of Jewish identity even while insisting upon their oneness. The community supported an Orthodox congregation for ritual traditionalists as well as Zionist and philanthropic societies for those more concerned with Jewish peoplehood. Secular sports and social clubs, especially for youth, preserved ethnic bonds. As the community grew more pluralistic, especially as it become more American, local Jews were factious in their unity.

7 Becoming Southern Jews, 1917 to 1929

I n the post–World War I years Durham's Jews established their identity as small-town southerners. Jews continued to be highly mobile, but a core persisted locally into the second generation. Native-born sons and daughters, they won honors in Durham's schools, played on its sports fields, voted in its elections, and fought in America's wars. Most had risen within a generation from poverty into the middle class. After a half century in Durham, Jews were now confident citizens and neighbors. A new brick, cathedral-style synagogue attested to their permanent civic place.

The American and Zionist flags that adorned the synagogue symbolized the dual identity Jews envisioned for themselves. Horace Kallen, educator and philosopher, advocated a cultural pluralism that challenged the hegemony of white, Anglo-Saxon Protestantism as the American norm. As Jewish Americans, the immigrants could assimilate into the political and economic mainstream while remaining culturally distinct. Identity was not monolithic. Jews did not need to blend into the melting pot to be fully American. Jews could preserve their collective identity while partaking of their rights as individuals.

Not only did Durham's Jews insist on their Americanism, but also they began representing themselves as Jewish southerners. As memories of eastern Europe eroded, especially with the second generation, local Jews began writing community histories that placed them in the southern narrative. As they invented an identity for themselves, Jews glossed over the contradictions of their Jewish American identity. They boasted of their wartime patriotism and their role as creators of the tobacco town while organizing societies to rebuild a Jewish homeland in Palestine and rescue their brethren in eastern Europe. They presented themselves as a modern, American people while they maintained traditional Orthodox worship imbued with Yiddishkeit.

Internal ethnic and religious conflicts absorbed Jews even more than their ties with their southern neighbors, with whom they maintained cordial if not close relations. The cohesiveness of the Durham community owed much to its nearly homogeneous east European ethnicity. In this regard it was representative of many southern Jewish communities. By the late 1920s almost three-fourths of the southern towns with more than one hundred Jews were largely east European. Typically, these towns were unable to sustain Orthodox religious life, but Durham held on more steadfastly. Generational changes, however, were at work. With high birth rates, by 1930 five-sixths of Durham's Jews were native born.[1]

Demographics imperiled community survival. After World War I Durham Jewry ceased growing, although the city boomed in the 1920s and withstood the depression relatively well. From 1920 to 1930 Durham grew from 21,719 to 52,037, a 140 percent increase. (Much of this growth reflected city annexations.) Jewish population increased but 7 percent, from 350 to 375. In 1900 3.1 percent of Durham's population was Jewish; in 1930 it was 0.72 percent. A 1936 survey reported the city's Jewish population at 344. Durham was exceptional in losing its Jews while the city grew. A study of communities during the era of mass Jewish immigration revealed that "local Jewish population trends tended to correspond to those of the larger society."[2]

In some measure Durham's lack of Jewish growth reflected transatlantic developments. In the aftermath of World War I and the Soviet revolution, the tide of European Jewish emigration abated. Moreover, public opinion turned decisively against unrestricted immigration. After resisting restrictionist legislation, Congress in 1921 and 1924 passed quota laws that placed caps on nationalities. In 1921, 119,036 Jews entered the United States; in 1925 that figure dropped to 10,292. Durham Jewry no longer experienced a flow of new immigrants to replenish its numbers or rejuvenate its Old World culture.

Southern Jewry declined from 1900 to 1930. The number of Jews in North Carolina remained very small, insignificant from a national perspective. The Jewish population of North Carolina fell from 8,252 in 1927 to 7,337 in 1937. North Carolina had the smallest proportion of Jews of any state in the country, about 0.21 percent of the total population in 1937, compared with a national figure of 3.7 percent. The state's rural character, with its family farms and small towns, attracted few Jews. Two tenements on the Lower East Side in New York housed as many Jews as lived in Durham, and one New York City ward contained fifteen times the number of Jews as resided in the entire state of North Carolina. North Carolina still lacked the urban center, an Atlanta or a Richmond, that could draw Jews in significant numbers.[3]

Southern Jewry continued to be mobile. After World War I North Carolina Jews dispersed into small towns. The perception was widespread that every town in the state contained a "Jew store." A 1929 study revealed the "exceptional fact" that 53 percent of North Carolina Jews lived in rural communities. They spread across 188 towns, mostly in the Piedmont. While Durham's Jewish population stagnated, smaller, neighboring towns grew. From 1933 to 1940, Henderson's Jewish population rose from thirteen to thirty-five, Oxford's from eight to seventeen, and Roxboro's from nine to eleven. Two or three Jews were reported in Carrboro, Graham, and Hillsborough. Chapel Hill's two Jews of 1916 grew to thirteen in 1927 and to thirty-two in 1937, establishing a permanent community.[4]

Durham's survival as a viable Jewish community was by no means certain. The Jewish communities of Tarboro and Statesville, where congregations had formed by the 1880s, faded by the 1930s, and their synagogues closed. An economic downturn in a one-industry town could devastate a small Jewish community. In Statesville many Jews were suppliers to the liquor industry, and Prohibition ended the community's viability.

Durham's economy was resilient. The city recovered quickly from the brief 1921 recession, and the town burgeoned as the textile and tobacco industries prospered. Durham's downtown underwent a building boom of banks, shops, and department stores. The new Washington Duke Hotel, at sixteen stories, towered over the other buildings. James B. Duke underwrote Durham's prosperity in 1924 with a $40 million endowment to Trinity College. A wholly new Duke University campus, replete with a Gothic cathedral, was built on pasture and forest on the edge of town. The campus construction, which lasted into the depression years, brought hundreds of workers to town and increased the faculty presence.

Jews benefited from the general economic boom. In 1910 the median wealth of Durham's Jewish households was $785. In 1925 that figure rose to $6,000. The 1925 tax rolls suggest that the town still contained Jewish poor, most of whom were grocers who arrived in the previous decade. In

1925, 31.4 percent of households listed property and real estate at less than $3,000. Nevertheless, Jews were working their way at least into the lower middle class, and several were wealthy. In 1925, 44.4 percent reported taxable assets between $3,000 and $20,000, and 20.3 percent had a net worth of more than $20,000 (see table 7.1).[5]

In the 1920s upward mobility was rapid. Newly arrived immigrant Ike Ornoff started as a peddler of fur pelts but soon opened a scrap iron and metal yard. The Hayti storekeeper Michael Margolis extended his wholesale grocery business to a half-dozen retail outlets. The baker Louis Jaffe sold his horse and wagon and bought a Chevrolet truck to deliver his bread. Some peddlers and shop owners who had arrived prior to World War I now owned real estate worth tens of thousands of dollars. Sam and Clara Swartz, nominally junk dealers, amassed fourteen lots. When Daniel Freedman died in 1926, the former peddler's holdings were valued at $46,500. Ben Kronheimer's property was taxed at $125,000. Second-generation Rosensteins, Gladsteins, and Freedmans followed the parental example and purchased farms and rental properties. As Chapel Hill's Franklin Street grew into a commercial district in the 1920s and 1930s, a row of Jewish stores opened on the street. In 1923 Sam and Mary Berman moved from a small wooden shop into a large, two-story brick store.[6]

No single rationale explains why Jews left, arrived, or remained in Durham. Economic opportunity was a significant but not an exclusive motive (see table 7.2). Statistics suggest that poorer and wealthier Jews were more likely to leave town and that artisans were more mobile than merchants (see table 7.3). Of the eight wealthiest Jews listed on the 1910 Durham tax rolls, only two persisted until 1925 (with one death). Success opened opportunities elsewhere even as failure removed the incentive to remain. This pattern of economic mobility also prevailed among Atlanta Jewry.[7]

Specifically, Jewish familial, communal, and religious factors pushed and pulled Jews. These factors suggest significant differences between Jews and ethnic southerners. Certainly the desire for a larger Jewish community, even more than economics, influenced Jews in choosing places of residence. Observant Jews who wished to attend daily prayer services and parents who were concerned about their children's futures as Jews headed north toward metropolitan areas. Barney Enoch, as a wealthy jeweller and landowner, had no financial incentive to leave Durham, but he was worried about his daughters finding Jewish husbands. The Enochs left for Baltimore. On the other hand, Eli and Jenny Nachamson moved from Kinston to Durham in 1926 for the very reason that the Enochs had left

TABLE 7.1. Value of Real Estate and Personal Property, 1925

Amount ($)	Aggregate		Real Estate		Personal Property	
	Eastern European	German	Eastern European	German	Eastern European	German
1–1,000	1		18	1	6	1
1,000–5,000	20		16	2	16	1
5,000–10,000	5	1	7		10	1
10,000–20,000	10				11	
20,000–30,000	3		2		4	
30,000–40,000	2				2	
40,000–50,000	4			1	2	
50,000–60,000					1	
60,000–70,000	2				2	
70,000–80,000		1			1	1
80,000–90,000		1				
90,000–130,000				1		1

Source: Durham County Tax Rolls, 1925, North Carolina State Archives, Raleigh.

TABLE 7.2. Persistence of Durham Jewish Residents by Occupation, 1902–1920[a]

Data	Professional	Self-employed trade	Self-employed artisan	Commercial employee	Manufacturer	Laborer
Present 1902	2	27	7[b]	17	3	
Present 1910	1	12	1[b]	5[b]	0	
Present 1920	1	11	0	5	0	
Present 1910	6	45	14	26		2
Present 1920	2	19[c]	5	14		0

Sources: *Directory of Greater Durham, 1902* (Durham: Samuel Adams, 1902); *Hill's Durham, North Carolina, Directory, 1909–10* (Richmond: Hill Directory Co., 1909); *Hill's Durham City Directory, 1919–20* (Richmond: Hill Directory Co., 1919); Durham County, North Carolina, Enumerated District Lists, Thirteenth Census of the United States, 1910, North Carolina State Archives, Raleigh.

[a] Not all the Jews in Durham in 1910 were residents in 1902; thus the lists convey different information.
[b] With one death.
[c] With four deaths.

TABLE 7-3. Persistence of Durham Jewish Residents by Aggregate Wealth ($), 1897–1925[a]

Data	0–100	101–500	501–1,000	1,001–3,000	3,001–5,000	5,001–10,000	10,001–15,000
Present 1897	1	9	5	2	2	3	
Present 1910	1	3	2	2	2	0	
Present 1925	0	2	2	2	2	0	
Present 1910	4	20	5	5	3	3	5
Present 1925	0	9[b]	2[b]	4	2[b]	1	1[b]

Sources: Durham County Tax Rolls, 1897, 1910, 1925, North Carolina State Archives, Raleigh, North Carolina.
[a] Not all the Jews in Durham in 1910 were residents in 1897; thus the lists convey different information.
[b] With one death.

TABLE 7.4. Places of Resettlement from Durham of Jewish
Households, 1885–1925

Location	Number	Percentage
Southern states	32	78.0
Georgia		
Macon	6	
Louisiana	1	
Maryland		
Baltimore	6	
North Carolina		
Asheville	2	
Chapel Hill	1	
Charlotte	1	
Goldsboro	1	
Graham	1	
Raleigh	6	
Roxboro	1	
Winston-Salem	2	
Texas	1	
Virginia		
Hopewell	3	
Norfolk	1	
Richmond	3	
South Boston	2	
Northern states	6	14.6
Illinois		
Chicago	1	
New Jersey		
Paterson	1	
New York		
New York City	4	

Continued on next page

TABLE 7.4. *Continued*

Location	Number	Percentage
Western states	1	2.4
California	1	
Other		
Palestine	1	2.4
Canada	1	2.4
Metropolitan areas		39.5
Small towns		47.4

Sources: Durham County Tax Rolls, 1897, 1910, 1925, North Carolina State Archives, Raleigh; oral histories and newspaper reports.

Durham. They were concerned about finding Jewish husbands for their daughters and believed that they would have better chances in the college town.

Nearly eighty of the Jews who departed Durham during the forty years preceding 1925 remained within southern states, and nearly half resettled in small towns. Forty percent headed for metropolitan areas. Baltimore, where many local Jews had family and business ties, was a favorite place to relocate. Synagogue president Jacob Kadis and community patriarch Moses Gladstein settled there in the 1920s. The fact that 42 percent found homes elsewhere in North Carolina suggests that the Jews were becoming a regional people. Jewish immigrants who abandoned Durham opened dry-goods stores in not-too-distant towns such as Graham, Roxboro, and Goldsboro, North Carolina, and South Boston, Virginia (see table 7.4). Census data confirm a dispersal of Jews into North Carolina's small towns during the 1920s.

The severest threat to local Jewry's survival came from the continuous departure of the second generation, who typically headed to metropolitan areas. The push from Durham was the desire to avoid a life of storekeeping in a tobacco town. "As soon as they graduated from high school, the boys went out," Pat Silver recalled. Women, too, found careers, education, or husbands outside the community. Professional opportunities and the allure of the big city pulled second-generation men and women. World War I drew twenty-four young men into the armed services. Sons and daughters went to college and did not return. Most attended Duke or UNC, but others headed to Smith, Yale, and Columbia. The children of immigrant tailors, grocers, and shoemakers were becoming artists, doctors, and professors. Parents left Durham to join their upwardly mobile children. The Brady and Greenberg families relocated to New York in the 1920s to be near their sons, who had enrolled at Columbia University Law School. (Henry Brady, too, quit Durham after a robber mugged him.)

Economic factors certainly explained the persistence of a core group. The Swartzes, Freedmans, and Rosensteins had invested heavily in Durham, and the second generation remained to run businesses and oversee property. Yet other former Durham families, such as the Bradys, the Enochs, and the Summerfields, held on to their local real estate while residents in other states. They were linked to their hometowns financially, if not sentimentally. A few second-generation Jews found occupational mobility in their hometowns as attorneys or managers.

New Jewish settlers pulled to town by family networks and business opportunities allowed Durham to sustain its Jewish numbers through the late 1920s and 1930s. The trade was mostly unequal, however. Durham Jewry was losing its college-educated youth, its few Jewish professionals, and gaining poorer immigrants, most of whom were coming to Durham as secondary or tertiary places of settlement. Typically, landsleit networks pulled them to the area. Ike and Rebecca Shapiro Ornoff were Lithuanian immigrants who had first settled in Newport News and Wilmington before relatives drew them to Durham. Nathan Lieberman, who had emigrated from Poland in 1923, arrived in Durham in 1927. Six years later he brought his brother Max to town. Family and business networks connected Jews across North Carolina's small towns. The Lacobs, who opened a Chapel Hill shoe store, were related to a Goldsboro family. These families followed a traditional path, beginning as peddlers and working their way up to stores. A growing student population in Chapel Hill provided a ready market of customers. In the 1920s Jewish-owned stores sprouted on Franklin Street, including Harry's Bar and Grill (owned by Abe and Harry Stern), which became a town fixture for generations.

A Cosmopolitan Community

William Boyd in *The Story of Durham* (1925) wrote proudly of Durham's "cosmopolitan" character: "Scarcely a town in North Carolina contained such a variety of humanity. This meant toleration." The foreign born comprised less than 1 percent of Durham's population. By 1930 the town also had fifty-nine Greek-born residents. The construction of the Duke campus brought some forty Italian artisans. A few Japanese, Chinese, and Indians also lived in town.[8] What Durham lacked were large numbers of Irish Catholics and Polish Catholics, who were the source of much anti-Semitic friction in the urban North. Relative to southern racism or the national anti-immigrant mood, Durham was benign.

Durham's Jews represented themselves as Americans to their Durham neighbors. When war came, Durham's Jewish boys rallied around the flag. At a time when Jews nationally were accused of being war shirkers, a 1921 Durham synagogue history, listing the names of twenty-four men in uniform, proudly claimed, "Every Jewish youth between the ages of 21 and 30 who was eligible for service was either in the army or navy." The War Bond, Red Cross, and Liberty and War Savings Stamps drives brought Jews and Gentiles together socially. On August 19, 1918, Governor Thomas Bickett proclaimed Jewish Relief Day in North Carolina, saying, "Let Jew and Gentile touch elbows and work together for the relief of these millions in distress." In a 1921 statewide effort for the national Jewish War Sufferers Fund, Lionel Weil raised more than $200,000, mostly from Gentiles.[9] The North Carolina plan became a national model. Historically, when North Carolina Jews approached civic and political elites on behalf of Jewish causes, they were well received.

The city's tolerance was tested in the postwar years. A national recession struck Durham in 1920–1921. Tobacco and cotton prices crashed, dropping local wages as much as 40 percent. The economic shocks exacerbated anti-immigrant feelings. World War I had aroused suspicion of aliens, and "100 percent Americanism" became a nativist rallying cry. Henry Ford's *Dearborn Independent* spread anti-Semitic propaganda into small-town America (although it was less well received in the South). Terrorist bombings fanned a Red Scare. Attorney General Mitchell Palmer led raids that arrested thousands and threatened hundreds with deportations—with a blatant disregard for their guilt or innocence. Jews were suspect as aliens and radicals. In well-attended revivals across the state in the 1920s evangelist Mordecai Ham pointed an accusatory finger at Julius Rosenwald as he denounced Jews for greed and vice.

Durham seemed largely removed from such passions, but Jews sought to separate themselves from the radicals. A Russian Jew, Joseph Goldman, appeared at the Temple Baptist Church one summer Sunday in 1921 to preach. The author of sixteen books, Goldman was identified as a "former rabbi" (without reference to his being a Christian convert) on his way to Jerusalem. He lectured "at his own expense" on the "horrors" and "deadly menace" of the Nihilists who had murdered his wife, parents, and six children in Russia.[10]

When Jews made their fund-raising appeals for a new synagogue in 1921, they described the building as a bastion against prejudice: "From the pulpit here we proclaim our collective faith and opinions, correct the misrepresentations of those who know neither our history nor religion and repel the insidious attacks and prejudice of those who know but maliciously distort."[11]

One dramatic case, a unique instance of anti-Semitic violence in Durham, revealed an undercurrent of popular prejudice. The grocer Harry Murnick had gone to the water company, a city agency, to pay his bill. He gave the bookkeeper a roll of fifty pennies. As the bookkeeper was counting the change, the manager, Harvey Bolton, stepped out, knocked the pennies to the floor and ordered Murnick to pick them up. "The bill is paid, and those pennies belong to you," Murnick responded. Bolton then locked the door, grabbed Murnick by the jacket, and called him a "Goddamned Jew." He hit him in the face and then slapped him. "Please turn me loose," Murnick pleaded. "I have to go home." Bolton shoved Murnick into a back room and began choking him with a towel. The bookkeeper looked out the window. Murnick dug into his pocket, gave Bolton a dollar, and took back his pennies. Bolton threw him out, warning him not to return. Murnick took Bolton to court, where he was convicted and fined.[12]

Murnick, represented by attorney R. O. Everett, sued the city for damages, and the case went to the state supreme court. Several Gentile witnesses testified to Murnick's good character. Murnick described himself to the court: "I live on Poplar Street, and conduct a grocery store. I have been living in Durham eleven years, coming here from Russia, and am a Jew. I am married and have a family of four. I own my home and two more houses." He never before had trouble paying his water bill. The court supported Murnick's right to sue the city and argued that the manager should have been fired, not just fined. "The only provocation given which we can infer from the language used by Bolton is the fact that the plaintiff was a Jew," supreme court chief justice Walter Clark asserted. He continued in the philo-Semitic vein of Zebulon Vance, citing Shakespeare and Walter Scott on the humanity of the Jew and quoting Disraeli's famous apologia on the Jew's ancient nobility; indeed, Clark noted, the Savior was of the tribe of Judah. "The world has long outlived this treatment of an historic race," the court summarized, "except perhaps in 'darkest Russia' when under the Czars." Justice Clark then sent an extract of his opinion—including Disraeli's defense—to attorney Everett, requesting him to have it printed in local newspapers to promote "good opinion" and "friendship" for Jews.[13]

When Jews were threatened, an attorney such as R. O. Everett or Percy Reade, a benefactor such as Julian Carr, or a judge such as Walter Clark stood ready to help or defend them. Everett, his son recalled, held "warm feelings" toward Jews both as his neighbors and, more abstractly, for their contribution to civilization. Durham contained an educated, upper class of professors, lawyers, and civic benefactors who were cosmopolitan and progressive, whose religious heritage was the Social Gospel.

A more pressing reason for Jews to feel anxiety was the rebirth in the 1920s of the Ku Klux Klan as a national movement. In the rural South it twisted its focus from blacks to Jews and Catholics. Although the Klan never became as strong a force in North Carolina as it did in Georgia or Indiana, it was a dramatic presence. Nonetheless, it was typical of Durham that the local Klan was relatively benign and that its public face was Americanism.

From 1922 to 1928 the Klan held rallies, parades, and banquets in Durham. Leonard Rapport, the optician's son, recalled one early Klan parade as a "big social event, everybody in town was there." Durham's Klan was far from intimidating, and it was not prone to violence. Blacks stayed off the streets, but Rapport could not remember receiving any parental warnings to stay away. He took a seat in the front row for the Klan rally.

In 1927 when the Georgia Klansman Dr. W. A. Hamlett, a minister and journalist, spoke at the new civic auditorium, more than two hundred Durhamites attended, Jews among them. The stage was set with a fiery cross above an American flag. "A spectacle of beauty rarely seen in Durham," the *Durham Morning Herald* reported. Hamlett was introduced by Mayor John Manning, a personal physician to many Jews. Hamlett appealed to the audience's patriotism and Christian honor. He warned against foreign elements and called for "true" Americanism. The newspaper observed, "Contrary to expectations . . . there was no fiery outburst of hate, no antagonism against any race or creed. . . . Members of the Negro race and the Hebrews who were present heard nothing which could offend them."[14]

"I don't think the Klan was anti-Semitic in Durham," Rapport said. "If the Jewish population didn't bother them, they didn't bother us." He believed that Roman Catholics were more of a target than the Jews. "The Klan in Durham was sort of bourgeois . . . a little sinister, below-the-belt Kiwanians," Rapport reflected, but "they were socially acceptable." He found them more "comical" than dangerous. A Klansman invited Melvin Gladstein to join the Durham group. The local Klan's rage was directed primarily at alleged violators of woman's honor, and its targets were both black and white. Two notable instances of southern anti-Semitic violence, the lynching of Leo Frank and the castrating of Joseph Needleman in eastern North Carolina in 1925, both involved alleged assaults on women.

In 1929 when Jews met at Beth-El Synagogue to mourn the massacre of Jews in Hebron, Dr. Manning, who regularly spoke at Klan rallies, rose from his sickbed to express sympathy from his church. Some Jews, however, felt anxieties. As a child, May Ornoff broke into a run when she passed a Klan home. Small-town Jewish folklore often depicts the Klan in bemused tones. Klansmen, who were frequently prominent citizens, remained customers and friends. A Jew in Muncie, Indiana, recalled that his father took him to Klan parades as a child, noting that the Klansmen railed against blacks and Catholics while remaining friendly to Jews.[15]

When anti-Semitism became overt, Jews dealt with it as neighborly, small-town southerners. Once a prominent Baptist preacher began delivering anti-Semitic sermons. Dr. Rosenstein approached a Baptist friend, a former judge, for a heart-to-heart talk. They then both met with the preacher, who was convinced to mend his views. Rosenstein also persuaded the publisher of the *Durham Morning Herald* to end its practice of identifying lawbreakers as Jews.

Campus Quotas

Jews who headed to college in the 1920s had found a changed atmosphere. Jews had arrived on campuses nationally in such numbers that prominent educators began speaking of a Jewish problem as a threat to Anglo-Saxon values. Led by Columbia and Harvard, northern colleges began imposing quotas. The South had too few Jews at its campuses to feel so threatened, but a quota system did operate. Henry Bane assumed Duke kept a quota, especially for Jewish women. "We weren't too affected here because I think they made exceptions for local residents," Bane said, echoing a community view that Duke accepted Durham students unconditionally in exchange for city services. State-supported UNC was regarded as more liberal in its admission policy, and it became the school of choice for North Carolina Jews.

Jewish students at UNC and Duke in the 1920s were certainly aware of the anti-Semitic mood nationally. At UNC E. J. "Mutt" Evans followed an unwritten rule that "no more than three or four of our boys could walk on campus in order not to attract attention to Jewish students. We wanted to be part of the scene without emphasis on the fact we were Jewish." Despite such heightened sensitivity and some very real prejudice, most Jews described their college days as harmonious. In the Trinity class of 1923 Durhamite Leo Brady served as president of the Hesperian Literary Society, and in 1930 for the first time a "New Yorker," Charles Rosen, was elected its president. UNC student Norman Block of Rocky Mount was president of the Order of the Grail, the prestigious secret society; vice president of the Dialectic Society; a varsity football player; and an officer of the lettermen's Monogram Club.[16]

Even as they aspired to Americanize and won academic and athletic honors, Jewish youth were still excluded socially from sororities and fraternities. Jews began forming their own Greek societies in the 1920s, a time of national institution building in American Jewry. The first Jewish fraternity at UNC, Tau Epsilon Phi, organized in 1924 and two years later comprised twenty-one members. E. J. Evans, a UNC student from Fayetteville, recalled some anxieties that a Jewish fraternity might provoke a "Jewish problem" on campus, and TEP initially had trouble receiving recognition from the fraternity council. In 1927 Zeta Beta Tau was established at UNC. In contrast to TEP, which attracted mainly the children of east European immigrants, ZBT was a preserve of Reform German Jews. The first Jewish fraternity at Duke, Pente, formed in 1926. It was so named because only five Jewish men were on campus. In 1929, it formally affiliated with the national Phi Sigma Delta.

Southern Jews

Despite the undertones of prejudice, the Jewish colony was recognized as an integral and respectable part of the community. The Jews attempted to minimize their difference to southerners by representing their Judaism as modern and American. In 1927 Abe Rosenstein wrote a community history for the *Durham Morning Herald,* taking the perspective of "a member of the Christian faith as he would look around the synagogue." He compared the scrolling of the Torah with the workings of a "typewriter ribbon" and described the mikva as a "baptismistry." Although the local congregation was still Orthodox and Yiddish speaking, Rosenstein observed how Reform Jews had dispensed with hats and added organ music. Rosenstein stated that younger Jews in Durham had abandoned such customs as separate gender seating. He stressed that the Jews "are practically all loyal boosters and actively identified with . . . civic affairs" and traced community origins to Duke's cigarette rollers. "Hebrew Congregation in Durham Had Its Inception with Tobacco Business," read the headline. In southern cities such as Savannah and Charleston, the presence of Jews in a city's formative years eased social acceptance of Jews in later generations. Whatever their history, Durham Jews were staking a claim as pioneers.[17]

No longer impoverished immigrants peddling or scavenging, Durham's Jews in the 1920s were middle-class shopkeepers and landholders with college-educated children. Families long settled in Durham often enjoyed intimate friendships with Gentiles. The Kronheimers maintained close ties to the Markhams, a socially prominent family. Mike and Fanny Gladstein named their daughter Hazel in honor of a friend in the Scoggins family. Families who lived outside the Roxboro Street neighborhood, such as the Silvers and Zuckermans in Trinity Park, became close friends with their Christian neighbors. Rosa Levin Silver brought wine and unleavened bread to the Episcopal church for use in the communion. In a sermon a priest praised this woman with a "Jewish heart" as an example of what a good Christian should be. Grocer Henry Brady and attorney R. O. Everett were friends; when the Everetts' son Robinson was born, Brady took him to the rabbi for a blessing. Jews donned the apron of the Masons and the fez of the Shriners.[18]

Jews rose in town society as they completed their move up the hill into their secondary place of residence. Although Jews spoke of Roxboro Street as the Jewish neighborhood, non-Jews did not perceive it to be a ghetto. The area was never exclusively Jewish. In 1921 in a three-block stretch of Roxboro Street extending from Canal to Dowd Streets, Jews occupied five of the fifteen homes. This figure remained stable for almost thirty years. Gentile merchants, artisans, and mill workers also lived in the area. Greek families settled nearby on Gray and Mallard Streets. Closer to downtown were the homes of prominent white Christian families such as the Markhams, Reades, Joneses, and Everetts.[19]

In the 1920s and 1930s some wealthier Jews moved to Trinity Park, a suburb that had been developed from Brodie Duke's estate near the Trinity College campus. College faculty, who were regarded as tolerant neighbors, favored this tree-lined, countrified neighborhood. The Kronheimers, the town's most affluent Jews, built a large Italian villa–style home on Minerva Street.[20] When the Evanses erected an international-style house among Trinity Park's traditional homes, they made a bold statement to provincial southerners. The break from the ethnic enclave was another sign of the Jews' acculturation as small-town southerners.

From a Shul to a Synagogue

Economic success, secular education, and residential integration brought Jews structurally into town society, but Jews would also need to establish a place in the town's religious community if they were to be respectable southerners. By 1918 synagogue leaders recognized that the community had outgrown the wooden house that served as the shul. They were spurred to action when the city decided to realign Liberty Street, which required demolition of the building. The members were divided between those who wanted only a modest wooden structure and those who argued for an impressive brick edifice. This decision bore directly on the community's identity as Jews and citizens, whether they were poor and transient or prosperous and permanent.

When the congregants gathered one evening at the old shul to debate the choices, Sam Margolis recalled, "pandemonium was in full sway." The arguing resounded loudly in Yiddish, punctuated with "lots of gesticulations." Attorney David Gladstone, who chaired the meeting, passionately argued for the wooden shul. Nathan Rosenstein, an advocate of a brick building, rose to speak, but Gladstone failed to recognize him. As shouts rang out, Gladstone stepped down. "Rosenstein went up to the *bimah* [altar] and took charge of the meeting," Margolis recalled. Quieting the crowd, Rosenstein called for a motion to build a brick synagogue, which carried unanimously.[21]

Although resentments lingered—Gladstone soon left town—the community was sufficiently unified to embark on its grandest project. A brick, cathedral-style synagogue located downtown would make a civic statement to the town's Christian community. New churches were rising across Durham, and downtown was undergoing a construction boom. Now Durham's Jews would stand on equal footing with the city's leading denominations.

The postwar years marked an era of extensive synagogue building as the immigrants grew in prosperity and solidified their communities. In 1918 Fayetteville's Jews erected a synagogue, and in 1920 an Orthodox congregation was founded in Asheville. In that year, too, Winston-Salem's

Orthodox Beth Jacob Congregation took title to a synagogue. In Raleigh Orthodox Jews purchased a building in 1914, and six years later Reform Jews began a drive to build a temple. Synagogues were erected in Greensboro in 1923 and in Gastonia in 1929. Nationally, some one thousand synagogues arose in the 1920s.

The congregation purchased a lot on the corner of Queen and Holloway Streets for $1,700 and awarded a building contract for $29,761. Such a commitment was seemingly unjustified, given the community's size, its constant divisiveness, and its finances. In 1919 the congregants had reasons for optimism, with seventy membership families and an annual income of $1,800. They supported a Hebrew school, a Sunday school, a Ladies Relief Society, Chevra Kadisha, and Hachnoses Orchim.[22] Yet families were leaving Durham. In 1921 the congregation claimed only fifty members. The success of the building campaign was by no means certain.

"It must . . . be borne in mind that we build for the future," the Building Committee declared. During the 1920s Jewish progressives, inspired by such innovators as Rabbi Mordecai Kaplan of New York, envisioned the synagogue not just as an Old World shul but also in broader terms as a Jewish cultural center that would house and affirm multiple forms of Jewish association, ethnic as well as religious. The Building Committee acknowledged such a role: "A synagogue, particularly in the South, is not only a House of Worship but equally as important a community center. Here convenes the women organizations, the various clubs, the Sunday school, the Hebrew school and the general community religious and social activities." The synagogue-center that brought worship, education, and social activities under one roof was a distinctly American invention. It developed from the ideology of progressive rabbis such as Kaplan, but it had precedents in classical Reform temples and contemporary Christian social churches. As a social and religious gathering place, it also had folkloric roots in the immigrant chevra.[23]

Progressive elements gave impetus to build the synagogue-center. Nathan Rosenstein had first come to Durham in 1904 because it had an Orthodox synagogue, but, as a Shriner, a professional man, and a bank director, he was also highly respected in the Christian community. The Building Committee's fund-raising strategy reflected the Jews' sense of themselves, the hierarchy of their identity as Jews and southerners: "Like all good charity, we began at home among our own, then solicited the aid of our Christian neighbors, and finally spread our solicitations throughout this state and country." In earthier Jewish terms, as Rosenstein's daughter

In 1921 Durham Jews built a downtown synagogue with cathedral-style architecture with the name Beth-El. As both a house of worship and a community center, it reflected postwar trend across the state and the nation. (Courtesy of the North Carolina Collection, University of North Carolina at Chapel Hill)

Ricky Rosenstein Lewin put it, "He *schnorred* [begged] the money." A goal of $30,000 required more than the *tzedakah* (charity) to sustain a small shul.[24]

On August 29, 1920, the day the cornerstone was laid, the congregation held auspicious ceremonies, with official Durham giving its benediction. A crowd of three hundred gathered at the construction site. President H. Sykes of the Chamber of Commerce introduced Dr. Abram Simon, rabbi of the Washington Hebrew Congregation, who addressed the audience on "Haticvo" (Hope), praising the purity of Jewish homes. As a native southerner and Reform Jew of German origin, Dr. Simon stood in stark contrast to the east European Orthodox Jews whom he was representing, but Durham Jews wished to project a public image of Jews as Americans. Dr. J. Elwood Welsh, pastor of the First Baptist Church, spoke for the Christian community, extolling the contributions of Jews to religion. He was followed by Willis Brogden, former Durham mayor and now a state supreme court justice. Rosenstein, assisted by Barney Enoch and Rabbis Simon and S. Bicovsky, laid the cornerstone.[25] It was filled with mementos that reflected the Jews' multicultural identity: a Durham news-paper, synagogue records, and Russian kopeks.

That night the Jews met at a lodge hall. The congregants bid for the honor of purchasing building materials for the synagogue. Doors were priced from $50 to $100 and windows from $22 to $75; for $18 (the num-ber eighteen being the traditional good-luck letter of *chai* [the eighteenth letter of the Hebrew alphabet, which represents the word "life"]), a con-gregant could purchase five hundred bricks. This practice derived from the bidding for ritual honors during the High Holidays. A large pledge was a means to achieve status, and public bidding put pressure on reluctant con-tributors to raise their donations or lose face. The *Durham Morning Herald* described the bidding as "lively." More than $14,000 was raised.[26] A sepa-rate women's committee under Sarah Shevel, widow of a wealthy mer-chant, took responsibility for furnishing and decorating the synagogue.

When the synagogue was completed in 1921, the congregation pub-lished a donors list that demonstrated the dominance of wealthy business-men. Fifty-one local Jewish donors pledged more than $100 each, and ten of these fifty-one gave more than $400. The largest was from long-time president Barney Enoch, who donated more than $1,000. The project in-spired some unusual Jewish unity in Durham, and Reform families, the Levys and Kronheimers, contributed.

Durham was a regional Jewish center, and "large numbers of Hebrew people" regularly joined the congregation for holidays. Gifts from nearby Henderson, Oxford, Graham, Mebane, Burlington, Roxboro, and Chapel Hill trace the geography of the synagogue's membership. Jews across the state also contributed. Goldboro's Weil family, though German and Re-form, sent several hundred dollars. Donations also trace the network of the ethnic economy as the merchants solicited their suppliers and wholesalers. Shoe companies and skirt manufacturers from Baltimore to Cincinnati sent token sums.[27]

In his solicitation letter Rosenstein reminded Durham that the Jews had made a civic sacrifice when the synagogue was condemned for a street widening. The town's benefactors were thus obliged to compensate them. Some fifty Christian individuals and businesses, led by $500 each from tobacco magnates Ben Duke and Julian Carr, contributed $1,700, almost 10 percent of the total. In so doing, they made a statement against anti-Semitism. For the Dukes the breach of forty years ago was healed, and Durham's Jews were now "our own people." Rosenstein took Ben Duke for a tour of the new building, and when the old man had trouble climbing the stairs, he told Rosenstein to install a handrail and send him the bill. Dozens of ordinary citizens, including African Americans, donated one or two dollars as tokens of goodwill. Church building in the South was a civic, not just a sectarian, duty, and Jews contributed to the building of churches, both black and white.[28]

"Durham," the Building Committee reported, "may lay claim to possessing the finest Orthodox synagogue in the South." The new synagogue, built of limestone and textured brick, totaled five thousand square feet with a sanctuary that could seat 350. It included a mikva "built strictly in accordance with the Orthodox law."[29] Like many urban, downtown synagogues constructed in the 1920s, this building was a "cathedral"; its eclectic architecture included Romanesque arches and a Classical pediment. Stained glass windows adorned the side. Only the Star of David on its roof distinguished it architecturally from several churches built at the time.

The board of directors in 1921 "resolved and declared" to change the name of Durham Hebrew Congregation to the more confidently ethnic Beth-El. Beth-El Congregation, Incorporated, under President Nathan Rosenstein and Secretary Henry Green listed as stockholders D. Freedman, N. Rosenstein, S. H. Hockfield, C. Wilson, M. K. Switzer, H. Brady, M. Zuckerman, and M. Margolis. All were European born. Its first High Holidays services, held in 1921, were led by Rabbi A. Zenovitz of Norfolk assisted by Beth-El's Reverend Max Shapiro.[30]

As the congregation proudly erected its new sanctuary, it suffered from attrition. Families who had provided leadership for a generation, people who had worked to build for Durham's Jewish future," abandoned the town in the 1920s. They included the synagogue president, Chevra Kadisha leader, and school principal. These departures hurt the congregation's social, religious, and financial stability. Generational changes were being felt. Although communal ties remained tight, religious ties loosened. The Jewish population stopped growing, and membership declined. Few younger, second-generation Jews joined. Board meetings were heated as members vied for offices. Arguments broke out on assigning honors during the High Holidays. Gibby Katz recalled, "They used to fight in the old shul over minor technicalities of how services were conducted."

The synagogue became the preserve of community elders, the immigrant traditionalists. On the High Holidays the men kept all-day vigils. Harris Abelkop stood by the bimah, loudly correcting anyone who made a mistake while reading the Torah. Services were times to both pray and talk. When the crowd was noisy, he hit his *siddur* (Sabbath prayer book) to shush them. The prayers were entirely in Hebrew with the sermon delivered in Yiddish. The men sat in the downstairs sanctuary and the women upstairs in the balcony. A *mehitzah* (partition) with a curtain separated the sections. The older women "would sit up there in their chairs and never move," Abe Stadiem recalled, even "in the summer when it was so hot you could die." Girls, understanding neither Hebrew nor Yiddish, peeked over the curtain at the boys below or gathered outside to socialize. Younger women began moving downstairs into the back rows on holidays when the synagogue was crowded. "My mother-in-law went upstairs," Molly Freedman recalled, but "downstairs I went and sat with my husband."

Jewish congregations typically placed more emphasis on philanthropy —fund-raising for a building, running welfare campaigns—than on the education of Jewish youth. In 1919 the Talmud Torah consisted of one teacher, thirty students, and three classes that met six times weekly after school. Rabbi Rabinowitz gave "goodboy" tickets to children who performed well whereas not-so-good boys received more painful instruction. "If you said 'v' for 'b,' you'd get a ruler across your hand or a big pinch in your cheek," Sam Margolis recalled. "You wouldn't make that mistake again." Parents were reported "unusually well pleased with the progress of the children," and several were able to converse in Hebrew. One student reflected, "I learned practically nothing."[31]

In some years the Talmud Torah faded, and parents employed tutors to prepare their sons for a Bar Mitzvah. Classes were reduced to four days, meeting in three half-hour, after-school sessions. As one group studied, the other boys played baseball or football, and the rabbi shouted to assemble the reluctant scholars. More than one child tried to sneak away. Although girls typically received no Jewish education beyond Sunday school, some parents arranged for their daughters to receive instruction.

The pulpit remained unstable. The Reverend Curlander arrived, but he left a year later after a dispute over distribution of kosher meat. In 1919 Rabbi Mordecai "Max" Shapiro was hired, and, except for a brief period in 1922 when Rabbi Meyerovitz (or Meyerson, as he changed his name) served, he remained until 1924. Shapiro, who had moved to Durham in 1913, had first served as a schochet and tutor. After his arrival, he brought his wife and daughter from Russia to his Roxboro Street cottage. His wife called him her *zadic* (righteous one), and as "Rebbe Zadic" he was recalled warmly as "a very, very gentle man." With a long, rabbinical beard, a black frock coat, and a large skull cap, he resembled a traditional east European rabbi. The Shapiros operated a delicatessen in the back room of their home, where they sold lox, schmaltz, and smoked salmon. In his backyard, he ritually killed chickens. The *rebbetzin* (rabbi's wife) roomed and boarded Jewish travelers and maintained a vineyard, selling kosher wine. Although Orthodox, Shapiro was "not rigid or fanatical,"[32] but after another round of community disputes, he took a pulpit in Wilson. In 1924 Rabbi Abraham Rabinowitz returned, but his stay proved stormy as resentments from the congregational split in 1913 remained. He left again after two years.

In 1925 Rabbi Jacob Aronson arrived from Brooklyn. A decade earlier he had served in Raleigh. The clean-shaven Aronson appeared modern, but he was another Yiddish-speaking immigrant who never mastered English. He was best remembered for a career-ending incident. In 1928 two con men gained his trust by appearing especially pious. Invited to the rabbi's home, they claimed to have invented a machine that could turn a one-dollar bill into a ten. Impressed by a demonstration, the rabbi withdrew his savings from the bank. A suspicious teller warned Charlie Wilson, a synagogue officer, about the rabbi's peculiar behavior, but Wilson arrived too late. The rabbi had been bilked and was an unwitting counterfeiter. To save the community from embarrassment, Dr. Rosenstein convinced him to leave. Aronson packed his belongings in a truck one night and left town.[33]

Ethnic Jews

In the 1920s the community bonded ethnically, but religious allegiances were loosening. The older Jews preserved their habits and customs, but the coming generation sought to escape the immigrant heritage, and their ritual observance eroded. Gibby Katz remembered as a child going around the Roxboro Street neighborhood waking the men at 5:00 so they could hold the morning service and be at work by 6:00. The family store occupied their lives, and that meant long hours six days a week. On the High Holidays stores closed, but for the Sabbath and other festivals they remained open. "We all went to the shul on Saturday to help them make a minyan," Abe Stadiem recalled, "and then as soon as shul was over we went to the store." Still, the men tried to fulfill their duties. On *Succoth* (Festival of Tabernacles), Jake Blankfield took a *lulav* (palm leaf) and *etrog* (citron) from store to store so that the merchants could fulfill the religious commandment to bless and shake them. A *sukkah* (tabernacle) was constructed next door to the synagogue, and the congregants gathered there to drink a ritual glass of wine. As the men walked home, they stopped by sukkahs up and down the street, arriving at their own homes in good holiday cheer. On Yom Kippur "Judge" E. Cohen performed the *kaporos* (scapegoat) rite, swinging a rooster around his head as expiation for sin.

The act was intended to drive away the evil eye, and one rebbe became enraged when a Gladstein boy refused to learn it. The young had little use for the old superstitions. A few older women regularly used the mikva, but the younger girls giggled or laughed when they passed it.[34]

Some older immigrants held to their Orthodoxy. Louis Gladstein rose every morning to put on his *tefillin* (phylacteries). He loved to chant synagogue melodies, and his chief pleasure was to hear a *chazzan* (cantor) in fine voice. Some men wore black hats, but many regarded a skull cap as an invitation for anti-Semitic taunts from the "lowlifers in East Durham," Sam Margolis recalled. A few continued to wear *tzitzis* (ritual fringes), which could be tucked inconspicuously under a shirt.

On Friday nights women gathered their families for Sabbath dinners. Sara Chai Miller, president of Ladies Aid, was considered so learned in Jewish law that she assumed the functions of a rabbinic court. Jews turned to her to resolve personal or marital disputes and to render judgments on social questions. She even issued a get. For traditional Jews, this showed an extraordinary deference to a woman's authority. " 'Bubbe' Miller ruled the roost with an iron hand," Sam Margolis recalled.

Although outwardly Orthodox, many fashioned a Judaism of their own making. Mike Gladstein would sneak home ham, which he guiltily called "Spanish corned beef." Although his wife did not keep a kosher kitchen, she kept separate dishes for Passover and burned the *chometz* (leaven) in a stove. Michael Margolis, son of a Latvian rabbi, moved to Queen Street because he wanted to be closer to the synagogue. But he was also a "free-thinker" who had abandoned such customs as wearing phylacteries. "He wanted to be Americanized," recalled his son Sam. Sam had a Bar Mitzvah, but he did not understand what he was reciting.

Jewish education had ignored women, and for men it consisted mostly of rote drills in ritual and prayer without much emphasis on the content of Judaism. In the 1920s Yetta Sawilowsky Brandt's parents moved to Durham from Augusta, Georgia, because they wanted to raise their children in a more Jewish environment. Yet, she remembered, "My parents did not really know a lot about the Jewish religion themselves. They could not possibly pass on to us what they did not know. . . . I guess that their parents, my grandparents, never taught them to be Jewish the way that they had learned in Europe." When the North Carolina Association of Jewish Women (NCAJW) formed in 1921, the women noted that "our parenthood is sadly deficient in the observance and teaching of Jewish home ceremonials and the religion which these embody."[35]

Immigrant culture persisted even as families Americanized. With the aging of the population, a grandparent often lived with the family, and multigenerational households became more common. Older Jews spoke Yiddish, which the younger generation could understand, if not speak. One described the language of the house as "pidgin Yiddish."[36] Fanny Gladstein, a college student, tutored some immigrant women in English, but many never mastered it.

Kashruth, the observance of the dietary laws, remained a dividing line between Gentile and Jewish Durham. Perhaps as many as forty-five of the seventy families kept kosher at home, and another dozen did so outside of it. Some kept kosher in deference to a parent or a grandparent who lived with them rather than from personal conviction. Ethel Mae Zuckerman Bernson recalled, "My mother always kept a kosher home because my grandfather always wanted her to." Kosher food was readily available in groceries and delicatessens. A Jewish merchant or Gentile butcher under rabbinic supervision served as ritual slaughterer. Traveling schochets also came down the railroad line. Herring was imported by the barrel from Norfolk, Richmond, and Baltimore. The pickled fish kept well, was rich in protein, and was cheap. When the grocer Elias Tabatchnick wheeled his herring barrels from the station to his store, the fish odor wafted through the streets, announcing his arrival. Many families kept backyard hen houses, chicken being a staple of the Jewish diet. Rabbi Shapiro drove his wagon through Hayti on Sunday mornings, stopping at Jewish homes and inquiring politely in Yiddish if they needed to have a chicken killed. For the women "flicking" chickens to render them kosher was a laborious process that offered opportunities to gather and socialize. The women spent countless hours boiling, delicing, and defeathering the birds. Mary Berman made a weekly trek from Chapel Hill—first by wagon, later by car—where she purchased kosher supplies and joined the flicking ritual. The Kronheimers' culinary tastes were German, and they savored wurst, sauerkraut, and pig's knuckles. They cooked their vegetables southern style with ham hocks, and on Sundays they indulged in chicken with oyster sauce.[37]

As ritual observance and synagogue membership declined, organizations formed to strengthen Jewish peoplehood. Durham Jews created a state network to strengthen their membership in the global Jewish community. Statewide systematic fund-raising campaigns for European relief had begun during World War I. The hostilities devastated Polish Jewry, and local newspapers reported in dramatic terms on the starving and homeless. Durham Jews felt especially helpless since the war had trapped their families. The community collected more than $12,000 for a statewide campaign on behalf of the National Jewish War Sufferers Fund. Durham's Jews, like east European Jews generally, were fervently Zionist. When Arab mobs in Hebron killed dozens of Palestinian Jews in 1929, Durham Jews gathered in the synagogue basement and raised $800.[38]

Jewish philanthropy in Durham was sensitive to the ethnic and Zionist conflicts that divided Jewry. The North Carolina Association of Jewish Women, founded by Sarah Einstein Weil of Goldsboro in 1921, with its German Jewish leadership drew but one Durham member, Lily Kronheimer. Under the leadership of Gertrude Weil, the NCAJW had a Zionist orientation, so the reluctance of local Jews to affiliate likely owed to social differences. Weil herself was a friend of Henrietta Szold, the founder of Hadassah, the women's Zionist organization. In February 1926, three speakers from prominent German families in Greensboro met with "interested" Jews in Durham to raise funds for a Joint Distribution Committee (JDC) campaign for European relief. Durham was assigned a quota of $10,000 in a national $13 million effort. Eight local workers began a three-day "systematic canvass among the Jewish population." After a week, they had raised $3,650, with "numerous contributions" from Christians.[39]

Durham's east European Jews may have felt some antipathy toward the JDC campaign with its non-Zionist, German leadership. In 1926 Rose Gladstein brought a Hadassah activist from Baltimore to Durham and organized a local chapter. Two days after the local JDC campaign began, the Hadassah chapter launched a fund-raising drive for the United Palestine Appeal. The presence of one new family, the Nachamsons, enhanced the local chapter. Jenny Nachamson had founded the first Hadassah chapter in North Carolina in Kinston, and she and her daughters served among Durham's early presidents. In 1933 Nachamson took her daughter Sara to Palestine to witness the rebuilding of the land and people. Eight of the twenty-four small-town Hadassah chapters in the South were in North Carolina. This statistic suggests the strength of Jenny Nachamson's Zionist leadership as well as the state's exceptional east European character.[40]

College Towns

As university towns both Durham and Chapel Hill were more cosmopolitan than similar southern communities. The Jews' "immigrant gifts" were appreciated.[41] Duke faculty who had cultivated a taste for rye and black breads in their European travels *discovered* Jaffe's kosher bakery. In Chapel Hill, Harry's, a kosher-style deli, became a hangout for campus literati and drew comparisons to cafes in Paris or Greenwich Village. Beth-El rabbi Chaim Williamofsky, a bibliophile, had an open invitation to the Duke religion department, where he enjoyed scholarly conversations with the faculty. In the 1920s Duke professors, regarded as community liberals, began assuming leadership in civic clubs such as the Lions, Rotary, and Kiwanis, and they welcomed Jewish members.

Children replicated much of their parents' experience. Some, especially those raised outside Roxboro Street, formed close friendships with their Gentile neighbors. Nonetheless, children also heard taunts that would have been unacceptable in polite adult company. The barbs of "Jewbaby" or "Christkiller" pointed to strains of anti-Semitism in the church or home. Many Jewish schoolchildren felt victims of a reverse discrimination: their teachers expected them to excel simply because they were Jews. Academic success did not always bring social acceptance. Girls felt a sense of isolation. Hazel Gladstein Wishnov recalled her school years as lonely: "I felt different. I felt isolated and alienated though I had a few girlfriends from the neighborhood. I felt a sense of singularness. It was particularly difficult for the Christian holidays. I felt there was something wrong with me." She was the last one chosen for children's games, if she was chosen at all, and she recalled how the schoolgirls would take drinks from the water fountain and spit at her. Yetta Sawilowsky was elected May Queen, but when people congratulated her parents, they added, "See, we love the Jews. We even picked one as May Queen." Such praise only emphasized a lack of acceptance.

Children who lived outside the Jewish neighborhood had non-Jewish playmates. "Until I got into ninth grade," Leonard Rapport recalled, "I was never in a class with a Jew or a Catholic." He found friends in a nearby white working-class neighborhood. Abe Stadiem, who lived on Liberty Street near but outside the Jewish neighborhood, "got along well with our neighbors," and as a child he recalled spending sleep overs with the children next door. When he reached high-school age his friends became exclusively Jewish, but when he returned to Durham after attending UNC he socialized with a mostly Gentile crowd. The middle-class neighborhood of Trinity Park, populated by Duke faculty, was regarded as tolerant. Children who attended Watts School there felt isolated, but they could not recall overt troubles. Leon Dworsky believed his social life was "definitely curtailed." Although he might join a neighborhood party, he was not invited to his classmates' homes. "We mixed with a group of Jewish people," Dworsky recalled. On Saturday nights Jewish kids gathered at each other's homes.

Schools made no distinction between church and state. In elementary school Jewish children stood uncomfortably with bowed heads as daily prayers were recited in Christ's name. Abe Stadiem remembered, "You go into the auditorium in the morning to say prayers and if you didn't bow your head down, they'd hit you, call you Jewbaby." He also recalled a "daggone teacher who used to hop on about the Jews." Stadiem added, "I didn't say nothing because I was scared to talk, I was the only one in there."

Social isolation and bouts of spite stood in contrast to expressions of sensitivity. When Joe Hockfield was asked to join the Hi-Y, the YMCA director exempted him from the Christian pledge. On Sunday afternoons the Reverend S. Bost violated his Sabbath rest to umpire the Roxboro Street baseball games. The 1933 baccalaureate service for Durham High School was held at the Baptist church, but Gibby Katz was touched when the principal expressed concerns about the feelings of Jewish students.

Durham held to its reputation as a fast-living town, and several Jews contributed to the local color. These were culturally hybrid, ethnic Jewish southerners. Roy and Dave Levy, third-generation southerners, operated a downtown pool hall that was a watering hole for the town's sportsmen. The pool hall remained off limits to college students. Professor Wannamaker of Trinity College wrote a letter to Henry and Ida Brady apprising them that if their son David were seen exiting Levy's rear door again, he would be expelled. Louis Stadiem's pawnshop did a thriving business with gamblers and ladies of the night who frequented a nearby red-light district. The ladies offered such fine collateral as a diamond ring or a Cadillac. One pawnshop customer was the infamously prodigal Brodie Duke, who would get the "biggest kick" by taking straw hats off the shelf and smashing them over people's heads. When the sheriff climbed a drainpipe and entered a second-floor window to break up a game at Sam Hockfield's store, he arrested Jew and Gentile poker player alike.[42]

Although the Jewish community prided itself on being exceptionally law abiding, Moses Levy remained an exception. The newspaper conceded his notoriety, observing that "Mose Levy . . . is almost as well known in Durham as a familiar tobacco sign is all over the world." In September 1926, the police raided his "combination store and dwelling house" on Fayetteville Street. Levy was surprised. He regarded himself as a friend of Durham's constabulary. Nevertheless, the police searched his premises, only to discover in an upstairs closet 192 fruit jars of corn liquor, totaling 48 gallons. Supported by four defense lawyers, Levy endured two mistrials and one guilty verdict. At a fourth trial the defense argued that Levy kept the forty-eight gallons for a "Hebrew celebration." Sacramental spirits, it seems, were exempt from Prohibition. The defense also pointed to the salubrious effects of drink, especially after a hard day's work. The *Durham Morning Herald* reported the surprising verdict: "Twelve of his peers, and all of them Gentiles, said Mose was not guilty of the charge of illegally possessing no less than eight full cases of copper-distilled, corn beverage which the 18th amendment sometimes humorously prohibits." Not merely content to be a free man, Levy wanted his sacramental corn liquor back. The newspaper regretted to report that there would be no "unofficial Jewish holiday" in Durham. The judge more wisely suggested that the sheriff should "pour it out" and reminded the defendant that federal authorities took a less tolerant view of moonshine than did the good citizens of Durham. Four years later, Levy was less fortunate when he masterminded a cigarette hijacking ring with several black colleagues, and he also felt the long arm of the law when he purveyed some ground meat of feline rather than bovine origin. Levy was always good for a game of cards in the rear of his "I'll Be Back" grocery store.[43]

Despite reports of petty lawbreaking, Jews were regarded as honest citizens. James Leyburn claimed extravagantly, "Every member of the Jewish community was scrupulously law-abiding; no Jew during the two decades [1900–1920] was arrested for any offense." A retiring police officer reported that he had never arrested a Jew.[44]

Sports was a primary vehicle of southern acculturation. Second-generation Jewish boys proved themselves as "muscle Jews." In the late 1920s, in "one of the most thrilling games ever played on the local Y court," Beth-El won the Durham Sunday school championship before hundreds of fans. Beth-El star Joe Hockfield led Durham High to a state basketball championship in 1930. Jews also won honors as boxers and as football heroes, the true test of southern manhood. Louis Sher, a shoemaker's son, in 1929 received national attention as a high-school fullback. Blocking for Sher at right guard was Hymie Dave. Harry Schwartz captained the UNC football team in 1928. Gibby Katz, a collegiate wrestler, joined the Durham Cardinals semi-professional football team. Durham's Joe Murnick was an undefeated boxer at UNC in 1937, succeeding as captain another Jewish fighter, Max Novich, a conference champion. By the 1930s, newspapers stopped identifying athletes as Jews, and, with the exception of church leagues, there were not any "Hebrew teams."[45]

None of the athletes recalled any anti-Semitism on the field. Hockfield heard taunts, but only from fans who thought he was an Indian. In his long athletic career Katz experienced only one conflict; a high-school coach asked him to fail French so that he could play another year, but Katz's mother said that was not permissible for a Jewish boy. Katz for years paced the sidelines at Durham High football games, taking a paternal interest in the players. Athletic prowess engendered Jewish community pride while marking their acceptance as ethnic southerners.

After World War I, Jews began identifying themselves as small-town southerners. Not only did they become Americans, but in their collective memory they constructed a narrative of community origins that placed them at the town's creation. The Jews were as integral to the city as Duke or tobacco, although virtually no Durham family was descended from the cigarette rollers. The Jews established their place collectively in the town's civic and religious communities, and they minimized their differences to their Christian neighbors. A new brick downtown synagogue attested to their permanence and their prosperity. As they became southerners, the Jews' adherence to traditional Judaism eroded, but they maintained their group identity and vestiges of their culture. The synagogue-center strengthened ethnic associations if not religious observance. On Roxboro Street they created a Jewish neighborhood. Now in their second generation, Durham Jews created a home and a history.

8 Crisis and Community, 1930 to 1941

The 1930s were uncomfortable times for Jews. Certainly North Carolina Jews shared national Jewish anxieties that anti-Semitism would break out locally as bigots vented against the "Jew Deal" and warned against a "Jew war." The anti-Semitic radio tirades of Father Coughlin and the anti-interventionist rhetoric of America Firsters aroused fears of popular anti-Semitism. Nazi propaganda revived discredited racial myths that Jews, like blacks, were biologically, not just religiously, different. Jews, like other Americans, also had to contend with the hard times of the depression. They defended Jewish interests at home and abroad while confronting a persistent discrimination that limited their opportunities in education, employment, and social relations. Fissures opened in the Jews' dual identity as their ethnic loyalty as Jews conflicted with their political reality as Americans.

The depression derailed what had seemed to be inexorable economic progress. The community was faced with the simple problem of survival. After graduating from the University of North Carolina, E. J. Evans enrolled at Harvard Law School for the 1929 term, but instead of attending he went into his father-in-law's Durham business. Sam Margolis, a history buff with ambitions to teach, wanted to continue his studies at Duke, but "everything fell apart." After classes he worked at the family grocery until 9:00 P.M. but finally had to quit college to support his family. His father had died, and his brother, Reuben, a Yale student, could not find a job. "You have to eat first," Margolis recognized. "To make a living was rougher than hell," Gibby Katz remembered. "You worked night and day literally, seven days a week, year in and year out. . . . I didn't know what a vacation was." Katz, another Duke graduate, became a grocer and butcher.

When the First National Bank failed, wealthier community members were wiped out. Nathan Rosenstein had invested his life savings in bank stock. His daughter Ricky Rosenstein Lewin recalled her father coming home, sitting on the steps, and sobbing, "Everything I have is gone except my friends." Benjamin Kronheimer closed his department store and retired to Richmond. The Mechanics and Farmers Bank managed to survive, so poorer Jewish grocers and merchants who invested with the black-owned bank were in better shape. The textile industry was devastated, but tobacco continued to prosper, which softened the depression's impact on Durham. The ongoing construction of the Duke campus also injected much needed cash into local coffers.

The Jewish internal credit system revived to preserve community survival. The Ladies Aid Society assisted families with their medical bills, helped pay for coal and food, and saved small businesses with no- or low-interest loans. The women also fed and housed poor transients. In 1932 several merchants formed a Free Loan or Hebrew Benevolent Society. Its long-time leader was Sam Daniel, a furniture store owner who had arrived from Chicago in the 1920s. The Polish-born Daniel was remembered as an "old-fashioned" Jew who ".worked for the good of the community." The society's leadership revolved over the years. Members purchased shares that allowed them to take loans. Few questions were asked for loans of $500 to $1,000. The merchants worked out a system of staggered paydays for their employees so that one merchant who needed money on a Monday was prepared to loan some on Thursday. One shop owner borrowed $20 and could not repay it for years.[1]

In hard times Jews returned to peddling. Maurice and Milton Julian, UNC students from Massachusetts, hawked shoes and rented bicycles to pay their way through school, eventually opening Franklin Street stores. Philip Cohen took to the road after his Chapel Hill bootery failed. At first he traveled a two-week route from the coast to the mountains, but the cost of purchasing local licenses led him to focus on a fifty-mile Raleigh-to-Greensboro route. He hitchhiked with a large satchel, finding customers at plants, gas stations, colleges, warehouses, or "any place where there is a crowd of men, especially on pay day." The summer, when college students were gone, was slow, but the fall, when tobacco markets opened, was lucrative. Cohen was a fixture at Durham warehouses. While the auctioneer began his chant and the farmers unloaded their trucks, Cohen spread out his "razors, blades, shaving cream, fountain pens, socks, pencils." Cohen kept "steady customers," which he attributed to his guarantee to "replace anything that goes bad." His ambition was to reopen a store.[2]

The 1930s were times of great labor unrest. The paternalism of Duke and Carr yielded to impersonal corporate bureaucracies. Decisions affecting Durham's economy were now made in executive offices in New York. Mill villages were turned over to private owners, and these properties deteriorated. Since the arrival of craftsmen to build the new Duke campus in the 1920s, unions had gained a foothold. Strikes rocked the town as the textile industry collapsed in the depression. A 1934 textile strike drew four thousand workers, all but closing the mills. Labor's hopes were revived by the election of Franklin Roosevelt, who was widely supported by local Jews. Durham Jews, for reasons of self-interest if not principle, supported the workers, who were their customers. Merchants donated food and tents and extended credit to the workers for shoes and clothes. Evans's United Dollar Stores joined eighteen businesses that signed a full-page advertisement in the *Durham Morning Herald* stating that "labor unions are America's greatest safeguard for economic progress" and calling for a "truly American brotherhood of Business and Labor."[3]

In their stores Jewish merchants formed social bonds with their customers, who were often farmers and factory workers. These friendships were noteworthy because working-class southerners, recently removed from the countryside, were susceptible to anti-Semitic appeals from rustic preachers who railed against Christ killers and from populist demagogues who fulminated against shylocks. Durham Jews sometimes complained about East Durham "lowlifers," uneducated mill workers, who harassed them. Yet warm feelings also developed. Jews depended economically on workers, both white and black, for their trade.[4]

Israel Freedman knew that when the economy improved, his customers would loyally repay him for the shoes and clothes that he sold them on credit in hard times. He piled groceries in his car to bring to the tenants who occupied farms that he owned in northern Durham County. Both Jew and Christian alike recalled him as a quietly generous man who endowed Duke scholarships for Durham students. Abe Stadiem, whose accent was thickly southern, found his customers to be "nice and polite," and he became friendly with the farmers who frequented his clothing store. "They'd invite me out to the farms," Stadiem recalled. "I'd go out there and eat with them. They considered me a southerner, one of them. But I told them I didn't eat bacon."

Phil Cohen, who peddled in the Durham tobacco markets, reported to Leonard Rapport of the Federal Writers Project that he had "no trouble" and experienced "little anti-Semitism." "The warehousemen are very nice to me," Cohen stated. "They say 'Get a truck and make yourself comfortable, you're always welcome here.'" Cohen, a short, stout, one-armed man, appreciated their "open-handed friendliness," and he found "touching . . . the regard of the people with whom he deals." When he hitchhiked, people recognized him and stopped to offer rides.[5]

Occupational Distribution

A 1938 occupational survey of North Carolina Jews by William Levitt, a UNC graduate student, demonstrated the persisting mercantile character of the Durham community. (Levitt's guide for his research was his father, a traveling salesman.) Of the seventy-eight Durham Jews listed, fifty-two were in retail businesses. At a time when 77.1 percent of Durham's working population consisted of wage and salary employees, 71.6 percent of the Jews were self-employed or worked on their own account. Jews, as was typical in small towns, continued to concentrate in groceries and dry-goods stores, but they were also branching into new fields. Two sold auto parts, and one, with Prohibition lifted, owned a liquor store. Seven ran scrap-iron yards. Four Jews listed themselves as manufacturers, as opposed to none in 1923. The town now contained a small number of Jewish professionals, including seven faculty at Duke and North Carolina College and one x-ray specialist. Two Jews (not listed on the survey) were lawyers. "Oddly enough," the report concluded, "there is no evidence of any Jewish people connected with the tobacco industry, the industry which brought the first large group of Jews to Durham."[6]

This fact was hardly odd at all. Certain business sectors were closed to Jews. In the depression years, when jobs were scarce, discrimination hurt all the more. The offices of American Tobacco and Liggett and Myers were considered off-limits. "I didn't take teaching because I knew that I would never get a job in the Durham school system," Hazel Gladstein realized when she chose her major at Duke. She applied for a position at Duke Hospital but was turned down by an interviewer who seemed excessively curious about the origins of the Gladstein name. Some downtown department stores simply did not hire Jews.

Yet, some Jews succeeded in fields that were regarded as closed. Ricky

Rosenstein taught in the public schools. Pat Silver felt welcome in various offices at Duke although the university did not hire Jews in administrative positions. In the 1920s American Tobacco employed Joe Dave, a second-generation Durhamite, as a clerk and offered to train him as an engineer. In the 1940s S. Algranti, a Jew of Armenian origin, served as a supervisor. The banking industry, considered hostile nationally to Jews, was open in Durham. After graduating from Duke in 1928, Harry Goldberg, a grocer's son, worked as a bookkeeper at the Depositors National Bank. Charles Zuckerman, an insurance officer, joined the board of George Watts's Home Savings and Loan. A half-dozen Jews served on bank boards. Harry Lehman, Kronheimer's nephew, as a third-generation southerner found easy entry into the highest circles of the civic and financial leadership. In 1930 Lehman was president of the Merchant's Association, director of the Central Carolina Bank, founder of the Carolina Textile Mills, and president of the Taxpayer's League.[7]

Persisting Jews tended to remain within the ethnic economic system, working in family stores or for other Jewish merchants before opening places of their own. In the state's thirteen largest Jewish communities, about half the employed Jews were "proprietors, managers, and officials," but in Durham the figure was two-thirds. The move from sales to store ownership was the principal means of occupational mobility. From 1900 to 1938, the percentage of local Jews working as clerks or salespersons dropped from 29.4 to 13.0 because clerks tended to become store owners or leave town. Established merchants upgraded their stores into specialty shops to appeal to a higher class of trade. Wilson's men's store and Sawilowsky's ladies' shop ranked among the town's finest. The United Dollar Store renamed itself United Department Store and improved its merchandise.[8]

Family owned groceries did not endure. The grocery capitalized more profitable enterprises such as a downtown dry-goods store or real-estate investment. From 1911 to 1938 the number of Jewish groceries dropped from twenty-one to nine. The grocers also faced increased competition from black merchants and from grocery chains. By 1938 the A & P had one main store and fourteen branches in Durham. Sam Margolis left the family's Hayti grocery to manage the Fayetteville Street A & P. Because of the depression, many youth had no choice but the family store. Family obligations to aging parents, Gibby Katz noted, frustrated ambitions to move on. Katz himself cared for his widowed mother.[9]

The growing presence of Jews in the professions followed national

trends. In 1938, 14.8 percent of local Jews were now employed professionally, compared with 5.8 percent in 1900. Jews flocked to colleges in the
interwar years as a changing economy created demand for white-collar
workers (see table 8.1). College-educated youth who aspired to break
from the store expressed frustration although doors did open for them professionally. David Jaffe, the baker's son, spoke a common sentiment: "For
someone with a college education, there were no opportunities" in Durham. Many local Jewish storekeepers had some college. Butcher Gibby
Katz, clothier Israel Freedman, and grocer Sam Margolis had all attended
Duke but found careers in the store. Jaffe, who earned a master of arts
degree from Duke in 1937, spent several years at the University of North
Carolina Press, and then the *Durham Morning Herald* hired him as state
news editor. He soon left for a New York publishing house. His friend
Leonard Rapport, the optician's son, also worked at the press and for the
WPA Federal Writers' Project, but he moved on to the National Archives
in Washington. Carol Goldberg, Kronheimer's niece and a Smith College
graduate, served as the *Durham Morning Herald*'s society editor, but she, too,
sought a journalistic career out of town. When Dr. Moses Stadiem, the
pawnbroker's son, was offered a position at Duke Medical School, he rejected it in favor of Tulane. The complaints about the lack of opportunity
spoke not just to job discrimination but also to the young Jews' large ambitions, which a small town could not contain.

The youth who left Durham for the cities reflected the changing demographic profile of Jewry as the second generation rose from the storekeeping of their immigrant parents to achieve success in law, medicine, and
other professions. In 1937, for example, Jews were a quarter of the population of New York but 65 percent of its lawyers and 55 percent of its physicians. David Brady, a Durham grocer's son, was a partner in a Roosevelt
law firm and head of the New York Selective Service Commission. Henry
Greenberg rose to a seat on the New York State Supreme Court. Harry
Primakoff, after graduating from UNC and interning at Watts Hospital,
practiced medicine in Baltimore where a hospital wing bears his name.
Rebecca Greenberg Lovenstein was the first woman to graduate from the
University of Virginia Law School and first licensed woman at the state
bar. The Washington Art Commission chose Nelson Rosenberg, a Durham
tailor's son, to decorate federal buildings, and in New York Nathan Ornoff,
son of a Durham scrap dealer, won a national art competition judged by
Edward Hopper.[10]

The pull of upward mobility from the region was a southern as well as

TABLE 8.1. Occupational Distribution of Durham Jews, 1887–1938

Profession	1887	1902	1910	1923	1938
Retail trades (%)	34.5	70.7	48.9	63.5	54.3
Dry goods/general merchandise	9	13	21	18	20
Grocer	1	13	14	18	9
Furniture		1	1		
Insurance agent				1	
Jeweler				2	1
Junk dealer			1	2	7
Auto parts dealer					2
Wine shop					1
News dealer				2	
Tobacconist					1
Milliner		1	4		
Landlord		1			
Loan agent			1		
Pawnbroker				3	2
Pharmacist				1	
Peddler		12	3		1
White collar (%)	31.0	10.3	36.9	17.6	14.8
Clerk/sales	9	6	32	10	7
Traveling salesman			1		1
Stenographer/bookkeeper				3	3
Bank employee					1
Skilled workers (%)	20.7	1.7	0.0	0.0	0.0
Garment worker		1			
Cigarette maker	6				
Unskilled workers (%)	0.0	0.0	0.0	1.4	0.0
Cleaner				1	

TABLE 8.1 *Continued*

Profession	1887	1902	1910	1923	1938
Self-employed artisans (%)	10.3	10.3	8.7	12.2	9.9
Baker			1	1	1
Butcher	2	1			2
Tailor	1	5	3	2	
Shoemaker			4	5	5
Watchmaker				1	
Manager/manufacturer (%)	3.4	5.2	1.1	2.7	4.9
Manager			1	2	
Manufacturer	1	1			4
Professional (%)	0.0	5.2	5.4	2.7	14.8
Optician		2	2	1	1
University faculty					7
X-ray specialist					1
Lawyer			2		2
Rabbi			1	1	1
TOTAL	29	58	92	74	80

Sources: Durham Business Directories, 1887, 1902, 1910, 1923, North Carolina Collection, University of North Carolina at Chapel Hill; William Levitt, "The Occupational Distribution of the Jews in North Carolina" (master's thesis, University of North Carolina, 1938).

a Jewish pattern. In a 1937 study, "The 'Drag' of Talent Out of the South," sociologist Wilson Gee noted that "the South is a region which has been and is being depleted severely of its best talent to the enrichment of other parts and to its own impoverishment." The professions most affected—editors, authors, artists, educators, lawyers, doctors—included fields that upwardly mobile Jews often favored. Educated youth saw around them the impoverished, illiterate South that Franklin Roosevelt declared "America's number one economic problem."[11]

Small numbers of second-generation Jews had acculturated as small-town southerners and persisted in Durham, expressing a typically southern pride of place. Several returned by choice after heading north. Nathan

Ornoff, who had moved to New York to study at the National Academy of Art, told a Durham reporter, "I want my friends back home to know that I didn't come up here to paint the city but to study, and as soon as I learn enough I'm coming back to North Carolina."[12] Ornoff returned to Durham to run an art school. After graduating from Duke in the 1930s, Ethel Mae Zuckerman and Hazel Gladstein left Durham for Philadelphia and New York, respectively, where they found careers, but they returned ten years later in measure because their husbands, who were northern urbanites, preferred small-town life.

Failure in the city also pulled Jews back home. Jake Nurkin sought fame and fortune in New York after winning local dance contests and being lauded for his imitations of Charlie Chaplin and Billie Richie. He returned to his father's Durham shoe-repair shop, later opening a dance studio. Abe Stadiem, after attending UNC, moved to Baltimore, but he disliked the city, missing the comforts and comraderie of a small town. Those who left and returned, though, were hard-pressed to name others who felt the pull of the South.

Durham's location on the New York to Florida axis brought a flow of Jewish migrants through town. Several families—the Greenbergs, Roses, and Bergmans—all told a story that had the ring of folklore. In the depression years they were en route between New York and Florida when they stopped in Durham overnight. Seeing tobacco workers pour from the factories, they decided to stay and open stores. In Chapel Hill students provided a similar market as tailors, shoemakers, and haberdashers opened stores. Brothers Sol and Jack Lipman came from New Bern to open shoe and tailor shops, respectively.

Jews on Campus

Durham was beginning its transition from a mill and market town into a medical and research center. Duke's $40 million bequest turned the university into an institution of national rather than just regional stature, especially after its medical school opened in 1930. In the 1920s the University of North Carolina had gained a national reputation for liberalism under the enlightened leadership of such men as university presidents Harry Chase and Frank Graham and sociologist Howard Odum.

In the 1930s American Jews, who were 3.5 percent of the nation's population, comprised nearly 10 percent of UNC's student enrollment. The Jewish percentage of the UNC student body was more than twenty times the Jewish percentage of the state's population. "I can't recall any family in Durham who had boys that did not go" to college, reflected Henry Bane, son of a Durham peddler who went to Trinity College and UNC Law School. "Not as many women as men" went, Ethel Mae Zuckerman Bernson observed. "I didn't think there was an expectation in a lot of families, but in my family there was." She and her sister enrolled at Duke.[13]

In the 1930s Jewish enrollment at UNC became numerically significant, rising to nearly 15 percent of the 1936 entering class. Duke did not experience such growth. A Methodist college in the small-town South had limited appeal to northern Jews, and the state's Jewish population was too small to have much impact. Statistics on Jewish undergraduates at Duke from 1930 to 1937 suggest that a quota was in effect. In 1933 Jews numbered 79 of 3,214 students, only 2.6 percent of the Duke student body, a quarter of the national percentage. Over a seven-year period Jewish enrollment at Duke remained consistently below 3 percent. In actual numbers there were between fifty-five and seventy-eight Jews on campus each year in a student body that fluctuated between two thousand to twenty-five hundred. Duke Medical School maintained a more liberal quota of 15 percent, with Jews numbering 28 of 170 students in 1933.[14]

In 1933 UNC was accused of maintaining a quota in its medical school. Morris Krasny, a northern student married to a Durham woman, was denied admission because the quota of four Jewish students had been filled. Krasny turned to Durham attorney R. O. Everett, who tried but failed to have the dean of the medical school, Isaac Manning, reverse his decision. Krasny then sent a letter and a petition of support from Durham's UNC alumni to President Graham. Graham promptly called Krasny to his office and then summoned the dean for "a brief but frank and friendly discussion."[15]

Manning, who had served as dean for twenty-eight years, admitted that he limited Jewish enrollment because he had difficulty placing Jewish graduates of UNC's two-year program into four-year medical schools. He maintained a quota of 10 percent, marking some applicants as "out-of-state Jews." Although Manning insisted that there was "no prejudice against Jews as such," he admitted Jews in pairs because he did not think that a Gentile would want to work as a laboratory partner with a Jew. Without a quota, Manning told Graham, Jews would swamp UNC. Although some Jews were "acceptable" students and qualified Jewish North Carolinians were never denied admission, Manning wrote in his memoirs, he believed that "rigid measures" were needed to control a nationwide

Jewish "problem." He found many Jewish students to be "exceedingly ob-jectionable," and at other medical schools they engaged in such deceits as changing their names or forging transcripts to gain admission.[16]

Manning and Graham became locked into a fierce public debate. Some alumni groups and all but one of the UNC medical school faculty sup-ported Manning, a respected physician from a distinguished North Caro-lina family. (His brother Dr. John Manning, a Durham mayor, was a warm friend and personal physician to many Jews.) Manning's defenders claimed that the issue was not prejudice but academic freedom and professional standards. Graham stood his ground, telling the dean, "I will have to over-rule you, and the young man will be admitted to your school." Manning resigned as dean although he remained on the faculty. Manning was suffi-ciently the southern gentleman that he did not let his prejudices affect his personal relations, and one Jewish alumnus recalled him as "a man of great honesty and character" and argued that it was "a grave injustice" to call him anti-Semitic. When medical schools asked Manning to identify the troublemaking Jewish student, he refused to release Krasny's name.[17]

The case aroused national publicity. Graham was praised editorially in the *New York Herald-Tribune.* E. J. Evans wrote a letter to Graham, his for-mer teacher: "You have earned the undying respect and admiration of millions of Jews throughout the nation. . . . At a time like this when Hit-ler and Nazis have ground under their heels the lives and hopes of . . . people whose only wrong was their Jewish blood, your action brings a breath of joy to despairing people." Graham's long-time friend Samuel Newman stated flatly that "Graham was a philo-Semite." Graham called Newman whenever a Jewish student needed money to finish college, and Newman regularly wrote and visited Graham to solicit his support for Jewish and Zionist causes.[18]

Despite Graham's liberalism, the position of Jewish students remained ambivalent. Bill Levitt, who received both a bachelor of arts degree and a master of arts degree in 1938, did not find the university to be "overtly" anti-Semitic but encountered prejudice when he "got into the inner workings." Levitt had ambitions to earn a doctorate and pursue an aca-demic career. He was heartened when sociologist Rupert Vance, a well-known southern progressive, agreed to write a recommendation until he discovered that Vance had described him as his "most brilliant Jewish student." Levitt believed that Vance had "dropped a bomb"; the label of Jew would deny him any chance of advancing in academia. He chose in-stead to work for the federal government. Levitt found it "a relief to get the hell out of there," yet he also recognized "good people," such as Graham, the playwright Paul Green, and the sociologist Howard Odum, founder of the pioneering Institute for Research in Social Science. Odum had gotten Levitt funding to study the occupational distribution of North Carolina's Jews, and he recommended Levitt as his "best student" without qualification.

Jewish racial stereotyping was incoherent and inconsistent, ignorant in its assumptions, but it was acceptable even in polite, educated society. When Mississippian Shelby Foote went to Chapel Hill in 1935 as a student, fraternity brothers, learning that his maternal grandfather was an Austrian Jew, questioned him on his "feelings about Jesus Christ." UNC medical school professor W. C. George, a world expert on blood, wrote Graham in support of admission quotas: "Restrictive measures agains[t] the Jews . . . might be necessary . . . to protect another race or racial culture." Without these restrictions, George predicted, a race war would ensue: one race is "going to dominate and determine the nature of the civilization, and the other will be submissive or it will be exterminated." Natural law worked against "different races living together." (George later became an infamous scientific apologist for segregation during the civil rights era.) In 1936 state bar president Kemp Battle, quoting a "liberal" southern academic authority, cited some dubious anthropology when he asked UNC president Frank Graham to limit Jewish enrollment. In a letter Battle explained that northern Jews came from Russia and Poland and were "racially . . . quite different and show the vices but not the virtues" of the southern Jews who were "Sephardim [*sic*] Jews" from Spain, England, and Germany. Battle endorsed quotas on "the type of Jew, known vulgarly as the Kike."[19]

Student Life
Northern Jews felt their outsider status on campus. When Milton Julian enrolled at UNC in 1936, his Orthodox parents did not want him to leave Massachusetts for a "heathen country[,] . . . a real treyfe society." UNC student Richard Adler, later a Broadway composer, recalled how the southern parents of his girlfriend Meg McKay reacted when he went to their home: "Here was his daughter, a lovely, promising twenty-three year old beauty. And her choice for a companion was a scrawny, badly clothed, nineteen-year old Jew from New York." He was "frozen out" of the house, his pride "demolished," but Adler's parents took his rejection for granted.[20]

In 1938 Len Rubin, a UNC student from New Jersey, explained in the

American Jewish Times why "a Northern boy comes South to school." He noted that Chapel Hill's growing reputation and liberalism were well known in the North, but his first two reasons were the low tuition and the desire to leave home and escape city life. He also acknowledged that sports and easier admission standards lured northerners. In 1938 more than 200 of the 249 Jewish students at UNC were from the North. Jews had "become an integral part of Southern campus life," Rubin noted, and Jews were "right at the top" in sports, academics, and publications.[21]

Yet, after surveying northern Jewish students on campus, he could not find one who expressed an "intention of establishing himself in the South. They all await the day that they can return to the North." Jews clustered in certain dormitories where they were a majority. Jews ate together, played together, and socialized together. In short, Rubin remarked, "they find themselves isolated." Jews did not "click" with southerners. Although incidents of prejudice were "few and far between . . . the Jewish boy is confronted by this stamp of Jew which he meets even in casual contact." Hillel and a YMCA interfaith group worked to lessen tensions. Curiously, Rubin said little about relations between northern and southern Jews, though he noted that southern Jews and Gentiles "find more interests in common." Rubin admitted that northerners often had chips on their shoulders. Sarah Cohen, a Jewish fraternity housemother, recalled that the southerners "were courteous. . . . The boys who came from New Jersey or New York were quite different. They were big mouthed."[22]

In 1934, when a committee of North Carolina Jews studied local campuses to establish a Hillel Foundation, they observed cultural differences between northern and southern Jews: "The Northern Jewish student, not being accustomed to the ways of the South, finds many difficulties in his path, and through misunderstanding, creates many more. Therefore it is our duty to bring about, through proper training, a better understanding."[23] Hillel's function was not just to ensure Jewish identity but to acculturate Jews into ethnic southerners. As the national mood turned anti-Semitic in the 1930s, southern Jews wanted to avoid unnecessary frictions.

Like their parents who were joining Hadassah or B'nai B'rith rather than affiliating with the synagogue, young Jews identified ethnically by joining fraternal or sororal societies. With the influx of Jewish students at UNC, Phi Alpha opened a house in 1933, and Pi Lambda Phi formed a chapter in 1939. Jewish houses, led by Tau Epsilon Phi, annually won awards for the highest grade point average among fraternities. Students who wanted to keep kosher could room at a boarding house operated by

Esther Jacobson, a Latvian immigrant who moved to Chapel Hill from Winston-Salem. At Duke a chapter of Zeta Beta Tau was founded in 1932 by Freddy Sington, a football coach. A loosely knit group, ZBT had only ten members in 1935. In 1931, five women formed Alpha Epsilon Phi, a Jewish sorority.[24]

After the Menorah Society faded from the collegiate scene, UNC students, in 1926, formed the Carolina Jewish Society. This society, too, waxed and waned. Visiting rabbis occasionally came to campus, but ad-hoc programs were inadequate to serve the growing Jewish student body. The local Jewish community had neither the size nor the resources to address the demand. In 1934 Rabbi Iser Freund of Goldsboro and Sidney Stern of Greensboro approached B'nai B'rith about establishing a Hillel Foundation in North Carolina. The North Carolina Association of Jewish Women responded by appointing a Committee on Student Activity to survey state campuses. At its 1935 convention Sara Evans reported that Duke enrolled 100 Jewish students and that UNC had 300, 189 of whom were North Carolinians.[25]

B'nai B'rith invited the national Hillel director, Abram Sachar of the University of Illinois, to address the 1935 NCAJW convention in Charlotte. The "meeting voiced its enthusiasm" to raise the necessary funds. Sachar went to Chapel Hill, where faculty and administrators received him "cordially." President Graham sent letters endorsing the project. A statewide campaign raised $6,000, the quota set by B'nai B'rith to begin a two-year probationary program.[26]

The foundation opened in Chapel Hill on October 9, 1936, and was the eleventh chapter in the country. For the dedicatory ceremonies Graham welcomed 275 students and dignitaries. Graham stated that "the University is a mingling of many currents and draws its strength from each. . . . This Foundation must be a part of, and not apart from, the University." He urged the students to hold fast to their Jewish heritage.[27]

Sachar selected as Hillel's first director Rabbi Bernard Zeiger of Michigan. In a report Zeiger observed that Jewish students were assimilationist. By a "strange paradox" university officials "warmly welcomed" Hillel while Jewish students were indifferent. "The average college student . . . knows little of Judaism and finds being a Jew a burden," Zeiger noted. "He tries to hide his identity by imitating the non-Jew." Their Jewish identity was in large measure imposed by the discrimination that marked them and pushed them into Jewish associations. Zeiger's successor, Rabbi Samuel Sandmel, a graduate of Hebrew Union College and a former assistant at The Temple in Atlanta, reported in 1939 on Hillel's inadequacies. Student attendance was inconsistent. Hillel still did not own a Torah, and the classrooms provided by the university for services lacked spiritual feeling. Rabbi Zeiger held "bull sessions" in the fraternity houses to impress upon students the beauty of their Jewish heritage. To raise the student's "self-esteem and pride," he brought distinguished speakers to campus, including historian and rabbi Bertram Korn. Two years after its founding, Hillel was described by student Len Rubin as "the most active, most energetic religious organization on the campus. It is awake; moving."[28]

When Hillel held its first High Holidays on campus in 1936, it began the first Reform services in the area. The service, with music department faculty performing Kol Nidre on violin and piano, was attended by 125 "students, faculty, and townspeople." A Passover seder drew 150, including President Graham. Campus Judaism was liberal and ecumenical. With separate Reform and Orthodox services Hillel pioneered the multiprayer group congregation that became a synagogue model a generation later.[29]

Jews did not appear on UNC or Duke faculty rosters in appreciable numbers until the 1930s. This situation was typical nationally. The liberal arts and professional schools were bastions of anti-Semitism. In 1932 Dean M. T. Van Hecke of the UNC Law School wrote that he doubted "the wisdom" of hiring a *Harvard Law Review* editor who was a Jew.[30] The paucity of numbers also reflected a Jewish prejudice against heading toward a South that Jews regarded as a backwater of provincialism and racial hatred. The opening of Duke Medical School brought the first significant number of Jewish faculty to the Durham campus. Prior to World War II both schools welcomed European émigrés, some of whom were scholars of international renown.

Before 1930 the UNC faculty included only a few members with Jewish names. Albert Shapiro taught Spanish from 1922 to 1926, rising to associate professor. Valdie Ephraim Levin was assistant professor of economics from 1929 to 1930. At Duke Jews were confined largely to the medical program. When Trinity College had first considered founding a medical school, President William Few had consulted the noted scientist Abraham Flexner, who had prepared a report on medical education for the Carnegie Foundation. The school's first faculty, imported from Johns Hopkins, included Jews, and several medical students remained as faculty. In 1932 Frederick Bernheim was appointed director of pharmacology, a post he would hold for thirty-two years.

William Perlzweig served as chief biochemist of Duke Hospital. The

Russian-born Perlzweig was a nationally recognized nutritionist, and his work with vitamins helped eliminate pellagra. Olga Marx, Perlzweig's wife, published poetry and translations of classical literature under her maiden name. In 1938 Philip Handler of the University of Illinois was appointed professor of physiology and nutrition. Handler was pointed to Duke by his friend Dr. Abram Sachar, national Hillel director, who encouraged him to become Duke's Hillel director, a position he held informally. The young, brilliant Handler published more than two hundred papers and the textbook *Principles of Biochemistry,* and he won decorations from Austria, Poland, and Belgium.[31]

UNC also began hiring Jews in the 1930s. Albert Suskin, who taught Latin at UNC from 1936 to 1945, was the son of an east European immigrant storekeeper in New Bern. His mobility, the move from small-town mercantilism to an academic career, anticipated generational changes that would transform North Carolina Jewry. Louis Osgood Kattsoff taught in the philosophy department from 1935 to 1945. He and his wife helped found Hillel, and he was recalled as a father figure to Jewish students. Edward Bernstein served on the faculty from 1934 to 1945, rising to professor of economics. A Reform Jew, he, too, was instrumental in establishing Hillel.

The most distinguished Jewish faculty member at UNC was Milton Rosenau, an epidemiologist who arrived in 1935 from Harvard Medical School. Rosenau was the first chairman of the Department of Public Health and in 1940 became its first dean when it was elevated to a school. Its building bears his name. "One of the most eminent men of science in the United States," Rosenau wrote hundreds of articles and more than ten volumes including, his definitive text, *Preventive Medicine and Hygiene.* As an American-born Reform Jew of German origin, Rosenau never affiliated with local Jewry, but he had been active in Jewish refugee work in the 1920s. In 1938 he held national board memberships with the American Jewish Committee and the Union of American Hebrew Congregations.[32]

In the 1930s, the UNC math and physics departments saw an influx of Jews. Nathan Jacobson of the Institute of Advanced Science in Princeton taught mathematics from 1937 to 1944, as did Reinhold Baer, a Swiss Jew, in 1937. Oscar Rice was professor of chemistry from 1936 to 1945. Nathan Rosen joined UNC's physics faculty in 1941. While at the Institute for Advanced Science, Rosen had formulated with Albert Einstein and Boris Podolsky the "EPR Paradox," an elaboration of the theory of relativity. Rosen spent eleven years at UNC, rising to professor.[33]

In the 1930s, while UNC wrestled with its medical school quota, several Jews served on the university's board of trustees. Leslie Weil, Laura Weill Cone, and Harriss Newman were all from German families whose North Carolina roots went back generations. Newman in 1933 was a state legislator who chaired the House Appropriations Committee. Cone, daughter of Solomon Cohen Weill, was a philanthropist who had married into the Greensboro textile family. Native southerners, they occupied positions of social as well as political prominence.

With the advent of Nazism local universities received émigré scholars. Southern universities, long regarded as academically inferior, courted émigré scholars, and their reputations rose accordingly. (This was truer for the sciences than for the humanities.) For the scholars their escapes from Europe were harrowing as they took tortuous routes to safety.

In 1934, Duke president William Preston Few received a letter from Edward R. Murrow, assistant secretary of the Emergency Committee in Aid of Displaced German Scholars, offering to place and supplement the salary of a scholar at Duke. Few requested Louis Stern, director of the Psychological Institute of Hamburg who had done pioneering research in the measurement of intelligence, coining the term *intelligence quotient.* Stern, remembered as an exemplary scholar and a kindly soul, died in 1938. At a memorial service in Duke Chapel, Rabbi Zeiger recited kaddish. Zeiger later speculated that Stern died of heartbreak over developments in Europe. He recounted an incident at a Chapel Hill fraternity house when the Sterns and an old friend, Joachim Prinz, the exiled Berlin rabbi, warmly reminisced and then spoke about the crisis abroad. A German exchange student, a Nazi, stood up to explain the Jewish problem, haranguing the crowd with talk of "Blood and Earth." Zeiger read in Stern's face "puzzled pity and sheer compassion" at the "babblings of a barbarian." Zeiger reflected on Stern's love of Germany, how the professor had found Chapel Hill to be "like a little park in Berlin." In 1934 Walter Kempner joined the Duke Medical School, and his rice diet program drew obese patients from around the world.[34]

UNC economist Edward and Edith Bernstein, with the assistance of local Quakers and Jews in Raleigh and Goldsboro, helped sponsor a "surprisingly large influx of refugees" to Chapel Hill from 1938 to 1940. The Bernsteins opened their small home to several families before the émigrés embarked on new lives. Frank Graham and Dean Carroll arranged academic appointments for émigré economists including Irvin Hexner of Czechoslovakia and Franz Guttman of Germany. Georges Lurcy, a Parisian financial advisor to the Rothschilds, entered UNC graduate school and later became a university benefactor.[35]

In 1939 Ernst Manasse of the University of Berlin came to Durham to teach at North Carolina College for Negroes. He had first fled Germany to Italy, where he tutored Jewish refugee children, then to England, and finally to the United States. Out of money and anxious to rejoin his wife and child, who had escaped first to Switzerland and then to Brazil, Manasse applied to more than one hundred colleges before Dr. James Shepard offered him a position. Manasse taught Latin and philosophy at NCC for more than thirty years, and his wife, Marianne, joined the art faculty.[36]

In 1939 Edith and Fritz London arrived in Durham. Fritz London, internationally known for his work in low-temperature physics and quantum mechanics, had taught at the universities of Berlin, Frankfurt, and Oxford. Duke chemist Paul Gross, on a visit to Paris, met London, who was then at the Sorbonne, and offered him a position. London came to Duke for a semester, returning to Paris to retrieve his wife and child who had been stranded there for medical reasons. Edith London, a curator at the Duke art library, was a widely honored artist whose work was collected by the North Carolina Museum of Art. After her experiences in Europe, she was shocked to learn at a meeting of faculty wives that Duke kept a quota for Jewish students.

In 1941 Raphael Lemkin of the University of Warsaw law faculty came to Duke. Lemkin stayed in Durham for two years, the Nazi persecutions having turned him into a driven man. As early as 1933 Lemkin, a public prosecutor, had anticipated a possible Holocaust and appealed to the League of Nations to ban mass murder. Wounded in the Polish resistance, Lemkin was carried through German lines to Lithuania and then fled to Stockholm. There he purloined diplomatic dispatches that proved the barbarity of German occupation policies. He took these to Moscow and after the German invasion fled to Siberia. Professor Malcolm McDermott of Duke, who had met Lemkin in Warsaw, by chance came across a French manuscript Lemkin had mailed far and wide in the desperate hope of finding a position. Duke cabled an offer to him. McDermott asked the local Jewish community to help put his case before the American government. Henry Bane interceded for B'nai B'rith. In 1944 Lemkin published *Axis Rule in Occupied Europe* in which he coined the word *genocide*. At war's end Lemkin, who lost forty-nine relatives to the Nazis, went to London and Nuremberg to prepare indictments against war criminals. Lemkin wrote the Genocide Convention that the United Nations adopted in 1948.[37]

Alfred and Hilde Brauer arrived at UNC in 1942. Brauer, who had served as a German artillery commander in World War I, had a faculty appointment at the University of Berlin, but he fled Germany after Kristallnacht in 1938. He spent three years at the Institute of Advanced Studies at Princeton, where he collaborated with Einstein before joining UNC's mathematics department. The Brauers felt "very welcome" and "loved Chapel Hill immediately," Hilde Brauer recalled.

Prejudice and Partnership

For southerners the Jew's racial identity was not fixed and, consequently, neither was their social place. Racial thinking confused biology, religion, and culture, and prejudice in practice reflected the incoherence of the underlying ideology. The newly founded Hope Valley Country Club included a restrictive clause in its charter but then invited the membership of two southern-born Jews of German origin, Ben Kronheimer and Harry Lehman. Although they passed muster as ethnic white southerners, they declined membership on principle as Jews. One newly arrived Durham merchant, a native North Carolinian of Dutch-Jewish ancestry, intermarried into a prominent Protestant family, converted to Christianity, and became a deacon of his church. Everyone in the community, except apparently for the man himself, regarded him as a Jew. When Jews complained about the exclusionary policy of Hope Valley, club officials referred to the membership of this converted Jew as proof that they did not discriminate. Southerners might open doors to "white" Jews, the acculturated Germans, while closing them to "black" Jews, the east European parvenus.

Small-town residents, regardless of region, often expressed a general anti-Semitism while believing in the exceptionality of the local Jew, who was friend and neighbor. Southerners drew lines between their Jewish neighbors and mythic alien New Yorkers. "The native North Carolina Jew is an entirely different personality from those in the large cities," Kemp Battle asserted. This "exemption mechanism" psychologically sanctioned anti-Semitism while allowing for warm personal relations with local Jews.[38]

A story told about two Chapel Hill characters—Seaton Lloyd, owner of a hardware store, and Dr. Simeon Nathan, the "Jewish veterinarian" from a southern family—illustrates this bifurcated attitude. Seaton's daughter had moved to New York to study voice and became engaged to marry a northern Jewish boy. Nathan walked into Brady's Restaurant, where he found Seaton sitting at the bar overcome by tears. When the "good doctor" inquired as to what the problem was, Seaton replied, "[My] best singing daughter is going to get married." Nathan offered congratulations, but Seaton rebuffed the compliment with the question, "What would you do if'n your daughter was going to marry with a damn Jew?" The anecdote ends with the comment that "Dr. Nathan was the first to go downtown and tell this story." Seaton obviously neither intended any insult to his Jewish friend nor recognized this fellow southerner as cut from the same fabric as the New Yorker. "Doc" Nathan, a massive man of three hundred pounds, was one of Chapel Hill's most colorful characters, and his veterinary offices served as a town social center.[39]

Although the anti-Semitic voices of a Father Coughlin or the America Firsters were not generally well received in the South, the North Carolina mountains were home to two of the nation's most notorious German sympathizers. William Dudley Pelley, a New Englander, headquartered his Aryan militia, the Silver Shirt Legion, in Asheville from 1932 to 1941. The "American Hitler" had little local following, and in 1941 he removed to Indiana, where federal authorities jailed him for sedition. More obnoxious was U.S. senator Robert "Our Bob" Reynolds. The bumptious Reynolds had stunned the state in 1932 by winning election as a throwback populist, a trust-busting champion of the working man. After his re-election in 1938 as a New Dealer, Reynolds broke with Roosevelt and turned virulently isolationist, the only southerner to vote against Lend-Lease. His anti-alien, anti-communist crusade revived suspicions of Jewish radicalism and populist canards of Jewish international conspiracy. The demagogic Reynolds played to nativist sentiment in North Carolina, which, as he often repeated, "had less aliens than any state." Although Reynolds denounced Nazi persecutions—his argument was economic rather than racial—from 1939 to 1942 his American Vindicator organization and newsletter made room for such Jew-baiters as Gerald L. K. Smith and Gerald B. Winrod. Reynolds employed a Nazi agent and appeared on a platform with Fritz Kuhn, leader of the German-American Bund. A fervid immigration restrictionist, Reynolds in 1939 opposed the Wagner-Rogers bill to admit twenty thousand mostly Jewish German refugee children. The *Voelkischer Beobachter,* a Nazi organ, quoted Reynolds: "I am absolutely against the United States waging war for the purpose of protecting Jews anywhere in the world."[40]

The state press joined the national media in reviling Reynolds. With its army bases and military traditions, North Carolina, like the South generally, tended to be interventionist though, as Henry Bane recalled, Reynolds spoke for a "segment." Back home his antics met with a "dump Reynolds" movement. When Reynolds lectured on immigration in Chapel Hill in 1940, the audience responded with derisive laughter. Facing certain defeat, Reynolds declined to run in 1944. The *Durham Morning Herald* expressed relief to be free of his "nauseating drivel."[41]

With heightened anti-Semitism here and abroad, local Jews acted, as did such national Jewish agencies as the Anti-Defamation League and American Jewish Committee, to enlist non-Jewish support in Jewish defense. A convocation of three faiths—Judaism, Catholicism, and Protestantism—became the standard forum to make a public statement against anti-Semitism. Judaism took its place as an American religion in a country historically defined as Protestant. The 1934 North Carolina Association of Jewish Women convention at the Washington Duke Hotel was an interreligious meeting aimed at fighting Nazi activities both in the state and in the country. A Jew, Protestant, and Catholic made declarations of faith.

Jews found a public champion in UNC president Frank Graham. The most prominent southerner in the National Conference of Christians and Jews, Graham hosted a three-faiths regional gathering in Chapel Hill in 1936. He lent his name to Jewish causes from the B'nai B'rith in Asheville to the Hebrew University in Jerusalem, and his correspondents included Professor Morris R. Cohen, physicist Albert Einstein, and novelist Ludwig Lewisohn. Graham supported a boycott of the Berlin Olympics and collaborated with Rabbi Stephen Wise in imploring the British to open Palestine to Jewish immigration. Secretary of the Treasury Henry Morgenthau Jr. wanted Graham to head the first War Refugee Board. The Hebrew Union College–Jewish Institute of Religion awarded Graham an honorary doctorate as a "disciple of the Hebrew prophets."[42]

In the 1930s Jews worked for the first time to build institutional links to the civic community beyond the personalism that had traditionally governed Jewish-Christian relations. Rabbi Israel Mowshowitz, who arrived in 1937, became the first Durham rabbi to join the ministerial association and to speak regularly before civic clubs. At the Rotary Club he denounced Hitlerism as a "contagious disease" and delivered an ecumenical address at the First Baptist Church. In 1938, the Seaboard Zionist Conference was cosponsored by the Durham Chamber of Commerce, and radio station WDNC broadcast the speeches. In the keynote address, Governor Clyde Hoey praised the Jews' contribution to civilization. When

University of North Carolina president Frank Graham (far right) was an indefatigable friend of the Jewish people, whether fostering Jewish student groups, fighting admissions quotas, or advocating Zionism. Here Graham poses with the left-wing Jewish Labor Committee, which agitated to open American doors to Jews from Nazi Europe. (From the Frank Porter Graham Papers #1819, Southern Historical Collection, Wilson Library, University of North Carolina at Chapel Hill)

Durham Mizrachi sponsored a speech by Rabbi Joseph Lookstein of Yeshiva University, Duke president Few introduced the speaker. The event was held in the horseshoe of Duke's football stadium to accommodate the crowd of Jews and Gentiles.[43]

Responding to the crisis of European Jewry, a revived United Jewish Appeal (UJA) launched a national drive in 1939. Locally, E. J. Evans recruited Marshall Spears, a retired judge, to serve as chairman. For the first time in twenty years Jews were asking the Gentile community to help them, Evans noted publicly, and he pledged that donations would assist both Jewish and non-Jewish refugees. At a breakfast meeting attended by one hundred Jews and Gentiles, it was reported that Jews had contributed $3,000 and that Christians had given more than $1,500. In 1940 the Durham Committee for the Care of European Children formed, with J. H. Marion Jr. as president and E. J. Evans as director.[44] This interfaith committee also pledged to assist non-Jews as well as Jews.

Nationally, Jews succeeded philanthropically in raising funds for refugee relief, but they failed to change public opinion or redirect Roosevelt administration policy to open doors to European Jewry. In universalizing an essentially Jewish problem, local Jews reflected the insecurity that Jews expressed nationally, that is, that popular anti-Semitism would infect America, too, if Jews pushed too aggressively to protect their own kind. Polls in 1937 and 1938 revealed that American Jews were sharply divided on easing refugee quotas and that a significant number were isolationist. Even such an ardent Zionist and rescue advocate as Stephen Wise, who spoke in Durham, still did not see the Jewish European situation as exceptional. In face of widespread public opposition to easing refugee quotas and fears of anti-Semitism, the national Jewish leadership preferred that non-Jewish agencies assume the lead in opening the quota gates for Jewish refugee children. Durham Jews were acting in concert with an organized national campaign to win pubic opinion and gain political support. While Senator Reynolds, as noted above, opposed the Wagner-Rogers bill that would admit twenty thousand refugee children, Frank Graham lobbied on its behalf. Wagner-Rogers died in Congress. American Jewry nationally was divided ethnically and ideologically, and it lacked the cohesion to rally American public opinion or to influence government policy.[45]

Despite the local Jews' success in enlisting the town's elites, one incident in 1940 revealed the presence of local anti-Semitism. Moses Levy, the acquitted bootlegger, was indicted on a bad-check charge. He claimed that a wholesaler had deposited his postdated check prematurely. Levy was convicted, and the judge, widely regarded as anti-Semitic, handed down a harsh sentence of three years. Attorney Henry Bane appealed the conviction to the state supreme court, which sustained Levy's guilty verdict but reversed legal precedents and established new ground in check-kiting cases still known as the "Levy Law." Rabbi Israel Mowshowitz pleaded in court for leniency for Levy, but the judge treated the rabbi with contempt. As the rabbi spoke, the judge sang, "I shall not be moved." Bane was appalled, as were other lawyers.[46]

Jews saw themselves as political outsiders. Not until 1936, when Simeon Nathan of Chapel Hill, the town coroner and a county health officer, won a two-year seat on the Orange County Board of Commissioners did a local Jew achieve electoral office. Nathan, however, was an acculturated southerner descended from Confederate soldiers. Several Jews from the east European community held appointed political posts but failed to win elections. Henry Bane designed the Recorder's Court, and by secret vote of the Durham Bar he was selected to be its first judge. When he ran for election, however, he was narrowly defeated. The newspaper identified Sigmund Meyer, who presided over the Durham County Board of Elections for more than a decade, as "among the better known young Durham attorneys" and speculated about his political future. After serving as an assistant judge of the Recorder's Court, he lost elections in 1940 and 1952 for a permanent seat. Several Jews ascribed these failures to backroom deals made by anti-Semites. The attitude in Durham's political establishment was that "you don't want a person of his kind sitting in judgment on people of our own kind," Lehman Brady believed. E. J. Evans's leadership in community fund-raising drives in the 1940s laid the groundwork for a postwar political career.[47]

Local Jews who aspired in electoral politics did not succeed. Despite their suspicions of anti-Semitism, Jews were making inroads into the hierarchy of leadership. Nationally, the election of Franklin Roosevelt brought Jews prominently into American political life, with Jews serving in the cabinet and as architects of the New Deal. This precedent would not be felt locally until the 1950s, when the barriers fell decisively.

Blacks and Jews: Conflicts of Interest

Black-Jewish relations reflected much of the ambivalence that prevailed in Jewish-Gentile relations. In their dealings with blacks Jews balanced feelings of prejudice, friendship, and self-interest. Poverty forced Jews into black neighborhoods where they encountered both resistance and acceptance. Race relations in Durham were not as embittered or as violent as elsewhere in the South. Southern civility was capable of transcending race. Durham, too, supported a black bourgeoisie that had common interests with Jews. Some Jews and blacks across class lines spoke of each other with respect and even warmth. Yet, Jews as whites inherited a racial code and an economic system that gave them advantage. They made profits from blacks as tenants, customers, or low-paid employees. In this regard Jews were like other white ethnic southerners. Nor did all Jews hold liberal attitudes toward the people whom they called coloreds or shvartzers. One dry-goods merchant was remembered for his blackface routines at community socials. Nonetheless, the Jews' own recent experience of poverty and discrimination also inspired sympathies. In the minds of Jews, at least, their racial attitudes were more liberal than those of their white Gentile neighbors.

If not politically allied, Jews and African Americans in Durham had a sympathetic relationship. When Jews built their synagogue in 1921, C. C. Spaulding and Dr. Aaron Moore of North Carolina Mutual contributed. Jews, too, donated to black churches. The sense of Jews as friends of blacks was reinforced by the Rosenwald Fund, which in the 1920s rebuilt eight Durham County schools. In 1939, when Durham Jews appealed for help from the Gentile community to assist European Jewry, Spaulding and J. H. Wheeler of the Mechanics and Farmers Bank led a UJA drive in the African American community. The sympathy of Durham blacks contrasts with the observation of George Schuyler of the *Pittsburgh Courier,* who upon touring the South, noted disapprovingly that "Negroes of all classes . . . are quite unconcerned about . . . the Nazi persecution of the Jews."[48]

With the exception of one or two Greek mercantile families Jewish grocers were the only whites to live in the heart of the black neighborhood. Living above or next to their stores, these Jews came to know blacks intimately. As a child Sam Margolis had black playmates, although he did not attend school with them. He walked two miles daily to attend the white Morehead School. Once his father, a short man, had an altercation with a black customer over the sale of sliced meat. The grocer pulled a gun from under the counter, and the customer tried wresting it away. The fight carried into the street, where a crowd gathered. Finally, a large black man, a railroad fireman, separated them, calming the crowd until the police arrived. The incident made young Sam a lifelong friend of black people. His father, who expanded his grocery into a food wholesale business, gave a black mill worker, Thomas Bailey, some food to peddle to earn extra cash. Eventually, Margolis turned over the ownership of a store to Bailey. When the "well known Jewish merchant" Israel Gordon was mugged at his Hayti grocery in 1938, the *Carolina Times,* the local African American newspaper, noted that he was "highly respected and much liked" and that "many have expressed their regrets."[49]

Lois Ray, an African American schoolteacher, recalled cordial relations with the Hayti Jews in the 1930s and 1940s. Local blacks, she noted, regarded the Jewish grocers as part of the community: "We didn't think of them as different." When her mother and she would meet the Katzes, Levys, or Margolises in their stores or at the Mechanics and Farmers Bank, they stopped to exchange family news. "They seemed to talk about whatever happened in the neighborhood as if they were a part of it," Ray recalled. Mose Levy was "super," Ray explained. "The store was well pa-tronized because we were glad to get a bargain and get good produce."

Jews, too, patronized African American businesses. Louis Stadiem pur-chased produce from black farmers who patronized his pawnshop. Poorer Jews turned to Mechanics and Farmers as the only Durham bank that would extend them credit. Immigrants, such as the grocer Morris Katz, felt more comfortable doing business with blacks than with the white, down-town bankers. A black contractor, a family friend, built the Katz's home.

"No matter how much we may have sympathized with the blacks," reflected pawnbroker Leon Dworsky, "we had to protect our own posi-tions first." For most Jews their relationship with blacks was that of em-ployer and employee. In southern fashion female houseworkers tended the children, and several Jews recall being raised by an "Aunt Molly" or an "Aunt Zola," black women who became "family." Some houseworkers picked up a few words of Yiddish and learned the art of making chopped liver or setting a Passover table. Jews were landlords in black neighbor-hoods, purchasing rental properties and then refinancing to increase their holdings. This practice was not confined to Jews and included much of the town's business and political leadership. A (non-Jewish) truck driver in 1938 commented that he intended to buy property in the black section because "nigger houses are the best paying."[50] Jews described their tenants as polite and reliable. Durham Jewish merchants hired black clerks well before it had become acceptable among Gentile storekeepers. In Chicago and New York, by contrast, blacks in the 1930s and 1940s rioted against Jewish merchants who refused to hire blacks.

Segregation and labor strife drew a few academic Jews toward the po-litical left. Chapel Hill since the 1930s had a reputation for progressive and sometimes radical politics. The campus supported a unit of the Young Communist League, later renamed the Carolina Youth Federation. Its leader in 1936 was Bill Levitt, a student from New York. Levitt worked with a group that supported a Burlington workers' strike. When Levitt and Professor E. E. Erickson met and dined with Durham's black leadership, they incurred public scorn for openly defying the racial codes. In the late 1930s the two men picketed white-owned stores in Hayti that refused to hire blacks. They succeeded in forcing some businesses such as the A & P to begin hiring black clerks. Sidney Rittenberg of Charleston had chosen to attend UNC in 1937 because of its "reputation for free expression and progressive thinking." Rittenberg, who called Graham one of the "great-est influences" of his life, quit school in 1940 to work in the labor and civil rights movements. (Rittenberg lived in Communist China after 1949, where he was imprisoned during the Cultural Revolution; he returned to UNC in 1982 to complete his bachelor of arts degree and later joined the faculty.) Student radicals did not consciously think of themselves as Jews in their activism, and other Jews regarded them as "too noisy."[51]

Ethnic Jews

Trends of Jewish disaffection observed in the 1920s became more pronounced in the 1930s. "Religiously inconsistent behavior, based on nostalgia and the communal elements of synagogue life, were incomprehensible to the immigrants' children born in America," historian Jeffrey Gurock observes.[52] The aging of the immigrant generation and the rise of an American-born youth transformed the religious character of the community. Older European-born Jews still clung to tradition. The synagogue—with its mikva, women's balcony, and Yiddish sermons—offered the security of the old ways. Jewish youth, eager to escape the immigrant heritage and to establish themselves socially and economically as Americans, turned away from the synagogue and its rituals. For secularized Jews in the 1930s, Judaism was not a pervasive way of life but was compartmentalized as a religion, an affiliation. To draw young, unaffiliated Jews into the congregation Joe Hockfield inaugurated a junior category with reduced dues. He organized children's services on Saturday mornings. Hockfield succeeded in bringing about ten families into full membership, but even then he had to overcome fears of older members that his efforts would compromise the congregation's Orthodoxy. The depression aggravated the problems of disaffection. Food and shelter became more urgent priorities than congregational dues. To keep the synagogue afloat, Ladies Aid paid the street assessment and heating bills and contributed to the mortgage payments. The synagogue resorted to bingo games to help pay the rabbi. In the evening the treasurer went door to door to solicit funds.

Women remained outside the ritual and governance but were entrusted with welfare and philanthropy. The Ladies Aid Society served as a congregational auxiliary, cooking for banquets and holding card parties. Their annual Purimspiels packed the hall. The plays were conducted in Yiddish, without scripts, and the ad-libbing provoked riotous laughter. Women reversed gender roles, donning patriarchal steel-wool beards to take revenge on the men. Ladies Aid sought to educate women, many of whom had received scant religious instruction. The rabbi was a frequent speaker, lecturing on such topics as Jewish history, the meaning of the *shofar* (ram's horn) and the fate of Jews in Germany. The cantor led them in singing holiday songs. Generational changes were at work as the older immigrant women yielded influence. In 1938 the society affiliated with the Orthodox Union, but younger women were pressing for membership in the Conservative Sisterhood. When Jeanette Fink arrived in 1940, Ladies Aid still held its meetings in Yiddish. Fink raised her hand to make a point, but when she answered in English these "pillars of the community" shouted at her, "*Reden* (Speak) Yiddish!" She could not speak Yiddish, however. Jews across generations were no longer speaking the same language.[53]

Durham's Americanized Orthodox congregation was typical of midwestern and southern communities outside metropolitan areas. American Orthodoxy on the Jewish periphery accommodated diversity. The Orthodox Union governing body lacked publicly defined membership criteria, and it enrolled congregations that no longer maintained gender-segregated seating.[54] At Beth-El synagogue governance remained in the hands of immigrant old-timers who resisted the demands of husbands and wives who wanted to share pews, American-born youth who wanted English-language prayers and sermons, and intermarried men who wanted to maintain membership. The struggle in Durham was whether to be inclusionary or exclusionary as Jews renegotiated the boundaries of Jewish identity.

Economic necessity exacerbated by the depression made adherence to Sabbath laws difficult. Shopkeepers were at the mercy of their clientele. For mill workers Friday was payday, and merchants stayed open late to serve them. Saturday was the farmers' market day. Orthodox Jews sought to preserve the spirit if not the letter of the law. S. H. Dworsky kept his pawnshop open on the Sabbath, verbally passing instructions to his Gentile employees but not handling money or touching a light switch. Some Jewish men attended services on Saturday morning while their wives and children ran the business. Most others simply worked as usual. Some Jews who employed Gentiles now kept their stores open on Rosh Hashanah. Attendance at services declined.

The second generation preserved Jewish associations, particularly for their children, but these often took culturally blended southern-Jewish forms. For most children, the Jewish community offered a network of friends, and because of community intramarriages cousins were plentiful. The congregation organized a Jewish girl scout troop, and the teenagers eagerly joined Junior Hadassah. The girls held "quarter parties" at each other's homes on Saturday nights; the entry fee was used for refreshments or contributed to charity.

For youth, their community extended beyond their Durham neighbors to Jews across the state. There were weekend trips to Asheville, Wilmington, Greensboro, Charlotte, and Raleigh for socials and dances. "A bunch of us would hop in a car and go to the dances that were arranged by synagogues and Jewish social groups all around the area," Sam Margolis remembered. Every Thanksgiving Durham and Raleigh Sisterhood alternated sponsorship of a dance that drew three hundred to four hundred from Virginia and the Carolinas. In the summers families rented homes in Carolina Beach, where the children met cousins and friends from other southern Jewish communities. "Everyone knew everyone else's business," Yetta Brandt remembered. "We were all really close." This social bonding network, reinforced by kinship ties, was a defining feature of southern Jewish identity.

The proximity of two universities alleviated one critical problem for small-town southern Jews: the lack of Jewish spouses. In one small Louisiana town, for example, sixteen of eighteen marriages from 1925 to 1955 involving Jews were interfaith. In Durham–Chapel Hill Jewish students and soldiers, whose numbers at times doubled that of the community, supplied a stream of potential spouses. Students piled into cars looking for dates. Durham families put up Duke and UNC students for Jewish holidays. "It was a great deal of fun, especially for the girls," several Durham women recalled. "There were so many boys from Carolina and Duke. . . . At the beginning of the year you went to the synagogue for the High Holy Days, you put on your best outfit, and the fellows from the university saw you and the phone calls would start coming. . . . We did not really need the Christians." For Durham boys it meant that at "winter time the girls didn't hardly look at us," Sam Margolis recalled. UNC student Sigmund Meyer met his future wife, Anna Switzer, when she came to Chapel Hill with a carload of Durham girls. On Saturday nights the Nachamson family, with eight daughters, held an open house for Jewish college boys looking for dates.[55]

Parents sought to Americanize their children, to adapt them to the world in which they would live. "When people used to ask my mother what nationality she was, she said American," Pat Silver remembered. Her sister Sadie Silver Goodman added, "Well, that's what she was. She was so proud of being American." Some parents were unhappy when their children brought home Christian friends, but the Silvers' mother always welcomed them.

The community held conflicting attitudes toward interdating and intermarriage. The prohibitions were stronger for girls than they were for boys, whom many parents assumed were less controllable. Expressing a common sentiment, Sarah Cohen believed it was beyond her power to stop her sons from interdating, but she refused to allow her daughter to do so. The Nachamson girls could not date Gentile boys. Hazel Gladstein Wishnov stated, "I never dated a Christian boy in my life." With all the local Jewish college students she always felt "very, very popular."

Not everyone felt this way. Interdating became more common. Intermarriages began occurring in the late 1930s. Several Jewish women married Christian men and converted, including at least one who became an active church member. Although no one openly degraded them, the converts incurred the community's disapproval. "You disgraced the whole family if you intermarried," Abe Stadiem recalled. When one of Charlie Wilson's sons declared his intention to intermarry, Stadiem added, "his father kicked him out of the house." He also recalled a religious boy from the Levin family who left town after he intermarried. One intermarried man who did not convert contributed generously to his wife's church until his divorce, but when he died the Chevra Kadisha buried him. He was an alcoholic, and the community regarded him as pathetic. Other intermarried couples found a degree of acceptance. When a Silver woman married a Christian, her mother was hurt but came to appreciate her son-in-law.

Two Jewish men who intermarried attempted to maintain congregational ties, even to raise their children as Jews, but the synagogue board would not allow non-Jewish spouses to be members. In at least two cases Christian women converted to Judaism after marrying Jews. One became a highly respected synagogue member, but the other turned to Christianity after her husband died, as did her sons, who had each received a Bar Mitzvah. Overall, intermarriages in the 1930s were still uncommon, numbering perhaps a half-dozen individuals in a community of 350.

Intermarriage was but one sign of changing community values. The Orthodoxy of the synagogue often alienated younger, liberal Jews, and disputes developed. On occasions a rabbi would not perform a funeral, circumcision, or Bar Mitzvah if he thought the family insufficiently observant. Ethel Mae Zuckerman Bernson recalled, "When my grandfather died, the neighbors had brought in non-kosher foods and sent potted plants. . . . The rabbi came in and said, 'You cannot hold a minyan here; it is not a Jewish home.'" In such cases congregation members versed in Jewish practice stepped forward to perform the rites.

Orthodoxy was under challenge. With restricted immigration there was no longer an influx of religious Jews to renew the community's Orthodoxy. The emerging second and third American-born generation was educated in public schools and less immersed in the culture of Yiddishkeit than their European-born elders. Parents wanted their children to think of themselves as Jews but were less concerned with ritual and practice.

Reform Jews

The effects of acculturation were seen even more strongly in the few Jews of German descent who persisted into the third and fourth generation, principally the Levy and Kronheimer families. Culturally they were southern, and their Jewishness also tended to be far more attenuated. None converted, though, and all readily acknowledged themselves to be Jews. The Kronheimers fit the stereotype of Germans as uptown Jews who were wealthy and cosmopolitan. Mattie Lehman Goldberg, Ben Kronheimer's niece, wrote that the family identified "proudly as Jewish." For many years Ben was listed as a special donor to the Jewish Publication Society. On High Holidays the Kronheimers closed their department store, and the family gathered in their living room, where Birdie Lehman, Kronheimer's widowed sister, read prayers in English.[56] This custom of parlor prayer gatherings was common among North Carolina's small-town Jews who lacked synagogue affiliation. As did the Levys, the Kronheimers turned to Richmond, where they had family ties if they needed a rabbi.

Simeon Nathan, who had moved to Chapel Hill in the 1920s, was unique among area Jews as an Old South Jew descended from Savannah and Charleston colonial families. His wife, Hattie, took their daughter on weekly treks to Temple Beth Or in Raleigh to be confirmed. Their two sons, however, received "not much" religious education, and Marx Nathan occasionally attended Protestant services with friends, although not from conviction but simply for companionship.

In contrast to urban Jewry, Durham's Germans and east Europeans were cordial if not intimate. Durham Jews spoke warmly of the Kronheimers, especially of Lily. A Sunday school teacher to the Orthodox Beth-El children, she was recalled as "a grand old lady." Durham Jews were well aware of the ethnic divide in Jewry and, with reason, suspected that North Carolina's *"Deitchen"* (Germans) looked down on them. Miriam Weil of

Goldsboro warned her niece in a letter about dating a Durham boy: "All of the Jewish people in Durham that I have ever heard of are of a very ordinary sort."[57] (This "very ordinary" boy, Louis Jaffe, would later win a Pulitzer Prize as a newspaper editor.) Although they did not form a local subcommunity, the Levys and Kronheimers maintained social and family links to German Jewish families beyond Durham.

Reform Jews were isolated. Kronheimer's grandniece, Carol Lehman Goldberg, once attended Rosh Hashanah services at Greensboro's Reform temple. She observed that it was a novel experience. Inspired, she returned home to make *latkes,* traditional pancakes, for the first time in her life (albeit with bacon grease). She eventually married a non-Jewish German. The Levy women held token membership in Jewish organizations, but efforts to enlist the Levy men in B'nai B'rith or Zionist campaigns received sharp rebuffs. Low birth rates diminished the subcommunity, and both the Levy and Kronheimer households included adult unmarried family members. Neither left Jewish descendants in town. Levy daughters found Jewish spouses out of town. Roy Levy, after his mother's death, intermarried. Spinsterhood and bachelorhood were a "social tradition" among German Jews, a study of Portland, Oregon, Jewry revealed.[58]

Several Reform Jews of German origin married into the east European community. Sigmund Meyer was raised in the eastern North Carolina hamlet of Enfield, where his German-born parents had settled in 1873. The young attorney had never set foot in a synagogue until his marriage to Anna Switzer, but Meyer, a tolerant man who was religiously liberal, became a long-standing officer of the Orthodox congregation.

For Reform Jews being observant or creating community would have required exceptional commitment. The few German Jewish families were aging, intermarrying, and dying, and none sustained itself in the area as Jews beyond a second generation. The local future of Reform Judaism lay in the hands of younger Jews descended from east European families who were religious liberals and felt alienated from Orthodoxy. Their numbers would be strengthened, as the Orthodox community had once been, by new migrations. Not until the early 1960s, however, would Reform Jews be sufficiently numerous to form a congregation.

In larger Jewish communities nationally in the 1920s and 1930s a more accommodating Conservative Judaism appealed to second-generation Jews, but Durham lacked numbers and resources to factionalize. Durham Jewry's profile was typical of communities that evolved toward Conservatism in its longevity, Americanization, and upward mobility, but the process lagged in Durham, which remained a cohesive ethnic enclave. It retained a nominally traditional synagogue for Jews who had largely abandoned Orthodoxy in their daily lives. "Hybrid synagogues" were typical in the South and Midwest, historian Jeffrey Gurock observes. Such religiously inconsistent behavior was typical of an acculturating Jewry. In a report titled "Orthodoxy in the South," a New Orleans rabbi noted the tendency of southern Jews to send their children to Reform Sunday schools. Durham Jews had no such alternative, however.[59]

Rabbi Chaim Williamofsky, who arrived from Hendersonville in 1930, recognized that his congregants were loosening their Jewish ways. The bearded Williamofsky was a rabbinic scholar who had attended the Slobodka yeshiva and been ordained in Lumseh. He had emigrated from Poland in 1925 and joined a brother in the North Carolina mountains. He, too, delivered sermons in Yiddish. On Friday afternoons women lined up at his home with chickens, which he slaughtered in his basement. A pleasant, well-liked man, Williamofsky was reappointed in 1934, becoming the longest-serving rabbi in three decades. The newspaper commented, "One of the most popular men ever to hold the synagogue pastorate, Rabbi Williamofsky is loved among Jews and Gentiles alike." In 1937 he left, chastising the congregants for their inability to pay him a salary that could support his wife and six children. During the depression he had been reduced to knocking on the doors of Jewish stores at closing hours to collect his salary.[60]

Rabbi Israel Mowshowitz, Williamofsky's successor, was a graduate of Yeshiva College. He was Durham's first college-educated rabbi, and Durham was his first pulpit. Although born in eastern Europe, he was culturally American. Young and newly married, the clean-shaven rabbi appealed to religious modernists. He enrolled in a doctoral program in psychology at Duke and took interest in college football. He read the congregation as "traditionalist": "The community was fairly Orthodox, Southern style. There was not really any Sabbath observance. Most Jews drove on the Sabbath, kept their stores open on the Sabbath, but they considered themselves an Orthodox congregation. Kashruth was observed by a large number of the congregants. There was a mikva in the synagogue, and it was used infrequently. . . . There was a great thrust on the part of some people to become Conservative, but there was no Reform tendency." Mowshowitz introduced change. He began late-Friday-night services, followed by an *oneg* ("joy," a social reception) Shabbat. More women moved down from the balcony. He delivered his sermons in English, which prompted an old-timer to storm down the aisle protesting, *"Ehr macht goyim fon unser!"* ("He's making Gentiles of us!"). Mowshowitz recognized "conflict within the Jewish community about ritual, about the nature of the congregation." To assist the rabbi, the Reverend Morris Klavan arrived from upstate New York in 1937 to serve as cantor and schochet. The Judaism that Mowshowitz instituted was closer to Modern Orthodoxy than to east European Orthodoxy. Modern Orthodoxy sought to adapt Jewish law to contemporary needs and was willing to find common ground with non-Orthodox Jews. Traditionalists suspected that Modern Orthodoxy was only a transitional stage to Conservative Judaism.

By 1938 a minority of American Jews belonged to synagogues. In Durham attendance at services declined. Friday night services, rather than the Saturday morning Torah reading, drew more people. "Once-a-year Jew" entered the Jewish lexicon. Yetta Sawilosky Brandt recalled, "We went to shul on the High Holy days and did not really feel pressure to be more active, religious, than that." At a Ladies Aid Society meeting the rabbi admonished the women that "the existence of the folk depends on coming to synagogue."[61]

The purpose of the synagogue as a community center was as much social as religious. It was home to every group from the Boy Scouts to the Ladies Aid Society. Religious celebrations were community events, a chance to "schmooze" with friends. For one fund-raiser each woman embroidered a napkin with her family's names; these were sewn together to form tablecloth quilts for use at banquets. For a Bar Mitzvah everyone gathered Saturday morning at the synagogue—invitations were unnecessary. A *kiddush* (sanctification with wine) was held after the service, and that evening the Ladies Aid cooked and served a banquet in the social hall. Ethnicity, group solidarity, rather than religion, was the bond that unified Jews.

As synagogue membership declined, social clubs, youth groups, and Zionist societies proliferated. Ethnic Jews who were not attached to synagogue ritual filled their need for Jewish association by affiliating with B'nai B'rith or Hadassah. "As a result of the growing catastrophe in Europe in the thirties and early forties, and the parallel crisis in Palestine," Nathan Glazer observed, "hundreds of thousands of Jews who had little or nothing to do with Jewish life were drawn into Jewish activities."[62] Local memberships reached record levels. This renewal was inspired by several families who had arrived in the 1920s—Evans, Nachamson, Lieberman, Rose, Daniel, Ornoff, and Dworsky among them. Strong-willed individuals such as Sara Evans and S. H. Dworsky quickly asserted leadership. Organizations became community power bases, the fiefdoms of families.

With anti-Semitism rising in the 1930s the North Carolina Association of Jewish Women began a statewide membership campaign, which overcame the Jewish ethnic divide. In 1932 a half-dozen women affiliated in Chapel Hill, and by 1936 more than forty Durham women had enrolled. East Europeans increasingly led the NCAJW, and local women achieved state office. Nathan Rosenstein would serve as state president of the men's auxiliary (NCAJM), which formed in 1930. Four years later NCAJM president E. J. Evans welcomed three hundred delegates to a NCAJW-NCAJM convention in Durham. One speaker warned that assimilation had left the German Jews unprepared for Nazism, and Abram Sachar, national Hillel director, delivered an ardently Zionist address. In 1937 the NCAJW passed a resolution calling for aid to German and Polish Jews and for the "upbuilding of Palestine." The NCAJW's twentieth annual convention in April 1941 brought nearly five hundred delegates to Durham after it was transferred from Wilmington for reasons of "national defense."[63]

The Jewish Men's Social Club formed in 1933 and opened second-floor clubrooms downtown. Four years later these clubrooms became home of a revived B'nai B'rith Lodge, Number 1249, named in memory of Nathan Rosenstein. B'nai B'rith anchored the community's social life. The club sponsored picnics, baseball games, and bowling tournaments. Businessmen gathered in the clubrooms for weekly luncheons and nightly card playing. Durham annually sent delegates to district conventions, and members rose in the B'nai B'rith hierarchy. In 1940 the lodge began the state's first chapter of Aleph Zadik Aleph, a fraternity for high school and college students. B'nai B'rith served as the guardian of the community's Americanism. In 1940, Henry Bane emceed a B'nai B'rith–sponsored Armistice Day program that featured an address by Congressman William Umstead on "Peace in America." Bernard Dworsky spoke on Jewish veterans of World War I. Two Durham veterans, Jake Nurkin and Sam Hockfield, presented colors as the audience sang "God Bless America."[64]

Mizrachi, the religious Zionist organization, was chartered locally in 1935 by Nathan Rosenstein and was followed two years later by a women's chapter under Dinah Dworsky. Durhamites traveled to national conventions. Mizrachi president Morton Rubenstein spoke in Durham, and S. H. Dworsky served on the Mizrachi national board. To protest the British government's White Paper limiting Jewish immigration to Palestine, twenty-eight local members signed a protest petition. Its social calendar included such Americanized entertainments as an annual linen show and a wiener roast. A Mizrachi meeting at Beth-El began with a prayer by the rabbi or rebbetzin, a singing of "Hatikvah" (the Zionist anthem) and a talk on the Jewish National Fund or Mizrachi's work in rescuing children. As the religiously Orthodox Zionist organization, Mizrachi complemented Hadassah, whose roots were in socialist Zionism.

In contrast to the "internecine strife" that characterized national Jewry, local Jews overcame religious and ideological differences. Although ideologically opposed in world Zionist politics, Mizrachi and Hadassah cooperated in Durham. Women from both groups went door to door together selling trees for Palestine. The high point of Durham's Zionist activity was the hosting of the Seaboard Zionist Conference in 1938. More than one thousand delegates arrived from eight states to hear a host of Jewish leaders, including Maurice Samuel, the noted author, and the national presidents of Hadassah and the Jewish National Fund. In 1940 Rabbi Mowshowitz led thirteen Durhamites to Washington to hear Chaim Weizmann speak. The spirit that existed locally owed both to the small-town Jewish cohesion and to southern codes of civility. The presence of North Carolina Jews on national boards attested to the democratizing of American Jewish life as rabbinic authorities and New York philanthropists yielded to grassroots advocates.[65]

Across the country local federations put pressure on the national leadership to heal the breaches between Zionists and anti-Zionists, German Jews and east European Jews. Various relief organizations—the Joint Distribution Committee, United Palestine Appeal, and the National Refugee Service—had conducted separate, and sometimes competing, local campaigns. When a national Council of Jewish Federations and Welfare Funds rapidly unified local affiliates across the country in 1932, a Federation of Jewish Charities formed in Durham and began conducting annual United Palestine Appeals. The Council of Jewish Federations finally succeeded in unifying the various campaigns in 1938, shortly after Kristallnacht in Germany. As a one-year experiment, a national United Jewish Appeal for Refugee and Overseas Needs was launched in 1939, and Durham responded immediately by organizing a local UJA campaign. This 1939 drive reflected the unprecedented crisis of world Jewry. Jews across the nation appealed to national organizations across sectarian and racial lines. The UJA became the Jewish community's primary philanthropy.[66]

In the 1930s Durham's Jews affirmed their membership in the global Jewish community by founding Zionist societies and working on behalf of European Jewry. These organizations culturally blended a traditional Jewish concern, the obligation that each Jew is responsible for the other, with an American spirit of democracy and volunteerism. Even though synagogue affiliation declined, the proliferation of Zionist and philan-thropic societies demonstrated a heightened ethnic consciousness. This Jewishness was a response to the international crises of the 1930s, which aroused fears of domestic anti-Semitism. Jews were secure enough as southerners to enlist the non-Jewish community in their efforts to save European Jewry, but, like Jews nationally, they were sufficiently insecure that they sought to universalize the Jewish crisis. The 1930s opened con-flicts in their dual identities as Jews and Americans, and it took a world war to heal the rift.

9 War, Holocaust, and Zion, 1940s to 1950s

World War II hit Durham with a boom. Just after New Year's Day of 1942, the federal government began construction of Camp Butner twelve miles north of the city. "Durham was a peaceful town," the *Durham Sun* reported, "then came the Army. . . . It swarmed down the streets in a never-ending tide, growling like a tidal wave." Camp Butner turned seventy-five thousand rural acres into a military training ground for some fifty thousand soldiers. Thousands of workers arrived to build and run the camp. Housing became scarce, and rents skyrocketed. Shops and restaurants were jammed. "It would be safe to say," the *Sun* observed, "that not a business firm in Durham faced bankruptcy during that first year."[1] Jews were counted among the thousands who served in and serviced Butner. Others came to open businesses in the thriving camp town.

For southerners, no less than for Jews, the war effort was an opportunity to demonstrate their Americanism, their commitment to national ideals. The South was still the most problematic of America's regions, exceptional for its poverty, rural character, and racial segregation. To raise the region to national norms, the Roosevelt administration funneled some $8 billion into the South for defense spending and military facilities. Southern port cities such as Norfolk, Newport News, Charleston, and Pensacola were homes to naval yards, and Marietta and Fort Worth developed aircraft industries.[2] Military camps arose across North Carolina, including massive facilities at Fort Bragg in Fayetteville and Seymour Johnson Air Base in Goldsboro. Durham was typical of southern camp towns. The infusion of money and people injected new life into its industrial and agricultural economy. New migrations allowed Durham to sustain its Jewish numbers. A dozen merchants, some of whom had first passed through town during their military duty, arrived from Michigan, New York, and New Jersey to open stores. Gordon's ladies' shop, Fink's jewelry store, Wolff and Zelon's loan agency, and Golden's pawnshops opened in the 1940s.

The war also transformed the Jewish campus presence. Duke housed army and navy training schools in finance and medicine that by 1943 had more than fifteen hundred men. The navy's Pre-Flight Pilot Training School at UNC by war's end would enroll 18,700 men. Labor shortages forced the campuses to retrench as the federal government raided faculties for the war effort. The Manhattan Project to build an atomic bomb depleted the hard sciences especially. Graduate students, many of Jewish origin, were enlisted to fill the vacancies.

As they had in World War I, Durham boys flocked to the flag, joining the recruiting lines the day after the bombing at Pearl Harbor. Rabbi Samuel Sandmel quit as UNC Hillel director in 1942 to become the navy's first Jewish chaplain. Altogether about thirty local Jews served, and several became officers. Sadie Silver Goodman's husband, Sanford, was killed at the Battle of the Bulge, and Fred Silver was severely wounded in action. In the military, rather than in their hometowns, local Jews felt the national anti-Semitic mood. Abe Stadiem recalled in his infantry training how the soldiers talked all night about "what the hell we fighting this damn war for all the damn Jews." Stadiem added, "I didn't want to say I'm one of them; liable to kill me."

The war effort intensified cooperation between Jew and Gentile as charitable agencies joined forces. An affiliate of the Army and Navy Committee of the National Jewish Welfare Board sought to "bring the homelike atmosphere of Judaism to the hundreds of Jewish soldiers stationed at Camp Butner and the trainees of Duke University." B'nai B'rith clubrooms were turned over to the U.S.O. for Sunday open houses. In 1942 Aleph Zadik Aleph cosponsored a Youth in Democracy high-school rally with a rabbi delivering the invocation. The women of the Chapel Hill Hillel Auxiliary were reported as "devoting all their time towards the war effort," wrapping bandages for the Red Cross and entertaining cadets at the pre-flight school.[3] In the synagogue vestry the Jewish Welfare Board prepared brunches of kugel, bagels, lox, and herring that proved popular among Christian as well as Jewish servicemen. Ladies Aid furnished a day room at Camp Butner, staffed the U.S.O. Center, collected books for the Red Cross, and shipped packages to servicemen at the camp and overseas. Jewish women worked with the Salvation Army Home, the Veterans Hospital, the Needlework Guild, and the Durham Council of Social Agencies.

The war effort harmonized the Jews' dual identities as Jews and Americans. As early as November 1941, local Jews began a round of parties, picnics, and brunches for Jewish servicemen. One dance drew one hundred soldiers. Twenty-seven Young Judeans traveled to Camp Butner for a Succoth picnic with Jewish soldiers. On one Passover, Sara Swartz organized a seder at Camp Butner. Kosher food was flown from New York. While the Jewish housewives prepared soup and kugel, German prisoners of war chopped vegetables. The sight of a German soldier holding a cleaver put the fear of death in Swartz, but one housewife held a friendly conversation with a prisoner in Polish. Camp Butner had its own Jewish chaplain, Rabbi Isadore Breslau, and a Jewish post control officer, Major Pinckney Bernstein.[4]

The community provided home hospitality, and the Dworskys and Swartzes put up servicemen for the High Holidays. "It wasn't unusual that between the two households there would be twenty-five soldiers sleeping on the floors," Leon Dworsky recalled. In Chapel Hill Sarah Cohen filled her house every weekend with servicemen and returned them to their bases loaded with cake. Sybil Macklin baked challahs and fed the servicemen frankfurters from Harry's deli. Local families also made room in their homes for the wives and children of the servicemen.

Like the college boys, the servicemen provided a steady supply of Jewish men for Durham's women. In 1940 a Fort Bragg soldier, Herman Wagner, met Sara Ornoff at a football game. Two years later they married, setting off a series of a half-dozen weddings between Jewish servicemen and local women. Most brides left town with their husbands although several, included Wagner, settled in local family businesses.

The war years marked the end of Jewish student apathy. In 1944, Arthur Goldberg, Hillel student president, observed that Jews currently on campus, either servicemen or students awaiting calls to duty, were more serious about their Jewishness than the generation of the 1930s, who was escapist and assimilationist: "The Jewish student wants to know what brought about the sufferings of his people in Europe. . . . In addition, the external pressure which has been brought to bear by the bigoted groups which are behind the many manifestations of anti-Semitism in America has brought many Jewish students into organized Jewish life. . . . They seem to be seeking strength to act, and are turning for this strength to their Jewish tradition." Friday night services drew unprecedented numbers. UNC student Louis Harris, later a political pollster, described the "spiritual beauty" of Sabbath dinner at the Tau Epsilon Phi house: "With chaos on every side of us, the Kiddush services Friday night strikingly bring home the utter need for peace and blessing." Hillel Rabbi Maurice Schatz opened Friday night services at the Presbyterian church to "civilians, students and servicemen." He added Sunday services for servicemen who could not come Friday nights, although some attended both sessions. A class in postwar Jewry and Zionist problems "strains the capacity of the room."[5]

Judaic Studies

In 1943 Duke became the first university in the South to establish a full-time position in Jewish studies. Although an academic appointment, it was also intended as an ecumenical gesture. North Carolina Jewish philanthropists, the Stern and Nachamson families, underwrote the position. The scholar and teacher would serve as a role model "thoroughly representative of the spirit of Judaism" both to Jewish and to Christian students. Rabbi Stephen Wise of the Jewish Institute of Religion recommended Theodore Gaster, a scholar of Canaanite texts from the University of London. Gaster, however, revealed to Duke administrators that he was an agnostic. Harvie Branscomb, dean of the Divinity School, responded that Duke did not want to hire "solely" a disinterested scholar but someone committed to community service, preferably a rabbi. Instead, Duke hired Judah Goldin, a Conservative rabbi who had been ordained at the Jewish Theological Seminary. As lecturer in Jewish Literature and Thought, Goldin taught a graduate course on Judaism in the first century and an undergraduate course on contemporary Judaism. (Duke had exempted Jewish students from the required religion course; many took the course, noting that they learned much about Judaism.)[6]

Goldin proved popular at Duke, especially among Jewish students, but his undergraduate course did not draw a large enrollment. Goldin's institutional status was shaky, and in addition Duke would not guarantee him tenure. Goldin experienced problems in Durham. Although he was theologically liberal, Goldin kept kosher, which proved "awkward." Branscomb noted that "the dietary matter created some difficulty in regard to social contacts in homes. Our scholar, I fear, felt himself a little isolated."[7]

Duke had too few Jewish faculty to support him, and after New York he found the local Jewish community too small and lacking in resources for his family. Goldin left in 1944 after two academic years. He became a distinguished rabbinic scholar at Yale and the author of *Living Talmud.*

Given the anti-Semitic mood in America and abroad, Duke, a Methodist school with few Jewish students, had made a philo-Semitic statement in instituting Judaic studies. Academic anti-Semitism had not only closed opportunities for Jewish professors but also denigrated Judaism as a subject worthy of study in itself. The choice of Goldin rather than Gaster reflected a national academic debate as to whether Judaic studies fell within the domain of a university's Semitic studies program or whether it more properly fit the mission of a seminary's religious advocacy. Jewish donors who endowed Judaic studies intended their gifts as a community service to counter anti-Semitism, and Duke followed the lead of such prestigious universities as the University of Chicago in hiring a rabbi for the post.[8] The movement of Jews from academic outsiders to insiders was tentative even as Judaism's place within the academic canon was still debated.

Southern Citizens
Communal efforts at ecumenicism breached racial boundaries. Rabbi Israel Mowshowitz became friends with the "outstanding black minister" Reverend Miles Mark Fisher of White Rock. Fisher, who held a doctorate from the University of Chicago, and Mowshowitz, a doctoral candidate at Duke, were both representative of the educated, professional clergy, men who were civically and politically progressive. For Race Relations Sunday in 1943 Rabbi Mowshowitz spoke "On Common Ground" to an interracial, interreligious gathering at Temple Baptist Church. This program, which the newspaper described as "unique" for Durham, was a local event for the National Conference of Christians and Jews' National Brotherhood Week. Mowshowitz described his relations with the black community as "excellent."[9] (The minister's daughter Ada, a physician, later converted to Judaism.) E. J. Evans led the steering committee for Lincoln Hospital, which served blacks. In 1948 as chair of the Community Chest Evans became the first white person to attend the kick-off banquet in the black community.

Hayti with its prosperous business district was a self-enclosed African American world, and Durham blacks enjoyed a vibrant communal life. Yet, to breach the racial lines carried the potential for violence, and several times during World War II Durham was on the verge of erupting. In 1944 a white Durham bus driver shot and killed a black soldier who refused to move to the back of a city bus. The incident provoked a near riot. In the late 1940s Jewish grocers in Hayti received threatening letters from blacks who did not want white merchants in Hayti. The Jews turned to attorney R. O. Everett, who was able to squelch any potential problems. In 1945 the *Carolina Times* printed an article titled "Jews in the South Must Stop Practices of Discriminating [against] Negroes in Stores," which called on Jews to break their solidarity with the "southern white" who, by custom, served blacks only in the rear of the store.[10]

As Jews moved into the mainstream of white society, they no longer lived in proximity to blacks. The Roxboro Street Jewish enclave began emptying rapidly in the early 1940s. The downtown business district was encroaching on the residential neighborhood, and the area was deteriorating. Large old homes were divided and made into rooming houses. The opening of an interstate bus station at the neighborhood's edge drew transients into the area. African Americans began occupying former Jewish homes. In 1947 only six of Beth-El's sixteen board members still lived in the old neighborhood. Jews soon entirely abandoned the area as they joined the exodus to the suburbs that sprouted in the postwar housing boom. Newly arriving faculty headed to wealthier, countrified developments such as Hope Valley.

The suburban exodus attested to prosperity and social integration. Traditional Jews regarded the move from Roxboro Street as a sign of assimilation. The trend in Durham was consistent with the national pattern that saw Jews move into middle-class suburbs in the postwar years. In the suburbs Jews could no longer walk to the synagogue on the Sabbath; they could no longer fulfill the Orthodox commandments. By the 1940s neither Jewish ethnic solidarity nor restrictive housing policies were forces dictating the Jews' places of residence. The Jewish community evolved with the city. The Jews moved to the city's center when downtown grew and abandoned it when the suburbs became ascendant. Increasingly, their residential patterns showed them behaving more as middle-class Durhamites than as clannish Jews committed to a traditional culture.

Jews found easier entrance into the Masons or Rotary. Sigmund Meyer, a southerner born and bred, joined virtually every civic club in Durham: the Masons, Elks, Moose, Sertoma, and the YMCA, where he served as a board member for more than twenty years. He also served as Exalted Ruler of the Shriners. After hobnobbing with Democrats whose clubroom was over his store, Jake Nurkin was appointed doorkeeper to the state legislature. Nurkin, a decorated World War I veteran, held state and national posts in the American Legion and Veterans of Foreign Wars. E. J. Evans, who became the acknowledged Jewish emissary to the civic community after Nathan Rosenstein's death in 1935, led the Durham Community War Loan Campaign, the Community Fund and Chest, and the boards of Watts and Lincoln Hospitals. In 1942 the Junior Chamber of Commerce named Evans its man of the year.[11]

Jews prospered with the growing postwar economy. By 1946 the Evanses' United Department Stores had expanded to six locations with seventy-five employees. The opening of Camp Butner had sent property prices spiralling, and in the postwar building boom Jews diversified their investments as duplex and apartment housing spread rapidly. As soon as one property was paid for, they would remortgage it to purchase another. The arrival of new business families did not slow until the late 1940s and early 1950s when Durham began declining as an industrial center.

Despite the postwar prosperity and their acceptance into civic elites—national polls revealed a declining anti-Semitism—Jews were conscious of their outsider status and sharply reactive to prejudice both imagined and real. In Chapel Hill Milton Julian, a World War II veteran, was invited to join the American Legion, only to have an anti-Semite blackball him. At UNC Charles Mangum, the medical school dean, quietly maintained the 10 percent quota of his predecessor, Isaac Manning. Art Shain, a student in the late 1940s, recalled a biochemist who, denying any prejudice, discouraged him from applying to medical school, repeating Manning's arguments that Jews were mercenary and that no medical school would accept him. A professor told a Jewish student that he did A work but that he had a policy of not giving an A to a Jew.[12]

Holocaust: A Homeland Lost

The Holocaust meant the death of one Jewish homeland even as Israel gave birth to a new. These events were for Jews everywhere defining events in constructing a new postwar identity. Like most Americans, Durham's Jews did not fully comprehend the systematic slaughter of European Jews. Not until early 1946 was the death count of six million Jews firmly established.[13] "We didn't know what was going on," Melvin Gladstein recalled. UNC student Arthur Shain echoed, "I was not really aware of the extent of the Holocaust." Yet, since 1941, Duke professor Raphael Lemkin, who had escaped occupied Poland, had lectured local Jewish groups as well as the Rotary, Women's Club, and state bar association on Nazi extermination policies. Local Jews were always responsive to crises in world Jewry. Whatever the disarray of national Jewish organizations, they had worked assiduously on the local level to raise funds for European relief and to enlist civic and political leaders in support of immigration.

News of the Holocaust struck Durham Jewry with personal force. "Everybody was in pain. We all had families," recalled May Ornoff Segal, who lost her grandparents. Mizrachi collected clothes to send overseas, and shopkeepers kept boxes in their stores for people to donate clothes, medicines, and canned goods. In 1944, sixty Durhamites pledged to support one immigrant child for a year as part of an international effort that saved eleven thousand children. Ben and Minnie Rose signed affidavits for more than twenty refugees, and Mutt and Sara Evans signed for fifty more, promising jobs, which entitled them to visas. George Lewin, a German émigré who held law degrees from the Sorbonne, met Evans by chance at the Hebrew Immigrant Aid Society in New York. Evans invited him to Durham. After his experiences in Germany, Lewin wanted to Anglicize his name to Lawson, but community volunteer Ricky Rosenstein convinced him that was unnecessary. In Durham Lewin found a home, a career, and—in Rosenstein—a wife. Doctors Alfred Apsler and Mortimer Taube worked in the Duke library. Simon Krynski, a Polish army veteran who held an advanced degree from the University of Poznan, first served as synagogue custodian before joining the Slavic Department at Duke. Others worked in the Evanses' department store before embarking on new lives. In 1948 Ricky Lewin headed a drive for SOS (Save an Overseas Survivor). A year later the United Services for New Americans sent to Durham three families who had survived the Bergen Belsen concentration camp. Jewish merchants hired the tailor, carpenter, and mechanic.[14]

After the war the trauma of Jewish persecution renewed efforts to educate the Christian community. "The Holocaust got Christians thinking," Gibby Katz reflected. In 1947, Rabbi Elliot Einhorn spoke at Oxford High School on the "Social and Cultural Contribution of Judaism to Mankind" and addressed the Durham Lions on "Brotherhood—Our Last Chance."[15]

Zion: A Homeland Found

Rather than discussions on the Holocaust, Arthur Shain recalled, most of the talk was on Zionism. Zionism dominated the Jewish community's agenda. Discussion groups were organized on Zionism and the United Nations. In 1944 E. J. Evans represented North Carolina at the American

Jewish Conference, which was convened to determine the direction of postwar Jewry. Its most notable act was to commit funds to establish a Jewish state, a move that precipitated a walkout by the anti-Zionists. In 1944 one hundred guests attended a Hadassah banquet at the Washington Duke Hotel to honor Rabbi Stephen Wise, head of the Zionist Organization of America and founder of the World Jewish Congress. He called Durham a "hotbed" of Zionism. Two local émigrés, Mrs. Alfred Apsler, an Austrian, and Mathilde Friedman, a German who had lived in Palestine, spoke on behalf of Youth Aliyah.[16]

Sara Nachamson Evans's organizing efforts across the region earned her the sobriquet of Hadassah's "Southern Accent." National vice president from 1954 to 1957, she brought the Zionist leadership to Durham. Hadassah "was the thing to do," Helen Stahl recalled. "You wore your gloves, you wore your hat, and you got to go to Sara Evans's house." The Hadassah calendar was a busy one and included sewing groups, a skit on "Jewish Welfare in Palestine," a poolside fashion show and Chinese supper, banquets at Harvey's Cafeteria, and dances at the Washington Duke Hotel. Once Sara Evans's friend Jennie Grossinger of the Catskills resort addressed the group. For youth, too, Junior Hadassah "was the thing," Yetta Sawilowsky Brandt remembered. "I could not wait until I was old enough to get in." A cultural group studied Jewish history and current events and entertained their mothers with Zionist songs. Young women were set on a lifelong course of volunteerism. Mizrachi addressed itself to both European relief and Zionism. In 1946 the chapter sent $470 to its children's home in Palestine and collected 419 cans of food, 15 cakes of soap, and 2 boxes of clothes for shipment to displaced persons camps in Europe.[17]

When the State of Israel was declared in 1948, Jews gathered at the synagogue to celebrate. Although Durham was ardently Zionist, Sara Evans recalled a man who complained to her, "Don't you know the headline 'Israel' in the newspapers will create anti-Semitism and put us in a very difficult position?" But it had a very different effect. The image of the Jew changed. From the Holocaust image of Jews as sheep who went to slaughter, the media now heralded Jews as fighters. Zionism created a new kind of Jew in America as well as in Palestine.

Jews intensified their efforts to generate support for Zionism in the Gentile community. The forum, again, was to fete a civic leader at a public event. In 1948 a Hadassah banquet attended by three hundred, including fifty Christians, honored Frank Daniels of the *Raleigh News and Observer*. Duke and UNC faculty added their names to a 1944 petition to President

Roosevelt, declaring their support for a Jewish state in Palestine. Nearly eighty doctors and scientists, most of whom were not Jewish, advertised in the Hadassah yearbook that they were "sympathetic" to the Hebrew University Medical School.[18]

Emissaries arrived in both Durham and Chapel Hill to give firsthand accounts of the Israeli War of Independence. In June 1949 Ben Foreman of Brooklyn, an *Exodus* crew member, spoke before the Jewish Welfare Association. Ruth Goldschmidt, a Czechoslovakian-born war correspondent for the Israeli Foreign Office, "held her audience spellbound" as she described battlefield action from Dan to Beersheba. The women welcomed the guests with Israeli songs. In 1951, 150 attended a tea at the Evanses' home to hear Mrs. Cecil Hyman of the Israeli embassy.[19]

The purpose of this Zionist activity was not just to build Jewish esteem but also to raise money. The social calendar included fund-raising banquets for Youth Aliyah at the Washington Duke Hotel and New Year's dances at the B'nai B'rith clubrooms. The events drew three hundred, virtually the entire community. Zionism linked this small, distant community to the historical saga of Jewish destiny.

The Zionist campaign also stirred Jewish campus life. A succession of speakers and programs marked campus calendars. In 1947 a Christian Zionist, Dr. Theodore Jackman, spoke at UNC before "a large audience of students and faculty." Jackman, introduced by President Graham, denounced the "British reign of terror" and stressed Arab-Jewish cooperation. Ralph Lowenstein of Danville, Virginia, spoke on his service in the Israeli army, and the students responded with "Palestinian songs." Duke and UNC supported chapters of the Intercollegiate Zionist Federation of America. In June 1949 sixty students gathered at UNC for a week-long celebration of Israel's first year of independence. UNC also held a UJA student drive that raised $1,600 in 1949.[20]

Jewish faculty who were otherwise unaffiliated greeted visiting Israeli diplomats and scholars and signed petitions in support of the Jewish state. Duke biochemist William Perlzweig was "more or less an assimilationist," but he was profoundly moved by the struggle to establish Israel and began studying Hebrew with the Beth-El rabbi. Perlzweig served as a Zionist spokesman at Duke. In August 1947 he left for Jerusalem as a "special adviser" to the Hebrew University–Hadassah Medical School. Perlzweig helped select the doctors who were later killed in the Mt. Scopus terrorist ambush. After recruiting replacements, he spoke at Duke's Friday night

Hillel services. Emotionally charged, he paced the aisle of York Chapel, galvanizing the students with his account of events in Palestine.[21]

Zionism unleashed latent bigotry on the Duke campus. Duke once hosted a panel discussion with three experts on the Middle East: a UNC political scientist who was an Arab, a Duke political scientist who had worked at the State Department, and Perlzweig. After the Arab representative spoke, the Duke professor rose and began delivering an anti-Zionist harangue that turned anti-Semitic. The professor began raving that the Jews would ruin the place, complaining that they stood out wherever they went. He claimed that he could pick out Jews: Jews from Miami, Jews from New York, all he had to do was look out in the audience and he could pick out Jews. Perlzweig banged the gavel to quiet the man, who remained unapologetic. Perlzweig rose to speak. He deferred to the expertise of the panelist as a political scientist, but as for the Jewish question he could assert that Palestine had transformed the Jews so that not even his colleague could recognize them. There the Jewish people regained their self-respect. Their backs stiffened, Perlzweig explained, turning to his antagonist, and, yes, even their noses straightened. The audience roared and clapped. Later, several Duke students complained to attorney Henry Bane, B'nai B'rith president, about the anti-Semitic outburst. Bane approached the departmental chairman, his former professor, who reprimanded the political scientist.[22]

Although the South with its German-Reform legacy has been stereotyped as non- if not anti-Zionist, Durham's ardor for the Jewish state was hardly atypical of the region. Hadassah and other Zionist societies arose not only in metropolitan areas but also in small towns from Virginia to Mississippi. Richmond was the home of the vocally anti-Zionist American Council for Judaism, but it nearly collapsed in 1948 as Virginia Jews rallied politically and philanthropically for the Jewish state. In Memphis, too, support for Israel was "almost universal" among Jews across ethnic and denominational divisions.[23]

The Jews' primary community remained a distant global Jewry rather than their non-Jewish neighbors. Historically, pogroms, the Holocaust, and Zionism led Durham's Jews to organize. Ethnic solidarity rose even as religious observance and synagogue membership declined. Besides their philanthropic purposes, the banquets, dances, and card parties created community bonds. Youth were enrolled in Jewish networks. These groups were intended as bulwarks against assimilation, but they also took culturally

blended, social forms—hotel banquets, wiener roasts, poolside parties—
that marked Durham's Jews as members in good standing of the southern
bourgeoisie. Meetings of the Ladies Aid, Hadassah, and the Zionist Organization of America regularly attracted forty to fifty members when the
synagogue was pressed to draw ten. Many Jews were nominally affiliated,
and others not at all, but a core group of committed families led to more
Jewish activity than the community's small numbers would suggest. Surprisingly, for a small, isolated southern town, local Jews achieved representation on national Jewish boards. Rabbi Mowshowitz recalled, "We
were, if anything, overorganized," and local Jews boasted that Durham was
the "Jerusalem of the South."

As Yiddish faded, Jews turned to Hebrew, the language of the Zionist
rebirth. Modern conversational Hebrew was taught in the religious school
and in adult-education classes. Children did not learn the Yiddish folk
melodies of their grandparents but rather the Hebrew songs of the *halut-*
zim, Israel's pioneers. Young Judea held picnics and oneg Shabbats where
the boys and girls studied Israeli life and practiced Israeli songs and dances.
At summer camp, Israeli counselors—farmers, artists, and soldiers—served
as role models of Jewish pride and self-sufficiency. Hebrew school classes
ended with Hatikvah and "Palestinian songs," and rabbis discussed Zionism at sabbath services. The rabbi was expected to be an expert on Israeli
politics and a public advocate of Zionism.[24]

A New Generation

The established Jewish community was undergoing a generational turn.
The European-born immigrants were aging and dying. The American-
born generation, especially women, raised in the 1920s and 1930s had received desultory Jewish educations. The second generation "saw the practices in the home but didn't get the education," Leon Dworsky observed.

What survived was a nostalgic or symbolic Jewish ethnicity, a sense of
heritage and belonging. At weddings Muriel Wilson serenaded the newlyweds with "Always," but she also sang "Abe Gezund." Jews answered to
such nicknames as "Yut" (Yossele) Levine, "Cup" (Cuple) Margolis, and
"Yankee" (Yankel) Zuckerman. Although kosher observance declined,
Jews retained a taste for ethnic delicacies available at a local deli and B'nai
B'rith clubrooms. Rather than a living culture, Yiddishkeit became a program, the subject of classes and lectures. Traditions were learned rather than
given. Blue Greenberg led Hadassah discussions on books of Jewish interest such as Maurice Samuel's *Prince of the Ghetto.* The women presented an

evening of "Songs Our Mothers Taught Us." In 1949 the women sang the cantata "What Is Torah?" at Hadassah and B'nai B'rith. This nationally popular work, a product of the Reconstructionist Foundation, celebrated Torah not just as the embodiment of the Zionist's *"Eretz Yisrael"* (Land of Israel) and the Orthodox's *"bet hamidrash"* (house of study), but in universal terms. Torah, according to the cantata, was "Israel's gift to humanity . . . the hope of the Negro people . . . the memory of Israel's struggle." Yiddishkeit, Zionism, and the American creed, the parochial and the international, all seamlessly blended without any sense of contradiction.[25]

Town and Gown

Local Jewry was growing ethnically and professionally diverse and religiously pluralistic. Jews flocked to campuses in record numbers in the postwar years. Colleges, led by Columbia University, began ending their quotas. Jewish servicemen took advantage of the GI Bill at levels that doubled the national percentage. When he arrived as Hillel director in 1948, Rabbi Samuel Perlman was given the task of implementing plans to erect a building that the war had delayed. B'nai B'rith embarked on a $50,000 campaign. A lot was purchased on Cameron Street a block from campus, and in 1951 construction began on the Hillel building. A year later Jewish enrollment was reported at 400 at UNC and 175 at Duke.

By the late 1940s the Jewish faculty were becoming numerically significant, but their relations with established Jews were tangential. The Evanses served as a bridge, entertaining academic families in their home. Beth-El rabbi Israel Mowshowitz, a Duke doctoral candidate, drew a few faculty into the congregation. Alfred Apsler, an émigré scholar at Duke, taught Sunday school. The Londons sent their children there, but they also arranged for tutoring with Rabbi Judah Goldin. Hillel served as a campus congregation. For many faculty, especially the German émigrés, Durham's southern-style Orthodoxy was unfamiliar. Hilde Brauer was raised in a small synagogue in her village, whereas her husband had attended Berlin's Great Synagogue. Marianne Manasse had been baptized as a child, and her family celebrated Christmas. The émigré scholars formed a circle among themselves. The Londons and Manasses resumed a friendship that had begun in Germany. They became close to the Brauers. These poets, artists, and scientists re-created their cosmopolitan culture in their southern hometowns.

The American-born faculty came from backgrounds that did not markedly differ from those of second-generation Durham Jews. Philip Handler's parents were Russian Jews who had immigrated to the United States in the 1890s. The professors, however, had broken free from the retail trades of their parents. When Handler first arrived he joined some local Jewish men for softball but felt little in common with them. In his own family "the ones who were in business all knew each other, and the few who went off in other directions didn't know each other," Lucy Handler recalled. "It took more than familial work or religious or ethnic ties to bring people together."

Some local residents looked on the faculty as elitists and assimilationists. Tensions developed. A professor recalled a merchant browbeating him as a Jewish slacker when he walked past his store. "Most of the faculty had a very peripheral relationship with the synagogue," Rabbi Simon Glustrom observed. "They were resented by members of the community because they didn't pull their weight." The conflict was not exclusively a Jewish problem. Town and gown generally remained apart. Ethnicity alone was insufficient to unite people whose education and professional interests were so diverse. Certainly some Jewish academics had little Jewish consciousness and held condescending attitudes. Durham resembled the places that they had left behind. Several had intermarried. Their social ties extended to the academic community where they could further their careers. Some Jewish faculty, in medicine especially, simply wished to assimilate, faced as they were with the career disabilities that afflicted Jews. Science and scholarship, not religion, shaped their values. Yet not all who remained unaffiliated were disaffected Jews. For Reform Jews Orthodox Beth-El was not an inviting place. A few faculty who remained outside the congregation, such as Milton Rosenau and William Perlzweig, served on national Jewish boards. Olga Marx's translations helped bring the writings of Martin Buber to the English-speaking public. Faculty wives joined the North Carolina Association of Jewish Women, Hadassah, or Hillel Women's Auxiliary. A few, such as the Bernsteins in Chapel Hill, headed for Raleigh's Reform temple. As Durham Jewry grew religiously pluralistic, its homogeneity as an east European, Orthodox community was breaking.

Conservative Jews
The Beth-El leadership remained in the hands of European-born traditionalists. S. H. Dworsky, who served as president for all but one year from 1937 to 1945, was a warm, Jewishly learned man who held rabbinical ordination from the Mir Yeshiva of Belorussia. As religious liberals raised their voices, Dworsky was pressed to maintain the congregation's Ortho-

doxy. In 1945 E.J. Evans, who would serve until 1952, succeeded Dworsky as president. The change was symbolic. In contrast to Dworsky, Evans was American born, college educated, and stumbled over Hebrew. Evans's task was to guide Beth-El toward Conservatism without alienating the Orthodox. The postwar board was a mix of young and old, liberals and traditionalists, immigrants and native born. In 1947 the Sisterhood president, Grace Gladstein, was elected to the board as women formally entered the leadership.

The religious splits were not purely generational; some younger members still wished to hold to Orthodoxy. Nor were all Orthodox Jews averse to compromise. Polish-born Max Lieberman, who would succeed Evans as president, was personally Orthodox, but he wanted services that were relevant to most congregants. "I was always trying to impress upon the rabbi to bring more English" into the services, he recalled. Lieberman, who spiced his conversation with talmudic citations and Jewish proverbs, believed that in praying in Hebrew he was "communing with God," but he knew that his wife, among others, did not know the language. He also wanted a rabbi who appealed to his children.

The Orthodox continued to dominate the synagogue's ritual. The older men sat in the front rows, reminding the rabbi to include all the required psalms and prayers and insisting that he use more Hebrew. Dworsky, wrapped in a large prayer shawl, followed the cantor through the liturgy, correcting him with a mutter or tap of his fingers. The older women held to their places in the balcony although most others had moved downstairs. Saturday morning Sabbath services were largely in the hands of the Orthodox because they were virtually the only ones who attended. At times there were difficulties making a minyan. For the High Holidays, when attendance was larger, the services tended to be more Conservative and included more English.

The decline of Orthodoxy was reflected in community kosher standards. The congregation paid the salary of a schochet, who slaughtered cows and chickens for a local butcher. Local beef was not overly appetizing, Leon Dworsky recalled. The schochet "would go out and buy a cow that stopped giving milk, and we would eat it the next day." When they traveled north, Jews returned with sides of beef packed in ice. In the 1940s, Morris Apter, who owned a delicatessen, repeatedly protested to the synagogue board that he could no longer afford to serve as kosher butcher, complaining that only twenty-five to thirty customers (about one-third of the community) purchased meat from him. In 1946 no butcher wanted the "Jewish meat concession," but Jones' Market agreed to sell poultry. With the advent of refrigeration, prime western beef was available. No longer could Durham support a schochet.[26]

Religious divisions provoked congregational debates. A member from a prominent family had married a Christian woman who, though she never converted, had a "Jewish attitude" and had given her children a Jewish education. The board argued whether to accept the man's monthly dues of six dollars. The rabbi agreed that the "exact Jewish status" was "delicate," stating that the congregant's wife was Jewish from a Reform viewpoint but not from a Conservative or Orthodox one. (The rabbi's perception of Reform Judaism at that time was mistaken.) A Chapel Hillian married to a Christian woman recalled that Beth-El would accept his membership but not his wife's although she wanted a Jewish education for their children. The elder men feared problems about burial of non-Jews in their consecrated cemetery, even in cases where women had converted. Others questioned the membership of Jews who kept their stores open on Yom Kippur or no longer kept kosher.[27]

The disputes, as they had in the past, owed to personal and family jealousies that were played out in synagogue politics. Younger members saw that the congregation's future lay with the new faculty at Duke, liberal Jews who might attend services if they were more meaningful and who might enroll their children in the Hebrew school if it were more progressive. Resentments arose between small and large donors, shopkeepers and wealthy businessmen. All arguments were passionately pursued, and, as Eli Evans noted, questions of membership in Beth-El were argued as if the survival of the Jewish people hung in the balance.[28]

Beginning in the 1940s, the Jewish upbringing of children was seen as the synagogue's primary responsibility. Parents believed that the cheder, with its Old World rebbe, was an anachronism. The Durham rabbis "were learned men in their ways but not in the American way of life," Sara Evans recalled. "These men . . . were responsible for the Jewish education of our community, but they brought with them a background of Poland." Parents wanted their children to have a Jewish consciousness, to have a Jewish "heart," and to respect tradition, but to many a strict adherence to *halacha* (Jewish law) seemed confining and unnecessary in an open, pluralistic society. Although dedicated to transcending their immigrant heritage and Americanizing themselves, these parents also grew concerned about their children's Jewish futures. Southern Jewish children were not being raised very differently from their Christian neighbors, especially as Jews dispersed into the suburbs. Harry Bergman, who had never had a Bar Mitz-vah, became the Hebrew school principal because he wanted his children to feel Jewish. For youth the synagogue, rather than the home, was the center of Jewish life.

By the 1940s Jewish education consisted of a culturally blended American program that borrowed from the public schools. National Jewish organizations responded to the challenge of an assimilating youth by offering technical support for curricula and educational materials. When the first annual Conference of Jewish Education was held in Richmond in 1948, rebbetzin Helen Glustrom and principal Harry Bergman attended. The teachers had access to magazines, records, film strips, and textbooks. Classes were coeducational. Students prepared book reports, took final exams, and received grades. The students elected a student council, and a board of education and parent-teacher group supported the school. The students published a school newspaper, the *Durham Israelite,* and the Beth-El Tigers competed against church teams in football, basketball, and baseball. At year's end Ben Rose's delivery truck was piled with hay, and the children scrambled aboard, parents following in their cars, for a picnic at Raleigh's Pullen Park. Molly Freedman noted that as a result of a new philosophy of "inculcating religion with pleasure," there had been a "marked improvement in decorum and attendance." Yet appeals to parents to discipline their schoolchildren were a perennial feature of temple bulletins.[29]

"People were very conscious about the school facilities, the education of the children," Leon Dworsky remembered about synagogue debates. "The one quality these young rabbis had," Eli Evans recalled, was that "they were great with kids. Their real survival would be the way they ran the Sunday school and Hebrew school." Mowshowitz's successor, Aaron Shapiro, was also Orthodox, but his tenure was short and stormy. When parents saw children running amok at one Sunday school, they fired the rabbi. After leaving Beth-El, he and the county coroner opened a restaurant near the synagogue and served unkosher food, embarrassing the community. In 1945, after prolonged debate, Rabbi Elliott J. Einhorn was hired. Einhorn had previously served a small, denominationally mixed congregation in Clarksburg, West Virginia. He remained until 1948, when the congregation began yet another search. Durham drew mostly young, novice rabbis for whom Beth-El was "training ground" for larger pulpits. Choosing a rabbi opened community divisions on religious identity.[30]

The immediate question was whether the board should ask for appli-

cants from Yeshiva University, which was Orthodox, or the Jewish Theological Seminary, which was Conservative. Sam Daniel, head of the
Chevra Kadisha, argued that a "man must be selected for himself and not
because he went to the Yeshiva, Seminary, or any other institution." E. J.
Evans added that the "congregation needed a man with liberal tendencies"
who would "make a modern showing." The European-born rabbis with
their Yiddish accents no longer met community needs because the rabbi
was now expected to join interfaith groups, to speak before the Kiwanis,
and to appeal to all-American children. Personality would override theological concerns. Ten rabbis applied for the position. The Jewish Theological Seminary sent a letter that called Simon Glustrom "one of the most
promising young men in the American rabbinate." Glustrom, still in his
twenties and newly married, was hired in 1948 as Beth-El's first Conservative rabbi.[31]

Glustrom had credibility for the Orthodox as a graduate of Yeshiva
University. He was a native of Atlanta, and Evans cited his "Southern
background" as a reason for hiring him. He replaced the Hebrew prayer
books with the bilingual Silverman editions and experimented with a
choir. He began a Sunday afternoon radio show on WDUK called "From
the Rabbi's Study." S. H. Dworsky, pillar of Orthodoxy, developed a "very
high opinion" of the Conservative rabbi as they studied Talmud together.
With Glustrom came the Reverend Benjamin Kaminetzky from Macon,
Georgia, who was hired as cantor, schochet, and religious school teacher.[32]

With a Conservative rabbi the congregation faced the question of affiliation. In 1948, women pushed the congregation toward Conservatism
when the Ladies Aid Society, affiliated with the Orthodox Union, also
joined the Women's League of United Synagogue of America and renamed itself Sisterhood. Two years later Nathan Lieberman questioned
whether the board should accept a charter from the United Synagogue, the
Conservative governing body. The expiration of Glustrom's one-year contract forced a decision.

At a board meeting S. H. Dworsky asserted that only Orthodoxy could
assure that "we should have a synagogue that everyone could attend."
Ricky Lewin countered that services as now conducted were more inter-
esting. Sara Evans spoke on behalf of the United Synagogue, adding that
"we want one congregation in this community, and only one." Women
were instrumental in pushing the congregation toward a Conservatism
that held the promise of a more egalitarian Judaism.[33]

On February 28, 1950, the Arbitration Committee drafted a letter to the Orthodox Union that vividly portrayed Beth-El's pluralistic religious character: "We are enclosing a check as a contribution for the services that you furnish our Rabbi. We are a community of diverse elements, Orthodox, Conservative, and Reform, and to maintain our unity we want to contribute to all organizations from whom we receive materials and literature. In view of our present situation affiliation with any one organization alone will disrupt our communal accord." The motion to endorse the letter passed by a vote of thirty-six to six.[34]

In 1950 Glustrom left despite a generous offer to induce him to stay. The Glustroms found Durham "very pleasant," but they did not see "potential for much growth." The rabbi moved to a larger community in New Jersey that was closer to the Jewish Theological Seminary.

The debate once again centered on the "qualifications" for a new rabbi. The board agreed to consider candidates from Orthodox, Conservative, and Reform institutions. The board wanted to preserve "one congregation, and all groups must be satisfied." The next rabbi, Pesach Krauss, was also Conservative. He, too, had a talent with children, instituting a children's choir that won regional honors, but he left after only two years. Beth-El then reverted to Orthodox leadership. The Reverend A. Miller, a graduate of Yeshiva University, arrived from Charleston to serve as cantor. Rabbi Solomon Shapiro from Houston followed. Although the Romanian rabbi and his French wife were foreign, his service as a war veteran and West Point chaplain attested to his Americanism. Active in refugee rehabilitation, he had helped prepare a new edition of the Talmud for Holocaust survivors. With his impressive resume Rabbi Shapiro left after two years. Durham's rabbinic instability was chronic. The small, distant congregation served as a stepping stone for rabbinic careerists.[35]

Affiliation was only one of the conflicts Beth-El faced. The crises of overseas Jewry had unified the community and diverted its attention. Even as Jews contributed to Palestine and European relief, Beth-El suffered from persistent financial problems. Perhaps only half the community affiliated. The practice of public fund-raising on Yom Kippur offended liberals, and many believed that it alienated faculty families who came for the High Holidays. In 1942, Beth-El was $1,000 in debt, and a few generous members bailed it out.

While the congregation struggled financially, it found itself pressed for space in thirty-year-old facilities. Sunday school classes overflowed into the kitchen and women's balcony. In 1948 the rabbi's home next door was converted into a religious school and community center. These ambitions were large because Beth-El's deficit had risen to $1,500. President E. J. Evans complained that the burden fell unfairly on a handful of members who signed financial notes and solicited dues.[36]

As early as 1942 plans were discussed for a new building. In 1943 Israel Freedman, a Durham clothier, donated $10,000 as seed money, which was followed by funds from the Evans family and Ladies Aid. The congregants, however, were divided on whether to improve the old synagogue on Roxboro Street or to relocate. Liberals argued that if Beth-El were to grow, it would have to attract faculty and younger Jews. Moreover, most Jews, including a majority of the board, now lived in the suburbs. Those who wished to preserve the old building felt the pull of nostalgia, but they also pointed to Beth-El's growing debt, now at $2,500.[37]

On June 28, 1950, Sara Evans, on behalf of the Community Center Committee, recommended moving to a new location. She cited "the deterioration of the present neighborhood and the inadequate space." An October 12 open meeting on the issue drew "record-breaking attendance." "There was much discussion both for and against moving and selling both for sentimental and financial reasons," the minutes recorded. Durham's Jews had sent thousands of dollars to Israel, Max Lieberman argued; they could do no less here. The board unanimously endorsed a new site. Leon Moel rose and delivered a "stirring speech," pledging $1,000. Others rose, too, and by evening's end $16,000 had been promised.[38]

In the time of Jacob, Lieberman recalled, seventy Jews entered Egypt and there they built a great nation. Several millennia later in Durham, North Carolina, seventy Jewish families were laying foundations for coming generations. "With the help of God and the help of the members of the congregation," Lieberman proclaimed, "we started to build."

The congregational history of Durham reflected larger transformations of American Jewry. In less than thirty years the Durham congregation had emerged from a rented hall to a wooden shul to a downtown cathedral. The chevra of the immigrants evolved into a community synagogue that stood on equal footing with Durham's churches. Durham's rabbis evolved from unordained "rebbes" and "reverends," who dispensed schmaltz and Torah, to college-educated professionals, from Lithuanian immigrants to native Americans. Increasingly, rabbis were civic-minded, acculturated religious leaders who could speak relevantly to their children and appear American to the non-Jewish community. In educating their children, Jews abandoned the traditional, authoritarian European models, the cheder and

Talmud Torah, for an American program appropriate for an assimilated youth. In the next decade Beth-El would take a step further as traditionalists lost their hold and modernists moved the congregation haltingly into the Conservative movement. In the suburbs the Jews would build a distinctly American Judaism.

If the crises of the 1930s caused conflicts in the Jews' dual identities as Jews and Americans, the war effort assuaged them. Jews and Christians expanded and intensified their personal and institutional contacts with a new appreciation of their shared values. In the postwar years brotherhood became a national credo. After attending schools and doing business together for three generations, Gentiles felt comfortable with Jews. The prosperity of the war and postwar years ameliorated economic tensions. Jews, now resolutely middle-class white people, no longer seemed different. The Holocaust discredited the demonizing of the Jews as a separate race. Abandoning their downtown enclave, Jews became friendly suburban neighbors. "After the war it was like someone opened a cold steel door and left it ajar just a bit," Gibby Katz recalled, "and said if you push it hard enough you might just get through." Younger Jews were now willing to push at the door in ways that a more vulnerable immigrant generation was not. "Jews were more willing to speak out and be noticed, and the Christians were more willing to listen and to take notice," Leon Dworsky observed. Jews began taking steps that would have been unthinkable a generation earlier. Parents protested Christian prayers in the schools. A rabbi fought to have the local election day moved from Saturday to Tuesday. In insisting on their rights as Americans, they also saw themselves as becoming better Jews.

Jews once again renegotiated their identities. Yiddishkeit was dying with the immigrant generation, and the Holocaust killed the Jewish Old World. The rising generation was educated in the values of their secular schools and universities. Jews no longer resided in an ethnic enclave, but they held to a nostalgic ethnicity, the warmth of group feeling and shared heritage. The Zionist rebirth offered Durham Jews a new identity that countered the forces of assimilation. Israel introduced a new culture of song, dance, language, and cuisine. As American Zionists, a term wrought with contradiction, Jews raised funds and lobbied politicians to rebuild their national homeland although scarcely a local Jew intended to resettle there.

The South was yet another homeland that Jews claimed. In 1944 a local Jew wrote a feature on Durham in the *American Jewish Times* that embellished the folklore that traced community origins to Duke's tobacco workers. Jews took "root" in Durham where they found a "permanent home," the writer claimed. Like southern agrarians, Jews lay "buried in the soil."[39]

10 Breaking the Boundaries, 1950s to 1960s

The composition and character of the Jewish community changed as Durham and Chapel Hill evolved from southern towns into a Sunbelt metropolitan area. The circle of established merchants was breaking as faculty and professionals arrived in increasing numbers. The ethnic enclave, bound by kinship ties, began yielding to a cosmopolitan Jewry. Durham–Chapel Hill, like the Sunbelt generally, was growing more demographically American. Jews were no longer confined largely to mercantile trades but integrated into the corporate economy, which locally was increasingly white collar and professional. The boundaries of community membership attenuated as unaffiliated and Reform Jews grew more numerous and asserted community leadership. Social relations with the non-Jewish community also evolved as discriminatory barriers were being breached. As Americans of the Jewish faith, Jews seemed less different. The declarations of three faiths, a community feature since the 1930s, gave way to dialogues on cultural pluralism as brotherhood became a civil religion. Certainly through the 1950s and early 1960s Jews continued to be identified as a distinct group, but Jews gained social acceptance in places where doors had once been closed. Politically, they were now insiders.

After the war Durham was unable to maintain its industrial base. Anti-smoking campaigns reduced tobacco consumption. The number of tobacco auction markets in Durham declined from thirteen in the 1950s to one in 1986. Textile mills were crippled by strikes and then ravaged by foreign competition.[1] Without a flow of workers into the downtown streets, storefronts boarded up, and businesses began a suburban exodus.

Small-town, southern Jewish storekeepers became an endangered species. In the 1960s suburban malls had opened in Lakewood, Northgate, Forest Hills, and Wellons Village. The downtown shop owner was no match for Sears or K-Mart, nor could the neighborhood grocer compete against the supermarket. Urban renewal in the 1960s cleared away the last Jewish stores in Hayti and dislocated many downtown merchants. Abe Stadiem and Harry Goldberg lost their S & G clothing store to a street realignment. Norman Schultz was given thirty days' notice to close his television repair shop before the city demolished the building.

Established merchants faced the choice of retiring, retooling, or relocating. Jake Margolis closed his grocery and opened an insurance agency. Pawnbroker Leon Dworsky turned to camera repair and then to computer programming. Mutt Evans, with his sons pursuing careers far from Durham, sold his department stores and joined a multiracial group of investors who won a franchise for a television station. The Evans, Bergman, Greenberg, and Rosenstein families also had extensive real-estate holdings that allowed them to weather the changing economic climate. Several merchants followed the economic expansion into the malls and highway strips. David and Israel Freedman closed their downtown stores and opened a men's store in the Northgate Mall. Harry Bergman brought his Record Bar into malls, eventually building a national chain. Robert Rosenbacher's men's store, The Hub, was a mainstay of downtown Chapel Hill, but it, too, spawned branches in local malls.

For other merchants it was time to close shop. Jacob Zuckerman, a community stalwart from an old Durham family, shut his furrier store and moved to Dayton. Virtually the whole generation of business people who arrived during the World War II boom—the Zelons, Fogels, Wolffs, Goldens, and Gordons, among them—also left. The Bloomfields, who had come in the 1930s, went "back home" to New Jersey. A steady stream headed for a Florida retirement.

Durham reinvented itself. The blue-collar industrial town was restyled as the "City of Medicine." A huge Veteran's Administration Hospital opened in 1950. A year later North Carolina Memorial Hospital was dedicated in Chapel Hill. The universities spearheaded the transformation of the area into a cosmopolitan Sunbelt center. Duke University and the University of North Carolina grew into nationally recognized research institutions, and with North Carolina State University in Raleigh, they formed the Research Triangle. A trickle of Jewish faculty in the 1950s grew into a stream in the 1960s and then into a flood in the 1970s. From their concentration in Duke's medical school, Jews began to be hired in the liberal arts and the social and physical sciences especially. In 1953, when Duke announced ninety-six faculty appointments, about a half-dozen Jewish-sounding names appeared on the list. As Arthur Hertzberg notes, "The universities became the first established American institutional arena in which Jews entered and even joined the elite." In 1938, 10 percent of local Jews were professionals. According to community lists, the percentage of households with a "doctor" doubled from 20 percent in 1958 (37 of 177 families) to 40 percent in 1964 (105 of 271).[2]

The founding of the Research Triangle Park in 1958 drew professionals into the area. In 1965 IBM opened a plant that grew to eleven thousand employees. Air-conditioning tempered the hot, humid climate. Research and office complexes replaced farmhouses and tobacco barns as features of the local landscape. Roads built as farm-to-market routes now served commuters heading from subdivisions to high-tech campuses. Durham, which a Jewish businessman called a "nickel-and-dime town,"[3] was now supported less by pocket money of farmers and workers than by megadollars from Washington. This process had begun with the building of Camp Butner and continued with the opening of the Veteran's Administration Hospital. Duke and UNC as national research institutions annually attracted grants in the tens and then in the hundreds of millions. The Environmental Protection Agency and the National Institute for Environmental Health Sciences built mammoth facilities in the park that employed thousands.

Suburban Jews

With the demise of the Roxboro Street ethnic enclave, Jews became suburbanites in new subdivisions that sprouted in the postwar building boom, especially in fast-growing Chapel Hill. As they held backyard barbecues and attended block parties, Jews and Gentiles got to know each other as friends and neighbors, and prejudices subsided. When Max Lieberman moved into a new home, his neighbor at first turned his back when he said good morning. Over the years their relations grew warmer, and he invited the neighbor to his son's Bar Mitzvah. "We had as many Gentile friends as Jewish ones," Ethel Mae Bernson recalled. In Chapel Hill Jews mixed easily. "I have never had negative feelings about being Jewish in this community," recalled Pearl Morrison, who came in 1946. Most people were politely curious. This pattern was typical in nonmetropolitan areas. A 1955 survey of Elmira, New York, revealed that Jews maintained distinct Jewish social cliques, but most also socialized with Christians.[4]

Doors once closed now opened. Whatever the paucity of numbers on campus, Jews reported a cordial welcome. Irving Alexander of the Psychology Department spoke for several arts and sciences faculty when he observed that he "never saw a sign of discrimination." Joseph Morrison, who had joined the UNC faculty after his war service, became one of the Journalism School's most popular teachers, the biographer of North Carolinians Josephus Daniels, W. J. Cash, and O. Max Gardner. Hope Valley Country Club abandoned its restrictive policies. The club had become insolvent, and Duke University bailed it out on condition that it accept whomever Duke recommended. This opened it to its first Jewish member, Duke pharmacologist Thomas Reamer. In the following decades, Hope Valley hosted Bar Mitzvah celebrations. Jews joined virtually all the civic clubs: Elks, Lions, Civitan, and Kiwanis. Some felt unwelcomed in downtown clubs, such as Rotary or Sons of Liberty, so they found other groups. The Masons, Shriners, and Elks especially had strong Jewish contingents, including their ladies' auxiliaries. Harry Bergman listed nineteen civic memberships. Molly Freedman was a PTA president, a Women's Club officer, and a member of the Red Cross, Tuberculosis Society, and United Fund.

After a century together, Jews and Gentiles knew each other as classmates, neighbors, and customers. Jewish difference lessened. "I don't think people thought of these individuals as Jewish or non-Jewish," Judge Robinson Everett reflected. "A lot of Jews had been very well assimilated. There weren't that many, and they weren't seen as a threat." Second- and third-generation Jewish residents participated in town life in ways that marked them as ethnic southerners. In 1953 B'nai B'rith entered a softball team in the city church league for the first time. Teen-aged girls donned formal gowns for a Jewish Debutante Ball. Annette Lieberman, the daughter of Polish immigrants, won the Miss Durham beauty pageant, cheered by shouts of "C'mon Hannah-la." When Durham celebrated its centennial, Jewish men grew sideburns, and women donned hoopskirts as if they, too, had been antebellum southerners. Despite their immigrant history and mercantile background, native southern Jews identified with the romantic myths of the plantation South.[5]

On campus, too, Jews blended into southern culture even as discrimination and group solidarity kept Jews distinct. Jewish campus life in the 1950s, as Eli Evans recounted in *The Provincials,* did not vary greatly from

At the Durham centennial celebration in 1953 Jacob and Dorothy Katz Zuckerman pose as a plantation lady and gentleman in front of their furrier shop. Second-generation children of east European immigrants, they identified culturally as southerners. (Courtesy of the *American Jewish Times Outlook* and the North Carolina Collection, University of North Carolina at Chapel Hill)

that of other southern students with its football weekends, cabin parties, and formal dances. Southern Jews on campus fell in with cousins or friends from summer camp and B'nai B'rith Youth. In the sports-crazed society Jews took pride in their big men on campus. Lenny Rosenbluth, the 1957 national basketball player of the year, led the Tar Heels to an undefeated season and a national championship. On the road he heard anti-Semitic taunts, but for Carolina fans he gave the epithet "New Yorker" a good name. In 1963 Larry Brown earned all-American honors as a UNC basketball player and later won an Olympic gold medal. At Duke Art Heyman, an import from Long Island, took the basketball team to the national finals in 1963 and was honored as the nation's most valuable player. A combative athlete, he, too, heard Jew-baiting jeers, especially at Clemson and Virginia. The heroics of Heyman and Rosenbluth entered the realm of southern folklore, and the players' numbers were retired and draped from arena rafters.[6]

Jews on campus played a traditional role as cosmopolitans among the provincials. Jonathan Yardley, the journalist who graduated from UNC in 1961, recalled that Jewish students "mostly from New York" were "the real force of intellectual excitement at Chapel Hill." Yardley, a self-described southern WASP, became the protégé of "urban Jews, which is one of the best things that ever happened to me." (Curiously, of Yardley's three inspirational Jews—Eli Evans, Joel Fleishman, and Allard Lowenstein—the first two were native small-town southerners.) Lowenstein was a disciple of Frank Graham and threw himself into every progressive cause from civil rights to world federalism. He was a wrestler, journalist, choir member, and Hillel officer. A classmate recalled, "This Jewish boy from New York knew more Southern Baptist hymns than the choir director at a tent revival." After attending Yale law school, he returned to UNC as a graduate student and later joined the North Carolina State faculty.[7]

Social Bias and Religious Prejudice

Jews remained conscious of their difference even as prejudice abated. Some social discrimination persisted, and even Christian friends did not always allow Jews to forget. Hazel and Elwood Wishnov bristled when a fellow Sertoma member introduced them as "my Jewish friends," wanting to be simply "friends." When an insurance agent demanded that Louis Stadiem pay a bill that he had settled, the agent snapped, "All you Jews are alike." For at least some Gentiles Jews remained "the Jews," not individuals but representatives of their group.[8]

Prejudice owed to traditional religious stereotypes. Fundamentalist Christians still looked on Jews as living relics of the Bible. Max and Isabel Samfield, native southerners, often sang or spoke in local churches. They were shocked to discover anti-Semitic lessons in a Baptist church school. Jeanette Fink enjoyed warm relations with neighbors who adored her children, but one woman, not recognizing that she was Jewish, asked how she could have married a man with horns. Once on his salesman's rounds Gibby Katz encountered a woman who had never met a Jew. She asked to touch him on the arm. When he asked why, she answered, "Because it would take me closer to Lord Jesus." "Honey," Katz responded, "you can touch me all over."

In the 1960s Beth-El experienced several anti-Semitic episodes including a swastika painted on its door and a brick thrown through a window during a Sabbath service. Rather than being seen as expressions of community sentiment, however, these incidents were regarded as calling cards of a hate group or a demented individual.

Until the early 1960s Duke continued to ask applicants to specify their religion. The fraternity and sorority system remained segregated into Jewish and Gentile houses. At UNC an administrator routinely assigned Jewish students to one dormitory because he thought "certain people would prefer to be together." Not until 1955 did the UNC placement office drop the religious preference question from its forms.[9]

Bias on campus in the 1950s and early 1960s was usually the legacy of a few older, entrenched faculty bigots. A newly arrived instructor at UNC overheard a senior professor remark that Zionism rather than English literature was the proper subject for him. A prominent Duke religion professor accused Zionists of maintaining dual loyalty and wanted modern Hebrew taught in the political science department. A Yale-educated medievalist believed that Jews had no future in Duke's English department as long as one anti-Semite remained to block his progress. He soon left. In certain departments of Duke Medical School, such as surgery, bias was more systemic, and Jews did not rise above junior ranks. "To become board certified you had to become chief resident. No Jew ever became chief resident," law professor Melvin Shimm observed of the colleagues of his wife, Dr. Cynia Shimm. He attributed the turnaround to the chairmanship of Eugene Stead, who instituted a meritocracy.

Melvin Shimm, who came to Duke in 1949, confronted anti-Semitic hiring practices in the Law School. At a faculty reception Shimm asked the dean if the Law School intended to hire a candidate named Bernstein. The dean, his tongue loosened by drink, conceded that the man "is all right. I think he's good. But there are members of this faculty who seem to think one Jew is enough." Another blatant case arose over the recruitment of a brilliant young Jewish scholar with an impressive publications record. At a faculty meeting a bigot, a Law School mainstay for thirty years, complained that the candidate's "work smells of commerce." When challenged, he confessed, "I'll make no bones about it. I have no love for the Tribe of Benjamin." An untenured professor, Jack Jackson, confronted the bigot, and the law faculty voted to extend an offer (which the candidate declined).

Certainly the relative paucity of Jewish faculty at UNC and Duke owed to continued Jewish prejudices against settling in a South that they regarded as alien terrain. In the 1950s and 1960s northern Jews who came to local campuses never intended to prolong their stays. "How could we raise our children in segregated schools?" asked Ruth Fein, whose husband taught at UNC in the 1950s. Myrna Schwartz broke into tears when her husband took a position at Chapel Hill in 1966. She thought that the South "was no place to raise a Jewish child" and resolved to move after a year.

In the postwar years problems persisted in the schools. Children were still taunted as "Christ-killers." At assemblies Jewish students mumbled "Onward Christian Soldiers." Sara Evans recalled a teacher who referred to her son as a "little Jewboy" and claimed she meant no offense. Robert Schultz's classes began each day with a Bible story. When the teacher read the New Testament, she reminded Schultz that his beliefs were wrong. A newspaper letter argued that students who did not believe in Jesus did not belong in public schools. The superintendent of schools, however, halted religious lessons in the classroom.

"They don't know us," Molly Freedman realized after a Christian woman expressed "surprise" to discover that Jews were "just like us." Freedman invited some Christian women to her home and arranged for the rebbetzin to answer their questions. In 1959 the Beth-El Sisterhood held a "Pageant of Festivals" at the synagogue for more than two hundred educators from Durham and Chapel Hill. Phyllis Dworsky set up tables, each of which focused on a holiday, and Dorothy Rose sang a song in English, Hebrew, and Yiddish. The newspaper saluted the event "for making a substantial contribution to better understanding."[10]

The McCarthy Era

The image of Jews as liberals and internationalists aroused nativist suspicions, always potent in the South. The McCarthy era stirred Jewish insecurities, especially after the Rosenberg affair. Northern intellectuals were suspected of leftist proclivities. Indeed, Hillel rabbi Maurice Schatz in a New Year sermon expressly linked Jewish destiny to progressive politics: "By our unreserved identification with liberalism and all humanitarian causes we can hope to recoup our incalculable losses of the past decade and emerge in our historic role of champions of forlorn hopes and unpopular causes." [11]

As they had in the Red Scare of 1921, local Jews in the McCarthy era asserted their Americanism. Henry Bane of B'nai B'rith warned the community that American Jewry must increase its activities in "defense of freedoms within our borders." B'nai B'rith maintained an Americanism Committee, and one prominent member, a lawyer, was a zealous hunter of Communist sympathizers. A popular sermon theme was "Democracy's Hebrew Roots," the subject of a 1952 lecture series by Rabbi Solomon Shapiro. [12] As president of the National Student Association, Allard Lowenstein spoke for the anti-Communist left, and his public debates with Communists sparked Chapel Hill politics.

A Jewish faculty member at Duke who was studying Russian recalled a law professor who complained to him that "we'll know when the Russians are coming when the Jews leave New York like rats leaving a sinking ship." Nathan Rosen, who had taught at the University of Kiev and at Black Mountain College before joining UNC, received word that an informant intended to implicate him before the House Un-American Activities Committee for allegedly associating with a Communist-front group during his student days at MIT. Although UNC asked him to stay, Rosen and his wife immigrated to Israel. He joined the physics department of the Technion and worked to bring blacklisted scientists to Israel. [13]

The leading local Communist was Junius Scales, a patrician North Carolinian, who married Sylvia Lacob, a Jewish woman from Chapel Hill. Scales claimed that his father-in-law, a hosiery salesman, "was subject to all the indignities reserved at that time for the non-rich Jew." His marriage ended in 1950, but at his 1954 trial for violation of the Smith Act, their Carrboro home was described as a "den of communism." [14] Local Jews felt anxiety about Lacob's leftist ties, Sarah Cohen recalled, "because of the stereotype that communists were Jews." The party organizer for North Carolina was Bernard Friedland of New York, and prominent academic Marxists, many of Jewish origin, visited Chapel Hill. Herbert Aptheker's well-publicized talk at UNC in 1966 provoked a challenge to the state legislature's anti-Communist Speaker Ban Law that ended in the U.S. Supreme Court.

American Civil Religion
Rabbis in the postwar years espoused a prophetic Judaism, a universalism that they asserted was the foundation of our republican government. The

best protection for Jews was to ensure that all peoples secured their rights. Brotherhood was America's civil religion. In 1960, when Beth-El conse- crated its new synagogue, Rabbi Herbert Berger wrote a statement, "One God and One Humanity," affirming the "fellowship of righteous people of all faiths and creeds." He drew parallels between "the gallant struggle to erect a lighthouse of freedom and democracy" in Israel and "the renais- sance of the prophetic spirit" in America.[15] Under the rubric of brother- hood, Judaism, Zionism, and Americanism were neither parochial nor con- tradictory but were universals worthy of tolerance.

When Max Samfield, an L & M research scientist, formed a chapter of the Toastmasters' Club in the early 1950s, he was greeted with silence when he said that he was not a church member, but the ice broke when he stated that he was a temple member. "The Christian community is much more able and willing and happy to accept a Jew who is honest about being Jewish than one who is trying awfully hard to pretend that he isn't," Samfield observed. The important thing in a southern town was to have a faith, any faith, and to be a member. When Judea Reform Congregation organized in 1961, churches opened their doors for its classes and services until it built a temple.[16]

The Holocaust had proven the results of enmity, and Jews appeared be- fore civic clubs and school assemblies to explain Judaism. Small-town Jews served as "ambassadors to the Gentiles," representatives of their nation to people who may have had little or no acquaintance with Jews. For Passover in 1953 a children's model seder was broadcast over radio station WTIK. Rabbi Berger spoke on "Brotherhood" as a "universal language" to the Durham Ministers Association and addressed the YMCA and YWCA on "Where Jews and Christians Meet." In 1968 Rabbi Joseph Asher of Greensboro delivered the baccalaureate address at the UNC commence- ment. Ministers were invited to the Beth-El pulpit on Friday nights, and in 1970 Berger was elected the Ministers Association's treasurer, the first rabbi to hold office.[17]

The campuses nurtured ecumenicism and progressive politics. Hillel directors of the 1950s and 1960s were social as well as religious liberals. Rabbi Samuel Perlman held a doctorate in sociology from Columbia University, and Rabbi Efraim Rosenzweig, who arrived in 1952, had worked in community relations in Montreal. Perlman stated that "we wel- come Christian students to all our functions" and conducted community model seders. Rosenzweig noted that a Hillel was vital on a southern campus "where everyone is usually 'church-directed.'" When Hillel hosted the Ministerial Alliance, some clergy reported that it was their first visit to a Jewish house of worship. Rabbi Rosenzweig was pleased to report that his Sabbath services brought together Moslems, Hindus, Christians, and Jews. Campus Judaism was inclusive and universalistic. Rabbi Joseph Levine, who arrived in 1962, taught courses on "Great Controversies in Jewish History" and held "dialogues" and "workshops" on such civil rights themes as "Passover and the History of Freedom."[18]

For Jews the ideal of brotherhood translated into political lobbying on behalf of Israel. The most popular forum continued to be a public event where prominent Gentiles were honored for their commitment to the Jewish state. In 1960, at a hotel banquet for three hundred that included Governor Luther Hodges, Durham Hadassah honored James and Mary Biddle Duke Semans with its Humanitarian Award and a plaque on Mt. Scopus. When Israeli ambassador Avraham Harman came to Durham in 1965, E. J. Evans brought Governor Terry Sanford to greet him.[19]

Southerners, polls showed, were receptive to Zionism, but sympathies owed more to religious and cultural affinities than to political support for the struggling state. In the 1960s Amnon Rapoport, an Israeli at UNC, spoke regularly at church dialogues with a Palestinian. He expressed shock at the ignorance about Israel that he encountered: "It was quite clear that I was a creature from another era and another continent." Nationally, the Six-Day War of 1967 strained Jewish-Christian relations. When fighting erupted, Mutt Evans led a delegation that rushed to Chapel Hill to confront Senator Sam Ervin. They came away feeling that he did not fully understand Jewish concerns for Israel's security.

Politics

The Jews' progress in politics reflected their movement from outsider to insider status. Demographic changes and the civil rights movement shifted the ethnic balances of power as the hegemony of white, Protestant, native southern males came under challenge. E. J. Evans's election as Durham mayor in 1950 set a precedent. Locally, Jews, many of whom were academic newcomers, would win local elections in numbers well beyond their proportion. The election of Jews coincided with the breaking of race and gender barriers. In 1951 women were first elected to the Durham town council, followed two years later by the first African American.[20]

When Evans first ran for mayor, religious and racial issues set the tenor of the campaign. Despite his origins as the northern-born son of Lithuanian immigrants, Evans belied stereotypes. Tall and athletic, with an

E. J. "Mutt" Evans and Sara Evans served as liaisons to both the Durham civic community and to global Jewish networks. Mutt Evans was Durham mayor from 1951 to 1963, and Sara Evans was a national figure in Hadassah, the women's Zionist society. (Courtesy of Eli Evans)

Americanized name, he had the courtly, courteous manner of his southern upbringing. Although a Yankee "by birth," a Chamber of Commerce publication declared, "Mr. Evans acts and thinks in the terms of a true Southerner and Tar Heel." It described Evans as "a tower of strength" to the Jewish community but added that "his active interest has transcended religious bounds to embrace" all Durham.[21]

As president of the Merchant's Association, Evans had served on the Citizens for Good Government Committee, a biracial group of labor and business leaders. After the incumbent mayor suddenly declined to seek re-election, the black faction, led by banker John Wheeler, advanced Evans's name. Conservative businessmen countered by nominating corporation lawyer James Patton. Although a member of the Durham Executives Club, Evans ran against the business establishment under the slogan "Equal Representation to All People." The newspaper described his campaign as "controversial." [22]

Evans aligned himself with southern progressives more committed to economic development than to racial politics. In 1948 Kerr Scott, a racial moderate, had been elected governor with a "Go Forward" campaign. Nevertheless, segregation and archconservatism remained deeply ingrained in North Carolina. In 1950 racists and Red-baiters pilloried Evans's mentor, UNC president Frank Graham, in an infamous senatorial primary.

Several anxious Jewish merchants expressed concern that Evans's campaign would arouse anti-Semitism and provoke racial unrest that might hurt their businesses. "Some of the old-timers . . . had perceptions of Jews as targets," Evans recalled. He attributed these fears to the immigrant generation. The Jewish community welcomed Evans's candidacy with pride.

One vocal anti-Semite did emerge. W. O. "Wimpy" Jones, publisher of the *Public Appeal,* ran *The Protocols of the Elders of Zion,* claiming that Evans's candidacy was one step toward world Jewish domination and linking him to the "communist" National Association for the Advancement of Colored People (NAACP). When New York attorney Joe Brady, a Durham native, sent a campaign donation, charges were made about outside Jewish influence. The Evanses were afflicted with obscene phone calls and personal threats. A pamphlet featured a picture of the Evanses' home with the admonition, "Do We Want a Goldberg or an Evans? What's the Difference? They're All Alike." Cooler heads prevented its distribution. Nonetheless, the police put the house under twenty-four-hour surveillance as election day approached. In his campaign literature Evans cited his service as Beth-El president and state UJA chairman because "people down here respect church work." [23]

Evans won the primary by eleven hundred votes, but two minor candidates forced a runoff. Newspaper ads condemned black bloc voting, and Evans called for an end to "prejudice, bigotry and hypocrisy." On the Sunday before election day, two prominent white Baptist ministers denounced from their pulpits the racial and religious divisions and declared their intention to vote for Evans. Evans won support in university precincts, but it was the black vote that provided the margin of victory. In the Hillside district Evans outpolled Patton by 1,241 to 64. The citywide tally was 6,691 to 5,916. The newspaper headline bannered, "Negro Vote Elects E. J. Evans."[24]

Evans proved popular and was comfortable as a public Jew. When asked if he found city council meetings rancorous, he replied, no, they were a cinch after synagogue board meetings. "Running a Church Trains for City Government" ran the next day's headline. Evans was unopposed in 1953 and in 1955. In 1957 he received a token challenge from the Reverend Julius Hicks, a radio evangelist, and a more serious one from Walter Biggs, a city councilman. Evans defended his accomplishments on a bond issue, downtown parking, and urban renewal, but the anti-Semitic fringe once again made noise. In May 1957 the mayor wrote an open letter to "Dear Voter" appealing for "fair play" and warning against hateful, unsigned handbills being distributed in the city. He reminded the voters that "the issues involved are neither racial, religious nor class" but the qualifications of the candidates. Evans won only six of twenty districts, but "aided by overwhelming support from three predominantly black precincts," he defeated Biggs 2,712 to 2,135. In 1957 Evans was selected president of the North Carolina League of Municipalities. Two years later, he was again unopposed.[25]

When Evans ran in 1961, he found himself challenged from the left and the right. The Central Labor Union and a deeply divided Committee on Negro Affairs endorsed his opponent, J. Leslie Atkins. In addition, Evans heard once more from Wimpy Jones, whose *Public Appeal* ran a weekly column, "Is the Mayor a Red?" Jones denounced the mayor's support of Anti-Defamation League Day as an anti-Christian plot of the "Zionist-dominated" Russians. He even blamed the mayor for religious divisions within the Jewish community. Evans, however, won by his largest margin ever, 5,507 to 4,207. Even without the endorsement of the leadership, he ran well in black areas and won support in every section of the city for the first time.[26]

With the election of John Kennedy as president in 1960 and Terry Sanford as governor in 1961, progressive elements in North Carolina came to the fore (although Durham voted for the segregationist candidate). Kennedy's election marked the ascendancy of minority Americans—Jews, Catholics, and blacks—over white Protestants.[27] Throughout the South, Jews won election to public office as never before. In North Carolina, Jews would also be elected mayors in Asheville, Elizabethtown, Fayetteville, Gastonia, Greensboro, Lumberton, Morganton, and Wilmington. In 1965 Jack Preiss, a Duke biochemist, was elected to the first of two terms on the Durham City Council, as Sunbelt newcomers began changing the political balances.

Civil Rights

The integration crisis confronted Jews with the contradictions of their place as white southerners. Jews regarded themselves as friends of blacks and contrasted their more enlightened attitudes and practices to those of white Gentile southerners. As a historically persecuted minority, traditionally regarded as a separate race, Jews believed themselves different. From their pulpits rabbis proclaimed the equality of all races. Whatever Jews believed, they did not want to jeopardize their hard-earned social and economic position by moving beyond public sentiment. Although the community remained generally cautious, some Jews, most of whom were newcomers, were in the streets protesting.

Local Jews may have been in a difficult position, but they did not feel so threatened as Jews deeper in the South. The late 1950s saw a rash of synagogue bombings. Undetonated sticks of dynamite were found at temples in Charlotte and Gastonia. North Carolina's leaders recognized that massive resistance and racial violence would hinder the economic development that they saw as the state's salvation. The state polished tokenism into a fine art as it minimally complied with court decrees.

The racial status quo prevailed through the 1950s and early 1960s. Durham's black capitalists represented a moderating force—several were prominent Republicans—who had improved their positions within a segregated society. While more militant blacks went to court to integrate UNC, President James Shepard gained professional programs at North Carolina College under separate but equal provisions. The threat posed by the militants led white civic leaders to cooperate with moderate blacks.

Blacks and Jews in Durham had a history of cooperation and goodwill. Jews patronized the black bank, which in turn made loans to the synagogue. Durham's Jews and black bourgeoisie shared class interests, and they had supported each other for reasons of both friendship and self-interest. A study of southern communities in the civil rights era noted that Durham came "closest to a real coalition of relatively equal [black and Jewish] partners." Jewish merchants, who often depended on black trade, believed that they were generous to black customers and gave more responsibility to their black employees than was the general practice. In Jewish stores black clerks waited on trade rather than just performed menial chores, Leon Dworsky noted. The Evanses' United Department Store had liberal check-cashing policies for blacks, permitted them to try on clothes, and installed restrooms for them. When a county judge told the Evanses that their biracial snack bar violated state segregation laws, the Evanses removed the seats, integrating it through a legal technicality. (Harry Golden saw it as a model for his Vertical Integration Plan, noting that southern laws permitted blacks and whites to stand together, but not to sit together.) Mary Mebane, an African American writer, recalled that the Evanses' stand-up luncheon counter was the only place downtown where she could eat without suffering the indignity of segregation.[28]

Yet, Jews and blacks remained socially apart, and their primary relations were economic. Jews and African Americans knew each other as landlords and tenants, merchants and customers, and employers and clerks or houseworkers. "In Chapel Hill you really didn't know a lot of blacks," Charlotte Levin recalled, "unless a black was your yardman or maid."

Southern civility and neighborliness ameliorated the harsher effects of segregation. Black customers recalled Jewish merchants as "very friendly, very nice people." Neil Johnston explained that the Jews "always treated us different, even if it was just a smile in passing. We never really saw them the same as we saw the other whites." Jews believed themselves to be compassionate employers. Levin recalled her maid telling her that she liked working for Jews because "they're so different than white people." Sam Gross, who moved from New York to Durham in 1960, offered an outsider's perspective: "The [Jewish] townspeople for the most part were much more sympathetic to the black community than the white Christian community, but still maintained some of the ethos of the white establishment."[29]

Certainly for some Jews, blacks were never more than "schvartzes." A Jewish woman expressed shock at walking into a store and overhearing the owner, a European-born merchant, shouting racial epithets into the telephone to a tenant who owed him rent. One Durham-born merchant and landlord commented, "We never had no trouble with them until they started integrating, and then we started having trouble." A wealthy businessman remarked that he did not pay the maid for her sick days because he did not want to encourage her to be shiftless. At least four times Jews were cited in newspaper headlines for owning substandard houses in black neighborhoods, an allegation that at least one vigorously denied. (Two of these articles were written by Jewish reporters and appeared in alternative newspapers published by Jews.)[30]

For Jewish southerners, sensitive to racial animosity and the potential

for violence, moderation seemed the wisest course. Jews were caught between their principles and their interests, between their sympathy for
blacks as an oppressed minority and their fears of white economic back-
lash. A rabbi stopping at a downtown newsstand overheard several mill
workers comment that the murdered civil rights workers Chaney, Schwer-
ner, and Goodman had gotten exactly what they deserved. Storekeepers depended economically on the mill workers, and self-interest dictated caution. In Chapel Hill the Jewish merchants were "silent" on civil
rights.[31]

Although established Jews were not civil rights advocates, they disdained the extreme of the segregationists. Jews knew that a racist who
hated blacks would have no love for Jews either. Local racists such as
Wimpy Jones regularly attacked Jews as Communists, and the state was the
home to several hate groups that mixed anti-Semitic diatribes in their
racist propaganda. Blacks were a shield for Jews, deflecting antagonisms
that could just as easily be directed against them.

By and large, Jews and blacks "went our own way," recalled Rabbi
Simon Glustrom, who came to Beth-El in 1948. Glustrom, a native Atlan-
tan, observed, "Most of the congregants were storekeepers who wanted
peace and quiet." Although they were "quite conservative" on race, "they
weren't rednecks." After living in New York, Glustrom and his wife,
Helen, a Canadian, felt "culture shock" coming to a society where restrooms and water fountains were marked "colored." When the rabbi invited a black Sunday school group to a Sabbath service, the cantor, who
had come from Georgia, became disconcerted, remarking to the rabbi in
Hebrew that the black faces made him think it was midnight. Some congregants thought that Glustrom was "too liberal" and "moving too fast,"
but the criticisms were mildly expressed, and his tenure was never threatened. Jews were "amenable to change," he noted, and he observed that he
and Mutt Evans worked to improve the racial climate.

The internal conflict Jews felt as southerners came to the fore in 1954
when the congregation interviewed a candidate for rabbi. "He seemed to
be the ideal for our community," a congregant recalled, and he had passed
the board and congregational reviews. At a final interview the board
learned that the candidate was a member of the NAACP, and he declared
his intention to continue his activism in Durham. "There was a lot of
discussion. We felt he was right," the congregant remembered, "but what
were we going to do?"[32] He was not hired.

North Carolina's rabbis were racial liberals. In 1955 the North Carolina

Association of Rabbis, acting in concert with Christian bodies, passed a resolution informing Governor Luther Hodges of "its whole-hearted support of the Supreme Court decision calling for de-segregation in the Public Schools." The rabbis stated, "We dare not permit the existence of laws which discriminate against any human being." The rabbis urged the governor to act "without undue delay." The timing of the resolution was significant. Only weeks earlier the governor in a radio and television report to the state had called on both races to continue segregation voluntarily, arguing that separate schools would serve the best interests of both races. A year later the rabbis passed a second resolution that called for "a swift end to segregation."[33]

In his Purim sermon of 1957 Rabbi Louis Tuchman, Beth-El's last Orthodox rabbi, lectured on "the problem of desegregation": "Purim teaches us that we must oppose all attempts at stifling man's freedom and his right to enjoy that freedom. . . . As Jews . . . we must speak out clearly and forcefully whenever the freedom of any individual is threatened." He reiterated this message on Hanukkah: "If we circumvent or pretend that it doesn't exist, then the problem of integration will not disappear. We must thrust ourselves into the fray and proclaim for every man his God given right to bask in the warm rays of freedom and equality." Commonly southern rabbis sermonized in favor of civil rights, even if they did not become activists. Tuchman's stand as an Orthodox rabbi in the South belies the stereotype that associates social justice with religious liberals, Reform rabbis in particular.[34]

Rabbi Herbert Berger, who succeeded Tuchman in 1957, was personally liberal, but he recalled that the congregants' attitude to civil rights was "not to rock the boat." At national rabbinical conventions Berger was asked to march with Dr. King. "I did not want to," he reflected. "I felt constrained. My congregation would be upset. I didn't want to fly in their faces." Yet, he noted that these same Jews also felt "closely allied" with blacks in rejecting inequality. Southern Jews were often quietly approving of the civil rights movement. At the Evanses' home and at interfaith services he met Durham's African American elite. The rabbi felt "honored" to meet these bankers and insurance executives. He invited UNC professor Richard Cramer, leader of the campus NAACP, to speak at Beth-El on civil rights. He confessed to Cramer the difficulty of speaking out when a prominent congregant was a slumlord. When demonstrations to open public accommodations tore apart Durham in 1963, Rabbi Berger joined nearly seven hundred citizens—including dozens of Jewish faculty—who signed a "pledge of support" to merchants who "adopt a policy of equal treatment to all without regard to race."[35]

In the 1950s white flight took hold in Durham, and the schools became predominantly black. Desegregation made token progress in the 1960s, but it was not until 1970 that federally mandated integration was implemented. Under court order, UNC desegregated its law, medical, and graduate schools. In 1955 black undergraduates were admitted. Duke, fearing a loss of federal funding, integrated its graduate programs in 1961 and its undergraduate colleges a year later (apparently dropping its Jewish quotas, too).[36]

In February 1960, black college students at North Carolina A & T began a sit-in at a lunch counter in nearby Greensboro, launching a protest movement that would transform the South. A week later similar sit-ins began in Durham and shortly thereafter in Chapel Hill. By 1963 the protest movement began targeting local hotels, restaurants, and theaters. Street protests and mass arrests rocked Durham and Chapel Hill. Violence simmered. The home of the chairman of Durham's human relations committee was bombed. Chapters of the Congress of Racial Equality (CORE), the NAACP, the Southern Christian Leadership Conference (SCLC), and the Student Non-Violent Coordinating Committee (SNCC) were on the scene, and Martin Luther King Jr., James Farmer, and Roy Wilkins visited town. Local activist Floyd McKissick, the first black graduate of UNC Law School, led the national Congress of Racial Equality.

As mayor of Durham, E. J. Evans interceded with the white business establishment to meet black demands. Evans appointed the city's first black policemen, firemen, and municipal supervisors. He pushed for an Urban Renewal Authority that won federal grants for low-income housing. In 1957 he instituted the biracial Committee on Human Relations. Evans's stand contrasts with the later resistance of another Jewish mayor, Henry Loeb of Memphis, who ran as a segregationist in 1959.[37]

Evans remained consistent to his principles as a peacemaker even as the civil rights movement grew increasingly militant; a liberal in the 1950s was a moderate by the 1960s. Nationally, the black-Jewish alliance was unraveling as black power advocates spurned white patronage. Evans recalled one incident when the police called his home to inform him that a sit-in was taking place at the downtown Woolworth's. He rushed to the store and assured the black demonstrators that he would press their demands with the business leaders if they would end their protest. They left, but that night windows were smashed up and down Main Street.[38] Evans's policies of conciliation may not have appeased increasingly militant blacks in the early 1960s, but Durham did remain quiet as it moved slowly and inevitably toward integration. Its racial moderation paralleled the Atlanta, rather than the Birmingham, model.

The Jews as a community did not take a stand on civil rights, but "a large number of Jewish people [were] actively involved in the elimination of racial segregation," Sam Gross observed. The civil rights revolution revealed divisions in the Jewish community between the established merchants, who tended to be conservative, and the newly arrived students and faculty, who were typically liberal. Unlike the merchants, who depended on the public for their livelihoods, the faculty were salary earners who had the security of their campuses.

These divisions came to the fore when Hillel rabbi Efraim Rosenzweig hired an African American woman as secretary and added his name to a list of Ministerial Alliance clergy endorsing integration. The state's B'nai B'rith hierarchy pressed him to resign. A Durham Jewish lawyer, intent on finding Communists and fellow travelers, turned his sights on the liberal Rosenzweig. The rabbi was warned that Jewish businessmen across the state would withhold their financial support of Hillel. In fact, B'nai B'rith groups in Virginia, Louisiana, and Mississippi had passed resolutions requesting the Anti-Defamation League to "reconsider its stand" in support of desegregation. Duke and UNC professors appealed personally on the rabbi's behalf to national B'nai B'rith Hillel headquarters in Washington. "The national office was supportive," Rosenzweig recalled, "but I had to live with the local situation." Hospitalized with ulcers, he resigned in 1962. Local Jews then asked him to lead the newly formed Judea Reform Congregation. Rosenzweig remained active, and the rabbi and a black Baptist minister, the Reverend Mr. Mosley, organized gatherings to bring their congregations together.[39]

For the most part, the business community did not resist integration. In 1961, when university students called for a boycott of segregated businesses, one or two Jewish-owned stores were on the banned list, whereas seven or eight were approved. Durham B'nai B'rith sponsored civil rights advocates, including attorney Morris Abram, for its installation dinner in 1956. Harry Golden, Charlotte's inimitable raconteur whose *Carolina Israelite* was outspokenly integrationist, also addressed the group. In 1960, the lodge honored two prominent African American civic leaders, Walter Hicks and John Wheeler of the Mechanics and Farmers Bank. Another program featured Duke law professor Melvin Shimm discussing civil rights in North Carolina.[40]

Several established Jews abandoned the usual caution in support of integration. In Chapel Hill Harry and Sybil Macklin desegregated their Franklin Street deli, the first restaurant in town, if not the state, to do so. Harry's became "a guerilla command post" for civil rights protestors, and a prosegregation radio announcer, Jesse Helms, denounced the place over the air. After living in the North, Hazel Gladstein Wishnov had returned to her native Durham as a member of the NAACP. She recalled warm relations with her black coworkers at Durham County Social Services. When an office banquet was scheduled at segregated Harvey's Cafeteria, she protested to her supervisor and boycotted the event. At a Chapel Hill meeting of the North Carolina Council of Women's Organizations, Molly Freedman, whose husband was a merchant, confronted a crisis when several black delegates unexpectedly appeared. She received heated criticism for accepting their credentials and welcoming them to the banquet. Running for UNC student body president, Eli Evans expected to lose when he called for desegregation of the dormitories, but he won by 250 votes.[41]

In Chapel Hill the civil rights crisis tested the character of a town that prided itself on liberalism. The response was, at best, cautious. In 1961 a school choice plan allowed for token desegregation while giving white parents an option out. A public accommodations law was hotly debated. Meanwhile, local blacks and student activists were beaten and arrested as they blocked store doors and sat down in streets. One black demonstrator was doused with ammonia.

Jewish activists drawn south by the civil rights movement did not cite a specifically Jewish motive for their commitment. Rosemary Ezra, a Californian who came to Durham–Chapel Hill as a CORE field worker, was "not connected to the Jewish community" in her activism. Other Jews noted that the movement had a Christian tone although Jews were invited to participate. Meetings were held in churches and led by ministers; protestors declared their intention to bear witness and invoked the example of Christ. One Jew who worked closely with Christian clergy was Allard Lowenstein, the former UNC student who returned to North Carolina as a graduate student and then taught at North Carolina State. Lowenstein organized sit-downs in Raleigh and helped plan strategy in

Chapel Hill. The governor denounced him as an "agitator," and Durham racist Wimpy Jones excoriated "the chief instigator . . . the cheapest little Jewish agitator we [sic] ever know—New Yorker Al Lowenstein."[42]

In 1964 when a judge sentenced a cadre of Chapel Hill protestors to jail for sitting in, blocking traffic, and resisting arrest (by going limp), a half-dozen were Jews. Rosemary Ezra received a six-month sentence in Women's Prison from a judge whom she thought anti-Semitic, becoming "the first Jewess ever to be locked up there." Ezra was unable to pay her $500 fine because she had mortgaged her car and home to finance civil rights activities. Joseph Tieger, an honors graduate of Duke, had, in the judge's words, the "dubious distinction of having the most arrests in Orange County" for civil rights. His twenty-three arrests earned him a twelve-month sentence, delaying his plans to enroll at Brandeis. Tieger was a CORE field worker, and the judge suggested that he was "being used by the international conspiracy who would destroy this country." Tieger's father came from New Jersey with a lawyer from the American Civil Liberties Union to secure his release. Shelly Blum, Carol Koplon, and Ellen Abrams also were convicted. UNC student Paul Wellstone became active after he saw Klansmen spit on demonstrators in downtown Chapel Hill. In the late 1960s he led a strike in support of black cafeteria workers who had been overworked and underpaid. The strike tore apart the campus, and the governor deployed the state police.[43]

Faculty did not cross the line into civil disobedience. They were liberals who picketed, signed petitions, and served on committees in support of integration. In 1961 UNC students published a declaration in the *Daily Tar Heel* asking why the faculty had not taken a stand. In response, faculty liberals, including more than a dozen Jews, signed a statement calling on local theaters "to admit all persons without regard to race." Professor Rashi Fein's support of the statement brought the wrath of his dean upon him. Rashi and Ruth Fein soon left town in measure because they found the episode so "distasteful." Ruth Fein recalled the verbal abuse she heard as president of the League of Women Voters when she sat with a black woman at a registration booth. Professor Dan Okun chaired the Committee of Concerned Citizens, which mediated between CORE and Chapel Hill town government on desegregating public accommodations. Richard Cramer, a UNC sociologist, served as the first faculty advisor to the campus NAACP. Larry and Miriam Slifkin, native small-town southerners, picketed a local theater. In Durham Sam and Hudi Gross's children became "token" whites in a desegregated school that became almost entirely black. Hudi Gross was taunted as a "honky" by her children's classmates. "It was a very trying period," she remembered. Grant Kornberg, son of a Duke professor, was the lone white student at Hillside High.

Women were especially active in confronting racism. Lucille Handler, a Duke faculty wife, was longtime president of the Durham League of Women's Voters, one of Durham's few integrated civic societies. As the lone Jewish member of Chapel Hill's Interchurch Council, Dorothy Blum, a socialist since her student days in Germany, tutored students at Lincoln High School and started the Progressive Teenagers Group at a black church. North Carolina native Charlotte Levin, a faculty wife, joined the multiracial, interdenominational Panel of American Women, which spoke on civil rights at local churches, schools, and social clubs. Levin received threatening letters, and several bigots told her pointedly that "all Jews are nigger-lovers."

Jewish Communal Life

In the immediate postwar years Durham Jews maintained their social circles as they always had. In the evenings they gathered at the B'nai B'rith clubrooms for television and card playing. Tuesday night bingo games were noisy, rollicking affairs. In the summers they vacationed at Virginia Beach or Carolina Beach, where they renewed ties with other southern Jews. Children were packed off to Camp Blue Star or Camp Tel Yehuda. The annual Thanksgiving dance drew teenagers from across the state. Unwelcome into the upper crust of North Carolina society, Jews held an annual debutante ball in High Point. Durham girls "came out" in a cotillion. This networking, reinforced by kinship ties, preserved the family feeling of southern Jewry.

The social columns reported weddings and Bar Mitzvahs as relatives gathered from down South and up North. Celebrations were held in the synagogue, and the women decorated, cooked, and served. These affairs had the character of a southern family reunion as out-of-town relatives arrived for a weekend of dinners and get-togethers. Rose Robbins and Mildred Margolis operated a kosher catering service, obtaining meat from a Charlotte market. For funerals mourners knew that community members would come to their home to fix meals. Chevra Kadisha leader Sam Daniel brooked no refusal when he called on a member to serve as a pall bearer or to make a prayer quorum.

Durham received a stream of emissaries, some of whom were rabbis, from domestic and foreign Jewish charities who went door to door ap-

pealing for funds. Not a few fit the Yiddish term *schnorrer* (beggar). To resolve this problem, the merchants developed an informal fund-raising system. "Yankee" Zuckerman walked into a Jewish store and shouted, "Give
me a dollar!" The merchant dug into his pocket to help build a yeshiva in
Brooklyn or an orphanage in Jerusalem. Itinerant Jews needing help wandered into the pawnshop of Sam and Florence Margolis near the bus station. The Margolises gave them a meal, a room, and bus fare to Miami or
New York.

By the 1960s Durham no longer supported a kosher baker or butcher,
and the intensity of Jewish ethnic life dissipated with the fading of the
immigrant generation and the increase in suburban dispersal. Mark Margolis recalled how as a teenager he would take his grandfather to synagogue on Saturday mornings. The old man pulled his arm to come make
a minyan, but the youngster would pull even harder to break away. Newly
arriving Jews, without family roots, felt the generational pull even less.

The small-town intimacy of Jewish community life did not endure. A
walk downtown had meant a round of friendly chats, Alfreda Kaplan recalled, but the days when "we knew everybody" were passing. As the business district emptied, the B'nai B'rith clubrooms closed. The immigrant
generation was retiring or dying. Pillars of the community pulled up
stakes, often for a Florida retirement. Youth continued to depart. The emptying of Roxboro Street and the sprawl into the suburbs broke the feeling
that the Jewish community was an extended family. "There wasn't that
oneness anymore," Sam Margolis lamented.

Academic Jews

"Had it not been for the academic community," observed Henry Bane,
"the Jewish community would have died." Unlike earlier mercantile migrants who had quickly integrated, the academic families remained at the
margin. Ruth Greenberg, who moved to Chapel Hill in 1949, noted that
many faculty "never denied they were Jews, but they just weren't dedicated." They were concerned with their careers and found social outlets
through their departments.

The small Jewish community in Chapel Hill revolved around Hillel.
"Those of us who were active in the Hillel Foundation felt this was our
synagogue," Pearl Morrison recalled. The Hillel director served as a community rabbi, performing weddings and baby namings and converting
Christian women who married Jews. The men met for Torah study and
bagels and lox while the women baked and held card parties to fund its

program. Sam and Mary Berman, who had lived in town since 1914, became surrogate grandparents for the community. The elderly, childless Bermans were a warm, endearing couple who took special delight in the Jewish children.

A concern for their children's Jewish futures drew academic families into congregational life. Pearl Morrison recalled, "We wanted our children brought up in the Jewish faith and have a good Jewish education." The Chapel Hill women established a cooperative Sunday school that met monthly in a member's home (and later at the Hillel house). They soon found that without a synagogue their program lacked "backbone" and began carpooling to Beth-El.

Unlike the previous generation, which tended to be careerist and assimilationist, the faculty who came to Duke and UNC in the 1950s included committed Jews who were unwilling or felt no pressure to compromise their Jewishness to advance themselves. This generation was shaped by World War II, the Holocaust, and Zionism. Jews no longer felt so strongly the discrimination to suppress their Jewish identities to advance their careers. Martin Lakin, a Duke psychologist, and Musia Lakin, a child educator, had resided in Israel in the late 1940s; he had served with the Haganah (pre-state Israeli army) and held a bachelor of arts degree from Hebrew University. Duke geneticist Sam Gross had attended Yeshiva Etz Chaim in Brooklyn, and Hudi Gross held a certificate from the Beth Jacob Teacher's Seminary. Economist Rashi Fein was the son of the Jewish historian Isaac Fein, and Ruth Fein's father was Rabbi Isadore Breslau, the former Camp Butner chaplain.

Jewish Revival

Jews were swept along in the national postwar religious revival. As Jews looked at their youth being raised as Americans in an open society, fears for Jewish survival grew. The European and Zionist crises had postponed local demands. With Israel established, Max Lieberman, long-time chairman of the United Jewish Appeal, recognized the need to look homeward: "I'm not saying we shouldn't send money to the UJA, but there comes a time when a man must think of himself." In Hebrew he recited Hillel's famous dictum, "If I am not for myself, who will be for me?"

The 1950s and 1960s were marked by synagogue building and congregation forming. A Hillel house rose in Chapel Hill in 1951; Conservative Jews built a new Beth-El Synagogue in 1957; and Reform Jews organized Judea Reform Congregation in 1961. The local situation reflected national trends. From 1945 to 1956 annual spending on churches and synagogues leaped from $26 million to $775 million. Jewish affiliation jumped nationally from 20 percent in the 1930s to nearly 60 percent in the 1950s; these figures were highest in small and midsized cities and lowest in metropolitan areas.[44]

Nationally, the establishment of Israel transformed American Jewish philanthropy; more than $200 million was raised in 1948 alone. Soliciting funds for the building of the Jewish state had been the community's principal philanthropic endeavor. The Durham Federation of Jewish Charities was primarily a fund-raiser for the United Jewish Appeal. The federation's annual banquets drew as many as two hundred to hear an Israeli general or journalist. UJA campaigns were dominated by a handful of downtown businessmen, and others gave only tokenly. E. J. Evans headed the state UJA for seven terms, a post also held by real-estate developer Abe Greenberg. In the late 1950s and early 1960s newcomers from Duke and the VA hospital assumed UJA leadership, and UNC faculty held a drive. Raising money for the UJA became a civil religion. The UJA, with its public testimonials, conferred community status.[45]

Durham, Molly Freedman reported, was the "Tel Aviv of the South. . . . It has been said that Durham has more Jewish organizations than any other city in the state" with its Junior and Senior Hadassah, Mizrachi, B'nai B'rith, Aleph Zadik Aleph, Sisterhood, North Carolina Association of Jewish Women–North Carolina Association of Jewish Men, Young Judea, United Jewish Appeal, and Jewish Federation. Local Jews rose to state and even national offices, and Durham hosted regional conventions. For women especially, philanthropic organizations became the focus of their social lives, a means to achieve community status.[46]

As newcomers took leadership from established southern families, the community restructured itself. Once vital groups such as Mizrachi and B'nai B'rith began declining in the 1960s while new populations created new institutions to serve their political and professional interests. Hadassah succeeded in sustaining itself as the community changed. Its concerns— children and health care—were perennial women's issues, and its legacy in socialism appealed to liberal faculty women. Hadassah was passed mother to daughter. Retirees brought their activism with them. By 1959 Chapel Hill formed a subgroup of fourteen. Junior Hadassah, which had expired, was revived in 1957 as Young Judea. The youth group, too, rose and fell with its leadership.[47] Until the early 1960s Mizrachi thrived, adding new members and raising several thousand dollars yearly. Its leadership was aging, however, and as an Orthodox organization its base of local support was dwindling. The Dworsky family continued as Mizrachi stalwarts, but the chapter ceased to be active.

B'nai B'rith also suffered from demographic changes. Its clubrooms remained the community's social center. Durhamites served as state presidents, and Robert Lipton rose to international director. For youth B'nai B'rith created the networking that ensured Jewish continuity. Their annual dances at Forest Hills Country Club drew teenagers from across the state. In 1952 a lodge formed in Chapel Hill with twenty members, including faculty and merchants. Women joined Hillel auxiliary. After the mid-1960s B'nai B'rith ceased to maintain itself as the old crowd aged and departed. The card-playing camaraderie did not appeal to newcomers, and the clubrooms closed. The Chapel Hill merchants were too few and the faculty too transient to sustain a lodge. Durham B'nai B'rith lingered, holding a softball game or picnic for hospitalized children, but it was a chapter in name only. The local struggles of B'nai B'rith, as well as Mizrachi and Hadassah, were typical of the national situation as its aging membership failed to replenish itself.[48]

A Suburban Synagogue

Beth-El Synagogue in the postwar years had not taken account of the generational changes that were transforming American Jewry. Ritual observance and practice of dietary laws had declined, yet only an Orthodox congregation served the community. Beth-El was struggling to maintain its cohesion as the community grew religiously pluralistic, especially as newcomers overwhelmed the smaller established community. In 1957 Beth-El moved irreversibly into the Conservative camp, and four years later Reform Jews established Judea Reform Congregation.

Beth-El's evolution from Orthodoxy followed national trends that saw Conservatism emerge as Judaism's dominant branch, growing from fewer than 200 congregations in 1945 to 443 in 1953. From 1955 to 1961, 269 more congregations joined the movement. The pace of change from Orthodoxy to Conservatism differed by locality. It correlated with suburbanization, economic mobility, and the extent of Americanization from immigrant culture. Downtown Orthodox synagogues were abandoned, and new suburban multipurpose centers arose. The postwar synagogue was attuned to middle-class families and focused on youth. The first priority was to preserve Jewish peoplehood. With Jews now dispersed, the synagogue became a social center with facilities for catered parties. A parking

Beth-El Synagogue, dedicated in 1957, was designed by Percival Goodman, a nationally prominent synagogue architect who popularized multipurpose floor plans for a religiously flexible people. (Courtesy of the Rare Book, Manuscript, and Special Collections Library, Duke University)

lot accommodated commuters. These striking new buildings attested to taste and prosperity. To design the Beth-El Synagogue-Center, Sara and E. J. Evans traveled to New York to engage the services of Percival Goodman, the nation's foremost synagogue architect. His "flexible plan" layout accommodated an adaptable Judaism. In contrast to the cathedral-style synagogue of 1921, which imitated church designs, Jews now erected an edifice that appeared distinctly and confidently different. Jews had left the ghetto behind them spiritually and materially.[49]

To see the project to fruition, the congregation needed to raise $150,000. The board secured a loan on liberal terms from the black-owned Mechanics and Farmers Bank. Abe Rosenstein, as his father once had, saved Beth-El financially by purchasing the old synagogue and two neighboring houses for the congregation's benefit. Businessmen dominated the twelve-member Synagogue-Center Steering Committee, but, of significance, the committee also included two women, Sara Evans and Edith Abelkop, the Sisterhood president. Of the 250 donors to the building fund, most were families who came to open stores in the 1920s, 1930s, and 1940s. A dozen were faculty. Sisterhood took its customary women's role, pledging $15,000 to furnish the kitchen and to air-condition the building. From the Gentile community donations came from John Sprunt Hill and Watts Hill, Durham bankers and benefactors.[50] In 1954 the congregation purchased a lot on the corner of Watts and Markham Streets in Trinity Park. The site was symbolic. It was one block from the Duke campus but distant from Roxboro Street.

Dedicated in 1957, Beth-El Synagogue-Center embodied the principles of American Judaism. The unornamented, functional architecture was modernist, but the post-and-lintel construction also evoked the Jerusalem Temple and the classical synagogues of antiquity. The "beautiful" building, as described in the booklet "Know Your House of Worship," united the "spiritual truths of Hebrew culture and religion and the dynamic impact of the teachings of American Democracy."[51] Its sculpture and stained glass attested to wealth and artistic sensitivity. The synagogue-center was a blended, multipurpose, Jewish American compromise. It included a mikva for Orthodox worshippers and a shower for basketball players.

Most congregants rejoiced when they gathered for the first High Holiday services, but the Orthodox were not pleased. There was no *mehitzah* (women's partition), nor did the mikva function properly. The ark was not oriented eastward toward Jerusalem as was traditional. The loudspeaker system, if used, violated Orthodox strictures on the use of electricity on Sabbath and holidays. "There was no way that we could have a truly Orthodox service in that building," a congregant protested. "Many of the old men were really angry when they saw the way the building turned out. The younger men had control of the money and the plans . . . and basically did what they wanted. They wanted the building to be more appealing to the university people so they built the congregation a nice, American synagogue."[52]

Certainly, synagogue leaders wanted to attract faculty families, but it was also true that the current members were middle-class, Americanized Jews. Orthodoxy's hold loosened as the immigrant generation declined. S. H. Dworsky, pillar of Orthodoxy, had died in 1955. The new synagogue was a symbol of the battle that Orthodox Jews were waging against what they saw as Conservatism's compromising spirit, its willingness to sacrifice sacred doctrine in a futile appeal for popularity. Orthodox men sat by themselves in a front corner, holding tightly to their old prayer books. Although the United Synagogue voted to permit women to read from the

Torah in 1955, not until 1958 did Beth-El conduct its first Bat Mitzvah. The young women led Sabbath services, but they were not permitted to chant the Haftorah, the biblical reading that marked acceptance as members.[53]

Rabbi Louis Tuchman, who had arrived from Charleston, was dedicated to maintaining Beth-El's Orthodoxy. In an article for the *American Jewish Times-Outlook,* "A Traditional Rabbi's View: The New Kesuba," he attacked the Conservative marriage contract because it permitted women to initiate divorce proceedings. He argued that Conservative rabbis, with their historical approach, denied the divine origins of the Torah. Orthodoxy, Tuchman continued, "remains the sole guardian and staunch upholder of tradition."[54] Tuchman ran an effective children's program and was well liked personally. Nonetheless, with the move to the new synagogue-center, Beth-El's days as Orthodox ended; the rabbi, too, wanted a Jewish day school for his children. In 1958, Beth-El's last Orthodox rabbi left for Freehold, New Jersey.

Rabbi Herbert Berger, who succeeded Tuchman, had appeal for every congregational faction. He was a graduate of Yeshiva University, the Hebrew Theological College in Chicago, and the Jewish Theological Seminary. Descended from rabbis, Berger had served as a Hebrew school principal, a Hillel adviser, university lecturer, and army chaplain. Although a native of Cleveland, he had spent twenty years in the South at pulpits in Memphis and Savannah. Quite extraordinary for a rabbi, he was divorced. In small communities such as Durham the rebbetzin took a lead in the school program and women's organizations. Apart from this disability, Beth-El was fortunate to find such a qualified leader, given the shortage of Conservative rabbis.[55]

Berger was a learned man, well versed in Talmudic literature as well as in secular subjects. For the old-timers he spoke fluent Yiddish. For the merchants he became a Rotarian and delivered invocations at civic clubs. For the Duke doctors he explained the intricacies of Jewish medical ethics. His sermon on love expressed a psychoanalytic viewpoint. Berger pushed adult congregants to learn Hebrew. At the same time he introduced more English into the services.[56]

With a new building and a new Conservative rabbi, Beth-El succeeded in attracting the academic community. With improved roads, Chapel Hill families began to join, enrolling their children in Sunday school. In 1959, Beth-El announced twenty-two new members, and a year later, a "Welcome Newcomers Sabbath" hosted ten more families, most of whom were faculty.

The 1960s were transitional years. In 1963, the board of trustees consisted of five merchants, three faculty, and two lawyers. In 1964 Bernard Greenberg became Beth-El's first university-connected president. Greenberg was a unifying force because he was Orthodox and a long-time resident. Duke law professor Melvin Shimm, who served from 1965 to 1970, noted that in his term "the balance had changed. The congregation was at least one-half university people." Henry Bane saw Beth-El evolve from a "shul into a synagogue."

Resentments arose as academic families made their presence felt, and some drew a line between "us-and-them." Northern urbanites had to adapt upon finding themselves among southern Jews. New Yorker Hudi Gross recalled her first Bar Mitzvah when a "dear little boy" stood on the bimah and declared, "Ah loves mah Torah." Her husband, Sam, was charmed by the "very pleasant" voice of lay cantor Jacob Zuckerman, but the "Southern accent" contrasted to the prayer style of his Brooklyn yeshiva. Businessmen regarded the faculty as incompetents when it came to managing the budget.

Jews, regardless of backgrounds, united in their concern for the Jewish education of an assimilated youth. The focus of the educational program was preserving Jewish peoplehood. Whereas earlier generations had been drilled in the behavioral mechanics of prayer and ritual, primarily for the Bar Mitzvah, the emphasis now was on Jewish identity defined as a consciousness. Adopting tenets of modern pedagogy, Jewish education borrowed from psychology as much as from religious tradition. Being Jewish meant developing an "awareness," a feeling of pride and self-esteem. School requirements included the ability to read three prayers in Hebrew and attend services, but, inspired by a new repertoire of Israeli song and dance, students were also encouraged to enhance their creativity. Confirmation, based on Protestant models, became an important event. The qualifying exam certified the students to be good Jews and committed Zionists. The student had to explain the Talmud and kosher laws, identify great rabbis from Hillel to Rashi to the Vilna Gaon, give the date and meaning of all Jewish holidays, and demonstrate knowledge of Israel's problems. At elaborate ceremonies on Shavouth (Festival of Weeks), the graduates recited the Confirmand's Prayer: "We are aware as never before of the meaning of the words, 'To Be a Jew.' May this sense of awareness remain with us during the coming years, so that we may be worthy of the great heritage that is ours."[57]

The children were imbued with a sense of Jewish communal responsibility. They were sent to national conventions of the United Synagogue Youth in Washington and Young Judea in Florida. As children matured, they progressed from Sunday school to Young Judea to Hillel and then on to Hadassah or B'nai B'rith.

How lasting an effect supplementary Jewish education had on students is questionable. Students learned to read Hebrew phonetically without comprehension. In the early 1950s the rabbi relied on a signed contract to ensure that students met their obligations. He admitted in a bulletin, "As you all know, working with the confirmands was, at times, exasperating." A 1954 student newspaper complained that parents did not attend services but expected their children to do so. Calls for decorum in religious school were constant across generations. Students retained vivid memories of classmates who flirted, cut up, giggled, and passed notes. A student in the 1960s recalled that he learned "very little" and that his friends "didn't take it seriously." Students were less than enthused about attending religious classes after a day in public school.[58]

Reform Congregation

Until the 1960s, Reform Jews had never been sufficiently numerous to form their own congregation. The few remaining early German Reform families were unobservant or were dying out. The impetus to found a Reform congregation came from the children and grandchildren of Durham's east European Jews. Ethel Mae Bernson was descended from two of Durham's oldest Jewish families, the Fagans and Zuckermans. Hazel Wishnov was the great-niece of cigarette roller Moses Gladstein. Both women had left Durham for the North, married, and returned.

They found allies among Reform Jews who moved to Durham in the 1950s. Max Samfield, descended from antebellum German immigrants, was the grandson and namesake of a Reform rabbi in Memphis. Jacob and Alfreda Kaplan, former New Yorkers, attended the Reform temple in Raleigh. Several families with Reform sympathies had joined Beth-El but felt uncomfortable there. With the new academic migration they now had the numbers to create a Reform congregation.

In October 1961, Richard and Ethel Mae Bernson convened a meeting in their home. The business families, the Bernsons and the Kaplans, provided leadership, but Duke Medical Center was well represented. Of the twenty-three people at the initial gathering, sixteen held doctoral degrees, and two others were faculty widows. Several were European émigrés. Fifteen also had children, a strong motive to organize. Once they committed to found a Reform congregation, the organizers scanned telephone books and began calling people with Jewish-sounding names. Although they inadvertently called some Gentiles, they more often received enthusiastic responses. News spread by word of mouth, and people began calling them. Max Samfield arranged an open meeting in a hall at Liggett and Myers. A representative from the Union of American Hebrew Congregations (UAHC), the Reform governing body, was summoned to address the group.

"That was when it really got started," Alfreda Kaplan recalled. More than one hundred people attended. The UAHC official was skeptical. First there was a territorial problem with Raleigh's Temple Beth Or because the UAHC would certify only one synagogue within twenty-five miles. After the meeting a group adjourned to the home of Alan Sindler, a Duke political scientist. They stayed until 2:00 A.M., by which time the UAHC official was so impressed with the group's enthusiasm that he agreed to recommend certification. This process of "spontaneous combustion" was being repeated across the country. In 1947 the UAHC claimed 364 congregations; this figure rose to 520 in 1955 and to 646 in 1963.[59]

At first, Judea Reform functioned without a rabbi. Hillel rabbi Efraim Rosenzweig was at this time embroiled with B'nai B'rith over his hiring of a black woman as secretary. Local Jews endorsed his civil rights stand and sought to retain him in the community. When asked to lead the new congregation, the rabbi was skeptical that the numbers were sufficient, but he agreed to work on a "trial" basis with a token salary. After one year, the rabbi "felt that this was a congregation with which I could happily share further years of my life as Rabbi." Rosenzweig, whose Russian-born parents had settled in Cincinnati, was raised in the milieu of midwestern classical Reform Judaism. As a child he had attended the religious school of Rabbi David Philipson, secretary of the Pittsburgh Platform. He graduated from the University of Cincinnati and received ordination from Hebrew Union College. A published poet and Judaica artist, Rabbi Rosenzweig was an inspirational figure.

Judea Reform quickly attracted new members. "People who had never been with anything joined," Alfreda Kaplan recalled. Rabbi Rosenzweig drew members of the academic community. At the start the congregants held monthly Sabbath services in homes, with High Holiday services in

Duke's York Chapel. Soon they moved to the Friends Meeting House. Judea Reform was do-it-yourself, and members took home the garbage and cleaned rugs after services. Later a minister offered the basement of the Temple Baptist Church. Judea Reform also oriented itself toward Chapel Hill, holding services at the Community Church and banquets at the Carolina Inn.

Congregational life at Judea Reform, like that at Beth-El, was attuned to middle-class suburbia. The emphasis was on Jewish peoplehood. The Women's Auxiliary held monthly meetings in members' homes where they planned fund-raising bazaars, fashion shows, square dances, and cocktail parties. The women sponsored a children's picnic for Lag B'Omer and a break-the-fast on Yom Kippur. Adult education groups studied the Talmud, Psalms, Hebrew, and the Sociology of American Jews.

In its ritual and ideology, Judea Reform expanded the boundaries of community. Its membership was extended to "families where at least one spouse is of the Jewish faith," an issue that had torn apart Beth-El. Judea Reform Congregation cast its lot with the "liberal interpretation of Judaism"; its handbook proclaimed, "Meaningful Judaism asserts that it is the moral and ethical principles which form the heart of our belief. . . . Judaism is dynamic and has changed with the ages." Jewish worship was not a matter of "nostalgia," and "observances may change when they are no longer relevant." Yet Judea Reform also pledged to "continue those lasting Jewish traditions and ideals that have stood for centuries." Its Friday night services were held in both English and Hebrew, but there were no Saturday morning services except for the Bar or Bat Mitzvah. Some congregants wore skull caps and prayers shawls, but others did not. Although the rabbi did not cover his head, he donned a white robe on Yom Kippur. For the High Holidays in 1965, an organist, tenor, soprano, and junior choir accompanied worship. From the first, Judea Reform integrated women into its leadership, with two serving on its founding board. (In the formative years women as temple officers served mostly as secretaries.)[60]

From the start, Rabbi Rosenzweig recalled, the congregants "were looking for a place for their children to get an education. I think that moved them more than anything else." Judea Reform established a religious or temple school with a principal and nine teachers. Children were expected to attend until tenth grade, when they were confirmed. Bar or Bat Mitzvah was "also available" but only as part of the process leading to confirmation. In 1965 Judea Reform had confirmed seven graduates but did not hold its first Bar Mitzvah until four years later.

Judea Reform experienced "continuous growth" in the 1960s, but with so many congregants from academia, its membership suffered from persistent turnover. Rabbi Rosenzweig lamented the "impermanence," the difficulty in sustaining community. Many faculty, Rabbi Rosenzweig observed, were outside the "mainstream of Jewish life." The perception in the community was that Beth-El was largely the mainstay of business people and that Judea Reform appealed mostly to academic newcomers. This generalization was only partly true. Several old Durham families affiliated, drawn to Judea Reform by their children. Three of its first four presidents were businessmen.

The decision to establish a Reform congregation was not well received at Beth-El, which, with its new building and rabbi, had liberalized to appeal to the very people that Judea Reform was now enrolling. There was reason for concern. Nationally, the Conservative movement was losing membership to the Reform.[61] Locally, the situation differed as unaffiliated and newly arrived families fueled Reform growth. In fact, only four of Judea Reform's fifty founding members had belonged to Beth-El. Fears were expressed that two congregations would divide the community, that Durham lacked Jewish resources to support both.

Some charges directed toward Judea Reform members reflected concern for the community's well-being; others vented resentments. A Beth-El leader visited the home of one organizer and suggested that the Reform Jews could hold separate services downstairs. Orthodox Jews, already upset about Beth-El's turn toward Conservatism, held prejudices against Reform Judaism. One questioned whether Rabbi Rosenzweig knew Hebrew, and another was convinced that Reform Judaism was merely a step to Christianity. "They called us goyim," Alfreda Kaplan recalled. When Judea Reform asked to borrow a Torah from Beth-El for its first High Holiday services, the request was denied. For some, Rabbi Rosenzweig reflected, a Reform congregation was "impossible . . . to accept."

The 1950s and 1960s were transitional years as new migrations and generational changes recast the community's demography and its identity. Jews were no longer confined to an ethnic mercantile niche. The Jewish community was diversifying with the changes in the regional economy. Unlike earlier migrations of trades people, who were readily absorbed, the newly arriving faculty and professionals differed in career, educational attainment, and religious orientation. This migration was also unprecedentedly large. Mobility had been a constant feature of local Jewry since its earliest days, but the salaried Sunbelt Jewish professionals lacked material attachment to their local community. Intellectual property was portable.

New populations expanded the boundaries of Jewish identity. An east European ethnic enclave with a nominally Orthodox congregation could no longer serve a pluralistic community. The unity of the Jewish community, its sense as a family circle, was breaking. For more than half a century the community had struggled to preserve congregational unity, but new migrations established Jewish pluralism as a permanent community feature. The evolution of Beth-El toward Conservatism and the forming of a Reform congregation were signs that the community was becoming more representative of American Jewish demography.

As religious liberals, Jews insisted on the congruity of Jewish and American values. Their Zionism upheld Israel as an exemplar of democracy. Jews and Christians alike proclaimed their common humanity under the banner of brotherhood. Rabbis welcomed non-Jews into their congregation. Yet, for all the professions of harmony, discrimination persisted. Native Jews in their civic associations still bore the mark of Jew, as Mutt Evans's political campaigns clearly revealed. As political liberals, Jewish faculty in the McCarthy era heard accusations of dual loyalty, some directed at them by fellow Jews. The civil rights movement further discomfited Jews, both native and newly arrived, as Jews wrestled with their status as white people. With integration and a changing economy, the South, too, was renegotiating its identity. For Durham–Chapel Hill Jews the 1950s and 1960s were a time of flux and disunity, and the community did not have a consensus on its own identity.

11 Sunbelt Jews, 1960s to 1990s

Of the many New Souths proclaimed, none so altered regional identity as the transformation into the Sunbelt. Although the South had been historically rural, by 1980 two-thirds of southerners lived in urban areas. The southern population exodus reversed itself. The Jewish population of the South grew commensurately as Jews emigrated from the Midwest and Northeast. From 1980 to 1990 the South gained 720,000 Jews, and the percentage of American Jewry residing in the region rose from 14.6 to 23.5 percent.[1] Atlanta and Houston developed into major Jewish communities, and Raleigh, Charlotte, and Greensboro began counting Jews in the thousands.

"Jewish population growth," the 1987 *American Jewish Yearbook* observed, "occurred precisely in those areas of the country that were experiencing the greatest economic development," especially places that were part of the "post industrial 'high-tech' economy." College towns such as Madison, Ann Arbor, and Berkeley also saw sharp rises in Jewish numbers as universities ended discriminatory practices and Jews flocked to the professions. A Sunbelt academic center such as Durham–Chapel Hill was thus doubly inviting to Jews. The Jewish population of Durham–Chapel Hill was 545 in 1964, 1,955 in 1984, and 3,358 in 1991.[2]

Jews might have been reluctant to move to a backward, segregated South, but they had few compunctions about living in the ethnically diverse Sunbelt. The Jewish influx must be seen in the context of a larger multiethnic migration that moved the area closer demographically to mainstream America. From 1970 to 1980 the number of foreign-born residents in North Carolina tripled. This trend was far more pronounced in the Triangle. The 3,333 Hispanics in the area in 1990 roughly equaled the number of Jews. The local Asian population grew more than 200 percent from 1980 to 1990, totaling 5,594. The descendants of Polish and Italian immigrants joined Jewish Americans. Of the seventy thousand local Catholics, fifty thousand were estimated to be recent transplants. As North Carolina integrated and prospered, African Americans who generations earlier had abandoned the South for Detroit, Chicago, and New York reversed their migration as one hundred thousand moved into the state between 1970 and 1980.[3]

Jews felt more comfortable moving into a cosmopolitan community. Rather than ethnic southerners, their neighbors were increasingly likely to be migrants from the Midwest and Northeast like themselves. Pressures to assimilate into the mainstream lessened as the hegemony of white, Anglo-Protestants declined. As Jews gathered for Israeli folk dancing and Yiddish lessons, the Polish Club sponsored a dance troupe and language classes. The Chinese-American Society and the Lebanese Association complemented the Jewish Federation. Echoing Jews, a Pittsburgh transplant reflected, "You take being Catholic for granted when you live in the North, . . . not here." Churches held Korean, Spanish, Ukrainian, and Polish services. A Greek Orthodox church built a sanctuary. Hindus and Buddhists organized worship. Local Arabs planned a mosque in Chapel Hill. "Immigrant" now meant not Jew but Arab, Asian, or Latino. Jews were no longer conspicuously alien, and, compared to African Americans or Native Americans, they were not particularly victims of discrimination.[4]

The Sunbelt brought the local economy into the global marketplace. Dutch investors financed hotel and office complexes. British, German, Swiss, French, Canadian, and Japanese firms built facilities in Research Triangle Park, including the corporate headquarters of pharmaceutical giant Glaxo-Wellcome. Raleigh-Durham International Airport offered nonstop flights to Paris and London as well as one-hour service for commuters to Atlanta, Washington, and New York. Located at the intersection of interstate highways 40 and 85, Durham–Chapel Hill was linked nonstop to California, New York, and Florida. Global communication and technology ended the sense of rural isolation, of living in the provinces.

The cityscapes of Durham and Chapel Hill were redrawn on a Sunbelt pattern. The cities that emerged were largely extended suburbs laid out to accommodate the automobile. Roadway spokes from downtown provided quick access to highway loops that encircled the city, creating rim economies. Construction of Durham–Chapel Hill Boulevard (Highway 15-501) in the 1950s drew the towns closer, and suburban sprawl erased town borders. Subdivisions bulldozed pasture and forest, and shopping malls marked every gateway.

Downtown Durham declined into a patchwork of postmodern office complexes and vacant lots, boarded-up stores, and abandoned factories. In 1986 American Tobacco closed its Durham plant, and L & M reduced its operations, throwing hundreds out of work. Historic preservation and neighborhood protection became political rallying cries. Brick warehouses were renovated into condominiums and upscale shopping arcades. Chapel Hill, which liked to call itself a village, sported a nine-story office tower on its main street. Because its business district bordered the UNC campus, downtown Chapel Hill thrived, but independent stores largely yielded to banks and national franchises.

North Carolina's Jewish growth was dramatic from the perspective of the state's history, but it still lacked a major metropolis to attract significant numbers. Although North Carolina ranked tenth among the states in population, it remained the most rural of industrialized states, with its people dispersed in small towns. Not one of its cities was counted among the nation's thirty largest. The state's Jewish population grew from an estimated 10,300 in 1960 to 14,945 by 1984, a rate nearly double that of the general population. On a percentage basis, North Carolina ranked fifteenth among the states in rate of Jewish growth, and the Triangle ranked among the top six fastest-growing Jewish communities. In way of comparison, however, Atlanta's Jewish population grew from 14,500 in 1960 to 33,500 in 1984. Jews comprised about 0.2 percent of North Carolinians, less than 1 percent of southerners, 1.9 percent of Durham–Chapel Hillians, and 2.5 percent of Americans. The trends suggested that the area would soon equal, if not surpass, national levels. From 1970 to 1990 the percentage of Jews in the local population quadrupled. From 1984 to 1991 alone the local Jewish population grew 71.8 percent (see table 11.1).[5]

Of the nearly thirteen hundred Jewish families who lived in the community in 1990, nearly 85 percent had arrived in the previous twenty years. Nine years later, the number rose to more than nineteen hundred families, with nine hundred households in Chapel Hill and seven hundred in Durham. Chapel Hill's rolling, countrified neighborhoods and superior public schools made the town especially attractive. As development spread,

TABLE 11.1. Durham–Chapel Hill Jewish Population, 1880–1990

Year	Durham pop.	Durham Jewish pop.	%	Chapel Hill pop.	Chapel Hill Jewish pop.	%	Durham–Chapel Hill Jewish pop.	%	N.C. Jewish pop.	N.C. %	Natl. %
1880	2,041	40	1.95	831					820 (1878)	.06	.50
1890	5,485			1,017							
1900	6,679	201	3.01	1,099					12,000		1.20
1910	18,241	305	1.67	1,149					1,500 (1907)		2.10 (1907)
1920	21,719	350	1.61	1,483					4,915 (1917)		3.30 (1917)
1930	52,037	375 (1927)	.72	2,699	13		388	.71	8,252 (1927)	.28	3.58 (1927)
1940	60,195	358 (1938)	.59	3,654	34 (1938)	.90	392 (1937)	.61	7,333 (1937)	.21	3.69 (1937)
1950	73,368	360 (1947)	.49	9,177					8,850 (1948)	.22	

1960	84,642	425 (1964)	.30	12,573	120 (1964)	.95	545 (1964)	.56	10,300	.23	3.08
1970	100,768	350 (1968)	.35	25,537	230 (1968)	.90	580 (1968)	.46	9,450 (1968)	.18	2.60
1980	101,149			32,421			1,955 (1984)	1.40	13,240	.20	2.70
1990	136,611			38,711			3,358 (1991)	1.90	15,800	.20	2.50

Sources: Jacob R. Marcus, To Count a People: American Jewish Population Data, 1585–1984 (Lanham, Md.: University Press of America, 1990), 165–66, 240–43; Durham–Chapel Hill Jewish Federation, 1990 Community List, Durham–Chapel Hill Jewish Federation, Durham.

Jewish households spilled into the adjacent country towns of Carrboro, Hillsborough, and Pittsboro.[6]

North Carolina's Jews concentrated in metropolitan areas along the Piedmont I-85 corridor. While Jews gravitated toward such Sunbelt cities as Greensboro, Charlotte, Raleigh, and Durham–Chapel Hill, agrarian communities languished. The eastern North Carolina towns of Tarboro, Goldsboro, Wilson, Jacksonville, and Lumberton closed their synagogues, in some cases after a century of Jewish communal life. Jews from small towns across the Southeast were drawn to the emerging Sunbelt centers. Retirees and second-generation professionals from rural Jewish communities in Virginia and the Carolinas resettled in Durham–Chapel Hill.

What remained constant among Jews was not so much a desire for roots and stability as a search for opportunity. Rates of persistence remained low. By 1998 only two of the nineteen hundred Jewish families—the Silvers and the Gladsteins—could trace their roots in Durham before 1900. The early German Jewish families died out locally. Another ten families went back before World War I, and about fifty traced to the 1920s, 1930s, and 1940s. In most cases these families consisted of a single person or an older couple, their children having long since departed. Of the 180 families listed by Beth-El Sisterhood in 1959, 125 were still in town in 1964, but only 45 remained in 1984. According to the 1990 National Jewish Population Survey one in five Jews lived in his or her city of birth. Because of "many children," the Durham–Chapel Hill figure was comparable; but of the 175 residents over age fifty-five, only 9 were natives, a figure closer to 1 in 20. In way of contrast, 70.4 percent of North Carolinians were born in the state.[7]

In the 1950s and 1960s the old pattern had held as youth continued to leave. As Eli Evans observed, fathers had built businesses for sons who did not want them. Optometrist Robert Rosenstein was the lone local Jew to carry a family business into a third generation. For youth Durham remained a "dead town." "I may be the only one who is still here," Norman Margolis reflected after recalling the names of Jewish classmates. By the 1970s, however, perceptions changed among youth. Durham and Chapel Hill supported lively arts and music scenes, sports calendars were full, and politics were liberal. The children found positions in local dance companies and computer firms. Rapid growth created opportunities for real-estate developers and health-care practitioners. This trend was true for the children of faculty as well as of mercantile families. As Calvin Goldscheider noted, "Since high levels of education and occupation have emerged for two generations of Jews, one potential source of generational conflict has lessened."[8] Anecdotal evidence suggested growing rates of persistence among youth. Sunbelt opportunities, the charm of a college town, or a desire to live closer to family kept them here. This choice owed to career and lifestyle factors, not to Jewish ethnic bonds.

A Sunbelt Professional Community

The Sunbelt Jewish migration into Durham and Chapel Hill reflected both the economic transformation of the area as well as the occupational and generational changes in American Jewry. The independent business-man largely yielded to the salaried professional. Durham–Chapel Hill Jewry became a well-educated, affluent community, representative to a high degree of the social and economic changes that had reshaped American Jewry. The Jewish professionals were highly representative, too, of the changing character of the area generally. In 1990, 56.7 percent of Research Triangle residents over the age of twenty-five had at least some college, and 11.6 percent held professional degrees, figures about one-quarter higher than national averages. In Orange County, home of Chapel Hill, 6.7 percent of those over age twenty-five held a Ph.D. Nationally, 71.4 percent of Jews over age twenty-five had some college, and 25.9 percent had graduate study.[9]

Jews were now pulled to the area for the same historical reason that they had been pushed away: professional opportunity. Durham–Chapel Hill exceeded national averages that showed Jews about equally divided between those who worked as "wage-earning professionals" and those who worked as "managers, agents, or retailers." A 1986 occupational survey of Judea Reform's membership revealed that nearly 70 percent (276 of the 369 employed congregants) were professionals. These included 65 physicians, 43 professors, 23 teachers, 15 engineers, 12 lawyers, and 23 administrators. Twenty worked in health care. Only two were dry-goods merchants, and another eleven were in retail fields. Five others worked in sales. The Sunbelt economy created opportunities for twelve real-estate agents and four financial advisors. Twelve were artists or musicians.[10]

Unlike those of previous generations, these Jews no longer had any sense of restriction in their career choices. With the demise of the ethnic mercantile niche, Jews were thoroughly integrated into the corporate economy, lessening one aspect of Jewish difference. Locally, Jews baked bread, bred cattle, patrolled as police officers, and published newspapers. With discounters and franchisers dominating dry goods, Jewish merchants opened specialty stores that catered to an upscale, cosmopolitan trade. Jews imported folk crafts, operated dance schools, purveyed rare books, and taught yoga. They owned Mexican cantinas, bookstore-cafes, and kosher-style delis and bakeries. Only one downtown Jewish dry-goods store survived.

Another change was the advent of the two-career professional family. In the 1950s and 1960s the husband's work dictated the decision to move to the area, and professional women often postponed careers for child rearing. Miriam Slifkin, a microbiologist whose physicist husband joined UNC, recalled that "it wasn't prevalent at all" for a woman to have a career in the 1950s. "I was criticized for wanting to get out of the house" and for choosing biology, a field not regarded as feminine, Slifkin reflected. Dr. Cynia Shimm, a graduate of Harvard Medical School, came to Durham in 1953 when her husband took a post at Duke Law School, but like many faculty wives, she worked only part-time as she raised children. With the children grown, Shimm took a position in Duke's Department of Psychiatry, and Slifkin completed her Ph.D. Other faculty spouses worked as schoolteachers. As gender discrimination weakened, two-career families became increasingly common. With five universities and numerous research facilities in the area they were able to find positions in disparate fields. On the 1986 Judea Reform list 140 of the 239 households were two-career families. In only sixteen cases did a woman describe herself as a homemaker (and twenty-five had no occupational listing).[11]

A growing segment of the Jewish population consisted of retirees lured by the climate, educational opportunities, and medical facilities. Many followed children who had taken professional positions locally. Statistically, 17.6 percent of local Jews in 1990 were over age 65, a figure equal to the national Jewish percentage but nearly double the Research Triangle percentage.[12] Irma and Manny Stein, who came in the early 1980s, spoke for many northern retirees when they described the appeal of the area: "With three universities there were always a lot of cultural activities. The people were very congenial. The climate was mild. After New Jersey we liked living in the woods." Memories of college or armed-service days drew others. One sign of the area's growing appeal to Jews was the presence of several retired rabbis, including Rabbi Nathan Perilman of New York's Temple Emanuel. Previously rabbis had left the area for larger, more resourceful Jewish communities. Local campuses responded to the retirees with elderhostels and continuing education programs.

On Campus

The universities spearheaded the migration of Jews to the South. Whether because of a quota or the reluctance of northern Jews to apply for admission, or both, Jewish enrollment at Duke remained around 5 percent through the 1960s. Mark Pinsky recalled that when he arrived as a freshman in 1965, "I probably knew or thought I knew every Jewish student who was at Duke, but by the time I was a senior . . . I sensed there was an explosion." What changed was Duke's policy of asking a religious preference question on its application. At once the percentage of Jews jumped as about 20 percent of registering students annually declared a Jewish religious preference. Duke, according to a cover story in the *New York Times Magazine,* was "hot." By 1992 the Jewish student body reached eighteen hundred. Meanwhile, UNC experienced a decline in Jewish enrollment as a percentage of its student body. In 1967, 5.7 percent of incoming freshmen were Jewish, but this figure dropped to 3.2 percent in 1970 and then to 1.8 percent in 1975. The absolute number increased from 400 in 1952 to 750 in 1994 as the campus expanded to 22,000 students. The trend reflected the state legislature's decision to limit out-of-state enrollment. Even so, the two campuses now held more than twenty-five hundred Jewish students, three-quarters of the number of the local Jewish community.[13]

The expanded Jewish presence at the universities was an index of Jewish movement from outsiders to insiders. Duke measured itself by Ivy League standards, and UNC became less a southern acropolis than a generic state university. When art historian Arthur Marks arrived in 1974, a "good-old-boys" network of North Carolinians "seemed to control the destiny of the institution," grooming its favorite sons for leadership. This clique loosened its hold, however. Marks cited the appointment to provost of Dennis O'Connor, an Irish American from northern Catholic schools, as a breaking of the ranks. Marks, who chaired the art department, doubted that UNC any longer allowed "bias" to override "merit." In the 1930s the UNC Law School dean doubted the "wisdom" of hiring a Jew; now a Jew served as dean. Duke Hospital, which once did not hire Jews, now had a Jewish director.

By the 1970s Jews no longer regarded Jewish origins as an impediment to academic advancement. At Duke Joel Fleishman, a former yeshiva student, founded the program in public policy studies and was appointed vice-president of the university. As Duke's chief fund-raiser, he held a highly visible post. Duke biochemist Phillip Handler in 1969 served as president of the National Academy of Sciences. In the 1980s, after nearly twenty years at Duke, religion professor Eric Meyers observed that "there are Jewish faculty all over the place. I can't keep track of them anymore." Martin Golding, a Talmudic scholar, headed the Philosophy Department. Kalman Bland, a rabbi, became chairman of the Religion Department. Allan Kornberg chaired both the Political Science Department and the Academic Council.

At UNC Cecil Sheps, who had first taught public health in 1947, rose to vice-chancellor for Health Services, the first Jew in the administration. In 1991, when a research center was dedicated in his name, Sheps publicly "thanked UNC officials for starting his medical career at a time when Jewish people were not always welcome in university communities." When Bernard Greenberg, dean of the School of Public Health, died in 1985, President William Friday of the UNC system hailed "this kind and gentle man" as a "great and good friend," and a building was named in his memory.[14] In 1970 Daniel Okun was elected chairman of the UNC faculty. E. J. Evans served as president of the UNC Alumni Association, and he and his son Eli were the only father-son pair to be conferred Distinguished Alumnus Awards. Jews served as deans of the schools of law, education, and social work.

In the 1970s barriers against women in academia began slowly lowering. Jess Fischer of UNC's School of Public Health observed only one or two Jewish women when she arrived in 1972. This number had increased marginally twenty years later. In the 1990s, only 21 percent of the UNC faculty were women even as the student body became predominantly female. Melanie Mintzer, who taught family medicine at UNC, observed, "My sense is that Jews are not under-represented." At Duke Judith Ruderman, a temple president, was appointed vice-provost.

Despite their numbers and insider status, Jews on campus still felt unease. The most disquieting reminder occurred in 1991 when California-based historical "revisionists" printed an advertisement in the *Chronicle,* the Duke student newspaper, denying that "the German state had a policy to exterminate the Jewish people." The ad called six million deaths an exaggeration and dismissed the gas chambers as propaganda. Outrage in the Jewish community was instant and palpable.[15]

The *Chronicle's* editors dissented from the ad's contents but defended printing it on First Amendment grounds, arguing that only open debate could decisively refute the Holocaust deniers. Duke president Keith Brodie and several law professors endorsed this position. After indignant students and faculty confronted Brodie, he issued a statement denouncing the "lies" but defending "our commitment to free speech." UNC's *Daily Tar Heel* also saw the issue in free-speech terms, but its advertising department rejected the ad.[16]

For Jews the academic defense of free speech was a license to anti-Semites. In response Hillel rabbi Frank Fischer, an émigré from Nazi Germany, addressed a Duke rally that drew four hundred. A campus "teach in" was held, and a Holocaust survivor addressed a student group. The library displayed an exhibit, "The Holocaust: Images and Reality," and David Wyman, author of *The Abandonment of the Jews,* was invited to speak. The History Department sponsored a counter ad that stated the "editors make a serious error when they confuse Holocaust deniers with historical revisionists." Divinity School faculty urged the *Chronicle* staff to apologize and asked Christian students to resign from the newspaper.[17] Despite the sympathetic voices, several Jews expressed bitter feelings toward the Duke administration. When a second revisionist ad was submitted, the *Chronicle* declined to publish it. Neither the issue nor the local response was distinctly southern, however, as Holocaust deniers provoked similar confrontations on campuses nationally.

University administrations instituted outreach efforts that ameliorated the pervasively Christian ethos of the campuses. Duke sponsored a Jewish baccalaureate service, resolving a problem that dated to the 1930s. In 1985 Duke began an annual Ecumenical Holocaust Memorial Service with candle-lighting ceremonies and addresses by Christian and Jewish theologians. At UNC students were given the option to remove "year of our Lord" from their diplomas. Calendars were full of interfaith lectures, seders, and services.

Barriers fell, and Jewish students joined sororities and fraternities that a generation earlier would not have let their parents in the door. In turn, Jewish societies opened their membership to non-Jews. UNC's Tau Epsilon Phi by 1986 was no more than half-Jewish, and the Zeta Beta Tau chapter closed. Sporadic efforts were made to revive Alpha Epsilon Phi. UNC, which once supported three exclusively Jewish fraternities, now had none. Duke's AEP welcomed non-Jews, but the fraternity was 90 percent Jewish. Jewish women freely chose among many sororities. With the lowering of discriminatory barriers Jews blended into the student body.

Judaic Studies

Duke's Judaic Studies program, founded in 1943, had died for lack of institutional support. In 1971 local B'nai B'rith members suggested reviving the program and designated contributions to Duke for it. At this time Eric Meyers, a professor of Bible and archaeology, was asking Duke to establish a program as a condition for his staying. Sara Evans, who had attended Duke, and E. J. Evans, a UNC alumnus, agreed to raise $500,000 from Duke and UNC alumni, and the Hebrew Culture Foundation and Z. Smith Reynolds Fund granted monies for faculty and offices. In 1972 Duke and UNC formed a consortium for a Cooperative Program in Judaic Studies. Duke's Judaica collection ranked among the country's twenty largest and, combined with UNC's, counted among the ten largest.

The success of Judaic studies, especially at Duke, reflected the national picture. Prior to 1948 only two secular universities, Harvard and Columbia, had full-time faculty in Jewish studies. By the 1980s, more than three hundred colleges were offering courses, and in 1997 there were eighty-five programs, with thirty granting graduate degrees. Still, it was extraordinary that a Methodist, southern university, far from metropolitan Jewish centers, made such a commitment. Judaic studies not only secured a place for Jewish culture in the academic canon but also offered a counterhistory that subverted the paradigm of western civilization as European and Christian. Like feminist and African American studies, Judaic studies walked a fine line between disinterested scholarship and advocacy, and its position among ethnic and gender studies was uncertain.[18]

Suitably endowed, the Cooperative Program in Judaic Studies expanded curricula at Duke and UNC. In 1973 Duke hired Kalman Bland, an authority on medieval Jewish mysticism. Carol Meyers, author of *Discovering Eve,* taught biblical literature with an emphasis on feminist perspectives. At UNC Jack Sasson, who had been teaching Near Eastern Studies since 1966, was joined in 1976 by David Halperin, a scholar of rabbinic Judaism, and later by Yaakov Ariel, a historian of American religion. Led by Eric Meyers and Carol Meyers, more than seven hundred local students traveled to Israel to participate in archaeological digs. The husband-and-wife team achieved celebrity when they uncovered the oldest known ark of the covenant in an early Galilean synagogue. They found themselves thrust before television cameras and posed in *People* magazine as "Raiders of the Lost Ark." Later, in a Galilean synagogue they unearthed a mosaic of an Israelite "Mona Lisa," which was removed to the Israel Museum.

Judaic studies placed the local community on the global Jewish map. Duke's program sponsored colloquia on such subjects as Ancient Biblical Prayer, Medieval Jewish Philosophy, and the Holocaust and Jewish-Christian Understanding. Israeli scholars held visiting appointments and included Hebrew University's Sidra Ezrahi, an authority on Holocaust literature; Yaron Ezrahi, a political scientist; and Yigal Shiloh, archaeologist of Jerusalem's City of David.

By the 1980s the Cooperative Program loosened because of administrative problems. UNC's Interdepartmental Judaic Studies Committee offered seven courses, and Duke's Center for Judaic Studies listed twenty-one. On the two campuses a dozen professors were teaching courses of Jewish interest ranging from archaeology to Yiddish. By the mid-1980s as many as five hundred students enrolled in the Duke program, including two hundred in a Hebrew Bible course.

As universities became centers of Jewish learning, Durham–Chapel Hill moved from the Jewish periphery closer to its center. The presence of Abba Eban, Elie Wiesel, and Isaac Bashevis Singer gave local Jews the feeling that they were no longer marginal. Jews turned out to hear Yosef Yerushalmi on Sephardic Jewry, Robert Alter on the Bible as literature, Thomas Friedman on Middle Eastern politics, and Irving Howe on immigrant culture.

Multicultural Southerners

As a relatively homogeneous community of east European background, Durham Jews traditionally had seen pluralism as a threat and struggled to preserve unity. Most new settlers had shared ethnic roots with the established community and were easily absorbed. In the case of the World War II émigré scholars, their numbers were too small to be unsettling. With a larger, more cosmopolitan migration, however, Yiddishkeit was no longer a pervasive communal binder. A community that strove to preserve its unity now sprawled and fractured. Jewish ethnicity did not imply a monolithic culture, and an American Judaism that upheld democracy and tolerance as religious values now affirmed its differences. Like the Asian and Hispanic communities, which divided into national subgroups, Jews also had allegiances to multiple homelands. Israelis, Russians, and South Africans were sufficiently numerous to form subcommunities.

With interfaith and conversionary marriages, new races and cultures entered the communal fold. Jews by choice lacked east European ethnicity. Jews now included people of Korean, Chinese, and African descent. Judea

Reform's black members included a physician and a college administrator, both of whom were Jews by choice. Beth-El's black worshipers, who were born Jews, included an Ethiopian physician and a Duke doctoral student who taught Hebrew school. Katya Gibel Azoulay, an Israeli of Caribbean descent, explored her complex roots in *Black, Jewish, and Interracial: It's Not the Color of Your Skin, But the Race of Your Kin and Other Myths of Identity.* Local Jews of African descent also tended to be highly educated professionals.

Small numbers of Sephardic Jews and Jews from Arab lands settled in the area, though never in sufficient numbers to form a subcommunity. A few Jews also arrived from Iraq, Iran, Egypt, and Lebanon, displaced by anti-Zionist politics. Syrian-born, Lebanese-bred Jack Sasson, a UNC religion professor, found himself constantly called on to be a local spokesperson for his heritage. Jews of Turkish or Greek Sephardic descent who had married Ashkenazi Jews simply blended into the larger community.

Nazism and the Holocaust continued to shape Durham–Chapel Hill Jewry. Having left France, Germany, Hungary, or Poland, these émigrés first found refuge where it was available—in England, Palestine, Cuba, Peru, Uruguay, or Guatemala—before arriving in Durham or Chapel Hill as secondary or tertiary places of settlement. These Jews traced to cosmopolitan origins, and, like American Jews, careerism drew them to the area. Local Latino Jews, a generation or two removed from eastern or central Europe, shared Ashkenazi roots with North Americans, but they retained some cultural difference as they remained attached to their Cuban, Chilean, and Peruvian homelands. Rosa Perelmuter, descended from Polish Jews, left Cuba to teach Spanish literature at UNC. She wrote and lectured on her dislocations. Sybil Sternberger, a native Yugoslavian, arrived from Uruguay when her German-born husband took an engineering post. Lazaro Mandel remained attached to his childhood Peru, where his German parents had settled.

Memory returned European émigrés to the nations of their births. They bore witness to lost homelands. Henry Fuchs, who had fled Hungary in 1956, revisited his native Tokaj to restore its synagogue and retrieve family memorabilia. German-born Henry Landsberger raised funds to rebuild the Dresden synagogue where his grandfather had been rabbi. Simone Lipman educated the community on her native Alsatian Jewish culture and her underground work rescuing Jewish children during the war. She, too, made nostalgic visits to Strasbourg. When Albrecht Strauss accepted a Fulbright professorship at the University of Erlangen, he did so consciously as a Jew who held conflicted feelings toward his native Germany. He also felt culturally at home in the England that had given him refuge.

In the 1950s and 1960s South Africans, dissatisfied with the apartheid regime, began taking positions at local campuses, particularly in the health sciences. A half-dozen, mostly younger families arrived in the 1970s after the Soweto riots. They affiliated strongly with the local Jewish community but maintained homeland ties as they gathered for teas and dinners. Most South Africans affiliated with Conservative Judaism, which more closely resembled the Liberal Judaism of their native land. South Africans became communal and Zionist leaders, expressing concern at the extent of assimilation that they saw among American Jews. Sharing east European roots and an Anglo culture, they blended into American Jewry.

The Israelis were a fluid group of ten to twenty families. They maintained community lists and gathered for communal celebrations. Unlike the Russians or South Africans, who settled permanently in America, the Israelis moved freely between the two countries. With global communication networks, exile no longer meant estrangement from homeland. Like postcolonial Asian and Hispanic peoples, Israelis could live in two worlds. The local Israeli typically was a graduate student or a professional at a university or research laboratory or the spouse of an American Jew. The National Humanities Center in Research Triangle Park hosted such noted Israelis as historian Jacob Talmon and linguist Benjamin Harshav for yearlong sabbaticals. Local Israelis tended to be secular Jews who were wary of religious institutions because of their experiences with the Orthodox rabbinate in Israel. They attended synagogue on holidays, however, and sent their children to the religious schools. As emissaries of Zion, Israelis taught Hebrew or Zionist history at Hillel and the synagogues.

Soviet Jewry had been a concern of the community well before the first émigrés arrived. In 1968, two years after Elie Wiesel had published *Jews of Silence,* a Beth-El confirmand spoke on "Remembering Soviet Jewry." In the mid-1980s the community participated in national petition campaigns in support of Soviet Jewish emigration, and youth groups met with North Carolina congressional representatives on behalf of the Student Struggle for Soviet Jewry. Starting in 1988 small numbers of Soviet Jews began arriving. The Russians directed to Durham–Chapel Hill by national resettlement programs tended to be well-educated scientists, musicians, and mathematicians. They, too, began the typical Jewish occupational climb. Engineers found work as mechanics and delivery persons until their English or vocational skills were sufficiently polished for them to find professional positions. By 1999 thirty-seven Russian Jewish families resided in the area.

Soviet Jews retained a Jewish consciousness, reinforced by anti-Semitism, but they lacked Jewish literacy. Simon Stompel, the first to arrive, had studied Hebrew in an underground cultural group in Moscow. He had celebrated Hanukkah and Passover but rarely attended synagogue. His mother, Raissa, who came two years later, recalled a few Yiddish words and some Jewish foods. Iosef Vaisman came from a "nonpracticing" family in the Ukraine but always considered himself to be Jewish. He and his wife, Shura, enrolled their daughter, Ester, in Hebrew school and attended services "as often as we can." "Genetic memory," Vaisman said, attached him to "the tradition of my ancestors," and he created a popular Yiddish web site, *Shtetl* (village). Jewish social agencies, which took care of the Russians' material needs, struggled to integrate them into the community socially and religiously. Of the dozen local families, only two or three consisted of two Jewish parents; most were intermarriages with ethnic Russians. The Russian language was a portable homeland, and Russian Jewish social circles also encompassed non-Jewish Russians.[19]

A Blended Sunbelt Culture

Jews and southerners alike continued to identify themselves as groups and insist on their differences, especially in their religious affiliations. Nevertheless, the boundaries of identity were being renegotiated and reconstructed as the region assimilated into the national—and global—economy. The ethnicity of Jews and southerners alike was eroding as the South evolved into the Sunbelt. The multicultural Sunbelt tempered the southerness of the place, now known by the nondescript title of Research Triangle. Mass culture—movies, television, fast food—leveled regional distinctions. A generic landscape of office complexes, commercial strips, and housing developments made no reference to regional identity.

"I was apprehensive about living in the South," quipped UNC psychiatrist Lee Marcus, "so we moved to Chapel Hill." Chapel Hill—with its antigun, antismoking, and gay-rights ordinances—was a liberal college town infamously out of step with the state. Jesse Helms once reputedly joked that a fence around Chapel Hill would be a cheaper alternative to a state zoo. Durham evolved from a southern mill town into a medical and academic center.

Southern culture Judaized as it became more mainstream American. The mass media had a large Jewish content. Woody Allen films drew crowds. Television brought Jewish comedians Jerry Seinfeld and David Letterman into southern living rooms. A half-dozen bagel bakeries competed for customers, but the southern biscuit had to be hunted. Newcomers established their urban Jewish culture locally. Andy Michaels opened Bentley's, a bagel and lox deli, and wrote on his placemats a credo that traced his restaurant's origins to his native New York: "As a commercial fisherman in North Carolina, I was inspired to recreate the tastes of my childhood." Sunday mornings for nominally southern Jews were spent with bagels and the *New York Times*. Exhibits of Israeli and Holocaust-inspired art, klezmer concerts, and Jewish film festivals appeared on cultural calendars. The state art museum in Raleigh housed a Judaica collection.

In a multicultural society identity was negotiable, and Jews picked and chose from an international menu. The New Age revival led some seekers to turn to the East for spiritual sustenance. In Chapel Hill Sy Syfransky published the *Sun,* a magazine with a national circulation, which featured Buddhist meditation and Hindu spiritualism. Local Jews ran an ashram for prisoners, sought release through rolfing, underwent polarity therapy, and led yoga and karate classes. Richard Adler, the Broadway composer who lived in Chapel Hill, wrote how his Indian mentor, gurumayi, sustained him through life-threatening crises.[20]

Some Jews, while retaining their names on Jewish Federation lists, joined the Society of Friends, the Community Church, the Unitarian-Universalists, or the Ethical Culture Society. These were progressive or loosely denominational churches dedicated to peace and social justice issues. With their tempered ritual and symbolism, they also appealed to interfaith families. The Community Church was so nonsectarian that in the 1980s, when a new minister began invoking the name of Jesus Christ from the pulpit, several Jewish members, without irony, asked a rabbi to intercede on their behalf. Durham's Unitarian-Universalist Fellowship held a Yom Kippur service and Kol Nidre ritual. Reform rabbi John Friedman observed "many" intermarried Jews among the members of mainline Christian churches who were raising children in their spouse's faith. At one time his temple included several families who were also church members.

Although some Jews consciously rejected Judaism or had "put it behind them," others were products of assimilated environments. Louis D. Rubin Jr., UNC's scholar of southern literature, noted that in his native Charleston the small, German, Reform Jewish community had largely faded, and "racial and religious origins and identity played a relatively small part in my childhood." The "perfunctory ritual" of Sabbath school interested him less than the noise and clatter out the window. He defined himself by the larger southern culture "that was so abundantly available." What he retained of Jewishness, he observed, was an "oblique" perspective that made him "conscious" of what other southerners took for granted.[21]

The universities drew a Jewish literati who acknowledged their Jewish origins but whose culture and community were internationalist. Several faculty wrote memoirs that traced their journeys from parochial Jewish upbringings to cosmopolitan society. Duke professor Alice Kaplan was "disturbed" by her grandmother's Yiddish, the language of "bad memories." Her own "need [was] to think in French." Feminist critic Eve Kosofsky Sedgwick wrote that her muse was "schooled . . . among assimilated Jews in the American creed," but she questioned "the Jewish choice of a minority politics based on a conservative reinscription of gender roles" and qualified her own identity as "in some regimes a Jew." Duke's Ariel Dorfman, the novelist and dramatist, acknowledged his Jewish immigrant ancestry, but as a native Chilean he defined himself as a multicultural Latino. Stanley Fish, chairman of the Duke English Department, was committed to critical theory that deconstructed ideologies and undermined stable identities. Others found value or community in feminism or academic marxism.[22]

The Persistence of Southern Jews

Although the Sunbelt attenuated southern culture, surveys indicated some persisting differences. Southerners continued to express a stronger "localism . . . a sense of place," a preference for their home communities, than did Americans in other regions. They were also measurably more religious. The South, in contrast to the North with its large Catholic population, was nearly 90 percent Protestant, almost all of whom, both black and white, were Baptist, Methodist, or Presbyterian. Southerners also tended to be more orthodox in their religious beliefs and more likely to be church going. There were noted differences, too, between northerners and southerners in the way of manners and pace of life.[23]

Native southern Jews who persisted in Durham became a subcommunity in their own hometowns. Elderly community members held to their social circles. Margolises, Gladsteins, and Liptons gathered for evenings of cards and mah jong. Native-born southern Jews were highly conscious of their local legacy. Cemeteries and memorial plaques testified to their roots. Lynne Gladstein Grossman, from the town's oldest Jewish family, proudly spoke of herself as a fourth-generation Sisterhood president, and Robert

Rosenstein continued his father and grandfather's legacy as a synagogue benefactor and B'nai B'rith state president. These families remained unique among Sunbelt Jews in their pride of local heritage. They spoke in regional accents, felt comfort with southern folkways, and maintained a pride of place. No Sunbelt Jew could buttonhole an African American state legislator as Sam Margolis once did, tell him in a down-home accent, "I knew your daddy," and recount a youthful escapade. Elderly Jewish Durhamites joined their Gentile neighbors as they chatted on park benches and strolled the malls. In contrast to the more numerous newcomers, they were woven into the hometown fabric with a tightness that only lifelong experience can create.

Native Jews recognized their southern difference from northern Jews in the way of manners. Eli Evans recalled on campus how well-bred southern boys were locked together with their northern brethren whose vulgarity, beer guzzling, and womanizing caused culture shocks. Not until Evans met northern Jews did he learn that *schmuck* was actually a term of endearment. "They corrupted me," North Carolinian Art Shain recalled with a wry smile of his northern fraternity brothers. "I find some northern Jews a little aggressive," Hazel Gladstein Wishnov noted. "We were more laid back. I think there is more softness and gentility in a southern woman. We were less abrasive." Ethel Mae Bernson recalled how her mother-in-law, a northern Jew, once urged her to push her way to the front of a line, but she protested that as a southerner she could not. A Duke student in 1980s contrasted southern Jews who were involved with "Jewish ethnics" to northern Jews who were committed to "capitalist ethics."[24]

Although some native southern Jews looked on the newcomers as interlopers, most felt a bond with their northern coreligionists. "I don't see a lot of difference other than the way we talk," observed Mark Margolis, a third-generation Durhamite. Although he and his brother, Norman, preferred to be called "southern Jews" rather than "Jewish southerners," neither had reflected greatly on that question of identity. "Family ties had a little bit to do with" keeping them in Durham, Mark Margolis reflected, but mostly it was the quality of life. What survived of their southern Jewish upbringing were their friendships with Jews across the state whom they had come to know in their teenage years of Jewish networking. Mark Margolis had first met his wife, Charlotte, at a B'nai B'rith youth convention. This social networking among southern Jews, reinforced by kinship ties, differentiated them from the newcomers.

The small-town southern Jew was a vanishing species. Henry Bane and

Gibby Katz, both bachelors, were members of a mostly Gentile old boys' club that habituated the downtown Palms Restaurant. There they joined their cronies—lawyers, merchants, and journalists—for good talk about city politics or high-school football. A *Durham Morning Herald* column described Bane, a dignified former judge, as the "doyen of the Palmists," and Katz, a husky, lumbering man with a ready smile, was "pure Southern" and "pluperfect Durham." Chapel Hill's Sam Berman, who died in 1961, became a "legend," the newspaper eulogized. "Berman," as he was known, was loved for his perpetual humor: "The little store keeper fellow playing dumb when all the time everybody knew he was knowing as a fox." Sybil and Harry Macklin, proprietors of Harry's Delicatessen, also entered Chapel Hill folklore. The kosher-style deli had long closed, but its clientele held such affection for the place that in 1986 more than three hundred gathered in Chapel Hill from as far as Europe and California to honor "the understanding couple who presided over the mayhem like a kindly aunt and uncle." By city proclamation Chapel Hill clothier Maurice Julian was honored as "Dean of Franklin Street." This generation, however, was dying or retiring from town.[25]

Native Jews who abandoned the region persisted in identifying themselves as ethnic southerners. They remained attached to their hometowns, the place of their memories. This nostalgia was reinforced by their local real-estate holdings, which kept them involved in the local economy. Durhamites told stories of relatives who had moved north years ago but remained thickly accented ladies and gentlemen. Ex-Durhamite Lehman Brady after a half century in New York retained his drawl and courtly manners, accentuated by a cane and broad-brimmed hat. He returned often to Durham to visit old friends, renew his Duke alumni ties, and oversee family property. Eli Evans, a Durham expatriate who lived in New York, wrote *The Provincials: A Personal History of Jews in the South* as a testimony to a distinct southern-Jewish identity. The book included a nostalgic evocation of his Durham childhood. Evans undertook *Judah Benjamin: The Jewish Confederate* as a task of self-definition. The title of his memoir, *The Lonely Days Were Sundays,* underscores the intensified religious awareness and difference typical of Jewish southerners. Evans recounted how when his son was born in a New York hospital, he clutched a vial of North Carolina soil, rooting him in the agrarian South. Clothing designer Alexander Julian, son of a local merchant, flew a Chapel Hill flag over his Connecticut home. Durham-born Ethel Mae Bernson, who had returned to her hometown after living in the North, declared flatly, "I'm proud to be a southerner." To these exiles, the South was homeland.[26]

Self-described southern Jews acknowledged the contradictions of their double identity, the hybrid aspects of "southern" and "Jewish" that did not blend. Steve Schewel, a native Virginian, had remained in Durham after graduating from Duke. In "Biscuits and Blintzes: Growing Up Jewish in the Fatback South," he reflected on his acculturation: "What does it mean that a committed Jew loves to eat pig so much?" During Passover week he eschewed leavened biscuits while lunching on chopped pork at Big Ed's country restaurant. "For this Jewish boy, that's fitting in," Schewel explained in his Virginia "twang." He would not, however, desecrate a bagel with barbecue nor a biscuit with chopped liver. He kept his two cultures "separate," delighting in "both."[27]

Several second- and third-generation Durhamites through intermarriage and acculturation had become so wholly southern that they vanished as Jews. They included a woman who had intermarried, converted, and become a pillar of her church, and a fireman, intermarried but unconverted, who bore the nickname "Snake." The children and grandchildren of intermarried second-generation Jews blended into the Christian community.

Sunbelt Jews as Southerners

The southern sense of place was problematic for mobile Jews. Sunbelt Jews lacked the kinship ties, agrarian roots, and ancestral legacy that were foundations of southern identity. Since Durham's founding, Jews had flowed in and out of town. Many families never remained long enough to establish roots, to acculturate, and the second generation typically left in search of opportunity. "I don't think that they thought of themselves as Southerners," Lynne Gladstein Grossman observed of her Jewish classmates who moved to Atlanta, Boston, and Washington. The thousands of newly arriving Sunbelt Jews were southern by geography, not by culture. Yet, the South made its mark.

Sunbelt Jews, too, expressed pride of place. After eight years, Myrna Schwartz, who once fretted about raising Jewish children in the South, was "happy about staying." With the end of racial segregation, the liberalizing of the local political climate, and the growth of a Jewish critical mass, Jews expressed comfort about raising families locally. Like southerners generally, Jews cited the pleasantness of the "physical environment." In 1976 Jo and Marc Cohen had arrived in Chapel Hill to attend graduate school. "When we moved down here I said, 'What are we doing here?'" Jo Cohen recalled. "After two years we didn't want to leave." Like many migrants they cited the beauty of the area, the cultural activity, and the healthy environment for children. They built a home in the country, planted fruit trees, and raised bees. With a doctorate in operations research Marc Cohen found work at a software firm. The pushing factor was, as former Miamians Joe and Susan Elinoff put it, the "crime and congestion" of their metropolitan hometowns. The Elinoffs decided to quit Miami after reading a lurid newspaper headline. The Elinoffs drove through Chapel Hill, "fell in love with the place," and sold their Miami home. In 1994 a *Money* magazine survey proclaimed the Triangle to be the best place to live in America. Jews, like southerners generally, ceased to be apologetic about living in the South, and they sought ways to stay. Quality of life, rather than economic necessity, was the decisive factor.[28]

Sunbelt Jews noted their southern acculturation, especially in manners. Newcomers habitually contrasted the friendliness of southerners with the rudeness of northerners. The relaxed pace was welcome relief from the freneticism they had left. "People tend to slow down here, personally and professionally, even when they get behind the wheels of their cars," observed Arna Lefkowitz, who came from Boston in 1973. Her accent "softened." Tourists in their hometowns, transplanted Jews educated themselves on southern culture. They sampled grits as an ethnic delicacy at nouveau southern cafes, collected folk pottery, and adorned their beds with quilts. Like southerners generally, they were sports fans devoted to their Tar Heels and Blue Devils.

A study of southern Jewish folklife noted that southern Jews differed from northern Jews in tending to have less elaborate Bar and Bat Mitzvah celebrations. In Durham–Chapel Hill an expensive affair was out of character, nor did it confer status on the hosts. "Money as a source of prestige and power plays little if any role in our congregational life," wrote Judea Reform president Peter Adland in a temple bulletin. The academic, rather than the southern, character of the community also explains these attitudes.[29]

The children of northern Jewish émigrés, who did not think of themselves as southern in their hometowns, confronted their difference when they went north to camp or college. They often expressed alienation from their northern Jewish peers. "I wasn't aware that I was a different kind of Jew until I went to camp and met kids from elsewhere," explained David

Schwartz, a Chapel Hillian whose parents were northern academic migrants. "They were pushy and crude." Miriam Ornstein, another Chapel Hill faculty child, complained about the "materialism" of the Long Islanders whom she met at Ann Arbor.

One aspect of southern culture that survived the Sunbelt changes was the more intense Jewish consciousness Jews felt on moving to the South, an awareness made all the stronger by the southerners' greater and more uniform religiosity. "You can't disappear here the way you can in New York, Chicago, or Los Angeles," observed Duke psychologist Martin Lakin, who arrived in the 1950s. After four years in Durham, Rabbi Eric Yoffie reflected, "You make a whole series of compromises down South that one does not need to make up North." Relative to those in other regions, southerners show greater rates of religious affiliation among educated and professional people, the very profile that described Jews. Like southern Jews generally, who led Jews nationally in rates of synagogue membership, local Jews also had a high degree of synagogue affiliation. Gallup polls in the late 1960s and early 1970s revealed that 35 percent of southern Jews had attended synagogue in the past week compared to 19 to 20 percent of American Jews. A 1991 Durham–Chapel Hill survey reported that 66.27 percent of the respondents were affiliated with a synagogue. By contrast the 1990 National Jewish Population Survey found that only 41 percent of "entirely Jewish households" were so affiliated.[30]

This intensified Jewish consciousness was felt most strongly among Jewish newcomers. New Yorker Lore Dickstein, who spent a sabbatical year in Chapel Hill, wrote in the liberal journal *Tikkun* in 1990 of her "Southern Discomfort." She observed, "The South is making me feel more Jewish, much to my consternation and surprise." She felt affronted by her southern-bred landlord, who greeted her with bagels. In the "white and Baptist" South, in contrast to the "ethnic stew" of New York, Dickstein found herself "still the Other to these people." She continued, "I am reacting badly to this sense of displacement," and she responded rudely to the Christian missionaries who knocked on her door.[31]

Relocated northern Jews were highly sensitive to perceived slights and insults. A Jewish couple from California settling in Chapel Hill took umbrage when a neighbor asked them what church they attended, UNC sociologist John Shelton Reed recounted. The question, Reed noted, was a "standard gambit" among southerners. "'We're Jewish'" was "a perfectly satisfactory response," Reed explained. In his wordbook of the southern vernacular UNC dramatist Paul Green defined the "Jewish disease" as

"over-sensibility . . . over-indulgence in self-brooding, self-pity." Such responses were consistent with national polls that demonstrated Jews suffered from a cultural lag, suspecting more anti-Semitism than can actually
be measured. The South accented these anxieties. Northern Jews brought
their antisouthern stereotypes with them, holding to an outdated image of
an agrarian, racist, illiterate benighted South even as they made homes in
a cosmopolitan, affluent Sunbelt metropolitan area. They expressed be-
musement at television evangelists and, as political liberals, disdain for conservative politicians such as Jesse Helms. Jews felt frustrated at the slow
pace of life, the way cashiers delayed supermarket lines with neighborly
chat. Wisecracking New Yorkers discovered that irony was not always appreciated, and Yiddishisms drew blank stares. Northern urbanites reacted
against the "smallness of the place."[32]

When southerners attempted to accommodate Jews, the results often
unintendedly emphasized cultural differences, sometimes comically. A supermarket stacked its shelves with extra challah in anticipation of Passover;
a "kosher" sandwich at a deli featured chopped liver and creamed cheese;
and a newspaper story on Yom Kippur described the traditional Kol Nidre
dinner. The Israel Festival at a local museum featured a Methodist choral
group singing selections from "Fiddler on the Roof."

If Jews felt discomfort, it owed to cultural dissonance, not anti-Semitism. Art historian Arthur Marks recalled that he had a "hard time" when
he arrived at UNC in 1974. As a Jew he retained "a sense of energy that
wasn't otherwise present and a manner of speaking, of forthrightness, that
didn't jell with their sense of gentility. . . . I suspect that my manner
was difficult for them." What united Jewish faculty was not so much religious solidarity as a sense of "northern urbaneness." Jews were prominent among campus liberals, joining labor or antiwar protests and advocating revisionist scholarship that emphasized race, class, and gender.

Beyond the Sunbelt enclaves of the Research Triangle extended the
agrarian South. Pick-up trucks with gun racks traversed country roads.
Although Jews did partake of the southern lifestyle as campers, boaters,
gardeners, and fishermen, it was rare to find a Jew who was an avid out-
doorsman, the hunter who was a stock figure of southern folk culture. As
Jews moved into subdivisions that bulldozed forest and pasture, they found
themselves culturally and politically distant from their agrarian neighbors.
Dr. Eva Salber, who practiced rural medicine, heard "a strong dislike for
liberal Yankees," particularly New Yorkers.[33]

The public schools no longer promulgated Christianity, and public anti-Semitic taunting had all but ceased. Paucity of numbers, however, continued to isolate Jewish children. David Schwartz, raised in Chapel Hill in the 1970s, did not feel "positive" about being Jewish. Yet, he could not recollect even one anti-Semitic episode. His closest friends were non-Jewish "kids in the neighborhood." Although Schwartz felt "very socially integrated," his high-school friends became a small circle from Young Judea. A number of his Jewish peers, he observed, were "socially maladjusted."

On campus Jews still felt discomfort as a minority in such a Christian milieu. Evangelists stood in UNC's "Pit" haranguing students as they changed classes. Jewish student government members provoked controversy when they sought to end funding for dormitory Christmas trees and parties. At Duke a cross on the university seal and the towering Duke Chapel were constant signs that Jews were outsiders. In 1983 student Tandy Solomon surveyed Jewish students for the *Chronicle*. Students spoke of "continual reminders" of their "otherness," of being "inundated" by messages announcing Christian fellowships, study groups, and square dances. One student described a dormitory advisor who did his best to convert him. Robbyn Footlick, a New Yorker, observed that "the South makes you feel your Jewishness stronger and you also . . . have to fight to keep it up." [34] At Duke's graduation the diplomas read "the year of Our Lord," and Christian Bibles were handed to students.

The multicultural agenda pushed forward group interests and intensified ethnic consciousness. "Pluralist principles . . . have been on the ascendancy at a time when ethnic differences have been on the wane," Stephen Steinberg observes. The declarations of three faiths in support of brotherhood, a community feature since the 1930s, gave way to dialogues on cultural pluralism, which by the 1980s evolved into multiculturalism, a global perspective sensitive to issues of race. On campus—at Duke especially, which earned notoriety for its allegedly "politically correct" faculty—Jews grew concerned that multiculturalism was creating frictions. Conscious of their minority status but no longer seen as a victim people, Jewish students sought to define a place for themselves in the multicultural spectrum. Jewish sensitivities were aroused as Duke's *Chronicle* and UNC's *Daily Tar Heel* featured letter and editorial skirmishes on Israeli-Palestinian issues. Jewish students held ongoing dialogues with Arab and African American students. At UNC Jewish and black college students discussed racial quotas, South Africa, and Louis Farrakhan. These talks, which were well attended, proceeded civilly without the rancor often found on metropolitan campuses. At a 1990 forum one black student defended his decision to join a mostly Jewish fraternity although some blacks accused him of lacking racial pride. UNC student David Kessel advocated women's and Afro-American studies in the *Jewish Tarheel* newspaper, but he concluded with an admonition: "On this campus, let's use multiculturalism as a catalyst for promoting racial, ethnic, and religious awareness and for diversifying our campus culture. Let's not use it as a vehicle for separatism and fingerpointing." The campus mood turned shrill over such issues as building a black cultural center on the UNC campus, but these conflicts were cast in racial rather than religious terms.[35]

In 1982 Chapel Hill public schools adopted a multicultural education policy that had the unintended effect of authorizing the observance of religious holidays. The Durham–Chapel Hill Jewish Federation "endorsed the concept" but warned against "an imposition of religion on our school children." Multiculturalism became so entrenched in Chapel Hill that in the winter of 1991 Christian parents protested when a school assembly included Kawanzaa melodies and Hanukkah songs but no Christmas carols.[36]

One sign of the community's maturing was the development of institutional rather than personal approaches to Jewish-Gentile relations, especially after the founding in 1977 of the Durham–Chapel Hill Jewish Federation and Community Council. Through such programs as an annual ministers' meeting, begun in 1981, the Community Relations Council (CRC) formalized outreach to the Christian community. The meetings were an update of the historical task of "explaining Judaism" and explored such ecumenical themes as the "rootedness of Christianity in the Old Testament." Jews more readily found Christian dialogue partners among urban black fundamentalists and white religious liberals than among rural white fundamentalists. The CRC lobbied school officials on such perennial problems as Christmas observances, prayer at school events, and scheduling conflicts on Jewish holidays.[37]

Jewish defense efforts took on some urgency in the 1980s when the state experienced a resurgence of Nazi and Klan groups. In 1982 Beth-El was defaced by spray paint and small bullet holes. To combat hate, the CRC appointed a Holocaust Committee to prepare programs for the public schools. As Israel became embroiled in Lebanon and the Palestinian intifada (uprising), Jews saw media assaults on the Jewish state as an affront to their group interest. In accord with national Jewish defense organizations, the local CRC sent delegations to newspaper publishers and radio broadcasters to protest allegedly biased reporting on the Middle East. CRC chair Elizabeth Gervais viewed Jewish defense holistically: "Better relations between the majority Christian community and ourselves . . . will strengthen our ability to aid Israel."[38]

Black-Jewish Breakdown

As integration took hold, the racial climate changed markedly. In 1969 Chapel Hill became the first predominantly white southern town to elect a black as mayor when Howard Lee defeated a white, conservative candidate. Increasingly, Jews knew blacks not merely as employees or customers but also as elected officials, colleagues in a university department, or personal bankers. The tenor of the local Jewish community on racial issues remained liberal even as the black-Jewish civil rights alliance unraveled nationally. Melvin Rashkis, a longtime Chapel Hillian, argued repeatedly and forcefully before the CRC that the only way to create harmony between Jews and blacks was by nurturing friendships with home visits. Although few blacks and Jews could claim intimacy, relations between the communities did not succumb to the racial strife that embroiled Chicago, New York, or Los Angeles. The issues that rended those cities—conflicts over neighborhoods, economic control, and political redistricting—did not exist locally. Durham had a large, empowered black middle class. The two communities shared a liberal agenda.

Most interactions occurred on institutional levels. Politically progressive Jews and blacks worked together in community-based programs and in groups such as Durham Congregations in Action or North Carolinians against Racist and Religious Violence. At North Carolina Central University the only two white professors to be conferred emeritus status, Ernst Manasse and Nell Hirschberg, were both Jews. Some native Jews held lifelong relationships with blacks whom they had known as customers, employees, or neighbors. A few Jews were personally committed to bridging the color line. Chapel Hill city councilman Joe Herzenberg, a former Mississippi civil rights worker, regularly appeared at black churches. Eva Salber, a physician who worked with the rural poor, felt an "immediate kinship" with the elderly black women whom she met in her work. She opened her home to them, and they invited her to christenings and funerals. Rabbi John Friedman formed friendships with black clergy, including an imam. Among the accolades awarded him for his human relations work was the Martin Luther King, Jr., Committee's "Keeper of the Dream" citation. Such efforts required commitment, and few Jews and blacks built relations beyond the workplace or issue-based forums.[39]

In the 1980s local Jews were highly sensitive to the much-heralded national breakdown of black-Jewish relations over such issues as affirmative action, the anti-Semitism of Louis Farrakhan, and Israeli relations with South Africa. Jesse Jackson's presidential campaigns of 1984 and 1988 found local Jews supporting and opposing the Rainbow Coalition. A local black labor leader asserted that Jewish administrative dominance of Duke Hospital was blocking African American progress. Black Muslim students confronted Rabbi John Friedman when he was invited to speak to a religion class at North Carolina Central University. The students denounced Judaism as a "perverted form of true African faith" and called Jews not the Chosen People but the "Children of the Devil." Friedman was shocked by the professor who, though disagreeing with the attacks, applauded the students for provoking discussion. The CRC gave high priority toward establishing a dialogue with the black leadership. A group of ten Jews and blacks began holding luncheon meetings to explore issues and to plan joint activities.[40]

In 1985 the CRC, under the impetus of UNC law professor Barry Nakell, opened a dialogue with black academic and political leaders that led to the forming of the Black-Jewish Roundtable. Its initial dinner meeting, which focused on affirmative action, drew fifteen Jewish and eight black participants, including Professor C. Eric Lincoln of Duke, Professor Harry Groves of UNC, and ex-mayor Howard Lee of Chapel Hill. Local Jews expressed approval of affirmative action in contrast to the position of national Jewish organizations. In sponsoring antiapartheid forums, Jews were able to express their opposition to South Africa's policies while defusing criticism of Israel. A 1984 synagogue gathering drew a large multiracial audience to hear Congressman Walter Fauntroy address the issue. To stress the nonracial character of Judaism, Jews brought to the area prominent black Jews, including Reuben Greenberg, police chief of Charleston, and Julius Lester, Judaic scholar and author.

Although some black leaders avidly participated in the roundtable, Jews felt increasingly that blacks were less interested than the Jews in pursuing a dialogue. The initiative usually came from the Jewish community. The roundtable discussants were drawn mostly from elites in both communities. The black professionals, many of whom were academic émigrés themselves, did not necessarily speak for the larger community. Nor did blacks share the Jews' perception of themselves as a fellow persecuted minority. Blacks were more interested in gaining political support for issues relevant to them than in discussions to create mutual understanding. In the late 1980s the roundtable focused on black concerns, primarily problems in the schools. A 1990 public forum held in a black church featured the superintendents of schools explaining the tracking program, a policy of identifying gifted children that blacks believed was discriminatory.

By 1990 the Black-Jewish Roundtable reached a dead end. Given the divisions within the black community, which lacked the cohesion of the Jewish community, the Jews found it difficult to identify and address black leadership. Periodic efforts were made to revive relations, with limited success. In 1991 black and Jewish groups cosponsored "Crossing the Broken Bridge," an interracial drama; the play and panel discussion drew more than one hundred Jews to North Carolina Central University, but only several dozen blacks. Even as civic and clerical leaders worked together on issues of mutual interest, blacks and Jews, like southern whites generally, remained socially and residentially apart.

Civic Insiders

As the community liberalized, Jews as white people took leadership positions that had been the sinecures of southern social elites. Zora Rashkis, a high-school teacher, became president of UNC's Friends of the College, and her husband, Melvin, served as president of the Chapel Hill Chamber of Commerce. As a Rotarian, he was asked to serve as chaplain because members enjoyed hearing Hebrew prayers. After a decade in town, developer Adam Abram served as president of the Durham Arts Council. He found the community welcoming. Being a Jew was never an issue.

In their civic affiliations Jews followed national trends as service clubs faded and environmental and social justice causes came to the fore. For the most part Jewish migrants gravitated toward liberal groups such as the National Organization of Women or the North Carolina Civil Liberties Union rather than to civic clubs such as the Lions or Kiwanis. Chapel Hill's Inter-Church Council and Durham's Central City Church Council, which ran shelters and community kitchens, rechristened themselves Inter-Faith Council and Durham Congregations in Action, respectively, and rabbis became involved. Jewish women served as presidents of both groups. Jews headed or helped found organizations such as the Hemlock

Society, Planned Parenthood, North Carolinians against Religious and Racist Violence, Physicians for Social Responsibility, and Women's International League for Peace and Freedom.

At formal dinners the governor presented research scientists Irwin Fridovich, Robert Lefkowitz, and Ernest Eliel with the state's highest honor, the North Carolina Award, alongside such notable native sons as Doc Watson, Billy Graham, and Charles Kuralt. Regional pride swelled when two Chapel Hillians, Gertrude Bell Elion and Martin Rodbell, won Nobel Prizes. As North Carolina tirelessly promoted its image as a high-tech center, it embraced these Jewish newcomers as its own.

Political Liberals

In both Durham and Chapel Hill conservative rural and business interests yielded to "citizen-power" coalitions of African Americans and white liberals.[41] Jews who aspired to political office invariably identified with black aspirations. When Ken Broun ran for Chapel Hill mayor in 1991, he cited his work as the founder of a legal training program for black South Africans. Durham politics were tumultuous and faction ridden as pro-business conservatives, blue-collar whites, academic liberals, working-class blacks, and middle-class blacks contended. In the 1980s a liberal black-white alliance dominated, climaxed by the election of a black mayor, Chester Jenkins, in 1989.

The election of Jews to public office far beyond their proportion was another sign of their insider status. When E. J. Evans ran for office in 1950, his Jewishness was an open issue. When Ken Broun won the mayoralty of Chapel Hill forty years later, the religious question was not once raised—except by Jews who took pride in his election.

The Sunbelt newcomers retained the traditional liberalism of their socioeconomic class and ethnic group. If anything, they seemed less influenced by national conservative trends. Local politics were hardly representative of either the South or the Sunbelt generally but, in Chapel Hill especially, reflected the liberalism of a college town. An archconservative such as Jesse Helms won statewide elections while drawing less than one-quarter of the local vote. Political surveys showed southern Jews to be more liberal than southern white Gentiles but less liberal than northern Jews.[42] The Sunbelt Jews who settled in Durham and Chapel Hill brought their northern politics with them. The caution that led small-town southern Jews to conform to conservative views was unnecessary in the college towns where a liberal political culture thrived. Contrarily in southern towns such as Knoxville, where Jewish businessmen had once held office, the newly arrived Sunbelt Jews were politically marginal.

In all cases Jews who aspired to political office identified with liberal factions. In 1988 Ellen Reckhow was elected to her first term to the Durham County Commissioners with the support of black groups. Especially concerned with planning and environmental issues, she was reelected in 1992 with broad backing. In Chapel Hill numbers of Jews served on the town council: Steven Bernholz (1967–1970), Sid Rancer (1973–1974), Gerry Cohen (1974–1979), Marvin Silver (1975–1976), Joe Herzenberg (1979–1980, 1987–1993), and Art Werner (1985–1993). Only Rancer, a businessman who had moved from New York in 1938, claimed long-time roots. And only Bernholz, a lawyer raised in Greensboro, was a southerner. Cohen and Herzenberg, UNC graduate students, were Democratic Socialists. If Herzenberg had any minority identification it was as a civil rights advocate and the only openly gay elected official in the South. In Carrboro, a mill town bordering Chapel Hill, attorney Steve Rose served as alderman in 1982 as liberals from the academic community wrested control from native conservatives. Jewish political activity was part of a broader movement that saw minorities break the hegemony of native white southerners. Names such as DeVito, Pasquini, Capowski, and Halkiotis appeared on local city and county boards. A Lebanese American succeeded a black as mayor of Chapel Hill. These candidates ran as individuals, and ethnic politics did not establish itself locally as it did in urban centers where Asian and Hispanic numbers were greater, although race issues were often in the forefront.

When Kenneth Broun, former dean of the UNC Law School, was elected mayor of Chapel Hill in 1991, he was the most liberal candidate in a three-person race that pitted him against a conservative businessmen and an environmentalist and fair-housing advocate. Broun focused on crime, finances, affordable housing, and downtown revitalization, and black, student, and environmental groups endorsed him. Neither ethnic loyalty nor religious prejudice played any role. Broun, a temple member, enjoyed wide and vigorous support from Jews, but his liberal opponent also listed Jews among her supporters. Broun won the election with a clear majority. In 1993 Broun was reelected without opposition.

Local Jewry remained liberal even as prominent national Jews espoused neoconservatism. In the 1986 congressional election, newspapers reported that the Republican incumbent, Bill Cobey, had received $11,000 from pro-Israel political action committees. Although the community appreciated Cobey's defense of Israel and Soviet Jewry, many were upset over his opposition to abortion and support of school prayer. In a fund-raising letter Cobey described himself as the "Christian" candidate. The community believed that his Democratic opponent, Duke political scientist David Price, was equally supportive of Israel while adhering to a liberal agenda. Local Jews confronted the American-Israel Political Action Committee (AIPAC), which supported Cobey, and rallied to Price's support. Price won the election handily. Price was reelected repeatedly with wide and public Jewish support even in 1998 when he ran against Tom Roberg, a Jew who was a conservative Republican. Liberal values proved stronger than ethnic loyalty. Jews also acted in the 1990 senatorial race to oppose Republican Jesse Helms and to support Democrat Harvey Gantt, a liberal African American. An ad hoc committee of prominent Jews raised funds, and Gantt spoke at a rally that overflowed the synagogue hall rented for the occasion.

On the community margin were Jews committed to alternative politics. Bob Sheldon operated the Internationalist bookstore, which featured leftist and Third World literature. Sheldon's outspoken advocacy of Palestinian rights occasionally rankled the Jewish community. (He was slain in 1991 during an apparent robbery at his store although some suspected political motives.) Dan Coleman was a leader of the Chapel Hill Greens, an environmental party, and edited a newspaper, the *Prism,* which featured left-wing journalism. The Progressive Jewish Network (PJN) supported causes from gay rights to Palestinian self-determination. Several joined Jesse Jackson's Rainbow Coalition. Steve Schewel, a former Duke student, founded and published the *Independent,* an alternative weekly with a progressive voice.

Veterans of the political radicalism that struck campuses nationally in the late 1960s and early 1970s continued their leftist activism. Jim Waller, Mike Nathan, and Paul Bermanzohn were former Duke students who organized for the Communist Workers Party while performing community service. Nathan served as a pediatrician at a clinic in Hayti, Durham's black neighborhood. In 1979 they drove to Greensboro with several black protesters for an anti-Klan, anti-Nazi rally. As they marched, Klansmen arrived in a motorcade and opened fire. The shoot-out left Waller and Nathan dead and Bermanzohn severely wounded.

The eventual acquittal of the Klansmen shocked the Jewish community—as it did the nation. Local attitudes were contradictory, however. None of the victims had affiliated with the Jewish community, and their politics were regarded as provocative. Nevertheless, they were Jewish victims of a violently anti-Semitic hate group. "There wasn't an enormous outpouring of sympathy," but there was a "grudging acknowledgement of an injustice having been done," recalled Rabbi Eric Yoffie. The victims themselves were conscious of themselves as Jewish radicals. Bermanzohn was the son of Holocaust survivors. Still handicapped by head wounds, he brought his newborn child to Beth-El for a naming ceremony. Congregants collected clothes for the family. Marty Nathan, widow of the slain pediatrician, appeared before local Jewish groups and pleaded for support.

Sunbelt Jewish Life

Jews were heading South, but so was much of America. Jews were in the vanguard of an emerging multicultural South. Although they still were highly sensitive of their difference, they felt less alien as the area became less ethnically southern and more cosmopolitan. In the way of acculturation Sunbelt migrants noted how the South softened their manners and heightened their religious consciousness. Typical of southerners, they became local boosters, citing national surveys that rated their hometowns high among the best places to live in America.

The social exclusion felt by earlier generations faded as Jews acculturated and the mainstream culture Judaized. If Jews as a people were assimilating into mainstream American culture, so, too, were southerners. The American mainstream was also turning southern as politicians from Jimmy Carter to Bill Clinton won national elections; country musicians Johnny Cash and Garth Brooks became national icons; and regional corporations such as Coca-Cola and Bank of America expanded into global markets. Jews differed from other southerners in their political liberalism and their concentration in professional fields.

As the small, relatively insular community was swept into the American multicultural mainstream, Durham–Chapel Hill Jews extended the boundaries of identity. Denominational definitions could not adequately delineate the varieties of Jewish belief or nonbelief. Local Jews included secular culturalists, New Age meditators, and Lubavitch Hasidim. New populations of retirees, converts, gay people, single parents, and interfaith families expressed differing communal needs. American Judaism was increasingly shaped by a personalism that held individual autonomy to be a higher value than religious or communal authority. Jews tailored religion to their lifestyles, selecting, ignoring, or reinventing traditions at their convenience.[43]

Congregations responded to consumer demands and market forces, extending outreach to bring outsider Jews into the communal fold. The old structures were no longer adequate for a sprawling, pluralistic community. As organizations faded, new ones arose. Where once the local Jewish community excluded members who did not conform to a nominally Orthodox standard, now Jews freely chose among alternative Judaisms. Historians of religion were at a loss to describe a normative Judaism or define a Jewish essence.[44]

In the 1960s and 1970s younger Jews, inspired by student movements, expressed frustration with suburban Judaism and turned to mystical texts to reclaim or invent what they saw as a spiritually authentic Judaism. This inward searching was followed in the 1980s by a renewed interest in Yiddishkeit, a Jewish response to the postmodernist, ethnic revival. Orthodoxy, which had expired locally, reestablished a presence. By the 1990s, the community was building new facilities and creating new Jewish structures. Congregations reshaped their sanctuaries and reconstructed their liturgies.

These efforts to revitalize were occurring while Jews were living with less Judaism. Most Jews were minimally involved, with perhaps 10 percent of the community attending weekly worship. Rabbis fretted over the Jewish illiteracy of their congregants and the indifference of youth. Courses that the rabbis offered on the Talmud or Midrash drew a core of ten to twenty dedicated participants but did not influence the larger community. The assimilated college generation of the late 1970s and 1980s was complacent about its Jewishness. A national Hillel study noted that most Jewish collegians were secure in their identities but religiously uninvolved. UNC student David Schwartz spoke for his generation when he observed, "I took my Judaism for granted. I was more interested in learning about other lifestyles." Only a "minority" of local youth were receiving Jewish educations, noted Brenda Ginsberg of Jewish Community Services. Surveying the contradictory trends in American Jewry at a 1997 UNC conference on "Judaism at the 21st Century," sociologist Samuel Heilman paraphrased Charles Dickens in describing it as being both the best and worst of times.[45]

As Durham–Chapel Hill became a Sunbelt community, it reflected national rather than just regional trends. Evidence of Jewish absorption into American society was open to conflicting interpretations: Were Jews assimilating or transforming themselves? Was Judaism dying or reviving? Were Jews expanding the boundaries of identity or eviscerating the Jewish essence? In Durham–Chapel Hill a vital, self-identifying core was Jewishly committed while larger numbers assimilated or tokenly identified, some breaking away. This disaffiliated group, however, was dynamic, with movement both toward and away from the core. Despite intermarriage and acculturation, local Jewish survival was not in doubt because of the large, constant migration.[46]

Changing Families

Intermarriage, once at the community's edge, entered its core. A rare occurrence in the 1920s became more frequent in the 1950s and commonplace in the 1980s. In 1980 less than 10 percent of Judea Reform's members were interfaith families, the rabbi estimated. By 1992 this figure had jumped to 25 to 30 percent. Conservative Beth-El counted perhaps one intermarried household among twenty members. Rising rates of intermarriage reflected, as one study observed, the "successful integration of Jews into American society and their achievement of a high level of social acceptance." A Reform congregation had organized in the 1960s largely because parents were concerned about their children's Jewish identities, yet none of the half-dozen graduates of its first confirmation class married a Jew. Historically, intermarriage had correlated with low levels of Jewish identification, with a desire to escape and assimilate, but intermarried Jews now served locally as UJA solicitors, Zionist spokespersons, and prayer leaders.[47]

As was true of Jews nationally, local Jews were late in addressing the intermarriage challenge. Communal efforts were ambivalent. Local rabbis were unwilling to perform interfaith marriages, yet they sought to bring these families into the Jewish fold. In earlier generations local intermarried Jews encountered rejection. In the 1990s workshops, lectures, and dialogues on interfaith marriage began appearing on community calendars. Jewish Community Services sponsored "One Couple–Two Faiths" workshops. Social worker Brenda Ginsberg noted that intermarriage was usually "more of an issue" for the Jew than for the Christian. Typically, she encountered a marginally Jewish male who felt a need to identify and pass on his heritage as his children grew older. The Christian wife often expressed frustration about raising Jewish children when her husband was unable to observe a Sabbath or conduct a Passover seder. In 1992 Rabbi Rachel Cowan, a Jew by choice who had coauthored *Mixed Blessings,* was brought to the community, where she chronicled her own spiritual journey and encouraged others to express theirs. The forums drew as many as two hundred people. One participant noted that the problem of interfaith marriage was more severe for a Jew who married a southerner because the likelihood was greater that the spouse's family would be committed Christians.

Not only had intermarriage and conversion from Judaism been rare; so too had conversion to Judaism. From 1976 to 1980 Reform rabbi Eric Yoffie averaged about one conversion a year, but his successor, Rabbi John Friedman, averaged about six. "Most" of these conversions were by persons contemplating marriage to a Jew. From 1978 to 1991 Beth-El rabbi Steven Sager performed about sixty conversions. Those wishing to become Jews, Sager observed, tended to be people with a "yearning of the spirit" who "grew up without any kind of faith or a faith that they were at odds with." They were especially drawn to the celebratory nature of Jewish holidays. Some had part-Jewish ancestry. Many were motivated because of a relationship with a Jew. The Reform and Conservative rabbis cooperated on a conversion course that included a ritual immersion in a lake.

Jews by choice tended to have high rates of Jewish identification. Locally, they served as heads of outreach committees, adult-education chairpersons, and prayer leaders. UNC medievalist Fred Behrends, whose German Jewish forebear had intermarried and assimilated, became president of Beth-El's Orthodox kehillah and led a Talmud study group. He spent his summers at an Israeli yeshiva. Maurice King, from an old Durham family, was drawn to Judaism after exploring local churches. He journeyed to Boston to be converted and studied in the B'nai Brak ultra-Orthodox community in Israel. He returned to North Carolina with his Israeli wife.

Another new dynamic was the changing profile of the Jewish family. The Durham–Chapel Hill community tended to be "more traditional" than national demographics, Rabbi Sager observed, although Rabbi Friedman noted that the community was "going in the direction of other communities" with growing rates of divorce and single-parent families. The destabilizing influences owed to economic pressures and high rates of mobility. Of the 1,250 households on the 1992 Jewish Federation list, 385 were listed as single persons. The single-parent family, the unmarried Jew living alone, and the elderly without family resources were recognized as growing segments of the local Jewish population. The federation and congregations responded with such programs as "Parenting after Divorce: A Two-Part Workshop" and new organizations such as JAZZ, Jewish Active Senior Citizens, and Chevra, a singles group. Chevra's mailing list extended to five hundred singles in the Triangle, and its happy hours and Sabbath dinners spawned some seventy marriages.[48]

The Holocaust and Israel

The Holocaust and Israel were embedded in Jewish identity. Yom Ha-Shoah (Holocaust Memorial Day) and Yom HaAtzamaut (Israel Independence Day) entered liturgical calendars as holidays. The annual Holocaust services, which featured testimonies of survivors, were among the community's best-attended events. They were organized by Generation to Generation, Triangle Sons and Daughters of Holocaust Survivors. Holocaust studies entered religious school curriculums, and busloads of students were sent on excursions to the United States Holocaust Memorial Museum in Washington.

The Six-Day War of 1967 brought a surge of Jewish self-identification locally as it did nationally, and the claim of Israel as homeland reasserted itself. Amnon and Aviva Rapoport, Israelis who lived in Chapel Hill, felt the difference. "From 1961 to 1966 hardly any attention was paid to us by the Jewish community," Amnon recalled, but after the war they were suddenly popular. He began teaching a class in Zionism. Local Jews were now likely to be more literate about Israeli politicians than about Torah sages. Raising funds for Israel and debating Israeli politics at forums were features of community life.

Israel was certainly an intense concern to a cadre of Jews—from academic as well as business families—but larger numbers were also indifferent. Conservative and Orthodox Jews tended to show more enthusiasm than did Reform Jews. "I can't say that I find Israel a burning topic among my Reform Jewish friends," Judith Ruderman noted. The Orthodox rabbinate in Israel alienated Reform Jews, as demonstrated by Knesset debates over "who is a Jew." Zora Rashkis added, "We are aware of the way they treat Reform Jews in Israel."

For youth Zionism served as a counterforce to assimilation. "My closest friends were kids in Young Judea," recalled David Schwartz. "Young Judea preyed on and encouraged a feeling of alienation. Israel is the only place we could have a Jewish life." Young Judea drew students for summer programs or year-long study where American teenagers farmed on a moshav, tutored Ethiopian immigrants, and served as community emissaries in dispensing charity. In response to a national Birthright Israel program to strengthen Jewish identity, a local Israel Experience endowment was created to send youth to the Jewish state. Campus Zionist student groups, supported by national organizations such as AIPAC and UJA, worked to develop student leadership by sponsoring missions and conventions. Prominent Israelis—Meron Benvenisti, Hirsh Goodman, and Amos Oz— appeared on campus venues.

The route between Durham and Jerusalem was well traveled. Rabbis led congregational tours to Israel. A state-sponsored North Carolina–Israel Partnership promoted trade and cultural exchanges. Unlike an earlier generation that was assimilationist, faculty now identified publicly as Jews and made institutional commitments to Israel. Morton Teichner, who came from Yeshiva University to serve as dean of UNC's School of Social Work, made twelve trips to Israel between 1965 and 1976 to advise Bar Ilan University, and Cecil Sheps visited Israel twenty-eight times to help Ben Gurion University build its medical services program. UNC philosopher George Schlesinger, an Orthodox rabbi, also taught at Bar Ilan. Duke and UNC sponsored programs and faculty exchanges with Israeli universities.

The Israeli contacts produced a significant emigration relative to the size of the community. After a sabbatical, the Lapkin family of Chapel Hill decided to remain. They were followed by the Rosenthals, who re- named themselves the Tals and settled in Haifa. In the 1960s and 1970s Israel's agrarian lifestyle and socialist principles drew college-aged Jews. UNC student Lee Siegel, a member of the Bayit commune in Chapel Hill, settled in Kibbutz Gezer. Several Orthodox Jews also emigrated in search of a religiously fulfilling life. Allan Dworsky, a third-generation Durhamite, remained in Israel after enrolling at Bar Ilan University.

The life of one young Israeli emigrant from Chapel Hill was a Jewish odyssey. Gregory Barry had been raised in an interfaith home, but at four- teen he decided that he wanted a Bar Mitzvah. His mother, Jess Fischer, joined Judea Reform and sent him to Hebrew school. A once-a-year Jew herself, she, too, started studying Hebrew and decided to take a belated Bat Mitzvah. Greg became a leader of Young Judea, visited Israel, and by 1981 joined a kibbutz. A year later his army unit was called to the Lebanon War. Early in the invasion Barry was killed in action.

The community grieved. Hundreds crowded Judea Reform for a me- morial service. "It wasn't just because my child was dead," Jess Fischer recalled. "It was a decidedly Jewish event. . . . At that moment I realized how strongly connected I was to the Jewish community." Fischer went to Israel. There she realized how isolated she had felt as a Jew in America, and she purchased a second home in Haifa. In 1991 she became president of the Durham–Chapel Hill Jewish Federation.[49]

Although Israel's rebirth instilled Jewish pride, as a political state it was subject to criticism. The romantic myths of the state's founding clashed with doubts on human rights policies and religious tolerance. The divisions within Israel proved contentious in North Carolina, too, and the relationship between Israelis and American Jews became less a hierarchy of homeland and exile than a dialogue among equals on issues of identity and democracy. As Israeli politics turned to the right in the late 1970s, local activists brought Palestinians and Israeli doves to Jewish audiences. American Professors for Peace in the Middle East sponsored campus forums. Chapters of Peace Now and the New Jewish Agenda conducted Arab-Jewish dialogues. The Peace Now chapter, which formed after the 1982 Israeli invasion of Lebanon, had a membership of 150 that included rabbis and federation leaders. An advertisement in a Durham newspaper in 1988 after the start of the Palestinian intifada, signed by 140 local Jews, expressed displeasure with Israeli policies and called for peace negotiations. Durham–Chapel Hill Jews were in the vanguard nationally in their peace advocacy. The activism was more representative of liberal college towns such as Madison or Berkeley than of conservative southern communities, which were habituated to caution and defensiveness when confronting Jewish issues.

Cycles of Renewal

Changing attitudes toward Israel was one aspect of a renegotiated Jewish identity as Jews sought to reconcile their secular and religious values. In the 1960s and 1970s disaffected Jews nationally coalesced into the Jewish Renewal Movement, which sought to reclaim a Jewishness that was spiritually authentic and politically subversive. As stated earlier, younger Jews turned away from the suburban synagogue, which they saw as a bastion of privilege and social convention, and looked to Judaism's mystical sources in search of personal fulfillment. The political alienation of the Vietnam War and the campus rebellions also brought them into conflict with Jews whom they saw as morally compromised by their assimilation into establishment elites. Leftist political ideologies motivated most activists, though a few saw themselves in the tradition of Jewish political radicalism. Jewishness was equated with political and cultural resistance. Duke student Mark Pinsky, a New Jersey native, had made the rites of passage from Bar

Mitzvah to United Synagogue Youth to Hillel. During the Six-Day War he left Duke to volunteer for the Israeli army. On his return Pinsky helped found a campus newspaper, *Irgun: The Radical Jewish Monthly,* later renamed *Hashomer.* On "Pesach, 5730," it declared, "We believe that Judaism in North America has degenerated from a rich and vital way of life into a desperate attempt to assimilate with a material culture. . . . Like the original Irgun we are committed to Jewish survival and self determination by any means necessary." It denounced by name a religion professor whom it accused of being anti-Zionist and anti-Semitic. It presented an "Uncle Jake Award" to a prominent Jewish businessman in Durham whom it labeled a slumlord. It supported Palestinian self-determination while demanding "no alliance with bourgeois nationalism."[50]

The newspaper's rhetorical terrorism and its foul language succeeded in rankling the "vacillating Jewish faculty," as Pinsky recalled. Several Jewish faculty were incensed. Nonetheless, Duke's campus radicals reflected a national resurgence of Jewish campus activism. In 1968 only two campuses supported Jewish newspapers; by 1972 that figure swelled to fifty-eight.[51]

The Jewish Renewal Movement peaked in the late 1960s and 1970s as political alienation provoked a spiritual inwardness, a breaking of conventional boundaries. As Hillel director, Reform rabbi Robert Siegel fit the times. On Friday nights students sat in circles, sang popular songs, and danced as their spirits moved them. The rabbi, who rode a motorcycle with a dog perched on the handlebars, taught an antiestablishment class, "Dilemma: The Jewish Money Game." In 1975 Hasidic troubadour Sholomo Carlebach roused Duke students with his spirited melodies, and Lubavitcher Hasidim visited campuses to celebrate holidays. A half-dozen UNC students formed the Bayit, a communal house, where they explored alternative living styles. The students kept kosher and celebrated Sabbath. Several immigrated to Israel, lured by the kibbutz movement, which seemed the fulfillment of their social and spiritual aspirations.

In the early 1970s students at the Duke Hillel and the UNC Hillel founded the Free Jewish University, which gave voice to their reawakening. Its catalogue began by quoting the "kabbalistic mystics" on *"tzimtzim,"* gathering the sparks of divinity, and *"tikkun olam,"* repairing the world. True to the universalism of the times, non-Jews were invited to enroll. The catalogue included a statement that spoke of a renewed, participatory Judaism: "[We] see ourselves as a community-in-formation, as individual Jews groping with questions of identity, feeling and knowledge."

. . . The Free Jewish University, you see is you." By 1974 the Free Jewish University program at Duke enrolled three hundred students and expanded to twenty-one courses.[52]

The student movements influenced congregations as Jews began to examine their beliefs and question their own religiosity. Even as Durham–Chapel Hill Jews had built new sanctuaries, less attention was being paid to belief and observance. Joel Smith, an early Judea Reform president, recognized that the institution building had often taken precedence over spirituality: "Judea Reform was as close to being a voluntary organization as you could imagine. Its religious function was secondary. A lot of members were not participating members at all and services were very poorly attended. . . . Its maintenance was an end in itself." The late 1960s and early 1970s were marked nationally by a "rise in Jewish theological interest." Judea Reform's statement of purpose called for a "meaningful" Judaism. Similar questions were also being raised at Beth-El. In 1968 one confirmand spoke on "Hasidism and Religious Experience," and another explained Martin Buber.[53]

One popular congregational forum became the Shabbaton, a community gathering pioneered by students. In 1971 Judea Reform Congregation held its first Shabbaton at Wildacres in the North Carolina mountains. Forty congregants gathered for a weekend of workshops, discussion, and services. A transcript of a 1973 Shabbaton on "The Individual and the Communal Jew: Getting It All Together" reveals an effort to reinvent Judaism.

The participants formulated a new ten commandments. Several themes emerged. One was an emphasis on ethics, an insistence on Judaism's universality. For Ruth Erickson being a Jew meant becoming "the very best Human Being one could be." As Howard Lewis put it, performing *mitzvot*, good deeds, was more important than developing an "explicit notion of God." Jerry Ruskin noted that "the prophets were social activists." The turn to prophetic Judaism led to discussions of Buber's views on the "I-Thou" encounter of individual and God and of individual and individual.[54]

Bert Kaplan saw a need to "come to grips with the mystical relationships in our lives." Kaplan was concerned that when "Reform threw out many of the emotional symbols and mystical aspects of Judaism," it lost "basic feeling." Erickson wanted a new kind of Sabbath observance where people could "get together, get into nature, sing and dance." The participants then attempted to reconcile their notions of self with their social obligations. Rabbi Rosenzweig introduced the example of the kibbutz, and Kaplan and Edward Clifford debated their own Israeli experiences where they met Jews who lived ethically without practicing ritual Judaism.[55]

The last commandment was to act " 'as though' we can contribute to the coming of a Messianic Age," which Rabbi Rosenzweig defined as "a maximum of justice, a social balance." The Shabbaton was participatory democracy; the rabbi abdicated his leadership to laypersons, and the children conducted services. The mystical yearnings, the encounter-group format, and the stress on "feelings" may seem more fitting for an Aquarian Age than a Messianic one, but the Shabbaton fit the times. Watergate and the Vietnam War were raising questions about the very foundations of the political and social order, and a rebellious, self-absorbed youth was everywhere challenging social conventions. Popular psychologies emphasized self-fulfillment. The Shabbaton reflected evolutions in American Judaism as Jews negotiated between faith commandments that were communal and obligatory and a personal spirituality that was private and freely chosen. "We should be rethinking our beliefs," Jacob Kaplan concluded.[56]

The Progressive Jewish Network

Some Jews, veterans of civil rights and antiwar struggles, were loosely affiliated, if at all, with the community while still remaining committed Jews. Gays especially felt Jewishly estranged. These Jews were wary of a Judaism that was patriarchal—sexist and homophobic in their view—and synagogues that seemed bastions of bourgeois privilege. They felt alienated as protestors for progressive causes bore Christian witness or demonstrated on Jewish holidays. As political activist Ron Grunwald stated, "I don't want to have to hide the fact that I'm doing that as a Jew." In the 1970s students and young professionals formed a chapter of the New Jewish Agenda.

The local New Jewish Agenda faded, but in 1985 fourteen people gathered in a Durham home to form the Progressive Jewish Network. They were a mixed group, "from religiously observant to profound revisionist secular, from liberal Democrat to socialist, from ardent Zionists to anti-Zionists." Their goal was "bringing a progressive voice to the Jewish community and a Jewish voice to the progressive community." Several were searching for a religious " 'home base' in the Jewish community," especially to celebrate holidays. They saw themselves as a "*chavura* [fellowship group], . . . building a sense of community." They allied themselves with the Jewish Renewal Movement, working toward "a Jewish liberation theology." [57]

Within three years the PJN had a membership of two hundred, and its monthly meetings drew twenty to thirty individuals. In 1987, it affiliated once more with the New Jewish Agenda. Members sat on the floor of a Durham home debating whether Zionism was a colonial or a national liberation movement. Speakers analyzed homophobia, studied Central American liberation movements, and warned about the resurgence of Klan and Nazi groups. PJN members joined the Martin Luther King birthday celebration at a black church and protested when a Nicaraguan Contra leader appeared at Duke. At Durham's Gay Pride '86 parade, the PJN marched under its banner.

After the upheavals of the 1970s social activists turned inward with a personal spirituality that radically reinterpreted tradition. On Purim PJN members debated the sexism of the Queen Esther Beauty Pageant and the morality of the Jews' revenge. Communal seders, which drew as many as seventy to the Friends Meeting House, included peace, feminist, and freedom *haggadahs* (Passover books). On Yom Kippur they held a meditation. The PJN attracted intermarried couples, and an interfaith group discussed such issues as "Raising Children in a Mixed Relationship."

After a Purim party, PJN members joined the festivities at Beth-El. "I think we were a big hit at the synagogue and the synagogue was a big hit with us," Grunwald observed. It was typical of the community that its establishment would embrace its outsiders. The Durham–Chapel Hill Federation was one of only two chapters nationally to invite New Jewish Agenda membership on its board. When Greg Robbins went to Nicaragua as a Witness for Peace, the federation helped defray his expenses. "We have different interests and emphases than the 'established' Jewish community," Robbins wrote, "yet we are also strongly connected" to it. [58] The insider status of the PJN reflected Durham's and Chapel Hill's evolution from southern to liberal college towns.

Interest in the PJN rose and fell with its leadership. By the early 1990s the group met sporadically. The New Jewish Agenda folded nationally. The PJN once again revitalized itself, but it was evolving into a *havurah* (fellowship group), more social than political. By the late 1990s it had disappeared.

Cultural Jews

Jewish organizations formed and disbanded with rapidity in response to community changes. Just as the social and political chaos of the 1960s and 1970s led to spiritual seeking, the suburban rootlessness and anonymity of the 1980s inspired a search for ethnic roots. As the immigrant generation was rapidly dying, third- and fourth-generation Jews wanted to remember what their parents had tried to forget. Jews constructed a postmodernist identity that reconnected them culturally to the Yiddishkeit of their lost ancestral homelands. Max Drucker, a retiree, gathered a small group weekly at his home to study Yiddish. The Triangle Jewish Chorale presented programs of folk and liturgical music in Hebrew, Ladino, and Yiddish. Fiddler Bert Chessin sought old-time musicians in New York and eastern Europe and founded a klezmer (east European Jewish folk music) band, Die Yiddishe Bande. The Magnolia Klezmer Band fused various traditions. Jewish Community Services offered cooking classes that taught a disconnected generation the lost arts of preparing kugel, blintzes, knishes, and chicken soup. The class, seminar, and workshop now formally instructed Jews in the skills and knowledge that the folk culture had once passed on traditionally from mother to daughter, father to son.

A handicrafts movement emerged locally as part of a general Jewish arts-and-crafts revival. Rabbi Efraim Rosenzweig crafted mezzuzahs and wall plaques, and Dorothy Heyman wove *tallesim* (prayer shawls) on a loom. Steve Herman was a national distributor of Sukkah kits. Galia Goodman gained a national reputation for her paper cuttings, a traditional Jewish art. Although a small-town southerner, she conducted training workshops at the Yiddish Scientific Institute (YIVO) in New York. The situation in Durham–Chapel Hill was consistent with studies that showed small-town Jews often enjoyed fuller Jewish lives than those in larger cities because less was taken for granted. "Isolation sometimes offers a greater sense of responsibility for group survival," observed Susan Rebecca Brown of small-town Jews.[59]

The Jews of Durham–Chapel Hill lacked the organizations typically found in American communities and supported groups that had only a token presence, if any, in most Jewish communities. Members of the Jewish Vegetarian Society and the Mosaic Outdoor Mountain Club sought to reconcile their personal ethical and environmental values with Jewish teachings. The Maimonides Society drew Jewish health care professionals. On the other hand, a branch of the National Council of Jewish Women never formed, and sporadic efforts to start an Organization for Rehabilitation through Training (ORT) chapter failed. B'nai B'rith was little more than a name. Among the older societies Hadassah alone sustained itself. A Chapel Hill group broke from Durham and received its own charter in 1976, growing to two hundred members. By the 1990s, both chapters had difficulty holding monthly meetings and developing leadership beyond a cadre of dedicated members. In 1996 the two chapters reunited.

A Jewish Federation

The centrifugal pull of Jewish diversity and suburban sprawl strained the bonds of community. The growing presence of elderly and single-parent Jews created demands for new organizations and social services. Moreover, Jewish identity entailed global as well as local communal responsibilities. Durham–Chapel Hill was late in responding to institutional developments in American Jewish philanthropy. After the Six-Day War, UJA fund-raising reached record levels as Jewish pride intensified. In 1973, with Israel again threatened, $660 million was raised. While Israel remained the focus, domestic needs had not been addressed. At national assemblies, students demonstrated for financial support. As the community grew to eight hundred families and sprawled into Chapel Hill, the need arose for an organization of greater structure and geographical scope than the UJA.

Efforts to create a local Jewish Federation were sporadic. Duke law professor Mel Shimm traces its origins to the aftermath of the 1973 Yom Kippur war when, in response to an ad hoc fund-raising campaign, meetings were held at Beth-El Congregation to systematize local Jewish philanthropy and draft bylaws. University people, mentored by Sara and Mutt Evans, inspired and led the federation. Gladys Siegel, whose husband taught at UNC, recalled an early meeting in her Chapel Hill home where organizers gathered in her living room without knowing exactly what a federation was supposed to do. Ultimately, they defined their mission as local Jewish welfare and defense, UJA fund-raising, and public relations for Israel. In 1976 Duke professors Melvin Shimm and Martin Lakin wrote a constitution for a Durham–Chapel Hill Jewish Federation and Community Council that gave representation to each of the community's Jewish organizations, including student groups.[60] Women took leadership roles, numbering perhaps half the board. In 1976 Gladys Siegel became its first president.

The Council of Jewish Federations through its general assembly linked local Jewry to a national network. The federation's increasingly professional campaigns included telethons, parlor parties, and an annual dinner gala. The federation nearly doubled its collections from 1981 to 1988, equaling rates of growth in UJA giving nationally. Nonetheless, year to year—excepting 1985 when the rescue of Ethiopian Jews inspired generous giving—the community rarely met its quotas. In 1983, 850 households appeared on the federation list, but only 367 donated. In 1987 the goal was $140,000, but only $133,000 was raised. Durham–Chapel Hill lacked the wealthy mercantile families typical of Jewish communities. One year a quarter of the total was raised by eighteen contributors, and more than half came from sixty-nine donors. Faculty lived on salaries and, unlike business people, did not aspire to status through public giving. Local Jews would rather debate politics than raise funds.[61] The primary Jewish philanthropy remained the congregations, and Beth-El and Judea Reform's combined budgets nearly doubled federation fund-raising totals.

Increasing professionalism was a national trend in Jewish philanthropy dating to the 1930s, but local Jewish charities had remained voluntary. Recognizing its limits, Durham–Chapel Hill in 1991 hired a professional UJA fund-raiser, and annual giving rose sharply. The federation raised $147,772 in 1990, but $234,854 in 1992. Six years later, when the federation had a staff of ten, it raised $448,415. The local federation was able to increase its fund-raising in contrast to national trends, which show a sharp decline since 1990.

Allocations created tensions as the community debated the conflicting priorities of Israel and domestic Jewry, issues that defined Jewish identity. Allocations reflected traditional Jewish concerns: the elderly, youth, and anti-Semitism. Major recipients were the Blumenthal Jewish Home (a home for the aged), the Anti-Defamation League, and the Hillel Foundation. Nevertheless, the primary recipient was the State of Israel. In 1980 Sara Evans had argued that fund-raising should be for Israel alone and questioned expenditures on a local ride service for the elderly. Local needs pressed forward, however. In 1985 the federation kept 20 percent locally, double the previous year's figure, and by 1988 that figure rose to 30 percent. Domestic needs were given greater priority after the National Jewish Population Survey of 1990 revealed alarming rates of assimilation. The local federation subscribed to the continuity agenda that the Council of Jewish Federations promulgated at its annual general assembly. In 1998, 57 percent was allocated locally, 5 percent remained in the state or country, and only 17 percent went overseas.[62]

The decreasing percentages sent to Israel reflected in some measure a growing ambivalence about the politics of the Jewish state. After the Israeli elections of 1977, followed by the 1981 bombing of Beirut and the 1982 Lebanese War, federation leaders noted that "many committed individuals are unhappy about Israeli policies" and felt alienated from the UJA. These concerns peaked in 1987 with the intifada. Concerns were also expressed that UJA funds were supporting Israeli Ultra-Orthodox groups that ostracized Reform and Conservative Jews. In 1987 the Durham–Chapel Hill Federation solicited support nationally in the Council of Jewish Federations to pass a resolution calling for increased Arab and Jewish cooperation and advocating greater tolerance for non-Orthodox Judaism in Israel. The federation began funding groups dedicated to Arab-Jewish coexistence, such as the New Israel Fund and the Interns for Peace. By publicly raising the issue the local federation had cast aside the focus on Israeli issues that tended to govern Jewish American politics.[63]

With a federation the community professionalized its social welfare. The primary need was caring for the rising number of elderly who, lured by the national media, were retiring to North Carolina. Many lacked family and communal ties to support them. After encountering an elderly Jewish woman lost in a supermarket, Dorothy Blum and Rishie Baroff oversaw the informal Friendship Circle for senior citizens. By 1978, however, the federation recognized that volunteerism and home hospitality were no longer sufficient and hired a social worker. The federation also assisted Jewish inmates at the federal prison in nearby Butner, arranging for Passover seders and High Holiday services. (Among the prisoners was the spy Jonathan Pollard.) With the arrival of Russian families, beginning in 1989, the community confronted numbers of economically distressed Jews for the first time in fifty years. The federation lent money, arranged host families, donated furniture, and found jobs for these new members of the community.

In the early 1990s American Jewry, alarmed by demographic trends, began belatedly addressing the problem of an assimilating youth. A Foundation for Jewish Student Life reorganized Hillel nationally as B'nai B'rith relinquished responsibility. North Carolina's Jewish federations increased their funding. Duke alumni raised $4,500,000 for a Center for Jewish Life. A director was hired, and an impressive facility replete with a mikva and kosher catering hall arose on the Duke campus. The Duke Hillel budget rose from $35,000 in 1995 to $150,000 in 1998. A reorganized UNC Hillel reported dramatically increasing levels of student interest in the 1990s, and it too embarked on a $3,600,000 endowment campaign. In 1999 UNC Hillel demolished its old building and broke ground for a new facility. This new center was designed with two chapels for Reform and Conservative services.

As Jews blended their secular and religious values, they restructured their institutions. Where Jewish groups once reflected the social conventions of the small-town South, they were now attuned to a larger, academically liberal community noted for its political, religious, and environmental activism. Jews harmonized the counterculture with rabbinic tradition. Gay rights, peace work, and backpacking reinforced Jewish identity. The Jewish organizational impulse continued unabated as a sense of ethnic identity and collective responsibility survived the community changes. Russian immigrants of the early 1900s were sheltered by a Hachnoses Orchim whereas those of the 1990s were welcomed by a subcommittee of the Durham–Chapel Hill Jewish Federation.

Democracy and Tradition

Synagogue membership remained the principal agency of Jewish affiliation. Of the 1,250 households on the Jewish community list in 1992, 745 were synagogue members, and a little more than 500 were financial contributors to the federation. Both congregations reported rapid growth. Nonetheless, fears of Jewish survival, reinforced by data from national surveys, were persistently expressed. A distinct minority of Jews were observant. Congregations wrestled with such issues as whether Christian family members of Jews could be given synagogue honors, whether children who were being raised in two faiths could be enrolled in the religious schools, and whether non-Jews could be buried in consecrated cemeteries.

Both congregations aspired to a Judaism that was democratic and participatory, reflecting a consensus of their membership's values while respecting minority rights. Beth-El, affiliated with the United Synagogue of Conservative Judaism, evolved into a religiously pluralistic congregation with a Reconstructionist rabbi. It housed two prayer quorums, one traditionalist but egalitarian and the other Orthodox. Judea Reform adopted a prayer book that offered alternative liturgies. In both congregations liberalizing trends were checked by returns to tradition.

Beth-El

Durham–Chapel Hill offered a paradigm of the dynamics that occurred across the Sunbelt as a new, large migration took control from established families who had built and sustained congregations. Tensions between liberals and traditionalists exacerbated as membership balances shifted. Older

families held proprietary feelings toward Beth-El as a keepsake of memories. A material contribution to the synagogue was the traditional means
to achieve status. Its plaques bore the names of these members' fathers and
mothers. As the academic families asserted leadership, it seemed to the
older families as if they were being evicted from their home. When in the
1970s president Norman Lefstein tried to organize a social dance, the
event turned into a disaster. No one wanted to come, and it was cancelled.
Conflicts arose over distributing honors for the High Holidays with families having held sinecures for generations. Board elections were hotly disputed, and resignations were threatened. Older residents sat together at
synagogue affairs, surprised to find themselves among strangers. Although
the congregation listed one hundred members, only about sixty paid full
dues.

The need to attract faculty families created pressures to modernize. In
1973 the Conservative movement allowed women to count equally with
men in the prayer quorum. Carol Meyers, who taught biblical studies at
Duke, petitioned the Beth-El board to expand women's participation. The
membership, however, was not wholly prepared to accept such a step. A
committee under Duke psychologist Irving Alexander reached a compromise, with the rabbi's approval, that allowed women to participate in a
monthly Sabbath service. For holidays observed on two days, the second
service would be egalitarian.

In the mid-1970s Beth-El was being pulled in contrary directions. The
Conservative-Orthodox split created tensions that kept the president's
phone ringing late at night. Moreover, Beth-El had kept its rabbi for an
unprecedented twenty years. The disputes over women's participation
were "pretty understandable," Gibby Katz reflected. "I had been reared in
such a strongly Orthodox environment." Nevertheless, Katz "got to think
about my own mother . . . a great lady" who had been a pillar of the Orthodox shul. "I got to having afterthoughts about women's participation
though she herself never would have. . . . I relented in my harsh stand."

Beth-El's rabbi, Herbert Berger, was admired as a "decent, kind" man,
but he was an "old-style Conservative rabbi of Orthodox background."
Judea Reform had recently hired Eric Yoffie, a dynamic young rabbi, and
Beth-El felt less competitive. Berger had supporters and opponents among
all factions, but in 1976 he left for Altoona, Pennsylvania.[64]

Choosing a new rabbi exacerbated tensions. An academic faction put
forward a candidate who was unacceptable to the others. "We were pretty
close to taking the key and locking the door and closing this place for

good," Gibby Katz recalled, "but we survived." Kalman Bland and Eric Meyers of Duke's Judaic Studies program agreed to serve as interim leaders. Both Bland, a rabbi, and Meyers, a cantor, were religious liberals. One Saturday Rabbi Bland turned the bimah to face the congregation rather than the ark as was customary in Orthodox synagogues. An Orthodox member interrupted the service, loudly demanding that the rabbi step down. The disputes were carried into board meetings, which turned "rancorous." [65]

In 1978 the search committee brought to Durham Rabbi Steven Sager, who had recently been ordained at the Reconstructionist Rabbinical College. A graduate of the University of Maryland, Sager was typical of the new generation of secularly educated rabbis. Sager and his wife, Sibby, still in their twenties, brought youth and vigor. Reconstructionism, based on the writings of Mordecai Kaplan, viewed Judaism as an evolving culture, asserting that Jewish law existed to maintain Jewish peoplehood. "You might not be a so-called religious person and still feel the need to join, a longing to identify with the community," Sager commented. "Judaism is a civilization, not just a faith." The search committee had an "explicit understanding" with Sager that women would participate fully, a stipulation that fit his own principles.

Sager recognized the divisions: "The socially cohesive community that built the building started to recede. An academic community that didn't feel it had any roots here became prominent." Several established families resigned, but others demonstrated their loyalty with new benefactions. Yet it was Gibby Katz, the lay cantor, whom the new rabbi found to be the "most profound influence because he represented a kind of continuity and stability." Katz, a warm, avuncular bachelor, "developed a great love for the kids," serving as a surrogate grandparent to newly arriving families.

As a Reconstructionist, Sager endorsed Jewish pluralism, holding that Judaism was open to a variety of expressions. To bridge the gap between the old and new membership, Sager suggested forming an Orthodox *kehillah* (community). With Orthodox members content to conduct services downstairs, Sager was free to innovate upstairs. He streamlined the "classical liturgical style" and replaced the sermon with open discussions. Rearranging the synagogue's sacred space, he brought the pulpit and reading desk from the platform to the floor. This arrangement replicated an Orthodox synagogue, but it was also a democratic gesture that brought rabbi and Torah closer to worshipers. To increase Jewish literacy, the rabbi led study groups on Midrash and Talmud. The forming of havurot also reflected another need. With the suburban sprawl, Beth-El's membership spread over four counties. Havurot were a means "to keep the synagogue together," redefining the synagogue as a "network of resources" rather than just as a sanctuary. By 1992 five groups had formed.[66]

A reinvented Judaism placed new emphasis on inclusion and participation. Efforts to revitalize education in the 1980s sought to empower children and families to take responsibility for Jewish observance rather than just fulfill rote requirements or defer to rabbinic authority. For the Bar and Bat Mitzvah the candidate and rabbi held a dialogue, a Talmudic exam, in place of the speech. A peer tutoring program had graduated students instruct the rising class. A more holistic approach sought to involve families in their children's education. *Mitzvah* (good deed) packets and how-to tapes and booklets were intended to strengthen Jewish home life and holiday observance.

In contrast to the dominance of elderly men in previous generations, women continued to assume more significant roles. The congregation fully embraced Conservative Judaism's option to accept women on equal standing with men in ritual and prayer quorums. In 1984 Gladys Siegel was elected the congregation's first female president. Ten years earlier, she had been narrowly defeated. In 1987 seven of the twelve board members were women, as were two of the five officers. The changing women's roles challenged the mission of Beth-El's Sisterhood, which historically had created community with its busy social calendar.

As Beth-El's membership rose from 150 members in 1978 to 325 in the 1990s, the congregation struggled to preserve its communalism. The conflict between the native and Sunbelt congregants ameliorated as the aging members were honored and memorialized. As president, Siegel made an effort "to reach out" to senior members who felt "disenfranchised." When Beth-El purchased the neighboring Mormon church for use as a school and a social hall in 1986, it was named for long-time benefactor Israel Freedman. The rancors of the past receded. "Differences . . . have drawn us together," the synagogue handbook asserted. "I think we have one of the most remarkable congregations today," Leon Dworsky reflected. "There is no 'us' and 'them.'" Some members, including the rabbi, moved freely downstairs and upstairs.[67]

Diversity was a "creative tension," as President Lewis Siegel put it, but it also raised questions of identity. In the mid-1990s congregants debated whether to remain formally affiliated with a Conservative movement that itself was divided between liberal and traditional factions. Whatever the

"Standards for Synagogue Practice" of the United Synagogue, only a minority of members kept kosher, observed Sabbath, or attended services regularly. With its Reconstructionist rabbi, Conservative affiliation, and Orthodox kehillah, Beth-El was highly representative of the emerging model of the American synagogue as a "mosaic of distinct and differing congregations," one that could accommodate differing religious identities.[68]

Judea Reform

Judea Reform in its early years had reflected the legacy of classical Reform Judaism. Over time, two trends grew pronounced. The first was toward a revitalized traditionalism, with Hebrew gaining ascendancy. The second was toward a more democratic liturgy with greater congregational participation, particularly from women. In the 1970s the Reform movement nationally, in response to membership surveys, was seeking to reinvigorate communal bonds and ritual practices.[69] Reform Judaism, too, was renegotiating the terms of its Jewish-American blending.

Having weathered the challenges of its founding, Judea Reform confronted the problems of a mature institution. The attitude of many academic families, Rabbi Efraim Rosenzweig noted, was, "Why should I build a sanctuary when I'll be moving on in a few years." From the start, Rabbi Rosenzweig recalled, the congregants "were looking for a place for their children to get an education. I think that moved them more than anything else." Plans were drawn to build in two stages. The first priority was a temple school. The congregation purchased land on Cornwallis Road in Durham near a highway exit convenient to Chapel Hill. The temple was to include a library, kitchen, rabbi's study, assembly hall, and classrooms. The hall, with an ark added, was a flexible space that doubled as a sanctuary. Rather than evoke classical Jewish forms and symbols, the architecture addressed the local environment. The structure was "beautifully designed to conform to the lines of the hill" and was faced with fieldstone to blend into the landscape. The multi-tiered parking lot demonstrated that its members would be commuting suburbanites. When Judea Reform dedicated its building in 1971, the president of the Durham Ministers Association and the mayors of Durham and Chapel Hill gave their blessings. Church building remained in the South both a civic and religious duty.[70]

In the early 1970s Judea Reform's membership growth was rapid. With worshipers sitting in hallways the temple could no longer accommodate

Judea Reform expanded three times since its opening in 1961, and it grew into the town's largest congregation. Educational needs dictated expansion as young families, drawn by opportunities in the Sunbelt, flocked to Reform Judaism. (Courtesy of the Judea Reform Congregation)

crowds. The congregants, however, were not wholly committed to expansion. Founding members feared that Judea Reform was losing its intimacy, its family feeling. Others were concerned about the expense. These conflicts were felt in many Sunbelt communities where newcomers overwhelmed small, established congregations.[71] At its annual meeting in 1977, the congregation authorized a building committee to proceed with expansion. The temple would be enlarged by twenty-five hundred square feet with a multipurpose sanctuary that could be expanded to seat 325.

When the temple was dedicated, Rabbi Rosenzweig was saluted at his retirement as an exemplary teacher who opened "the eyes of Jew and non-Jew alike to the richness and relevance of Jewish culture to modern life." He was honored especially for his commitment to minorities.[72] As rabbi emeritus, Rosenzweig remained an active and eminent presence.

Rosenzweig's successor, Rabbi Eric Yoffie, turned the congregation toward tradition. Yoffie was a graduate of Brandeis and of Hebrew Union College's New York campus, and Durham was his first pulpit although he had served as an assistant rabbi on Long Island. Traditionalism "was my own orientation," Rabbi Yoffie stated, "and I made no bones about that." Unlike Rosenzweig, Yoffie wore a skull cap and prayer shawl during services. He and his family kept kosher, an uncommon practice in the Reform rabbinate. Although Rosenzweig performed intermarriages under "certain circumstances," Yoffie categorically did not, to the consternation of many congregants. Conscious of the lack of Jewish literacy among his members, Yoffie instituted a Jewish conversion course for Jews. Previously, the education program focused on tenth-grade confirmation with Bar or Bat Mitzvah "also available" on request. Judea Reform confirmed seven graduates in 1965 but did not hold its first Bar Mitzvah until four years later. Yoffie redesigned the educational curriculum with a three-year program to emphasize Bar and Bat Mitzvah. Teenagers were enrolled in the Reform movement's Middle Atlantic Federation of Temple Youth. They traveled to conventions in Greensboro and Charlotte to discuss such topics as "Jews in Modern Society" and "Dissent and Civil Disobedience."

In Yoffie's four years membership rose from about 100 to 170. As was often the case, a young, promising rabbi soon left Durham to advance his career. In 1980 he moved to St. Louis to pursue organizational work on behalf of Reform Judaism. Always committed to Israel—more so than his congregants—Yoffie rose to the directorship of the Association of Reform Zionists of America. In 1995 he was elected president of the Union of American Hebrew Congregations.

Rabbi Yoffie's successor was Rabbi John Friedman, a Kansas City native and graduate of the Hebrew Union College–Cincinnati. Friedman had attended Hebrew Union College's one-year program in Israel, an experience that had strengthened his Zionist and traditionalist leanings. Friedman was also an energetic civic activist committed to interfaith relations. He served as president of the Durham Congregations in Action, an interfaith welfare group, and chairman of the Central Conference of American Rabbis Interreligious Affairs Committee. Outspoken on Israeli issues, he hosted Arab-Jewish dialogues and invited Israelis from Peace Now and Interns for Peace.

In liturgy and education Friedman was a liturgical innovator committed to making services more democratic and participatory. He instituted cantorial training to create lay prayer leaders. Like Rabbi Yoffie, he refused to perform intermarriages but worked strenuously to bring interfaith families into the fold. He also recognized the need for the synagogue to serve family needs. He instituted a toddler's program and Saturday morning children's worship. The religious school extended from kindergarten through high school with a weekly after-school Hebrew school. Despite the expanded program Friedman readily acknowledged the inadequacy of biweekly sessions to impart learning and inspire a Jewish commitment. Parents pushed children to attend, and discipline remained a perennial problem.

After some stagnation in the late 1970s, the congregation continued to grow in numbers and prosperity in the mid-1980s. With a preponderance of academic families, membership turnover remained high. Older members with business backgrounds regarded the academic leaders as spend-thrifts, and disputes and threatened resignations marked board meetings. As two-career families became the norm, volunteerism also became more problematic. Women, who historically had been responsible for education and philanthropy, no longer had the time to commit to charitable work. The Judea Reform Women's Group faded by 1983. Women were now so well integrated, serving regularly as congregational presidents, that an auxiliary seemed unnecessary. With the tempering of gender roles, a similar fate fell to the Men's Club. Judea Reform struggled to preserve continuity and communal feeling as membership rose to five hundred households. Rabbi Friedman experimented with the havurah, and by 1992 a dozen groups enlisted more than one hundred families. The groups consisted of retirees, young families, and intermarried families.

Judea Reform remodeled its spartan, cinder-block building into a temple of American Judaism. The interior repeated a theme of spiritual light. Starkly white walls gave the sanctuary a brighter feeling. After much debate a proverb was inscribed on the wall in Hebrew and English: "The Mitzvah of the Lord is Clear, Giving Light to the Eyes." A curtain for the ark repeated a pattern of Magen Davids rising from darkness. To emphasize the democratic character of Jewish worship, the remodelers placed two pulpits at the sides, which gave equal status to the rabbi and lay cantor.

Judea Reform quickly overtaxed its facilities. The congregation moved its High Holiday services from the Community Church to the larger Chapel Hill High School auditorium. The religious school had only five classrooms for 160 students, necessitating split sessions. Plans were drawn for a new building that would contain offices, kitchen, classrooms, and library. Its fifty-seven hundred square feet would double the temple's size.

In 1986 Judea Reform embarked on an ambitious campaign to raise

In 1961 Rabbi Efraim Rosenzweig (center) became Judea Reform's
first rabbi. His successors, Rabbis Eric Yoffie (right) and John Friedman (left), moved the congregation toward traditionalism. (Courtesy of Rabbi John Friedman)

$400,000. On April 10, 1988, in ceremonies led by Rabbi Friedman, Judea
Reform broke ground for the Mel and Zora Rashkis Building. The celebration affirmed Reform Judaism's renewed commitment to both Jewish
peoplehood and universal values, Zionism and Americanism. The Durham
sanctuary was likened to King David's Temple, which set the "pattern" for
future generations. The speakers invoked the spirits of Abraham and Sarah;
Jacob, who dreamed of a ladder to heaven; and Moses, the teacher, who
stood on holy ground. It called on the "spirit of the exiles . . . to build
again the Zion of old, the Zion of today, the Jerusalem on earth." The

congregation also recalled the "spirit of the fountain of learning that was European Jewry, destroyed and extinguished by Amalek" in the Holocaust. Then in a southern, biracial, ecumenical vein the congregation sang "Gonna Build a Mountain," an African American spiritual. The lay cantor concluded in Hebrew with the traditional *Shehechiyanu* (blessing of thanks). The ceremonies celebrated Reform Judaism's blended, multicultural values.[73]

With its willingness to be inclusive and democratic, Reform Judaism confronted questions of Jewish boundaries. The temple bulletin declared, "We especially welcome interfaith couples who want to be part of the Jewish community and are raising their children as Jews."[74] Although non-Jews were accepted as members and a few became active, questions were raised as to whether they could serve on the Ritual Committee, become officers, or be awarded liturgical honors. The congregation adhered to Reform Judaism's decision to accept paternal as well as maternal descent as the criterion of Jewish origin. The Outreach Committee—led by a Jew by choice—drew interfaith families into congregational life. Rabbi Friedman did "everything I can" to encourage non-Jewish spouses to convert. A 1991 Sabbath service featured conversion testimonies.

The rabbis observed a high degree of Jewish illiteracy among their well-educated members. To encourage "democratic singing," Isabel Samfield, a voice teacher who served as a cantor, attempted to teach liturgical singing but confronted problems with members from "so many different types of congregations." A fair number had little Jewish education or were converts or intermarried spouses. Rabbis passed out transliterated sheets so that worshipers could follow the Hebrew. For adults who had not received a Bar or Bat Mitzvah, Judea Reform held an Anshe Mitzvah program with a curriculum in theology, ritual, and Hebrew. In eight years more than 125 congregants enrolled. The Torah Corps led discussions of the Sabbath reading. For gender equality, "sexist" language was removed from the prayers, which now were spoken on behalf of "humankind." Matriarchs as well as patriarchs were invoked. In the mid-1980s Rabbi Friedman switched from the Union prayer book to the innovative *Gates of Prayer,* which allowed him to create a service from five alternate texts. These efforts succeeded, and Friday night services typically drew two hundred attendees.[75]

The migration of retirees created another need, a cemetery. As Rabbi Rosenzweig wryly observed, the Sunbelt reversed the historical pattern of Jewish community development where the cemetery preceded the congregation. The Durham Hebrew Cemetery was problematic for Reform

Jews because Beth-El's Chevra Kadisha held to Orthodox standards. Interfaith couples or those wishing cremation had difficulties. In 1982 the Cemetery Committee under Herb Posner purchased 3.4 wooded acres south of Chapel Hill. The forest setting was preserved with headstones set flush to the ground. Posner found arrowheads on the site and was comforted that Jews as a venerable people "have joined forces with the most ancient inhabitants." For a mobile people, a cemetery symbolically and materially rooted Jews to a place.[76]

Judea Reform's evolution reflected postwar Reform Judaism's traditionalist revival. This renewed emphasis owed in part to the influx of second- and third-generation descendants of east European immigrants of Conservative and Orthodox background. Rabbi Emeritus Rosenzweig saw it as a reaction to the Holocaust: "Now it is time to restore what has disappeared." The changes also reflected the new climate of ethnic consciousness of the 1980s. More Hebrew was introduced into the liturgy. Bar and Bat Mitzvah assumed more importance than confirmation. Without neglecting Reform Judaism's historical emphasis on a rational, ethical Judaism, the rabbis sought to strengthen Reform's emotional appeal. In a 1990 temple bulletin, Rabbi John Friedman wrote, "Our Reform congregation has introduced many rituals once anathema to Reform Judaism. It is partly an effort to reclaim the spiritual side of Jewish life which is our legitimate birthright." Members debated whether to change their name from Judea Reform Congregation to Judea Reform Synagogue. President Peter Adland noted that Jews were evolving "in the opposite direction" from their "nineteenth-century American Reform Jewish ancestors who wanted a less distinct identity within American society." A 1992 Shabbaton focused on "Judaism and the Irrational" and featured Duke Judaic Studies professor Kalman Bland, an authority on mysticism.[77]

Reflecting Reform Judaism's commitment to social justice, Judea Reform's members also participated more fully in the civic life of the non-Jewish community than did Conservative Jews. Reform rabbis were activists dedicated to interfaith efforts. Congregants worked in soup kitchens and homeless shelters and on Christmas delivered turkey dinners to the homebound. The sanctuary hosted ecumenical programs for Baptist bell choirs and black Islamic scribes.

In thirty years Judea Reform had grown from a small, informal gathering of alienated Jews meeting in a church basement to the area's largest congregation with a synagogue three times expanded. The growth reflected more than increasing population. With the rising numbers of interfaith couples, an assimilating youth, and a rootless membership, the congregation's outreach programs and inclusionary policies embraced new kinds of Jews and even non-Jews.

Reconciliation

The historical impulse toward Jewish unity worked to heal divisions between Beth-El and Judea Reform. "A primary thrust of my activity was to overcome the old animosities," Rabbi Yoffie observed. "We made some substantial progress." This relative harmony attested to the persistence of the community's small-town, southern legacy. When Rabbi Friedman arrived at Judea Reform in 1980, he and his wife, Nan, published a letter of introduction in the *Beth-El Bulletin:* "After all, there are not so many Jews in our community that we can remain strangers for very long. . . . The unusually congenial spirit which exists between our two congregations is most refreshing. As many of you know, this is generally not the case in many large metropolitan areas."[78]

Differences between the congregations narrowed as Beth-El's membership, too, became mostly professional. Each congregation as a matter of policy opened its doors to members of the other. The congregations held joint observances of Israel Independence Day, Holocaust Memorial Day, and an annual Sabbath service. Sharing a concern for youth, Judea Reform and Beth-El Congregation in 1989 cooperated on a high-school program, Midrasha. Students were educated in the Bible and Rabbinics, Jewish Culture, and Jewish Philosophy. Jewish Culture emphasized the Holocaust and Israel. The curriculum reflected a communal consensus on the elements of Jewish identity. From 62 students in 1991, Midrasha grew to 150 in 1999.

Beth-El inclined toward the liberal side of Conservatism; Judea Reform had grown traditional. The reason to join one or the other often had less to do with theology than with location, nostalgia for a worship style, or preference for a rabbi. Reflecting national Jewish trends, the Reform temple, with 500 members, was growing more rapidly than the Conservative one, which had 325 households. The lifestyles and Jewish identities of most local Jews were more amenable to a less religiously rigorous, more Americanized Reform Judaism, which was also more open in its outreach to marginal Jews and more committed to social justice in the general community. The Conservative congregation differed in its more intensive educational program for children and its more traditional, Hebrew-language holiday and Sabbath services. Both congregations adhered to a Judaism that had largely acculturated to American democratic values.

Without strong ideological cores, the congregations were inclusionary and embraced considerable internal diversity. The lifestyles of most Reform and Conservative Jews did not markedly differ.

Both congregations in the 1990s showed incipient signs of a renewed Jewish spiritualism, a theological interest that complemented the postwar emphasis on Jewish peoplehood. Rabbis observed that their congregants spoke more comfortably and unabashedly of God. Judea Reform responded by opening a Beit HaMidrash where congregants could learn how "the presence of God may be found in study," and Beth-El sponsored such programs as a "Meditation Retreat" on the cabalistic techniques of prayer.[79]

By the mid-1990s both Beth-El and Judea Reform confronted problems of growth. Membership overtaxed facilities, and each embarked on expensive fund-raising campaigns to compensate. Judea Reform purchased twenty-two acres to create a campus, and Beth-El engaged in a $1 million renovation. Growth alienated some members as the congregations struggled to preserve communal feeling. By institutionalizing change, broadening the definition of Jewish identity, the congregations responded to a Jewish marketplace where Jews were autonomous in their religious choices. Women reading from the Torah or havurot for interfaith families may seem departures, even ruptures from the Jewish past, but, in fact, Jews were reinventing their traditions. The very lack of definition of a Jewish essence allowed the broadest possible membership, but it also raised questions of a Judaism that was emptying its content.

Orthodox Revival

Orthodoxy's surprising resurgence throughout the Jewish world was felt in Durham, too. Children reverted to practices that their parents had left behind them. Sam and Florence Margolis put *mezzuzot* (cases holding Torah writings) on the doorposts of their home and kept kosher so that their son Jay, a cantor, could visit them. Roslyn and Monroe Wall, founders of Judea Reform, saw their daughter marry an Orthodox Jew and establish a traditional home. Beth-El's Rabbi Sager noted that newly arriving families tended to be increasingly observant, suggesting traditional Jews no longer regarded the South as an uninviting place.

Duke physician Ed Halperin and his wife, Sharon, who came to Chapel Hill from Boston in 1983, found living in the area as Orthodox Jews to be "problematic." There was no yeshiva or working mikva. The few Orthodox Jews who did not live within walking distance of the synagogue were isolated. Still, some Jews maintained traditional Judaism. A kosher meat co-op trucked provisions quarterly from Maryland. Nearly fifty families, about 3 percent of the community, subscribed. Its organizer, Mardi Zeiger, also served as a kosher caterer. The Duke Center for Jewish Life was designed to include a kosher restaurant and a community mikva.

When Beth-El granted women equality, Orthodox members found themselves unable to attend services. In 1979 an Orthodox kehillah organized, with Leon Dworsky serving as its mainstay. The kehillah attracted twenty-five to thirty members to its basement chapel, which preserved gender segregation (though side to side rather than front to rear). On the chapel walls were ark ornaments and a marble founders' plaque from the 1921 synagogue. The kehillah affiliated with the Union of Orthodox Jewish Congregations.

Several old Durhamites joined the kehillah, but newly arrived students and professors sustained it. Some pointedly lived within walking distance of the synagogue. They were joined by Israelis who, though not Orthodox, felt more comfortable with the traditional Hebrew service. A half-dozen women regularly attended. The kehillah functioned much like the immigrants' chevra as a place where traditional Jews could gather "to schmooze" as well as to pray. Observant members who tried to bring more prayer ritual or daily services did not succeed. For funerals Dworsky oversaw the Chevra Kadisha, Durham's oldest Jewish organization, which remained steadfastly Orthodox.

In 1995 Rabbi Carey Friedman, supported by Yad Avraham and the Judy and Michael Steinhardt Foundation, was sent as an emissary to Durham to strengthen the community's Orthodoxy. A charismatic teacher, he established the Duke Jewish Learning Experience, which featured Talmudic study and daily prayer services. His more rigorous Orthodoxy created tensions with the southern-style traditionalism of the kehillah, and in 1996 Rabbi Friedman formed a separate congregation, Ohr Torah. Durham was feeling the larger ideological conflicts between an accommodationist Modern Orthodoxy and an exclusivist Orthodoxy. Ohr Torah did not survive Rabbi Friedman's departure, but the Jewish Learning Experience continued its educational mission. In 1998 Rabbi Pinny Lew, a Lubavitcher Hasid, established a Chabad House in Chapel Hill near the UNC campus. The house hosted traditional Shabbat and weekday services.

Jewish Pluralism

Local Jewish factionalism was consistent with national trends that saw the dominance of movement-affiliated congregations challenged by rising numbers of independent groups. Several dozen havurot met as small fellowship groups to pray, study holy texts, or discuss politics. In Fearrington, a planned community built on a dairy farm ten miles south of Chapel Hill, a havurah of forty-five members formed in 1991. Alvin Schultzberg, its leader, had been an activist with the National Havurah Committee in New York. The Fearrington havurah included both affiliated Jews and "Jewish agnostics." Although they held seders and Hanukkah parties, they were a "strictly cultural, educational group," Schultzberg explained, and did not conduct worship services. Their concern, as was true of many Jews who lived in areas of low Jewish density, was "identity and heritage."

In 1996 a dozen families gathered to form the Chapel Hill Kehillah, planting the seeds of the town's first community synagogue. Within three years its membership grew to 110 households. The religious school, which met at UNC Hillel, enrolled forty children. High Holiday services at the Community Church drew three hundred. The kehillah rented a facility, hired an administrator, and obtained cemetery space. In 1999 it engaged rabbinic student Leah Richman from the Reconstructionist Rabbinical College, the first woman to serve a local congregation. The kehillah's services were egalitarian, and its members wrestled with questions of identity. The kehillah complemented its traditional liturgy with a monthly "creative" service. The impetus for a Chapel Hill congregation was a response to growth and geography, but it also offered yet another choice between Reform and Conservatism.

Secular Jews—some were quick to call themselves atheists—who were uncomfortable with the religiosity of the synagogue but wanted their children raised with Jewish cultural values joined the Triangle Cooperative Schule. Milt Kotelchuck, who taught public health at UNC, had operated such a school at the Workmen's Circle in Boston and started a program in his Chapel Hill home. By 1992 it included thirty-four children in four age groups, meeting monthly on Sunday mornings. The Triangle Cooperative Schule, imbued with a spirit of Yiddishkeit, focused on social justice issues. At assemblies parents and children sat together singing Yiddish songs. For a Bar or Bat Mitzvah, the student had to spend a year working in a community-based service program and then make a report to the "congregation."

Sporadic efforts to establish a Jewish day school locally had failed. In the 1990s national Jewish philanthropy was committed to a continuity agenda that refocused resources on Jewish education. Survey data demonstrated the insufficiency of supplementary Jewish education to instill Jewish identity and commitment. In 1992 some twenty Jewish parents gathered to organize the Jewish Community Day School to "teach children about their heritage and instill pride in their Jewish identity." Parents launched a campaign to erect a building, with a goal that grew to $2.1 million. As part of a national effort, the Judy and Michael Steinhardt Foundation of New York granted seed money. In 1995 the school opened temporarily at Judea Reform with thirteen students. Adding a grade each year, the school grew to eighty children in a preschool to fifth-grade program. In 1998 the school dedicated the fourteen thousand square foot building, named for the Sandra E. Lerner donor family, on a hilltop adjoining Judea Reform. The establishing of a day school linked Durham–Chapel Hill to the Jewish Community Day School Network, which enrolled some twelve thousand students in sixty programs.[80]

The school's mission statement asserted that "children will be taught to respect Jewish diversity at home and in the community." Reform, Conservative, and Orthodox Jews wrestled with curricular issues to satisfy diverse beliefs, and a committee struggled to compose its own prayer book. Although the intent was to integrate Jewish and secular studies, the school developed a dual curriculum. Like many Jewish schools nationally, it was challenged to find professional Jewish educators. In contrast to denominational schools, the Community Day School was nondoctrinaire and sought to impart the values of both tradition and personal autonomy. "We are not telling our children what to believe," director Simone Solitan observed. "We are teaching Jewish literacy and showing them the variety of possibility within Judaism. Hopefully, they will make their own decisions." The goal was to "encourage celebration of diversity." American Jewish identity, children were taught, is freely chosen.[81]

With its greater numbers and diverse institutions and with the growth of the region into a metropolitan area, Durham–Chapel Hill Jewry no longer could be described as small town, but it still maintained a spirit of accommodation and heightened Jewish awareness that were typical of southern and small-town communities. The community was southern in its civility, maintaining internal harmony as it grew religiously diverse. Reform, Conservative, and Orthodox Jews enjoyed friendly relations that reflected good will and mutual respect. When parents gathered to organize a Jewish day school in 1992, Leon Dworsky, whose father had argued that only Orthodoxy could preserve communal unity, insisted that it be nonsectarian to embrace all Jews. This tolerance was significant considering past conflicts and the religious divisiveness found in Israel and American urban communities. Although disputes arose on such issues as building a mikva, local Jewry was simply too small, and the environment too Christian, for Jews to exacerbate their differences. This inner tolerance was typical of communities in areas of low Jewish population density.

The transition from a small-town to a Sunbelt Jewry was marked by both change and continuity. Jews lived comfortably with the contraries and contradictions of their multicultural identities. Their Americanism had created a democratic Judaism that was tolerant of diversity. They redefined the Jewish essence to include gender equality and patrilineal Jews. In response to consumer demand, their congregations sought outreach to interfaith families. They subscribed to an American Jewish continuity agenda that focused on the education of youth and the strengthening of Jewish identity through Israel. Yet, beyond the committed core, most Jews were minimally involved. Extending boundaries and accommodating diversity raised concerns that Judaism was emptying its content to be all things to all people. What in their collective memory bound Jews as a community? Holocaust memory alone could not sustain a living culture, and Israel's religious value as the agency of Jewish redemption succumbed to politics.

As tradition eroded, Jews reinvented a past for themselves, insisting on their continuity with former generations. Sunbelt Jews affirmed local roots and wrote themselves into the southern narrative. They did so as native southern Jewry was dying and losing its regional distinction. With diverse backgrounds, Sunbelt Jews turned to history to create a communal memory. The Rosenzweig Museum and Jewish Heritage Foundation of North Carolina, which had a Judaica gallery at Judea Reform, launched a custodianship project to collect artifacts that documented the state's Jewish history. In 1986, when the community held celebrations to commemorate its centennial, members of the professional community organized the observances. Its leader, Albert Heyman, a Duke neurologist who had arrived in the 1950s, acted to honor the community founders, emphasizing the continuity between the Sunbelt newcomers and older southern families. Local Jews held a Purim Ball to commemorate an event first held in 1887. The Southern Jewish Historical Society had its 1987 convention in Durham, and historian Leah Hagedorn presented a lecture series on regional issues titled "South of Hester Street: Reflections of Three Centuries of Southern Jewry." Finally, a book was undertaken to create a single, continuous narrative of local Jewish communal life. Sunbelt Jews, no matter how recently they had arrived, sought to validate their own presence in the area, to plant the South in their collective memory.

12 Conclusion: Exiles at Home

Durham–Chapel Hill's Jews were east and central Europeans who labored to reestablish a Jewish homeland in Palestine while they built houses in the North Carolina Piedmont. They acculturated to a South whose own regional identity was problematically American. They were mobile in a society that honored place. They were cosmopolitans among southerners, provincials among Jews. The identity of the southern Jew was fluid, relative, and multiple.

"Is there an American Jewish culture?" Robert Alter asks. "The question is nearly imponderable because each of its component terms is so clearly problematic." When *southern* is added, the question is further confounded. In significant respects "Jewish," "southern," and "American" blended, and in other ways they "braided," remaining structurally distinct. Sociologist John Shelton Reed, analyzing survey data, writes of the compatibility of "Jewish Southerners," and folklorist Carolyn Walker-Lipson, conducting interviews, notes the incongruity of "Southern Jews."[1]

Migrations, the constant arrival and departure of peoples, made definitions even less stable. Given their mobility, many Jews never remained long enough in the South to assimilate. The narrative of southern Jews is a story of changes and continuities, progress and disruption, borders and broken boundaries. "American Jewish culture has no essence, and has never been autonomous," Stephen Whitfield writes, "but it does have a history."[2]

The Jews who sojourned in North Carolina during the colonial, early republic, and antebellum years were few and transitory. Jews as a class were identified with commerce, but North Carolina was too undeveloped economically to draw sufficient numbers to form a community. The rare family that did persist tended to assimilate into Christian society. When Jews protested the state's religious test for public office, they echoed an internationalist rhetoric of Jewish emancipation. They were not a distinctly regional people.

In the mid-nineteenth century the state's commercial economy began developing just as German Jews were immigrating to America. As new market towns sprouted along rail lines, peddlers and storekeepers came from Baltimore, Richmond, and New York. Southerners welcomed their capital and services, and as individuals German Jews found social as well as economic place. When southern nationalism asserted itself with the advent of Civil War, these young German immigrants expressed their regional loyalty by defending the Confederacy.

The German Jews who arrived in Durham starting in the mid-1870s maintained an economic niche as dry-goods merchants. Durham was a colonial outpost of Richmond and Baltimore, which served not merely as credit and distribution centers but also as surrogate Jewish homelands where Jews found spouses, rabbis, and congregations.

For a small-town Jewish community to survive, it needed to maintain a viable economy and draw east European immigrants. Tobacco was the lure that first pulled significant numbers of immigrant Jews to Durham. As young proletarians, the Jewish cigarette rollers who arrived in the early 1880s were typical of the mass of Jews newly settling in the United States. The South was not receptive either to immigrants or organized labor, however.

The east European peddlers and storekeepers who arrived between 1880 and 1910 founded an enduring Jewish community. These immigrants, who came largely from the Ukraine and Latvia-Lithuania, arrived through family chains. Abandoning Baltimore or New York, where they had first settled, they were young families in search of economic security and independence. The self-employed storekeepers were the representative Jews in small towns nationally and in the South particularly. Typical of Jews outside metropolitan areas, they established an economic niche as middlemen between town and country, black and white, and capitalist and laborer. Their concentration in mercantile trades differentiated them from other southerners, especially in a working-class town such as Durham.

Jews acted to reconstruct their immigrant Yiddishkeit. Despite the

Americanized name of Durham Hebrew Congregation, their synagogue was an Old World chevra where they could socialize in Yiddish and pray in Hebrew. Although they were highly mobile, Jews remained sufficiently numerous to sustain communal life. Jews organized a congregation, social clubs, and Zionist societies.

Durham–Chapel Hill Jewry was tightened by its homogeneous east European ethnicity. Absent from Durham were the social and religious tensions between Germans and east Europeans that rended urban communities. A common heritage of Yiddishkeit, secured by family ties, united the community. Group solidarity strengthened feelings of warmth and intimacy, but such familiarity also impassioned conflicts. The community began fragmenting along personal, religious, class, clan, and generational lines, and dissident congregations formed in 1901 and 1913. The community struggled to preserve its unity even as it institutionalized itself with a new synagogue and communal societies.

Culture and religion separated east European Jews from native southerners, and relations were not intimate. Traders without an agrarian past, southern Jews had very different personal histories from their neighbors. In their collective memories they mourned Jerusalem and Kishniev, not Appomattox. Jesus did not save them. Bacon and barbecue, staples of the southern diet, were forbidden foods. Jews were respected as flesh and blood of the savior, but they were also damned as Christ killers. Situated in the racial divide between blacks and whites, Jews formed relationships of both friendship and self-interest with African Americans, but Jews also complied with the racial codes.

Jews who settled outside metropolitan areas generally found acceptance. In Durham Jewish immigrant upward mobility harmonized with the New South's ethic of progress and uplift. To succeed in business Jews needed to cultivate goodwill and know their place. Southerners customarily extended hospitality to the stranger even as they suspected aliens. Jews were too few and too accommodating to present any threat to the existing social or political order, in contrast to the upheavals that large immigrant populations caused in such places as Boston or New York. Jewish institutions took culturally blended forms that minimized differences. A Hebrew baseball team preserved ethnicity. Like their Christian neighbors, Jews sent their children to Sunday school.

By World War I, with their high birth rates Durham Jews were increasingly native-born southerners who had been educated in the public schools and, for growing numbers, at the universities. Jews readily adopted southern folkways. As they acculturated they began breaching the structural separation that kept Jew and Gentile apart. Real estate and banking integrated Jews into the town economy. A Jew ran for public office in 1908. The children of east European immigrants became beauty queens, football heroes, and champion debaters. Yiddish inflections yielded to southern drawls.

After World War I, as Americanism campaigns encouraged assimilation into Anglo-Saxon society, Jews endorsed a cultural pluralism that sanctioned a dual identity as Jewish Americans. The Beth-El Synagogue-Center, dedicated in 1921, preserved ethnic bonds and religious tradition, but it also served as a Jewish church in a town where respectability meant religious affiliation. By being more Jewish, as Reed suggests, Jews were also more southern.[3] With prosperity, Jews had risen into the middle class. No longer sandwiched in a ghetto between black and white Durham, they moved uphill to Roxboro Street. Although not an exclusively Jewish neighborhood, Roxboro Street became a Jewish enclave with a kosher deli and bakery.

As they Americanized, Jews also began representing themselves as ethnic southerners. In the 1920s, in newspaper articles and the dedicatory booklet of their new synagogue-center, local Jews constructed narratives that traced community origins to the cigarette rollers although few families could claim such descent. Durham Jews described themselves as "civic boosters" who had lived there since the town's "inception."[4] They identified with the South and impressed this history in their collective memory. This folklore was passed along for generations.

In the 1930s the depression and renewed anti-Semitism both in the United States and abroad heightened Jewish consciousness and tightened communal bonds. Nazism and isolationism compelled Jews to choose among the competing loyalties of their dual identity. Discrimination on campus and in the corporate economy reminded Jews of their outsider status, especially as second-generation Jews were moving into the professions.

What remained constant among Durham–Chapel Hill Jews across generations was their effort to preserve Jewish identity by organizing themselves locally and maintaining networks to Jewry beyond the locality. "A concern for Jewries abroad virtually defines the American Jewish persona," notes historian Henry Feingold.[5] Although religious observance and synagogue membership had declined since the 1920s, Jews affiliated with social and Zionist societies that maintained their ethnicity outside their religion. Durham supported an astonishing array of organizations from Aleph Zadik Alpha to the Zionist Organization of America that linked North Carolinians to Jewish destiny. As southerners, they worked strenuously to enlist the town's civic leadership in support of European Jewry, but they were sufficiently anxious in their social place that they downplayed publicly the Jewish aspect of the crisis.

The war effort brought both Jews and southerners into the American mainstream. As their youth enlisted in the armed forces, Jews and Gentiles cooperated to support the troops at local military camps. Social barriers lowered. The Holocaust finally discredited racial stereotyping of the Jews. After the war brotherhood was upheld as a national credo, and Judaism took its American place as one of three faiths. Jews no longer lived residentially apart but integrated into new suburbs arising in the postwar building boom. Discriminatory barriers began lowering at the universities, and Jews enrolled on local campuses in unprecedented numbers. Israel gave American Jews a new, assertive identity, and Jews enlisted their southern neighbors in building the Jewish state, which they represented as a beacon of liberty and democracy.

Just as E. J. Evans's election as mayor of Durham in 1951 marked the Jews' acceptance as southerners, however, the civil rights movement aroused insecurities. Jews and African Americans in Durham had a history of cooperation and goodwill, and blacks repeatedly voted for Evans. Nonetheless, Jews also knew that a forthright stance might endanger their hard-earned business success. The conservatism of many established families differentiated them from the newly arriving professional Jews, who were often overtly liberal.

In the 1960s as Durham evolved from a southern mill and market town into a postindustrial academic and medical center, Jewish population grew from the hundreds to the thousands. Where once Jews had been a mercantile people, now they were becoming disproportionately professional. In this regard they were very much like the new populations flocking to the Research Triangle. The Sunbelt welcomed the engineer and the professor as harbingers of economic progress just as the New South had welcomed merchants.

With population growth the community grew ever more pluralistic. The ethnic cohesion that had previously bound local Jews as an extended family was broken. Increasingly, Jews became autonomous in their religious choices. Jews constantly renegotiated their Judaism and reinvented their institutions as they mediated between personal and traditional religion. As American Jews, they broke from the nominal Orthodoxy of their immigrant parents and adopted a moderate Conservatism that was more accepting of women and more appealing to children. The new Beth-El Synagogue-Center with its flexible plan was designed to accommodate the social as well as the religious needs of suburban families. The organizing of Judea Reform Congregation in 1961 attested to the community's growth in numbers and diversity. Rapidly growing into the area's largest congregation, Judea Reform encouraged a democratic, more inclusive Judaism. Orthodoxy also enjoyed a resurgence with several new worship groups. The intensified religious awareness that is a defining feature of southern Jews worked to preserve communal unity, a pattern dating to the community's earliest days. A federation and community day school united Jews across denominational boundaries. Local Jewish survival relied not on an unshakable allegiance to an immutable faith but on flexibility. New organizations, from burial societies to backpacking clubs, formed in response to changing populations and new understandings of Jewish identity. Neotraditional revivals countered secularizing trends as Jews resisted a complete assimilation.

The old-time Jewish community in Durham–Chapel Hill was dying out as it was in small towns across the Midwest and Deep South. The local Jewish community survived because the area transformed itself economically. Durham grew into a midsized city, and with Chapel Hill it formed part of a Sunbelt metropolitan area totaling approximately one million people. With population growth Durham–Chapel Hill no longer fit the definition of a small town. The overwhelming number of the nearly four thousand Jews of the late 1990s were Sunbelt migrants whose mobility might soon take them elsewhere.

Jewish growth was but one sign that the South, like the rest of America, was evolving into a multicultural society. Jews were no longer the most conspicuous of the region's alien groups, and Arab, Asian, and Hispanic immigrants repeated the Jewish pattern of economic niche and family economy. Like these postcolonial peoples, Jews remained connected to distant homelands. Although outside Jewish metropolitan areas, Durham was not geographically isolated, and Jewish transients constantly flowed in and out of town. Kinship ties kept them connected to Florida and northern states—and to Israel. Like southern blacks, who had reversed their great migration from the urban north, Durham–Chapel Hill Jews traveled frequently to Baltimore, Philadelphia, and New York, places that they also called home.

Multiculturalism gave Jews and southerners the sanction to assert their distinct identities. Local, ethnic, and regional studies and societies are proliferating even as the differences erode. The Southern Jewish Historical Society, the Museum of the Southern Jewish Experience, and the Jewish Heritage Foundation of North Carolina arose to preserve a vanishing heritage. In Virginia, Arkansas, Kentucky, Mississippi, and South Carolina, books and exhibits focused on each state's Jewish histories. America was increasingly described as a federation of regions and peoples rather than as a melting pot with a uniform national culture.

As historian Mark Bauman emphasizes, the narrative of southern Jewry is essentially an American story.[6] Durham–Chapel Hill Jewry follows the conventional paradigm of American Jewish acculturation. The evolution from Orthodoxy to Conservatism to religious pluralism, although retarded locally, is consistent with national trends. Immigrant shuls became American synagogue-centers. Their congregation forming and synagogue building in the 1880s, 1920s, 1950s, and 1990s follow the American pattern, as did their religious disaffection in the 1930s. Israel and the Holocaust were twin pillars of the postwar Jewish identity. Jews responded to the zeitgeist in the spiritual seeking of the 1960s and in the ethnic revival of the 1980s.

The educational and occupational mobility of local Jews, the rise from retail trades into the professions, is highly representative of the changing national Jewish profile. The timing of their move from a ghetto to an ethnic middle-class neighborhood to the suburban dispersion follows the classic tertiary pattern of Jewish settlement. The growth of Durham and Chapel Hill reflects the national redistribution of Jewish population southward. Across the community changes, local Jews affirmed their membership in the global Jewish community. Durham–Chapel Hill was one link in the national Jewish Federation structure. As rates of assimilation and intermarriage began approaching national levels, the community subscribed to a national agenda dedicated to Jewish continuity by founding a day school and rebuilding campus programs.

Even though Durham–Chapel Hill Jews were representative Americans, they were also conscious of themselves as living in the South, however attenuated its regional culture. A small, aging core group persisted as acculturated, small-town southern Jews, and a few assimilated to become wholly southern, lost to Jewry. Mobile second- and third-generation native Jews who abandoned Durham and Chapel Hill continued to identify themselves as ethnic southerners. Alumni and family ties returned them to the area. This attachment was more than sentimental because real-estate holdings kept them materially tied to their hometowns. Southern identity was a matter of ethnicity rather than of geography. Indeed, a survey revealed that 20 percent of North Carolinians did not describe themselves as southerners, whereas 6 percent of Michigan residents did so.[7] With their mobility, Jews claimed many homelands, wherever their actual place of residence. For self-identifying southern Jews, Durham–Chapel Hill was home.

What was most distinct about Durham–Chapel Hill Jewry as southern was its local color, those places of attitude and custom that owed specifically to the southerner's sense of place. Native Jews spoke in Piedmont accents. Their manners displayed the grace and courtesy of a southern upbringing. However mobile, southern Jews felt a loyalty to place. Durham, its air redolent of tobacco and auctioneers' chants, its streets crowded with farmers and mill workers, was vivid. This was the South of Mose Levy bootlegging sacramental corn liquor and Rosa Silver sharing matzoh with her friend the minister. It was Yetta Sawilowsky being crowned May Queen and cantor Gibby Katz pacing the sidelines of high-school football games. It was a black Aunt Zola setting a Passover table and Sam Margolis recalling his days in "chedah."

The sense of small-town southern Jewry as a culturally unique community has been largely lost even as the region is being transformed. Most Jewish families residing in the area since its earliest days did not remain beyond a generation. The thousands of Sunbelt transplants who migrated more recently have acculturated to an attenuated South. Sunbelt malls and subdivisions have bulldozed the southern cultural landscape. Durham–Chapel Hill Jewry in its demographics and patterns of community development now reflects mainstream national trends. Sunbelt migrants—who remain long enough—do recognize some southern softening of their manners, some slowing of their energies, and some heightening of religious consciousness. Such attitudes suggest some persistence of a distinctly southern identity. Even this blending is problematic, however. If their Jewishness is nothing more than a symbolic or nostalgic ethnicity, than their southernness, given their mobility and lack of local history, has even less content. The Durham–Chapel Hill Jewish community is unprecedentedly large and vibrant. Whether it is symbolically or essentially Jewish, whether it becomes southern by culture as well as by geography, whether indeed either peoples retain their distinction, is the unwritten final chapter of this book.

Notes

1. Introduction: More or Less Southern

1. Martin Cohen, "Structuring American Jewish History," *American Jewish Historical Quarterly* 57, no. 2 (December 1967):140; Ewa Morawska, *Insecure Prosperity: Small-Town Jews in Industrial America, 1890–1914* (Princeton: Princeton University Press, 1996), xviii.

2. Mark Bauman, *The Southerner as American: Jewish Style* (Cincinnati: American Jewish Archives, 1996), 5; Elizabeth Fox-Genovese, "The Anxiety of History: The Southern Confrontation with Modernity," *Southern Cultures* (Inaugural Issue, 1993):65.

3. John S. Reed, *My Tears Spoiled My Aim and Other Reflections on Southern Culture* (Columbia: University of Missouri Press, 1993), 15, 21, 29–32.

4. Lee Shai Weissbach, "East European Immigrants and the Image of Jews in the Small-Town South," *American Jewish History* 85, no. 3 (Sept. 1997): 231–32.

5. Bauman, *Southerner as American,* 29.

6. Fred Hobson, "The Savage South: An Inquiry into the Origins, Endurance, and Presumed Demise of an Image," in *Myth and Southern History,* ed. Patrick Gerster and Nicholas Cords (Urbana: University of Illinois Press, 1989), 134, 146.

7. Morawska, *Insecure Prosperity,* xiv; Murray Polner, "Smalltown Rabbis: Is Anyone Listening Out There?" *National Jewish Monthly* 92, no. 1 (Sept. 1977):18; Howard Epstein, *Jews in Small Towns: Legends and Legacies* (Santa Rosa, Calif.: Vision Books International, 1997).

2. The North Carolina Background, 1585 to 1870s

1. Jacob R. Marcus, *Early American Jewry: The Jews of Pennsylvania and the South, 1655–1790,* vol. 2 (Philadelphia: Jewish Publication Society, 1953), 272.

2. Gary Grassl, "Joachim Gans of Prague: The First Jew in English America," *American Jewish History* 86, no. 2 (June 1998):195, 203, 209.

3. Derek Penslar, "The Origins of Jewish Political Economy," *Jewish Social Studies* 3, no. 3 (spring-summer, 1997):27 (quotation); David Goldberg,

"An Historical Community Study of Wilmington Jewry, 1738–1925" (seminar paper for Dr. George Tindall, University of North Carolina at Chapel Hill, spring 1986), 6.

4. Virginia B. Platt, "Tar Staves and New England Rum: The Trade of Aaron Lopez of Newport, Rhode Island, with Colonial North Carolina," *North Carolina Historical Review* 48, no. 1 (January 1971):1.

5. William Powell, *North Carolina through Four Centuries* (Chapel Hill: University of North Carolina Press, 1989), 126; Goldberg, "Wilmington Jewry," 1; Leon Huhner, "The Jews of North Carolina Prior to 1800," *Publications of the American Jewish Historical Society* 29 (1925):142–43; Francis Salvador was a South Carolina Jew. Richard Rapely was his Gentile friend.

6. Goldberg, "Wilmington Jewry," 1; Ira Rosenwaike, "An Estimate and Analysis of the Jewish Population of the United States in 1790," *Publications of the American Jewish Historical Society* 50, no. 1 (Sept. 1960):23–67.

7. Jacob R. Marcus, "Light on Early Connecticut Jewry," in *Studies in American Jewish History* (Cincinnati: Hebrew Union College, 1969), 90–91.

8. Robert Kenzer, *Kinship and Neighborhood in a Southern Community: Orange County, North Carolina, 1849–1881* (Knoxville: University of Tennessee Press, 1987), 30–33; Huhner, "Jews of North Carolina," 142; Brent Holcomb, *Marriages of Orange County, 1779–1868* (Baltimore: Genealogical Publications, 1983), 251.

9. Myron Berman, *Richmond's Jewry: Shabbat in Shockoe, 1769–1976* (Charlottesville: University Press of Virginia, 1979), 115; see Myron Berman, *The Last of the Jews?* (Lanham, Md.: University Press of America, 1998), 28, 41; Jacob R. Marcus, *The American Jewish Woman, 1654–1980* (Cincinnati: American Jewish Archives, 1981), 53–54; Goldberg, "Wilmington Jewry," 13–15 (quotation); Malcolm Stern, "The Function of Genealogy in American Jewish History," in *Essays in American Jewish History to Commemorate the Tenth Anniversary of the Founding of the American Jewish Archives under the Direction of Jacob Rader Marcus* (Cincinnati: American Jewish Archives, 1958), 83–86, 94, 97.

10. Marcus, *Early American Jewry*, 500.

11. Guion Griffis Johnson, *Ante-Bellum North Carolina: A Social History* (Chapel Hill: University of North Carolina Press, 1937), 429; Jonathan Sarna, "The Impact of the American Revolution on American Jews," in *The American Jewish Experience,* ed. Jonathan Sarna (New York: Holmes and Meier, 1986), 23; Morton Borden, *Jews, Turks, and Infidels* (Chapel Hill: University of North Carolina Press, 1984), 40–44 (Henry quotations); Mary Hollis Barnes, "Jacob Henry's Role in the Fight for Religious Freedom in North Carolina," March 19, 1984, typescript, North Carolina State Archives, Raleigh.

12. Steven Hertzberg, *Strangers within the Gate City: The Jews of Atlanta, 1845–1915* (Philadelphia: Jewish Publication Society of America, 1978), 14; Powell, *North Carolina*, 250.

13. Malcolm Stern, "The Role of the Rabbi in the South," in *"Turn to the South": Essays on Southern Jewry*, ed. Nathan Kaganoff and Melvin Urofsky (Charlottesville: University Press of Virginia, 1979), 24; Hertzberg, *Strangers within the Gate City*, 14–15; Berman, *Richmond's Jewry*, 136.

14. Arthur Durden, *Joseph Fels and the Single Tax Movement* (Philadelphia: Temple University Press, 1971), 7–11.

15. Werner Sollors, *The Invention of Ethnicity* (New York: Oxford University Press, 1989), xi.

16. Morris Speizman, *The Jews of Charlotte, North Carolina: A Chronicle with Commentary and Conjectures* (Charlotte: McNally and Loftin, 1978), 4–5; for Wallace, see Gary Freeze, "Roots, Barks, Berries, and Jews: The Herb Trade in Gilded-Age North Carolina" (paper presented at the Economic and Business Historical Society, April 28–30, 1994); for Grausman, see Charlotte Litwack, "The Jewish Community of Raleigh," in *The Heritage of Wake County, North Carolina, 1983,* ed. Lynne Belvin and Harriette Riggs (Winston-Salem: Hunter, 1983), 78.

17. Goldberg, "Wilmington Jewry," 33; *Jewish South*, March 19, 1878 (quotation).

18. Moses Rountree, *Strangers in the Land: The Story of Jacob Weil's Tribe* (Philadelphia: Dorrance, 1969), 5.

19. Borden, *Jews, Turks, and Infidels*, 46–47 (Smith quotations); for Orange County Know-Nothings, see Kenzer, *Kinship and Neighborhood*, 64–65.

20. Daniel Grant, *Alumni History of the University of North Carolina, 1795–1924* (Chapel Hill: University of North Carolina Press, 1924), 47, 362, 553.

21. *Hillsborough Recorder*, Nov. 15, 1851.

22. Ruth Blackwelder, *The Age of Orange: Political and Intellectual Leadership in North Carolina, 1752–1861* (Charlotte: William Loftin, 1961), 182; North Carolina, vol. 19, p. 23K, R. G. Dun & Co. Collection, Baker Library, Harvard University Graduate School of Business Administration (quotation).

23. John Hope Franklin, "'As for Our History . . . ,'" in *The Southerner as American,* ed. Charles Sellers, Jr. (Chapel Hill: University of North Carolina Press, 1960), 4–5.

24. Speizman, *Jews of Charlotte*, 4; Simon Wolf, *The American Jew as Patriot, Soldier, and Citizen* (Philadelphia: Brentano's, 1895), 301–5, 419; Matthew Karres, "Alfred Mordecai," in *Dictionary of North Carolina Biography*, vol. 4, ed. William Powell (Chapel Hill: University of North Carolina Press, 1991), 313; Hugh B. Johnston, Jr., "Oettinger's Dependable Store," 1976, unpublished typescript, Wilson County Library, Wilson, North Carolina.

25. Wolf, *American Jew as Patriot,* 303.

26. Leon Dworsky, interview with author, Jan. 5, 1987. Wolf lists seventeen Jewish soldiers who served in regiments that were in Chapel Hill at war's end.

27. Borden, *Jews, Turks, and Infidels,* 49–50.

28. Kenzer, *Kinship and Neighborhood,* 102–4.

29. Quoted in Hertzberg, *Strangers within the Gate City,* 34; quotation from *Goldsboro Argus* in Harry Golden, *Our Southern Landsmen* (New York: G. P. Putnam, 1974), 180.

30. North Carolina, vol. 12, p. 453; vol. 8, p. 406; vol. 9, p. 446, 504; vol. 25, p. 87, R. G. Dun & Co. Collection, Baker Library, Harvard University Graduate School of Business.

31. Stephen Mostov, "Dun and Bradstreet Reports as a Source of Jewish Economic History: Cincinnati, 1840–1875," *American Jewish History* 72, no. 3 (March 1983):342, 352.

32. Wolf, *American Jew as Patriot,* 390; *Hillsborough Recorder,* Nov. 3, 1866. The 1860 census lists an M. E. and A.D. Cohen in Hillsborough, but Cohen was a Christian minister.

33. Sydney Nathans, *The Quest for Progress: The Way We Lived in North Carolina, 1870–1920* (Chapel Hill: University of North Carolina Press, 1983), 12; Orange County, North Carolina, R. G. Dun & Co. Collection.

34. Orange County, North Carolina, R. G. Dun & Co. Collection; Jean Anderson, *Durham County: A History of Durham County, North Carolina* (Durham: Duke University Press, 1990), 130.

35. Hasia Diner, *A Time for Gathering: The Second Migration: 1820–1880* (Baltimore: Johns Hopkins University Press, 1992), 25–26; Berman, *Richmond's Jewry,* 40, 139, 154, 264–65.

36. Harry Golden, "The Jewish People of North Carolina," *North Carolina Historical Review* 32, no. 2 (April 1955):211.

37. Martin Weitz, ed., *Biblio . . . Temple of Israel, Wilmington* (Wilmington: Temple of Israel, 1976), 12–17.

38. Anderson, *Durham County,* 126, 139.

39. Kenzer, *Kinship and Neighborhood,* 180; Hugh Lefler and Albert Newsome, *The History of a Southern State: North Carolina* (Chapel Hill: University of North Carolina Press, 1973), 130.

3. A German Jewish Colony, 1870s to 1880s

1. Quoted in Mena Webb, *Jule Carr: General without an Army* (Chapel Hill: University of North Carolina, 1987), 94; Anderson, *Durham County,* 163–64; E. J. Ayers, *The Promise of the New South: Life after Reconstruction* (New York: Oxford University Press, 1992), 55; see Jacob Rader Marcus, *To Count a People: American Jewish Population Data, 1585–1984* (Lanham, Md.: University Press of America, 1990).

2. Lefler and Newsome, *History of a Southern State,* 715; Marcus, *To Count a People,* 165.

3. Robert Durden, *The Dukes of Durham, 1865–1929* (Durham: Duke University Press, 1975), 115.

4. Ayers, *Promise of the New South,* 67, 469.

5. Kenzer, *Kinship and Neighborhood,* 126; Durden, *Dukes of Durham,* 15.

6. Tenth Census, 1880, Orange County, North Carolina; Orange County Tax List, 1875, North Carolina State Archives and History Search Room.

7. *Durham Herald,* March 22, 1876; *Hillsborough Recorder,* Nov. 3, 1866.

8. *Durham Tobacco Plant,* Dec. 11, 1888; May 10, 1896; Maurice Weinstein, ed., *Zebulon Vance and "The Scattered Nation"* (Charlotte: Wildacres Press, 1995), 64, 89, 93.

9. North Carolina, vol. 19, pp. 238, 268, 274, 280, R. G. Dun & Co. Collection.

10. North Carolina, vol. 19, p. 280, R. G. Dun & Co. Collection; Kenzer, *Kinship and Neighborhood,* 113–14. A similar pattern existed in Keystone, West Virginia, where Jews occupied a variety of mercantile trades but remained outside the coal industry. See Deborah Weiner, "The Jews of Kingston: Life in a Multicultural Boomtown," *Southern Jewish History* 2 (1999):1–25

11. *Durham Tobacco Plant,* Jan. 26, 1876.

12. *Durham Morning Herald,* March 22, 1876; *Durham Tobacco Plant,* Oct. 19, March 28, 1877.

13. North Carolina, vol. 19, p. 238, R. G. Dun & Co. Collection; Weinstein, *Zebulon Vance,* 82.

14. *Durham Business Directory, 1876,* Durham County Library.

15. Quoted in *Durham Recorder,* Sept. 18, 1889.

16. *Durham Tobacco Plant,* June 10, 1879.

17. *Durham Tobacco Plant,* March 28, 1877 (Mohsberg ad); *Durham Tobacco Plant,* June 21, 1881 (Levy ad).

18. Durham County Tax Rolls, 1883, 1884, North Carolina State Archives.

19. Sigmund Meyer, "Story of Durham Jewry," 1951, 4B, typed manuscript, Perkins Library, Duke University.

20. Anderson, *Durham County,* 169, 171 (quotations); Ayers, *Rise of the New South,* 417.

21. Meyer, "Story of Durham Jewry," 4B; *Bradstreet's Reports of the State of North Carolina* (New York: Bradstreet, 1888), 77; *Durham Daily Globe,* Oct. 10, 1885.

22. Kemp Battle, *History of the University of North Carolina,* vol. 2 (Raleigh: Edwards and Broughton, 1912), 346.

23. Weinstein, *Zebulon Vance,* 80; *Durham Recorder,* Sept. 15, 1889; Meyer, "Story of Durham Jewry," 4B; *Durham Morning Herald,* March 22, 1876; Edgecombe County, R. G. Dun & Co. Collection, 446–47.

24. Anderson, *Durham County,* 227.

25. *Occident* 18, no. 50 (March 8, 1860); Weitz, *Biblio* . . . , 12–17; Charlotte Litwack, *Recollections: Conversations about the House of Jacob* (Raleigh: N.p., 1976), 2.

26. Weitz, *Biblio* . . . , 17; Herbert Ezekiel and Gaston Lichtenstein, *The History of the Jews of Richmond from 1769 to 1917* (Richmond: H. T. Ezekiel, 1917), 277; Rountree, *Strangers in the Land;* Saul Viener, "Edward Calisch," *Encyclopedia Judaica,* vol. 5 (New York: Macmillan, 1971), 62.

27. Stern, "Role of the Rabbi in the South," 25; Howard Sachar, *A History of the Jews in America* (New York: Knopf, 1992), 112; Michael Meyer, "German-Jewish Identity in Nineteenth-Century America," in *American Jewish Experience,* 56 (quotation).

28. David Goldberg, "Samuel Mendelsohn," in *Dictionary of North Carolina Biography,* vol. 5, ed. William Powell (Chapel Hill: University of North Carolina Press, 1991), 252; Weitz, *Biblio* . . . , 17; [Tarboro] Congregation B'nai Israel Congregational Minutes, Sept. 24, 1882, American Jewish Archives, Cincinnati; Weinstein, *Zebulon Vance,* 10.

29. *Jewish South* (Atlanta), April 10, Oct. 14, 1877; Rountree, *Strangers in the Land,* 60; Congregation Emanuel, Statesville, North Carolina, Centennial Celebration, North Carolina Collection, Wilson Library, University of North Carolina.

30. *Jewish South* (Atlanta), July 12, 1878; *Durham Tobacco Plant,* Oct. 1, 1878; Michael Meyer, *Response to Modernity: A History of the Reform Movement in Judaism* (New York: Oxford University Press, 1988), 252. Some German still persisted in the Goldsboro, New Bern, and Wilmington synagogues.

31. Meyer, "Story of Durham Jewry," 10C.

32. *Durham Recorder,* May 13, 1885; Greenberg, *Through the Years,* 21; *Durham Tobacco Plant,* Nov. 17, 1886; March 9, 1887; Sept. 5, 1888.

33. Meyer, "Story of Durham Jewry," 5; *Turner and Company's Durham Directory for the Years 1889 and 1890* (Danville, Va.: E. F. Turner and Co., 1889), 22.

34. Kenzer, *Kinship and Neighborhood,* 124; *Durham Tobacco Plant,* Nov. 15, 23, Dec. 1, 1888; for Kronheimer family, see Mattie Lehman Goldberg Papers, Manuscript Room, Perkins Library; *Durham Daily Sun,* Nov. 21, 1899.

35. Weissbach, "East European Immigrants," 236; Elliott Ashkenazi, *The Business of Jews in Louisiana, 1840–1875* (Tuscaloosa: University of Alabama Press, 1988), 163.

4. Russian Tobacco Workers: A Proletarian Interlude, 1880s

1. Sydney Nathans, ed., *The Quest for Progress: The Way We Lived in North Carolina, 1870–1920* (Chapel Hill: University of North Carolina Press, 1983), 23.

2. Joseph Robert, *The Story of Tobacco in America* (Chapel Hill: University of North Carolina Press, 1967), 141; Lefler and Newsome, *History of a South-*

ern State, 521; Walter Fleming, "Immigration to the Southern States," *Political Science Quarterly* 20 (1905):283–88; *Nativities of the Foreign-born Population,* 57th Congress, 2d sess., 1902–1903, No. 12 Series, Doc. No. 15, Part 12, House Documents Vol. 42, 4390.

3. Eli Evans, *The Provincials: A Personal History of the Jews in the South* (New York: Atheneum, 1976), 15–17. Accounts vary on the number of Jewish workers. Duke stated 125, whereas local Jewish histories cite 300; the larger number may include dependents and Jews hired by Blackwell. A smaller number seems justified.

4. Hiram Paul, *History of the Town of Durham, North Carolina* (Raleigh: Edwards and Broughton, 1884), 117–18; Meyer, "Story of Durham Jewry," 4A.

5. Bernard Goldgar, "Autobiographical Memoir," 1, 51–52, unpublished typescript, Perkins Library. Gus Kaufman of Macon, Georgia, brought this manuscript to my attention, and Harry Goldgar of New Orleans granted permission to cite it.

6. *Durham Morning Herald,* Jan. 17, 1926; Melton McLaurin, *The Knights of Labor in the South* (Westport, Conn.: Greenwood Press, 1978), 62.

7. *Durham Morning Herald,* Jan. 17, 1926; Southgate Jones, "The Handrolled Cigarette Industry," Jan. 22, 1945, typescript, Rare Book, Manuscript, and Special Collections Library, Duke University.

8. Nannie Tilley, *The Bright Tobacco Industry: 1860–1924* (Chapel Hill: University of North Carolina Press, 1948), 520.

9. Kenzer, *Kinship and Neighborhood,* 122; Dolores Janiewski, "From Field to Factory: Race, Class, Sex, and the Woman Worker in Durham, 1880–1940" (Ph.D. diss., Duke University, 1979), 215–16; *Progress: Journal of the Cigar Makers Progressive Union,* Sept. 26, 1884; Dec. 20, 1884.

10. *Durham Tobacco Plant,* Jan. 11, 1882; *Durham Morning Herald,* Jan. 17, 1926.

11. *Progress,* Sept. 26, Dec. 5, 1884; McLaurin, *Knights of Labor,* 31–33.

12. Tilley, *Bright Tobacco Industry,* 519; James Buchanan Duke Letter Book, Feb. 8, March 16, 1886, No. 1 (1885–1889).

13. *Progress,* Jan. 24, 1884; May 29, 1885.

14. *Durham Tobacco Plant,* Feb. 2, 1887; *Progress,* May 29, 1885; McLaurin, *Knights of Labor,* 62; Tilley, *Bright Tobacco Industry,* 519.

15. McLaurin, *Knights of Labor,* 63.

16. Ibid., 52 (first quotation); Janiewski, "From Field to Factory," 216 (second quotation); Dolores Janiewski, *Sisterhood Denied: Race, Gender, and Class in a New South Community* (Philadelphia: Temple University Press, 1985), 85.

17. Paul, *History of Durham,* 98–100.

18. *Durham Tobacco Plant,* July 10, 1888.

19. McLaurin, *Knights of Labor,* 42; *Durham Tobacco Plant,* Feb. 2, 1887; Sept. 15, 1888; Janiewski, *Sisterhood Denied,* 19–20.

20. *Progress,* May 29, 1885; *Bureau of Labor Statistics, State of North Carolina,*

1887 (Raleigh: Josephus Daniels, 1887), 83; Janiewski, *Sisterhood Denied*, 71.

21. *Raleigh News and Observer*, April 5, 1896.

22. See Robert Ingalls, *Urban Vigilantes in the New South: Tampa, 1882–1936* (Knoxville: University of Tennessee Press, 1988); Irving Howe, *World of Our Fathers* (Harcourt Brace Jovanovich, 1976), 109–10.

23. Janiewski, *Sisterhood Denied*, 87.

24. *Durham Tobacco Plant*, Sept. 15, 1886; Paul Seligson, letter to author, Jan. 8, 1988.

25. *Progress*, Dec. 20, 1884.

26. For Edelsohn, see *Durham Tobacco Plant*, Feb. 2, 1887; for Harris, see Tilley, *Bright Tobacco Industry*, 519.

27. Gerald Sorin, *A Time for Building: The Third Migration, 1880–1920* (Baltimore: Johns Hopkins University Press, 1992), 110; Paul Seligson, letter to author.

28. Paul, *History of Durham*, 99–100.

29. Janiewski, *Sisterhood Denied*, 3–4; William Boyd, *The Story of Durham: City of the New South* (Durham: Duke University Press, 1925), 135.

30. *Durham Recorder*, May 13, 1885; Paul, *History of Durham*, 117.

31. Meyer, "Story of Durham Jewry," 5A.

32. *Durham Morning Herald*, March 20, 1927.

33. *Progress*, Dec. 20, 1884.

34. Ernest Seeman, *American Gold* (New York: Dial Press, 1978). The novel was published some forty years after it was written.

35. Foster Fitz-Simons, *Bright Leaf* (New York: Rinehart, 1948). Jews were obvious models for Fitz-Simons's Ukrainians. His description of Ukrainian customs, black relations, and peasant spirit are fanciful.

36. *Report of the Building Committee of the Beth-El Congregation upon the Completion of the Beth-El Synagogue* (Durham: Beth-El Congregation, 1921); "Jewish Communities in the South: 9. Durham, N.C.," *American Jewish Times* (August 1944):7; Evans, *Provincials*, 13, 17.

37. Evans, *Provincials*, 13.

38. Hertzberg, *Strangers within the Gate City*, 248; Ayers, *Promise of the New South*, 453.

5. **East European Immigration: From Old World to New South, 1886 to 1900**

1. Weissbach, "East European Immigrants," 237.

2. *Directory of the Business and Citizens of Durham City for 1887* (Raleigh: Levi Branson, 1887); *Directory of Greater Durham, 1902* (Durham: Samuel Adams, 1902).

3. Lee Shai Weissbach, "Stability and Mobility in the Small Jewish Community: Examples from Kentucky History," *American Jewish History* 79, no. 3

(spring 1990):361, 371; Dwight Hoover, "Introduction: To be a Jew in Middletown," in *Middletown Jews: The Tenuous Survival of an American Jewish Community,* ed. Dan Rottenberg (Bloomington: Indiana University Press, 1997), xvii.

4. Harold Geisert, "The Trend of the Interregional Migration of Talent: The Southeast, 1899–1936," *Social Forces* 18 (October 1939):67.

5. *Raleigh News and Observer,* April 5, 1896.

6. Quoted in Sachar, *History of the Jews in America,* 112.

7. W. J. Cash, *The Mind of the South* (New York: Vintage, 1941), 58–59; *Durham Morning Herald,* Dec. 1, 1909; W. J. Cash, "Jehovah of the Tar Heels," *American Mercury* (July 1929):310; Ruth Simand Malis, letter to author, n.d. (Heillig quotation); Hazel Gladstein Wishnov, telephone interview with author, Nov. 19, 1987 (Levy quotation).

8. *Durham Tobacco Plant,* Dec. 11, 1888; May 10, 1896; Weinstein, *Zebulon Vance,* 89–90; quoted in Leonard Dinnerstein, *Uneasy at Home: Antisemitism and the American Jewish Experience* (New York: Columbia University Press, 1987), 113; Walter Weare, *Black Business in the New South: A History of the North Carolina Mutual Life Insurance Company* (Urbana: University of Illinois Press, 1973), 21.

9. Marcus, *To Count a People,* 240–41; Richard Sanders, *Shores of Refuge: A Hundred Years of Jewish Emigration* (New York: Holt, 1988), 143–44.

10. Durham County Naturalization Papers, North Carolina State Archives.

11. Chester Cohen, *Shtetl Finder* (Los Angeles: Periday, 1980), 1, 109, 123. The shtetls are spelled variously. Vidzh is Witz, Widze, or Vidzy; Akmian is Akmene, Okayman, or Agmean; Zagear is Zager, Zhagar, or Zagare. John Briggs, *An Italian Passage: Immigrants to Three American Cities* (New Haven: Yale University Press, 1978), 70; Howard Rabinowitz, *Race, Ethnicity and Urbanization: Selected Essays* (Columbia: University of Missouri Press, 1994), 233–34; Durham County Naturalization Papers, North Carolina State Archives.

12. Litwack, *Recollections,* 35–42.

13. *Durham Morning Herald,* Nov. 12, 1915; Jack Glazier, *Dispersing the Ghetto: The Relocation of Jewish Immigrants across America* (Ithaca: Cornell University Press, 1998), 196.

14. *Durham Daily Sun,* Aug. 5, 1904.

15. Arthur Goren, "Jews," in *Harvard Encyclopedia of American Ethnic Groups,* ed. Stephan Thernstrom (Cambridge: Harvard University Press, 1980), 581; "Statistics on Population," 1900 Census Lists, North Carolina State Archives.

16. Morawska, *Insecure Prosperity,* 32; W. C. Dula, *Durham and Her People* (Durham: Citizen's Press, 1951), 90; Litwack, *Recollections,* 35.

17. Janiewski, *Sisterhood Denied,* 71; *County Population Trends, North Carolina,*

1790–1960 (Chapel Hill and Raleigh: Carolina Population Center, UNC, and Statistical Center, State of North Carolina, March 1969), 37.

18. *Directory of the Business and Citizens of Durham City for 1887; Directory of Greater Durham, 1902; Durham Morning Herald,* July 11, 1904.

19. *Directory of the Business and Citizens of Durham City for 1887; Directory of Greater Durham, 1902; Durham, North Carolina, Directory, 1911–1912* (Richmond: Hill Directory Co., 1911); Sadie Silver Goodman, May 19, 1986, untitled typescript, Perkins Library; *Durham Sun,* July 3, 1895; April 28, 1903; May 11, July 12, 1904.

20. Hertzberg, *Strangers within the Gate City,* 187–88.

21. *Durham Morning Herald,* Dec. 2, 1915 (quotation); *Durham Sun,* Feb. 26, 1897.

22. Leon Jick, "The Reform Synagogue," in *The American Synagogue: A Sanctuary Transformed,* ed. Jack Wertheimer (New York: Cambridge University Press, 1987), 85, 88–89; Weissbach, "East European Immigrants," 233.

23. Carolyn Gray Lemaster, *A Corner of the Tapestry: A History of the Jewish Experience in Arkansas, 1820s to 1990s* (Fayetteville: University of Arkansas Press, 1994), 78.

24. Goldgar, "Autobiographical Memoir," 52.

25. Leonard Rogoff, "Synagogue and Jewish Church: A Congregational History of North Carolina," *Southern Jewish History* 1 (1998):60–62.

26. Howe, *World of Our Fathers,* 195; Jeffrey Gurock, "The Orthodox Synagogue," in *The American Synagogue,* 53.

27. Meyer, "Story of Durham Jewry," 1C; *Report of the Building Committee,* 5; Abraham Karp, *Haven and Home: A History of the Jews in America* (New York: Schocken Books, 1985), 90.

6. Creating an American Jewish Community, 1900 to 1917

1. C. Vann Woodward, *The Burden of Southern History* (Baton Rouge: Louisiana State University Press, 1968), 18.

2. *Durham Morning Herald,* June 13, 1909; June 23, 1907. For Jews Wittkowsky was hardly a "wonderful Hebrew." He replied with an insult when asked to contribute to Charlotte's synagogue, changed his name to Whitson, and converted to Christianity.

3. See Weare, *Black Business in the New South.*

4. Janiewski, *Sisterhood Denied,* 57.

5. Morawska, *Insecure Prosperity,* 32, 41; Joel Perlmann, "Beyond New York: The Occupations of Russian Jewish Immigrants in Providence, R. I., and in Other Small Jewish Communities, 1900–1915," *American Jewish History* 72(March 1983):369–94.

6. *Durham Sun,* Sept. 21, 22, 1901.

7. Durham County, North Carolina, Enumerated District Lists, Thirteenth

Census of the United States, 1910, North Carolina State Archives; Morawska, *Insecure Prosperity,* 41.

8. Richard Lansburgh, "Remembering 'Pa' " *Generations* (fall 1999):19, 24.

9. E. J. Ayers, *Promise of the New South,* 67, 95, 469.

10. Litwack, *Recollections,* 42.

11. *Durham Morning Herald,* Jan. 9, 1902; July 20, 1906, Jan. 9, Feb. 11, 1908; May 8, 1912.

12. *Durham Morning Herald,* May 17, 1913; Dec. 31, 1938; *Durham Sun,* May 23, 1912.

13. *Durham Sun,* Oct. 19, 1907; March 9, 1919.

14. *Durham Sun,* Sept. 21, 1901.

15. Irving Howe and Kenneth Libo, *How We Lived: A Documentary History of Immigrant Jews in America, 1880–1930* (New York: Richard Marek, 1979), 327–28.

16. *Directory of Greater Durham, 1902; Durham, North Carolina, Directory, 1911–1912.*

17. *Durham Sun,* July 11, 1904.

18. Durham County Tax Rolls, 1897, 1910, 1925.

19. Henry Brady, Durham County Real Estate Deeds and Records, Durham County Courthouse; Max Shevel, Durham County Probate Records, Will Book 3, March 16, 1917, 44, Durham County Courthouse.

20. *Durham Sun,* May 14, 1904.

21. Benjamin Kronheimer, Durham County Probate Records, Will Book 6, 149; Will Book 11, June 6, 1939, 320.

22. Sam Margolis, conversation with author, Nov. 14, 1992; *Durham Daily Globe,* June 10, 1879.

23. *Durham Morning Herald,* July 3, 1902; Oct. 9, 1906; *Durham Sun,* June 10, 1904.

24. *Durham Morning Herald,* Dec. 4, 1910.

25. *American Jewish Yearbook, 1917–1918* (Philadelphia: Jewish Publication Society, 1918), 408; Anderson, *Durham County,* 230.

26. *Chanticleer* (Durham: Organizations of Trinity Colleges, 1916).

27. Benjamin Harshav, *The Meaning of Yiddish* (Berkeley: University of California Press, 1990), 122; Joseph Dave, "Interview," oral history transcript, American Jewish Archives; Samuel Newman, "Frank Graham," *American Jewish Times* (October 1955):9–11.

28. Hillel Halkin, "Henry Hurwitz," *Encyclopedia Judaica,* vol. 8 (New York: Macmillan, 1972), 1371; Newman, "Frank Graham," 7; *Durham Morning Herald,* May 12, 1914.

29. Henry Bane, interview with author, Nov. 1986; quoted in Golden, *Our Southern Landsman,* 222; *Raleigh Times,* Dec. 29, 1927.

30. Arthur Abernethy, *The Jew a Negro* (Moravian Falls, N.C.: Dixie Publish-

ing, 1910), 107; Simmons quoted in John Higham, *Strangers in the Land* (New Brunswick, N.J.: Rutgers University Press, 1988), 164; Cash quoted in Rowland Berthoff, "Southern Attitudes toward Immigration, 1865–1914," *Journal of Southern History* 17, no. 3 (August 1951):348–49; Vance quoted in Alfred O. Hero, Jr., *The Southerner and World Affairs* (Baton Rouge: Louisiana State University Press, 1965), 66.

31. Cash, *Mind of the South,* 58, 342; Wittkowsky quoted in Howe and Libo, *How We Lived,* 327–28; Richter quoted in Golden, *Our Southern Landsmen,* 159.

32. Cash, *Mind of the South,* 59; *Durham Recorder,* May 13, 1885; *North Carolina Reports,* vol. 181 (Raleigh: Mitchell Printing Company, 1921), 181–96; George Tindall, *The Ethnic Southerners* (Baton Rouge: Louisiana State University Press, 1976), 11.

33. Meyer, "Story of Durham Jewry," n.p.

34. *Durham Morning Herald,* May 30, 1904; Jan. 17, 1926; Jones, "The Hand-rolled Cigarette Industry," 3.

35. *Durham Morning Herald,* Feb. 9, 1905; Feb. 20, 1914.

36. Daniel Patterson, interview with the author, April 13, 1992.

37. *Durham Sun,* April 19, 1901.

38. Dave, "Interview"; *Durham Morning Herald,* Dec. 20, 1914.

39. *Durham Morning Herald,* Feb. 7, 1904; July 14, Aug. 11, 1906; July 16, 1914; *Durham Sun,* March 30, 1904.

40. *Durham Morning Herald,* Dec. 27, 1912; Paul Green, *Paul Green's Wordbook: An Alphabet of Reminiscence,* vol. 1 (Boone, N.C.: Appalachian Conservation, 1990), 604.

41. *Durham Morning Herald,* May 2, 1915; March 29, Aug. 4, 22, 1911; Daniel Patterson, interview with author, April 13, 1992.

42. *Durham Morning Herald,* Aug. 22, 1911.

43. *Durham Morning Herald,* Nov. 16, 1901; Sept. 14, 1909; Jan. 28, 1910; *Durham Sun,* Dec. 18, 1903.

44. Morris Schappes, ed., *A Documentary History of the Jews in the United States, 1654–1875* (New York: Citadel, 1950), 510; *Durham Morning Herald,* April 14, 1909; Jan. 29, 1910.

45. *Durham Morning Herald,* Jan. 6, 1911.

46. Meyer, "Story of Durham Jewry," n.p.

47. *Durham Morning Herald,* Feb. 19, 1915; July 27, 1915.

48. *Durham Morning Herald,* Aug. 26, 1913; Dec. 9, 1915.

49. *Durham Sun,* July 27, 1901; Dula, *Durham and Her People,* 55; Meyer, "Story of Durham Jewry," n.p.; Nathan Summerfield, letter to author, April 30, 1987; Ayers, *Promise of the New South,* 310.

50. *Durham Morning Herald,* March 27, 1913.

51. Ibid.
52. *Durham Morning Herald,* Aug. 16, 1913.
53. Mattie Lehman Goldberg Papers; James Leyburn, *The Way We Lived, Durham, 1900–1920* (Elliston, Va.: Northcross, 1989), 154–56.
54. Leyburn, *Way We Lived,* 156.
55. Leyburn, *Way We Lived,* 144.
56. Sigmund Meyer, conversation with author, Sept. 25, 1986.
57. Meyer, "Story of Durham Jewry," 6B; *Durham Morning Herald,* March 31, 1905.
58. Ruth Simand Malis, letter to author, n.d.; *Durham Morning Herald,* Aug. 16, 1903; Anderson, *Durham County,* 262.
59. Howe and Libo, *How We Lived,* 328.
60. Pauli Murray, *Song in a Weary Throat* (New York: Harper and Row, 1987), 33–34.
61. *Durham Morning Herald,* March 14, 1908.
62. *Durham Morning Herald,* June 13, 1907; Jan. 5, 1908; Feb. 4, 23, 1910; Meno Lovenstein, letter to Leonard Rogoff, Oct. 18, 1986.
63. Leonard Dinnerstein, *Uneasy at Home: Antisemitism and the American Jewish Experience* (New York: Columbia University Press, 1987), 223; *Durham Morning Herald,* July 26, 1912.
64. *Durham Morning Herald,* Oct. 10, 1909; March 22, 1911.
65. Ayers, *Promise of the New South,* 309.
66. *Durham Morning Herald,* April 28, 1903; Oct. 11, 1904; July 11, 1906; April 10, 1907.
67. *Durham Sun,* Sept. 24, 1901.
68. *Durham Morning Herald,* Aug. 15, 1908.
69. *Durham Morning Herald,* Aug 12, 1908.
70. *Durham Morning Herald,* Aug. 15, 1908.
71. *Durham Morning Herald,* Aug. 11, 1908.
72. *Durham Morning Herald,* Aug. 22, 1908.
73. *Durham Morning Herald,* April 20, Aug. 23, 1908.
74. For description of Lovenstein indictment and trial, see *Durham Morning Herald,* July 28, 29, 31 (Reade quotation), 1910. See *Durham Morning Herald,* Sept. 1, 1910, for references to his religious "heterodoxy" and Sept. 2, 1910, for newspaper attacks. *As I Saw It* is mentioned in the *Durham Morning Herald,* Oct. 20, 1910, but no copy has been located. Lovenstein's political career was unknown to his son.
75. *Durham Morning Herald,* Sept. 9, 1903; March 19, 1911; June 30, 1907; *American Jewish Yearbook, 1914* (Philadelphia: Jewish Publication Society, 1914), 118; Stephen Whitfield, *In Search of American Jewish Culture* (Hanover, N.H.: Brandeis University Press, 1999), 242.

76. Weissbach, "East European Immigrants," 252.

77. Karp, *Haven and Home,* 60.

78. Anderson, *Durham County,* 224.

79. Lehman Brady, interview with author, Jan. 1, 1987.

80. *American Jewish Yearbook, 1900–1901* (Philadelphia: Jewish Publication Society, 1900), 400; Sorin, *Time for Building,* 175.

81. *Durham Sun,* Aug. 15, 1901; Karp, *Haven and Home,* 175.

82. *Durham Morning Herald,* Aug. 10, 1902.

83. Durham Hebrew Congregation Company Certificate of Incorporation, Perkins Library.

84. *Durham Morning Herald,* March 19, 1904.

85. *Durham Morning Herald,* Sept. 27, June 22, Aug. 17, 1905.

86. *Laws, Rules and Regulations of the Durham Hebrew Congregation Company,* Perkins Library, June 17, 1907; for Haskell, see Meyer, "Story of Durham Jewry," n.p.

87. *Durham Morning Herald,* Feb. 9, 10, 17, 1906.

88. For reports on the trial, see *Durham Morning Herald,* July 12, 13, 14, 15, 1906; for the Norfolk rabbinic court, see *Durham Morning Herald,* July 21, 22, 1906; for the property sale, see *Durham Morning Herald,* Oct. 14, 1906.

89. Karp, *Haven and Home,* 104.

90. *Durham Morning Herald,* Feb. 9, 1906.

91. For Kruger-Haskell fight, see *Durham Morning Herald,* January 9, 1907; for Nurkin-Morris, see *Durham Morning Herald,* August 4, 1911; for Levy-Lovenstein case, see *Durham Morning Herald,* May 24, 1908; for Greenberg case, see *Durham Morning Herald,* July 27, 1910.

92. *Durham Morning Herald,* Dec. 12, 1904; Dec. 18, 1906.

93. *Durham Morning Herald,* July 26, 1912; June 6, 1913.

94. For Rabbis Ben Mosche and Rabinowitz, see Meyer, "Story of Durham," 7; for Rosenberg, see *Durham Morning Herald,* Oct. 6, 1909; also for Rabinowitz, see *Durham Morning Herald,* June 7, 1914.

95. *Durham Morning Herald,* June 24, 1913; Meyer, "Story of Durham Jewry," 4C.

96. *Durham Morning Herald,* March 31, 1912; June 24, 1913; Meyer, "Story of Durham Jewry," 4C.

97. *Durham Morning Herald,* Sept. 30, 1914; Sept. 18, 1915.

98. *Durham Morning Herald,* June 7, 1914; Aug. 26, 1913.

99. *Durham Morning Herald,* March 20, 1915.

100. Meyer, "Story of Durham Jewry," 5C; Henry Bane, interview with author, Nov. 1986.

101. Lehman Brady, telephone interview with author, Jan. 1, 1986; George and Ricky Rosenstein Lewin, interview with Robin Gruber, Jan. 29, 1986;

Sam Margolis, interview with Robin Gruber, Nov. 15, 1985; Lewin and Lewin, interview with Robin Gruber.

102. Judith Pilch, "Education," *Encyclopedia Judaica,* vol. 6 (New York: Macmillan, 1972), 440.

103. Frances Wynne, *Durham, North Carolina, Marriage Register, 1881–1906* (Baton Rouge: Oracle Press, 1983); *Durham Morning Herald,* July 6, 1905; Gilbert Katz, interview with author, Sept. 23, 1986.

104. *Durham Morning Herald,* March 12, 1904.

105. *Durham Sun,* Aug. 15, 1902; *Durham Morning Herald,* April 19, 1911; June 4, 20, July 17, Aug. 9, Oct. 23, 1913; Jan. 3, 1914.

106. *Durham Morning Herald,* April 19, 1911; *Durham Sun,* Nov. 26, 1903; *Durham Morning Herald,* April 7, 1904.

107. *Durham Morning Herald,* Jan. 30, 1913; May 26, Jan. 3, 1910.

108. *Durham Sun,* April 24, 1901.

109. *Durham Sun,* April 19, 1901; June 15, 1902.

110. Meyer, "Story of Durham Jewry," 14B; *Durham Morning Herald,* June 24, 1906.

111. Ayers, *Promise of the New South,* 334.

112. Lehman Brady, interview with author, Feb. 23, 1987; Hannah Sinauer, Memorandum on Lodge in Durham, N.C., to Marilyn Bargteil, Oct. 28, 1986, Perkins Library; see Karp, *Haven and Home,* 223–32.

113. Weissbach, "East European Immigrants," 247.

114. *Durham Morning Herald,* Aug. 10, 1911; Jan. 7, 1914 (quotation); Jan. 11, 1915.

115. Milton Gordon, *Assimilation in American Life* (New York: Oxford University Press, 1964), 235.

116. Eli Lederhendler, "Historical Reflections on the Problem of American Jewish Culture," *Jewish Social Studies,* 5, nos. 1 and 2 (fall 1998/winter 1999):48–49; Harshav, *Meaning of Yiddish,* 122.

7. Becoming Southern Jews, 1917 to 1929

1. Weissbach, "East European Immigrants," 237, 252; *American Jewish Yearbook, 1919–1920* (Philadelphia: Jewish Publication Society, 1919), 523.

2. "President's Report," *North Carolina Association of Jewish Women Yearbook, 1935–1936* (Greensboro: NCAJW, 1936), 13–16; Lee Shai Weissbach, "Decline in an Age of Expansion: Disappearing Jewish Communities in the Era of Mass Migration," *American Jewish Archives* 49, nos. 1 and 2 (1997):49.

3. *American Jewish Yearbook, 1940–1941* (Philadelphia: Jewish Publication Society, 1941), 656; William Levitt, "The Occupational Distribution of the Jews in North Carolina" (master's thesis, University of North Caro-

lina, 1938), 26; Paul Johnson, *A History of the Jews* (New York: Harper and Row, 1987), 372.

4. *American Jewish Yearbook, 1928–1929* (Philadelphia: Jewish Publication Society, 1929), 190–91. See also Marcus, *To Count a People,* 165–68.

5. Durham County Tax Roll, 1925.

6. Daniel Freedman, Durham County Probate Records, Will Book 7, December 9, 1926, 22; Durham County Tax Roll, 1925.

7. Hertzberg, *Strangers within the Gate City,* 142.

8. Boyd, *Story of Durham,* 160–61; Anderson, *Durham County,* 343.

9. *Report of the Building Committee,* 6; *We Save Them or They Die: American Jewish Relief Committee, North Carolina Conference* (Raleigh: Mitchell, 1922); Frederick Rypins, "North Carolina," *Universal Jewish Encyclopedia* (New York: Universal Jewish Encyclopedia, 1928), 240.

10. *Durham Morning Herald,* Aug. 31, 1921.

11. *Report of the Building Committee,* 3–4.

12. Meyer, "Story of Durham Jewry," 12C.

13. *North Carolina Reports,* 181–96 (Murnick quotation); R. O. Everett Diary, April 22, 1921, Duke University Manuscript Department (Clark quotations). Robinson O. Everett granted permission to cite the diary.

14. *Durham Morning Herald,* Jan. 25, 1922; Sept. 7, 1927.

15. Dan Rottenberg, ed., *Middletown Jews: The Tenuous Survival of an American Jewish Community* (Bloomington: Indiana University Press, 1997), 50.

16. *Chanticleer,* 1923, 1927, 1928, 1929; *Yackety Yack,* vol. 18 (Chapel Hill: Union of the University of North Carolina, 1928), 32.

17. *Durham Morning Herald,* March 20, 1927.

18. Sadie Goodman, May 19, 1986, untitled typed manuscript, Perkins Library; Robinson O. Everett, letter to author, Dec. 19, 1991.

19. *Hill's Durham, North Carolina, Directory, 1921* (Richmond: Hill Directory Co., 1921).

20. Claudia Roberts, Diane Lea, and Robert Leary, *The Durham Architectural and Historical Inventory* (Durham: City of Durham, 1982), 205.

21. *Beth-El Bulletin,* Jan. 1992.

22. *American Jewish Yearbook, 1919–1920* (Philadelphia: Jewish Publication Society, 1919), 523.

23. *Report of the Building Committee,* 3; see David Kaufman in *Shul with a Pool: The "Synagogue-Center" in American Jewish History* (Hanover, N.H.: Brandeis University Press, 1999).

24. *Report of the Building Committee,* 3, 6, 7.

25. *Durham Morning Herald,* Aug. 29, 1920; Similarly, Charlotte's Orthodox Jews brought a Reform rabbi from Savannah to dedicate their synagogue. See Marc Lee Raphael, "The Thought of Rabbi Abram Simon, 1897–

1938," *American Jewish Archives* 49, nos. 1 & 2 (1997):62–77. Simon saw Judaism and Americanism as "twin children of our consciousness."

26. *Durham Morning Herald,* Aug 29, 1920; Aug. 31, 1921.

27. *Durham Morning Herald,* Oct. 1, 1913.

28. George Lewin and Ricky Rosenstein Lewin, interview with Robin Gruber, Jan. 29, 1986.

29. *Report of the Building Committee,* 3.

30. Meyer, "Story of Durham Jewry," 3; *Durham Morning Herald,* Sept. 28, 1921.

31. Meyer, "Story of Durham Jewry," 10C; Sam Margolis, interview with Robert Klein and Karen Feldman, March 25, n.y.; Lehman Brady, telephone interview with author, Jan. 1, 1986.

32. Hannah Teichman Daniels, letter to author, n.d.

33. Joe Hockfield, telephone interview with author, Nov. 8, 1988.

34. Gilbert Katz, interview with author, Sept. 23, 1986; Abe Stadiem, interview with author, April 8, 1992; David Jaffe, telephone interview with author, n.d.; Melvin Gladstein, interview with Lynne Grossman, n.d.; Meyer, "Story of Durham Jewry," 10C; May Ornoff Segal, interview with Mollie Fridovich, April 1, 1986; Emma Edwards, *North Carolina Association of Jewish Women* (Greensboro: NCAJW, n.d.), 2; Leah Hagedorn, ed., *Jews in the American South, 1860–1965* (Durham: Duke Office of Continuing Education and the Durham County Library, 1987).

35. Emma Edwards, Condensed Minutes (March 18, 19, 1928), North Carolina Association of Jewish Women, North Carolina Collection.

36. Hazel Gladstein Wishnov, interview with author, April 27, 1982.

37. Mattie Lehman Goldberg Papers.

38. Glazer, *American Judaism,* 105; *We Save Them or They Die; Durham Morning Herald,* Dec. 6, 1905; "Jewish Communities in the South: Durham, N.C.," *American Jewish Times* (August 1944):7.

39. *Durham Morning Herald,* Feb. 19, 1926.

40. Karp, *Haven and Home,* 263–64; *Durham Morning Herald,* Feb. 22, 1926; Weissbach, "East European Immigrants," 249. Weissbach defines a small town as a general population under 100,000 and a Jewish population under 1,000.

41. Higham, *Strangers in the Land,* 251.

42. Lehman Brady, interview with author, Feb. 23, 1987; Abe Stadiem, interview with author, April 8, 1992; Joe Hockfield, interview with Robin Gruber.

43. *Durham Morning Herald,* March 30, 1927.

44. Leyburn, *Way We Lived,* 156; Henry Bane, interview with author, Nov. 1986.

45. On "muscle Jews," see Walter Laqueur, *A History of Zionism* (New York: Holt, Rinehart, and Winston, 1972), 485; Beth-El game reported in undated newspaper clipping owned by Joe Hockfield.

8. Crisis and Community, 1930 to 1941

1. Gilbert Katz, interview with author, Sept. 1, 1986.
2. "Phillip Cohen, Peddler," Federal Writer's Project Interview with author, Dec. 1, 1938, Southern Historical Collection, Wilson Library.
3. *Durham Morning Herald,* Sept. 2, 1934.
4. Gilbert Katz, interview with author, Sept. 23, 1986.
5. "Phillip Cohen, Peddler," 8.
6. Levitt, "Occupational Distribution," 26, 47–48; U.S. Bureau of the Census, *Sixteenth Census of the United States: 1940; Population, North Carolina,* vol. 2, part 5, *Characteristics of the Population* (Washington, D.C., 1943), 399.
7. Mattie Lehman Goldberg Papers.
8. Levitt, "Occupational Distribution," 47.
9. *Durham, North Carolina, Directory, 1911–1912.*
10. Goren, "Jews," 589.
11. Wilson Gee, "The 'Drag' of Talent Out of the South," *Social Forces* 15 (March 1937):343; "President's Report," *North Carolina Association of Jewish Women Yearbook, 1935–1936,* 13–16.
12. *Durham Morning Herald,* Feb. 27, 1938.
13. Henry Feingold, *A Time for Searching: Entering the Mainstream, 1920–1945* (Baltimore: Johns Hopkins University Press, 1992), 14; Marcia Synnott, "Anti-Semitism and American Universities: Did Quotas Follow the Jews?" in *Anti-Semitism in American History,* ed. David Gerber (Urbana: University of Illinois Press, 1986), 246.
14. "Jewish Students at Duke University Undergraduate Schools, 1930–1936" and "Jewish Students at Duke University Medical School, 1930–1936"; typescripts held by the Duke Archives.
15. Quoted in Edward Halperin, "Frank Porter Graham, Isaac Hall Manning, and the Jewish Quota at the University of North Carolina Medical School," *North Carolina Historical Review* 67, no. 4 (Oct. 1990):394–95.
16. Halperin, "Frank Porter Graham," 393–94.
17. Otto Steinreich, "For the Record," *North Carolina Medical Journal* 8, no. 53 (Aug. 1992):392.
18. Warren Ashby, *Frank Porter Graham: A Southern Liberal* (Winston-Salem: Blair, 1980), 128–29; quoted in Halperin, "Frank Porter Graham," 393–94; Samuel Newman, "Frank Porter Graham: An Appreciation," *American Jewish Times* (May 1972):9.
19. Bland Simpson, "His Way from the Start," *Carolina Alumni Review* 83, no. 2 (summer 1994):38; W. C. George, letter to Frank Graham, Sept. 30, 1933,

Southern Historical Collection; Kemp Battle, letter to Frank P. Graham, Nov. 17, 1936, Southern Historical Collection.

20. Richard Adler, *You Gotta Have Heart* (New York: Donald and Fine, 1990), 137.

21. Leonard Rubin, "On a Southern Campus: The Jewish Boy's Problem," *American Jewish Times* (April 1938):30–31, 70.

22. Ibid., 31, 70.

23. Ibid., 70; *North Carolina Association of Jewish Women Yearbook, 1935–1936,* 51–53; The NCAJW figures contrast with those of Rubin's survey, which show northern Jews to be the majority.

24. Ben Patrick, *The Front Line: Materials for a Study of Leadership in College and After* (Durham: Duke University, 1942), 108, 116; Evans, *Provincials,* 86; "The Resurgence of TEP at Chapel Hill," *American Jewish Times* (July 1947):6–7; Alvan Duerr, *Baird's Manual of American College Fraternities* (Menasha, Wis.: Collegiate Press, 1940), 252–54.

25. *North Carolina Association of Jewish Women Yearbook, 1935–1936,* 51–53.

26. Ibid.

27. *American Jewish Yearbook, 1936–1937* (Philadelphia: Jewish Publication Society, 1937), 19.

28. I. H. Jacobson, "Hillel and the Jewish Student," *North Carolina Association of Jewish Women Yearbook, 1937–1938* (Greensboro: NCAJW, 1938), 44; Herbert Goldberg and Horace Richter, "Hillel and the Jewish Fraternity," *American Jewish Times* (June 1938):2–3, 11; "Durham, N.C.," *American Jewish Times* (Sept. 1939):10; Rubin, "On a Southern Campus," 31.

29. *Daily Tar Heel,* Sept. 18, 26, 1936.

30. Quoted in Synnott, "Anti-Semitism and American Universities," 263.

31. Durden, *Dukes of Durham,* 222; Leon Dworsky, interview with author, Jan. 5, 1987.

32. *Charlotte Observer,* Dec. 7, 1939 (quotation); *Durham Morning Herald,* Nov. 23, 1941; "Durham, N.C.," *American Jewish Times* (Dec. 1939):23.

33. *Register of the Faculty of the University of North Carolina, 1795–1945,* North Carolina Collection.

34. Edward R. Murrow, letter to William Preston Few, Jan. 1934, Perkins Library; "Durham, N.C.," *American Jewish Times* (June 1938):5, 7.

35. Edward Bernstein, "Welcoming New Arrivals to Chapel Hill," in *They Fled Hitler's Germany and Found Refuge in North Carolina,* ed. Henry Landsberger and Christoph Schweitzer (Chapel Hill: Academic Affairs Library, 1996), 52.

36. Arthrell Sanders, "Former NCCU Prof Recounts Odyssey," *North Carolina Central University Newsletter* 1 (fall 1984):3, 5.

37. *St. Louis Dispatch,* Dec. 19, 1948.

38. Battle, letter to Graham, Nov. 17, 1936; for discussion of exception mecha-

nism, see John Dean, "Jewish Participation in Middle-Sized Communi-ties," in *The Jews: Social Patterns of an American Group,* ed. Marshall Sklare (Glencoe, Ill.: Free Press, 1958), 314–16, and Peter Rose, *Strangers in Their Midst: Small-town Jews and Their Neighbors* (Merrick, N.Y.: Richwood Pub-lishing, 1977), 77.

39. Leonard Huggins, *Anecdotes* (Chapel Hill: n.p., 1981), 264.

40. For southern attitudes on the war, see Alfred Hero, Jr., *The Southerner and World Affairs* (Baton Rouge: Louisiana State University Press, 1965), 92; Julian Pleasants, "The Senatorial Career of Robert Rice Reynolds, 1933–1945" (Ph.D. diss., University of North Carolina, 1971), 465–66, 494, 496–97, 545 (Reynolds quotations).

41. Pleasants, "Senatorial Career of Robert Price Reynolds," 575; Robert Reynolds, "Threats to America become Realities," Jan. 18, 1940, speech to Carolina Political Union, typescript, North Carolina Collection; *Durham Morning Herald,* Nov. 10, 11, 1943.

42. David Wyman, *The Abandonment of the Jews* (New York: Pantheon, 1986), 217; Frank Porter Graham Papers, Southern Historical Collection, May 30, 1946; Samuel Newman, "Frank Porter Graham," *American Jewish Times Outlook* (May 1972):8.

43. "Durham, N.C.," *American Jewish Times* (March 1943):24 (quotation); *North Carolina Association of Jewish Women Yearbook, 1934–1935* (Greens-boro: NCAJW, 1935), 14; *North Carolina Association of Jewish Women Year-book, 1936–1937* (Greensboro: NCAJW, 1937), 14–15; *Durham Morning Herald,* May 23, 1938.

44. *Durham Morning Herald,* May 27, 1939; Evans Papers, July 10, 1940, Perkins Library.

45. Henry Feingold, *Bearing Witness: How America and Its Jews Responded to the Holocaust* (Syracuse: Syracuse University Press, 1995), 213, 173, 229, 231, 247.

46. Henry Bane, interview with Robin Gruber, Nov. 19, 1985.

47. Dula, *Durham and Her People,* 163; *Durham Morning Herald,* Feb. 26, 1938; Lehman Brady, telephone interview with author, Oct. 1, 1986. Meyer was a native North Carolinian of German origin, but he had married into an East European family and strongly identified with the Jewish community.

48. Weare, *Black Business in the New South,* 81, 120; Anderson, *Durham County,* 324; *Report of the Building Committee;* George Schuyler to Walter White, Dec. 22, 1935, NAACP Papers, II L 7, Library of Congress, Washington, D.C.

49. *Carolina Times,* Jan. 22, 1938.

50. "John Rogers, Produce Truck Driver of Chapel Hill," interview by Leonard Rapport, Federal Writers Project, Sept. 19, 1938.

51. William Levitt, telephone interview with author, Dec. 11, 1991; Martha

Holland, "Sidney Rittenberg: An American Perspective of China" (master's thesis, University of North Carolina, 1986), 5; William Levitt, telephone interview with author.

52. Gurock, "The Orthodox Synagogue," 52.

53. George and Ricky Lewin, interview with Robin Gruber, Jan. 29, 1986; May Ornoff, interview with Mollie Fridovich, April 1, 1986.

54. Gurock, "The Orthodox Synagogue," 62.

55. Benjamin Kaplan, *The Eternal Stranger: A Study of Jewish Life in the Small Community* (New York: Bookman, 1957), 96–98; quoted in Robin Gruber, "From Pine Street to Watts Street: An Oral History of the Jews of Durham, North Carolina," Oral History Seminar of Dr. Lawrence Goodwyn and Dr. Eric Meyers, Duke University Archives, 42.

56. Mattie Lehman Goldberg Papers, 1943.

57. *Durham Israelite,* Feb. 1940; letter from Miriam Weil, Feb. 1910, Weil Papers, North Carolina State Archives.

58. Mattie Lehman Goldberg Papers; William Toll, *The Making of an Ethnic Middle Class: Portland Jewry over Four Generations* (Albany: SUNY Press, 1982), 52–55.

59. Jack Wertheimer, "The Conservative Synagogue," in *The American Synagogue,* 117; for "Orthodoxy in the South," see Jeffrey Gurock, *American Jewish Orthodoxy in Historical Perspective* (Hoboken, N.J.: KTAV, 1996), 94–95.

60. *Durham Morning Herald,* May 1, 1934; "Durham, N.C.," *American Jewish Times* (Sept. 1937), 85.

61. Nathan Glazer, *American Judaism* (Chicago: University of Chicago Press, 1957), 105; Ladies Aid Society Minutes, Nov. 3, 1937, Perkins Library.

62. Glazer, *American Judaism,* 114.

63. *North Carolina Association of Jewish Women Yearbook, 1936–1937,* 10; Edwards, *History of the North Carolina Association of Jewish Women,* 17.

64. "Durham, N.C.," *American Jewish Times* (Dec. 1940):16; Dula, *Durham and Her People,* 163.

65. *Durham Morning Herald,* May 25, 1938.

66. For the United Palestine Appeals, see "Durham, N.C.," *American Jewish Times* (Jan. 1938):14; "Durham, N.C.," *American Jewish Times* (May 1938):5; Charles Silberman, *A Certain People: American Jews and their Lives Today* (New York: Summit, 1985), 187.

9. War, Holocaust, and Zion, 1940s to 1950s

1. *Durham Sun,* June 13, 1943.

2. David Goldfield, *Promised Land: The South since 1945* (Arlington Heights, Ill.: Harlan Davidson, 1987), 5–8.

3. "Durham, N.C.," *American Jewish Times* (Jan. 1944):42; "Durham, N.C.,"

American Jewish Times (Aug. 1944):7 (first quotation); "Durham, N.C.," *American Jewish Times* (April 1942):26; "Durham, N.C.," *American Jewish Times* (May 1943):16 (second quotation).

4. "Durham, N.C.," *American Jewish Times* (Oct. 1944):25; "Camp Butner, N.C.," *American Jewish Times* (April 1945):23.

5. Arthur Goldberg, "Report from the Campus," *American Jewish Times* (June 1944):11; Louis Harris, "Kiddush at Chapel Hill," *American Jewish Times* (April 1940):26; *Durham Morning Herald,* Nov. 22, 1944; "Hillel-Jewish War Board Cooperation," *American Jewish Times* (Oct. 1944):50.

6. Paul Ritterband and Harold Wechsler, *Jewish Learning in American Universities* (Bloomington: Indiana University Press, 1994), 127–28.

7. Harvie Branscomb, "A Note on Establishing Chairs of Jewish Studies," in *The Teaching of Judaica in American Universities,* ed. Leon Jick (Waltham, Mass.: Association for Jewish Studies, 1970), 97–98.

8. Ritterband and Wechsler, *Jewish Learning in American Universities,* 127–28.

9. "Durham, N.C.," *American Jewish Times* (March 1943):24.

10. Gilbert Katz, interview with Robin Gruber, Jan. 25, 1986; quoted in Cheryl Greenberg, "The Southern Jewish Community and the Struggle for Civil Rights," in *African-Americans and Jews in the Twentieth Century: Studies in Convergence and Conflict,* ed. V. P. Franklin et al. (Columbia: University of Missouri Press, 1998), 131.

11. W. C. Dula, *Durham and Her People,* 163.

12. Bonnie Wexler, "Seek a Real Cure," *Carolina Alumni Review* 86, no. 5 (Sept./Oct. 1997):23.

13. Feingold, *Bearing Witness,* 272–73.

14. "Durham, N.C.," *American Jewish Times* (April 1943):55; "Durham, N.C.," *American Jewish Times* (May 1948):43.

15. "Durham, N.C.," *American Jewish Times* (April 1947):55.

16. "Durham, N.C.," *American Jewish Times* (April 1947):17; *Raleigh News and Observer,* May 30, 1944.

17. "Our First Twenty-Five Years," *Durham Hadassah Yearbook, 1951* (Durham: N.p., 1951), n.p.; Eli Evans, interview with Robin Gruber, March 9, 1986; Evans, *Provincials,* 111, 113; *Durham Morning Herald,* March 24, 1986; *Durham Sun,* March 24, 1986; "Durham, N.C.," *American Jewish Times* (May 1938):5; "Durham, N.C.," *American Jewish Times* (April 1940):23; "Durham, N.C.," *American Jewish Times* (May 1938), 5; "Durham, N.C.," *American Jewish Times* (April 1946):16.

18. "Durham, N.C.," *American Jewish Times* (Jan. 1946); *Raleigh News and Observer,* March 19, 1948; *Durham Hadassah Yearbook, 1948–1949* (Durham, 1948), n.p.

19. "Durham, N.C.," *American Jewish Times* (Feb. 1940):22; "Durham, N.C.," *American Jewish Times* (June 1949):21–22 (quotation); "Durham, N.C.,"

American Jewish Times (May 1953):34–36; *Durham Morning Herald,* June 14, 1943; "Durham, N.C.," *American Jewish Times* (Nov. 1951):24.

20. "Chapel Hill, N.C.," *American Jewish Times* (Sept. 1947):79 (Jackman quotations); "Durham, N.C.," *American Jewish Times* (Jan. 1949):36 (Lowenstein quotation); "Durham, N.C.," *American Jewish Times* (June 1949):34.

21. Simon Glustrom, telephone interview with author, July 12, 1992 (first quotation); *American Jewish Times* (Sept. 1949):57 (second quotation); Leon Dworsky, interview with author, Jan. 5, 1987.

22. Leon Dworsky, interview with author; Henry Bane interview with Robin Gruber, Nov. 19, 1985.

23. Weissbach, "East European Immigrants," 248; Melvin Urofsky, *Commonwealth and Community: The Jewish Experience in Virginia* (Richmond: Virginia Historical Society, 1997), 164–66; Selma Lewis, *A Biblical People in the Bible Belt: The Jewish Community of Memphis, Tennessee, 1840s–1960s* (Macon: Mercer University Press, 1998), 175–76.

24. Molly Freedman, "Durham, N.C.," *American Jewish Times Outlook* (June 1953):47–49; Leon Dworsky, interview with Robin Gruber, Nov. 6, 1985.

25. Roberta Rosenberg Farber and Chaim Waxman, *Jews in America: A Contemporary Reader* (Hanover, N.H.: Brandeis University Press, 1999), 303. Sociologist Herbert Gans identifies a "symbolic ethnicity"; "Durham, N.C.," *American Jewish Times* (March 1953):29–30; Ira Eisenstein and Judith Kaplan Eisenstein, *What Is Torah: A Cantata for Uni-Chorus and Piano* (New York: Jewish Reconstructionist Foundation, 1942).

26. Beth-El Congregation Minutes, Sept. 5, 1943, May 9, 14, 1944, Perkins Library. Meat concession debated Feb. 14, 1946.

27. Beth-El Congregation Minutes, Feb. 14, 1946.

28. Evans, *Provincials,* 117–18.

29. "Durham, N.C.," *American Jewish Times* (Dec. 1948):18; "Durham, N.C.," *American Jewish Times* (Jan. 1949):22.

30. Eli Evans, interview with Robin Gruber, March 9, 1986.

31. Beth-El Congregation Minutes, 1948.

32. Beth-El Congregation Minutes, Feb. 28, 1950; "Durham N.C.," *American Jewish Times* (Dec. 1948):18.

33. Beth-El Congregation Minutes, Nov. 10, 1949.

34. Beth-El Congregation Minutes, Feb. 28, 1950.

35. Beth-El Congregation Minutes, July 6, 1950; Simon Glustrom, letter to author, May 13, n.y.

36. Beth-El Congregation Minutes, 1948.

37. Beth-El Synagogue Building Committee Report, 1961; Beth-El Congregation Minutes, 1950.

38. Beth-El Congregation Minutes, June 28, 1950.

39. "Jewish Communities in the South: Durham, N.C.," *American Jewish Times* (Aug. 1944):7.

10. **Breaking the Boundaries, 1950s to 1960s**
1. Anderson, *Durham County,* 400.
2. Arthur Hertzberg, *The Jews in America: Four Centuries of an Uneasy Encounter* (New York: Simon and Schuster, 1989), 311; Beth-El Sisterhood Membership Lists, 1958, 1964, Perkins Library.
3. Mark Margolis and Norman Margolis, interview with author, April 30, 1992.
4. Dean, "Jewish Participation," 314–16.
5. Evans, *Provincials,* 117.
6. Evans, *Provincials,* 196–98; Art Shain, interview with Myrna Schwartz, n.d.
7. Jonathan Yardley, "An Interview with Jonathan Yardley," *Carolina Alumni Review* 7, no. 82 (summer 1989):40–41; Wade Smith, "A Memorial Service for Allard Kenneth Lowenstein, Class of 1949," 22, typescript, North Carolina Collection.
8. Abe Stadiem, interview with author, April 8, 1992.
9. Richard Cummings, *The Pied Piper: Allard K. Lowenstein and the Liberal Dream* (New York: Grove Press, 1985), 19–20.
10. Molly Freedman, interview with Naomi Kirshner, April 1, n.y.; Mrs. Sam Freedman, "Durham, N.C.," *American Jewish Times Outlook* (Jan. 1960):12, 41.
11. "Durham, N.C.," *American Jewish Times* (Oct. 1944):10.
12. Hannah Lieberman, "Durham, N.C.," *American Jewish Times* (April 1949):10; "Chapel Hill, N.C.," *American Jewish Times Outlook* (Nov. 1952):52.
13. Joseph Straley, conversation with author, Sept. 19, 1988.
14. Junius Scales and Richard Nickson, *Cause at Heart* (Athens: University of Georgia Press, 1987), 122; *Durham Morning Herald,* April 15, 1955.
15. Herbert Berger, *Report of the Building Committee of Beth-El Congregation* (Durham: Beth-El, 1961), n.p.
16. Judea Reform presidents, interview with Sheldon Hanft and author, July 31, 1986.
17. Rose, *Strangers in their Midst,* 76 (first quotation); Mrs. Sam Freedman, "Durham, N.C.," *American Jewish Times Outlook* (April 1961):10, 58 (second quotation); "Durham, N.C.," *American Jewish Times Outlook* (April 1953):77; *Beth-El Bulletin,* March 24, 1962.
18. Samuel Perlman, "Hillel at the University of North Carolina," *American Jewish Times* (Sept. 1949):7; Efraim Rosenzweig, "Hillel at Chapel Hill,"

American Jewish Times Outlook (March 1955):6; Joseph Levine, "Hillel in North Carolina," *American Jewish Times Outlook* (Dec. 1962):36, (May 1963):19.

19. Mrs. Sam Freedman, "Durham, N.C.," *American Jewish Times Outlook* (May 1960):8, 33; "Durham, N.C.," *American Jewish Times Outlook* (Jan. 1971), 10, 15–16; Melvin Shimm, interview with author, Dec. 15, 1986.

20. Anderson, *Durham County,* 398.

21. Dula, *Durham and Her People,* 289.

22. *Durham Morning Herald,* June 1, 1952.

23. Evans, *Provincials,* 6; Eli Evans, *The Lonely Days Were Sundays: Reflections of a Jewish Southerner* (Jackson: University of Mississippi Press, 1993), xxi.

24. *Durham Morning Herald,* May 7, 1951; for "Palestinian songs," see "Durham, N.C.," *American Jewish Times* (Jan. 1949):36.

25. *Durham Morning Herald,* June 1, 1952; E. J. Evans, "Dear Voter" letter, May 1957, Evans Family Papers, Perkins Library; *Durham Morning Herald,* May 19, 1957.

26. *Public Appeal,* March 1, 1961; *Public Appeal,* March 28, 1962; Evans, *Provincials,* 11.

27. Arthur Hertzberg, *The Jews in America: Four Centuries of an Uneasy Encounter* (New York: Simon and Schuster, 1989), 348.

28. Mark Bauman and Berkley Kalin, eds., *The Quiet Voices: Southern Rabbis and Black Civil Rights, 1880s to 1990s* (Tuscaloosa: University of Alabama Press, 1997), 15; Anderson, *Durham County,* 434–41; Harry Golden, "The Golden Vertical Plan," *New South* 11, no. 11 (Nov. 1956):12; Mary Mebane, *Mary* (New York: Fawcett, 1981), 220.

29. Quoted in Gruber, "From Pine Street to Watts Street."

30. Dwight Yarborough, telephone interview with author; quoted in Gruber, "From Pine Street to Watts Street," 49; Abe Stadiem, interview with author, April 8, 1992; Barry Yeoman, "Landlord Hall of Shame," *Independent,* May 30, 1991, 9; *Hashomer* 1, no. 2 (May 20, 1970).

31. Ruth and Rashi Fein, telephone interview with author, April 27, 1995.

32. Leon Dworsky, telephone interview with author.

33. "Resolutions of the North Carolina Association of Rabbis," *American Jewish Times Outlook* (Dec. 1955):31.

34. Louis Tuchman, letter to Jacob Rader Marcus, March 26, 1957; Bauman and Kalin, eds., *Quiet Voices,* 5.

35. Mrs. Sam Freedman, "Durham, N.C.," *American Jewish Times Outlook* (May 1956):13–14; "Durham, N.C.," *American Jewish Times Outlook* (Dec. 1960):17; *Durham Morning Herald,* May 2, 1963.

36. William Snider, *Light on the Hill: A History of the University of North Carolina at Chapel Hill* (Chapel Hill: University of North Carolina Press,

1992), 246–49; Douglas Knight, *Street of Dreams* (Durham: Duke University Press, 1989), 97, 99.

37. Patricia LaPointe, "The Prophetic Voice: Rabbi James A. Wax," in *Quiet Voices,* 162.

38. E. J. Evans, "The Jewish Experience in Durham and Chapel Hill: Conversations with Long-Time Residents," Joel Schwartz, moderator, Sept. 27, 1987, Perkins Library.

39. Greenberg, "Southern Jewish Community," 151.

40. Mrs. Sam Freedman, "Durham, N.C.," *American Jewish Times Outlook* (May 1956):13–14; "Durham, N.C.," *American Jewish Times Outlook* (Dec. 1960), 17.

41. Bob Brown and Roy Pattishall, "The Trouble with Harry's," *Spectator,* Aug. 7, 1986, 5; *Daily Tar Heel,* March 26, 1957; *Durham Morning Herald,* April 2, 1964.

42. Rashi Fein, telephone interview with author; Rosemary Ezra, telephone interview with author; William Chafe, *Never Stop Running: Allard Lowenstein and the Struggle to Save American Liberalism* (New York: Basic Books, 1993), 29; *Public Appeal,* April 20, 1960.

43. John Ehle, *The Free Men* (New York: Harper and Row, 1965), 276, 287 (Tieger quotations); see also *Durham Morning Herald,* April 2, 1964; David Schwartz, "U.S. Senate Gains a Controversial Voice," *Carolina Alumni Review* 80, no. 2 (summer 1991): 30.

44. Marc Lee Raphael, *Profiles in American Judaism: The Reform, Conservative, Orthodox, and Reconstructionist Traditions in Historical Perspective* (San Francisco: Harper and Row, 1984), 72; Hertzberg, *Jews in America,* 323.

45. "Durham, N.C.," *American Jewish Times Outlook* (July 1958):52–53.

46. Molly Freedman, interview with Naomi Kirschner, April 1, n.y.; "Chapel Hill, N.C.," *American Jewish Times Outlook* (June 1952):53.

47. Beryl Slome, telephone interview with author, Dec. 30, 1986.

48. "Chapel Hill, N.C.," *American Jewish Times Outlook* (June 1953):50; *Carolina Handbook, 1959–1960* (Chapel Hill: YMCA, 1959), 139.

49. Hertzberg, *Jews in America,* 323, 332–38; Whitfield, *In Search of American Jewish Culture,* 204.

50. *Report of Building Committee of the Beth-El Congregation* (Durham: Beth-El, 1961).

51. Molly Freedman, "Know Your House of Worship," *Report of the Building Committee of the Beth-El Congregation* (Durham: Beth-El, 1961).

52. Leon Dworsky, interview with Robin Gruber, Nov. 5, 1985.

53. Joe Hockfield, telephone interview with author, Nov. 9, 1988.

54. Louis Tuchman, "A Traditional Rabbi's View: The New Kesuba," *American Jewish Times Outlook* (April 1955):15, 23.

55. *Beth-El Bulletin,* March 24, 1962.

56. *Beth-El Bulletin,* March 24, 1962.

57. "Durham, N.C.," *American Jewish Times Outlook* (July 1952):22; Beth-El Confirmation Exam, May 29, 1960, Perkins Library.

58. *Beth-El Bulletin,* Oct. 1990; *Mahrud,* 1954 (Durham Young Judea student newspaper); Robert Schultz, telephone interview with author, Oct. 5, 1992.

59. Raphael, *Profiles in American Judaism,* 71, 197–98.

60. Judea Reform Congregation, *Shalom* (n.p., n.d.), 1, 8.

61. Steve Sharot, *Judaism: A Sociology* (New York: Holmes and Meier, 1976), 164.

11. Sunbelt Jews, 1960s to 1990s

1. Randall Miller, "The Development of the Modern Urban South: An Historical Overview," in *Shades of the Sunbelt: Essays on Ethnicity, Race and the Urban South,* ed. Randall Miller and George Pozzetta (Westport, Conn.: Greenwood Press, 1988), 2; Barry Kosmin et al., *Highlights of the CJF 1990 National Jewish Population Survey* (New York: Council of Jewish Federations, 1991), 25.

2. Barry Kosmin, Paul Ritterband, and Jeffrey Scheckner, "Jewish Population in the United States," *American Jewish Year Book, 1987,* ed. David Singer (Philadelphia: Jewish Publication Society, 1987), 170.

3. *Raleigh News and Observer,* Feb. 21, Oct. 11, 1991; Powell, *North Carolina,* 528.

4. *Raleigh News and Observer,* Oct. 11, 1991.

5. Marcus, *To Count a People,* 49–50; Kosmin, Ritterband, and Scheckner, "Jewish Population in the United States," 169.

6. George Fishman, "Retirement Planning Survey," fall 1991, 16, Durham–Chapel Hill Jewish Federation, Perkins Library.

7. Beth-El Sisterhood Membership Lists, 1959, 1964; Sidney Goldstein, "Profile of American Jewry: Insights from the 1990 National Jewish Population Survey," *American Jewish Year Book, 1992,* ed. David Singer and Ruth Selden (Philadelphia: Jewish Publication Society, 1992), 102; Fishman, "Retirement Planning Survey," 2, 52.

8. Calvin Goldscheider, *Jewish Continuity and Change: Emerging Patterns in America* (Bloomington: Indiana University Press, 1986), 180.

9. "Population Characteristics," *Metropolitan Statistical Area: Raleigh–Durham–Chapel Hill, 1990,* Greater Durham Chamber of Commerce, Chapel Hill Public Library.

10. Karp, *Haven and Home,* 310; Judea Reform Congregation, Nov. 8, 1986, typescript, Perkins Library.

11. *Chapel Hill Newspaper,* March 6, 1992.

12. Fishman, "Retirement Planning Survey," 11; "Population Characteristics."

13. Michael Winerip, "Hot Colleges," *New York Times Magazine,* Nov. 18,

1984. Statistics derive from surveys by the University of California at the UNC Office of Institutional Research.

14. *Chapel Hill Herald,* June 19, 1991; *Chapel Hill Newspaper,* Nov. 25, 27, 1985; Patrick O'Neill, "Climb for the Summit," *Chapel Hill Newspaper,* June 7, 1992.

15. *Chronicle,* Nov. 5, 1991.

16. "Holocaust Revisionism: Protest and Response at Duke," Perkins Library.

17. "An Open Letter to the *Chronicle,*" *Chronicle,* Nov. 15, 1991; "The History Department Responds to Holocaust Ad," *Chronicle,* Nov. 13, 1992.

18. Silberman, *A Certain People,* 226; Berel Lang, "Jewish Culture," *American Jewish Year Book, 1998* (New York: American Jewish Committee, 1998), 151.

19. Jackie Hershkowitz, "Soviet Jews Flee Homeland for Chapel Hill Hospitality," *Daily Tar Heel,* Jan. 28, 1982.

20. Adler, *You Gotta Have Heart,* 343–44.

21. Arthur Marks, interview with author, April 16, 1992 (first quotation); Louis D. Rubin, Jr., *A Gallery of Southerners* (Baton Rouge: Louisiana State University Press, 1982), xii (second quotation); Louis D. Rubin, Jr., *The Golden Weather* (New York: Atheneum, 1961), 22–23 (third and fourth quotations).

22. Alice Kaplan, *French Lessons* (Chicago: University of Chicago Press, 1993), 12–14 (first quotation); Eve Kosofsky Sedgwick, *Fat Art, Thin Art* (Durham: Duke University Press, 1994), 3 (second quotation); Eve Kosofsky Sedgwick, *The Epistemology of the Closet* (Berkeley and Los Angeles: University of California Press, 1990), 72, 63 (third and fourth quotations).

23. John Shelton Reed, *One South: An Ethnic Approach to Regional Culture* (Baton Rouge: Louisiana State University Press, 1982), 136 (quotation); Abraham Lavender, "Jewish Values in the Southern Milieu," in *"Turn to the South,"* 130; John Shelton Reed, "Instant Grits and Plastic-Wrapped Crackers: Southern Culture and Regional Development," in *The American South: Portrait of a Culture,* ed. Louis D. Rubin, Jr. (Baton Rouge: Louisiana State University Press, 1980), 32–33.

24. Evans, *Provincials,* 196–98; Tandy Solomon, "Being Jewish at Duke: The Sizeable Minority," *Chronicle,* Feb. 16, 1983.

25. *Durham Morning Herald,* Dec. 16, 1986; *Chapel Hill Weekly,* Aug. 3, 1961; *Raleigh News and Observer,* July 7, 1986; Brown and Pattishall, "The Trouble with Harry's," 5, 7, 8.

26. Evans, *The Lonely Days Were Sundays,* 332.

27. Steve Schewel, "Biscuits and Blintzes: Growing Up Jewish in the Fatback South," *Durham Independent,* Oct. 7, 1992, 10–11.

28. Reed, "Instant Grits," 36; "The Best Places to Live in America," *Money,* September 1994, 126–30.

29. *Judea Reform Today* (Feb. 1992).

30. Carolyn Walker-Lipson, *"Shalom Y'All": The Folklore and Culture of Southern Jews* (Ann Arbor, Mich.: University Microfilms International, 1986), 118; for statistics on affiliation, see Reed, *One South,* 111. The data exclude Florida. Reed, "Instant Grits," 34; for 1990 statistics, see Kosmin et al., *Highlights of the CJF 1990 National Jewish Population Survey,* 37.

31. Lore Dickstein, "Southern Discomfort," *Tikkun* 5, no. 6 (Nov./Dec. 1990):25, 106.

32. John Shelton Reed, "Whistlin' Dixie," *Spectator,* April 12, 1992, 8; Green, *Paul Green's Wordbook,* 604; Leonard Fein, *Where Are We?* (New York: Harper and Row, 1988), 148; Arthur Marks, interview with author, April 16, 1992.

33. Eva Salber, *The Mind Is Not the Heart: Recollections of a Woman Physician* (Durham: Duke University Press, 1989), 222.

34. Solomon, "Being Jewish at Duke."

35. Stephen Steinberg, *The Ethnic Myth: Race, Ethnicity, and Class in America* (Boston: Beacon, 1981), 254; *Raleigh News and Observer,* April 30, 1992; David Kessel, "Integrate or Isolate," *Jewish Tarheel* (spring 1992):3.

36. Chapel Hill–Carrboro Public Schools Multi-Cultural Education Policy, Chapel Hill Public Library.

37. Durham–Chapel Hill Jewish Federation Community Relations Council Minutes, March 1981, Dec., 13, 1982, Perkins Library.

38. Community Relations Council Minutes, Feb. 17, 1981, Perkins Library.

39. Salber, *The Mind Is Not the Heart,* 222.

40. John Friedman, interview with Sheldon Hanft and author, July 31, 1986.

41. Paul Luebke, *Tar Heel Politics: Myths and Realities* (Chapel Hill: University of North Carolina Press, 1990), 171.

42. John Shelton Reed, "Ethnicity in the South: Observations on the Acculturation of Southern Jews," in *"Turn to the South,"* 138.

43. Whitfield, *In Search of American Jewish Culture,* 198.

44. Whitfield, *In Search of American Jewish Culture,* 247; Yosef Yerushalmi, *Zakhor: Jewish History and Jewish Memory* (Seattle: University of Washington Press, 1996), 92.

45. William Rudolph, "Our Changing Constituencies," Nov. 12, 1985, typescript; Samuel Heilman, "Judaism at the Turn of the Century" (Judaism at the 21st Century Conference, University of North Carolina at Chapel Hill, Oct. 26, 1997).

46. Stephen Cohen, *American Assimilation or Jewish Survival?* (Bloomington: Indiana University Press, 1988), 1–3; Rabinowitz, *Race, Ethnicity, and Urbanization,* 245.

47. Peter Medding et al., "Jewish Identity in Conversionary and Mixed Marriages," in *American Jewish Yearbook, 1992,* ed. David Singer and Ruth

Seldan (Philadelphia: Jewish Publication Society, 1992), 3 (quotation); Kosmin et al., *Highlights of the CJF 1990 National Jewish Population Survey,* 14; "Alyenu," Feb. 22, 1992, Judea Reform Congregation, Durham; "Raising Children in an Interfaith Marriage," Rachel Cowan, Feb. 23, 1992, Judea Reform Congregation, Durham.

48. 1992 Durham–Chapel Hill Jewish Federation Name and Address List, Durham–Chapel Hill Jewish Federation, Durham.

49. Quoted in Barry Yeoman, "Strangers in a Strange Land," *Independent,* March 10–23, 1988, 8.

50. *Irgun* 1, no. 1 (Pesach 5730); *Hashomer* 1, no. 2 (May 20, 1970). The newspaper's name change may reflect the students' belated recognition that the Irgun was nationalist and militaristic.

51. Charles Silberman, *A Certain People,* 226.

52. *Free Jewish University of North Carolina Catalogue,* fall 1973, Duke Archives, Perkins Library.

53. Karp, *Haven and Home,* 316.

54. "The Individual and the Communal Jew: Getting It All Together," June 22–24, 1973, typescript, Judea Reform Congregation Fifth Shabbaton.

55. Ibid.

56. Charles Liebman, "When Prayer Becomes Leisure," *Forward,* June 11, 1999; "The Individual and the Communal Jew."

57. *PJN Newsletter* (Dec. 1987).

58. *PJN Newsletter* 10 (Nov. 1986):3, 4.

59. Susan Rebecca Brown, "As They See Themselves," in *A Coat of Many Colors,* ed. Abraham Lavender (Westport, Conn.: Greenwood Press, 1971), 31–34.

60. *Durham–Chapel Hill Jewish Federation and Community Council Constitution, Draft II,* June 1979, Durham–Chapel Hill Jewish Federation, Durham; "Minutes," Sept. 1, 1977, Durham–Chapel Hill Jewish Federation and Community Council.

61. Harold Strauss, "Minutes," Jan. 8, 1981, Sept. 15, 1983, March 10, 1988, Durham–Chapel Hill Jewish Federation.

62. "The Durham–Chapel Hill Jewish Federation 1999 Information Packet," Durham–Chapel Hill Jewish Federation.

63. "Minutes," March 10, 1988, Durham–Chapel Hill Jewish Federation Board Meeting.

64. Melvin Shimm, Beth-El Presidents Forum, Sept. 14, 1986.

65. Melvin Shimm, Beth-El Presidents Forum, Sept. 14, 1986.

66. *Raleigh News and Observer,* Sept. 20, 1987; Melvin Shimm, Beth-El Presidents Forum, Sept. 14, 1986.

67. Beth-El Synagogue Handbook, Perkins Library; Lior Moriel, "Two-tiered Temple," *Spectator,* Sept. 24, 1987, 35–38.

68. Abraham Karp, "Overview: The Synagogue in America—A Historical Typology," in *The American Synagogue,* 28.
69. Jick, "The Reform Synagogue," 105–6.
70. Efraim Rosenzweig, "Dedication of New Building: Judea Reform Congregation, Durham," *American Jewish Times Outlook* (July 1971):6.
71. Sharot, *Judaism,* 164.
72. Rosenzweig, "Dedication of New Building," 6.
73. "Groundbreaking Service, Mel and Zora Rashkis Wing, Judea Reform Congregation," typed manuscript, Judea Reform Congregation, Durham.
74. "Judea Reform Congregation," 1987, brochure, Judea Reform Congregation.
75. Max and Isabel Samfield, Judea Reform Presidents Forum, n.d.
76. *Chapel Hill Newspaper,* Nov., 11, 1984.
77. John Friedman, "From the Rabbi," *Judea Reform Today* (August 1990); Peter Adland, "From the President," *Judea Reform Today* (May 1992).
78. *Beth-El Bulletin* (August 1980).
79. *Judea Reform Today* (Jan. 1997); *Beth-El Bulletin* (March 1997).
80. Minutes of the Durham–Chapel Hill Jewish Community Day School Steering Committee, Sept. 23, 1992, Jewish Community Day School, Durham; Durham–Chapel Hill Jewish Community Day School Mission and Goals Statement, Jewish Community Day School, Durham; *The Jewish Community Day School of Durham/Chapel Hill Report Card* (spring 1999), 1; *Raleigh News and Observer,* Nov. 9, 1998.
81. "The Jewish Community Day School: Capital Campaign," booklet, Perkins Library; *Raleigh News and Observer,* Nov. 9, 1998.

12. **Conclusion: Exiles at Home**
   1. Robert Alter, "The Jew Who Didn't Get Away: On the Possibility of an American Jewish Culture," in *American Jewish Experience,* 269; Stephen Whitfield, "The Braided Identity of Southern Jewry," *American Jewish History* 77, no. 3 (March 1988):363; Reed, *One South,* 111; Walker-Lipson, *Shalom Y'All,* 152.
   2. Whitfield, *In Search of American Jewish Culture,* 31.
   3. Reed, *One South,* 111.
   4. *Durham Morning Herald,* March 20, 1927.
   5. Feingold, *Bearing Witness,* 253.
   6. Bauman, *Southerner as American,* 5, 18.
   7. John S. Reed, "South Polls: Where Is the South?" *Southern Cultures* 5, no. 2 (summer 1999):118.

Glossary

bet hamidrash/Beit HaMidrash	house of study
beth din	rabbinic court
bimah	altar
chai	Hebrew for "life"; related to eighteenth Hebrew letter
chavura	fellowship group; variant spelling
chazzan	cantor
chevra	society or "fellowship of cronies"
Chevra Kadisha	Holy Brotherhood
chometz	leaven
Deitchen	German Jews
Eretz Yisrael	Land of Israel
etrog	citron
get	divorce
Hachnoses Orchim	Welcoming Society
haggadah	Passover prayer manual
halacha	Jewish law
halutzim	Zionist pioneers
haskalah	Jewish enlightenment
havurah (havurot)	fellowship group(s)
kaporos	Yom Kippur expiation rite with rooster as scapegoat
kashruth	observance of dietary laws
kehillah	community
ketubah	marriage contract
kiddush	sanctifying prayer over wine
landsleit	homeland folk
landsmanshaftn	societies of countrymen
latkes	traditional pancakes
lulav	palm leaf

mehitzah	women's partition
mensch	morally responsible man
mezzuzah (mezzuzot)	doorpost plaque(s) containing prayers on parchment
mikva	ritual bath
mitzvah (mitzvot)	good deed(s)
mohel	ritual circumciser
numerus clausus	quota
oneg	joyful reception
rebbetzin	rabbi's wife
schnorrer	beggar
schochet	ritual slaughterer
semicha	rabbinic ordination
Shehechiyanu	blessing of thanksgiving
shofar	ram's horn
shtibel	small synagogue in rented room or store
shvartzers	black people (Yiddish slang)
siddur	Sabbath prayer book
sukkah/Succoth	tabernacle/Tabernacles
tallesim	prayer shawls
tefillin	phylacteries
tikkun olam	"repairing the world"
treyf	unkosher
tzedakah	charity
tzim-tzim	"gathering the sparks of divinity"
tzitzis	ritual fringes
Yiddishkeit	ethnic Jewishness
zadic	righteous one

Bibliography

Books, Journal Articles, and Unpublished Works

Abernethy, Arthur. *The Jew a Negro.* Moravian Falls, N.C.: Dixie Publishing, 1910.

Adland, Peter. "From the President." *Judea Reform Today* (May 1992).

Adler, Richard. *You Gotta Have Heart.* New York: Donald and Fine, 1990.

Alter, Robert. "The Jew Who Didn't Get Away: On the Possibility of an American Jewish Culture." In *The American Jewish Experience,* edited by Jonathan Sarna, 269–81. New York: Holmes and Meier, 1986.

American Jewish Year Book. Philadelphia: Jewish Publication Society, 1899–1998.

Anderson, Jean. *Durham County: A History of Durham County, North Carolina.* Durham: Duke University Press, 1990.

Ashby, Warren. *Frank Porter Graham: A Southern Liberal.* Winston-Salem, N.C.: Blair, 1980.

Ashkenazi, Elliott. *The Business of Jews in Louisiana, 1840–1875.* Tuscaloosa: University of Alabama Press, 1988.

Ayers, Edward. *The Promise of the New South: Life after Reconstruction.* New York: Oxford University Press, 1992.

Barnes, Mary Hollis. "Jacob Henry's Role in the Fight for Religious Freedom in North Carolina." March 19, 1984. Typescript. North Carolina State Archives, Raleigh, North Carolina.

Battle, Kemp. *History of the University of North Carolina.* Vol. 2. Raleigh: Edwards and Broughton, 1912.

Bauman, Mark. Introduction to *The Quiet Voices: Southern Rabbis and Black Civil Rights, 1880s to 1990s,* edited by Mark Bauman and Berkley Kalin. Tuscaloosa: University of Alabama Press, 1997.

———. *The Southerner as American: Jewish Style.* Cincinnati: American Jewish Archives, 1996.

Bauman, Mark, and Berkley Kalin, eds. *The Quiet Voices: Southern Rabbis and Black Civil Rights, 1880s to 1990s.* Tuscaloosa: University of Alabama Press, 1997.

Berger, Alan, ed. *Judaism in the Modern World.* New York: New York University Press, 1994.

Berger, Herbert. *Report of the Building Committee of Beth-El Congregation.* Durham: Beth-El, 1961.

Berman, Myron. *The Last of the Jews?* Lanham, Md.: University Press of America, 1998.

———. *Richmond's Jewry: Shabbat in Shockoe, 1769–1976.* Charlottesville: University Press of Virginia, 1979.

Bern, Ronald L. "Utilizing the Southern-Jewish Experience in Literature." In *Turn to the South: Essays on Southern Jewry,* edited by Nathan Kaganoff and Melvin Urofsky. Charlottesville: University Press of Virginia, 1977.

Bernstein, Edward. "Welcoming New Arrivals to Chapel Hill." In *They Fled Hitler's Germany and Found Refuge in North Carolina,* edited by Henry Landsberger and Christoph Schweitzer. Chapel Hill: Academic Affairs Library, 1996.

Berthoff, Rowland. "Southern Attitudes toward Immigration, 1865–1914." *Journal of Southern History* 17, no. 3 (August 1951).

Beth-El Synagogue. *Building Committee Report.* Durham: Beth-El Synagogue, 1961.

———. *Report of the Building Committee of the Beth-El Congregation upon the Completion of the Beth-El Synagogue.* Durham: Beth-El Synagogue, 1922.

Biale, David. "Jews and the Politics of American Identity." In *Insider/Outsider: American Jews and Multiculturalism,* edited by David Biale, Michael Galchinsky, and Susannah Heschel, 17–33. Berkeley and Los Angeles: University of California Press, 1998.

Biale, David, Michael Galchinsky, and Susannah Heschel. Introduction to *Insider/Outsider: American Jews and Multiculturalism,* edited by David Biale, Michael Galchinsky, and Susannah Heschel, 1–16. Berkeley and Los Angeles: University of California Press, 1998.

Blackwelder, Ruth. *The Age of Orange: Political and Intellectual Leadership in North Carolina, 1752–1861.* Charlotte: William Lostin, 1961.

Borden, Morton. *Jews, Turks, and Infidels.* Chapel Hill: University of North Carolina Press, 1984.

Boyarin, Jonathan, and Daniel Boyarin. *Jews and Other Differences: The New Jewish Cultural Studies.* Minneapolis: University of Minnesota Press, 1997.

Boyd, William. *The Story of Durham: City of the New South.* Durham: Duke University, 1925.

Bradstreet's Reports of the State of North Carolina. New York: Bradstreet, 1888.

Branscomb, Harvie. "A Note on Establishing Chairs of Jewish Studies." In *The Teaching of Judaica in American Universities,* edited by Leon Jick. Waltham, Mass.: Association for Jewish Studies, 1970.

Brettschneider, Marla, ed. *The Narrow Bridge: Jewish Views on Multiculturalism.* (New Brunswick, N.J.: Rutgers University Press, 1996).

Briggs, John. *An Italian Passage: Immigrants to Three American Cities.* New Haven: Yale University Press, 1978.

Brown, Bob, and Roy Pattishall. "The Trouble with Harry's." *Spectator,* Aug. 7, 1986.

Brown, Susan Rebecca. "As They See Themselves." In *A Coat of Many Colors,* edited by Abraham Lavender. Westport, Conn.: Greenwood, 1977.

Bureau of Labor Statistics, State of North Carolina, 1887. Raleigh: Josephus Daniels, 1887.

Cash, W. J. "Jehovah of the Tar Heels." *American Mercury* (July 1929).

———. *The Mind of the South.* New York: Vintage, 1941.

Chafe, William. *Never Stop Running: Allard Lowenstein and the Struggle to Save American Liberalism.* New York: Basic Books, 1993.

Chyet, Stanley F. "Reflections on Southern-Jewish Historiography." In *Turn to the South: Essays on Southern Jewry,* edited by Nathan Kaganoff and Melvin Urofsky, 13–20. Charlottesville: University Press of Virginia, 1977.

Cigar Maker's Official Journal (December 1895):3.

Cohen, Chester. *Shtetl Finder.* Los Angeles: Periday, 1980.

Cohen, Martin. "Structuring American Jewish History." *American Jewish Historical Quarterly* 57, no. 2 (December 1967):137–52.

Cohen, Stephen. *American Assimilation or Jewish Survival?* Bloomington: Indiana University Press, 1988.

County Population Trends, North Carolina, 1790–1960. Chapel Hill and Raleigh: Carolina Population Center, UNC, and Statistical Center, State of North Carolina, March 1969.

Crow, Jeffrey J., and Larry Tise. *Writing North Carolina History.* Chapel Hill: University of North Carolina Press, 1979.

Cummings, Richard. *The Pied Piper: Allard K. Lowenstein and the Liberal Dream.* New York: Grove Press, 1985.

Davidowicz, Lucy. "The Jewishness of the Jewish Labor Movement in the United States." In *The American Jewish Experience,* edited by Jonathan Sarna, 158–66. New York: Holmes and Meier, 1986.

———. "What Is the Use of Jewish History?" In *Insider/Outsider: American Jews and Multiculturalism,* edited by David Biale, Michael Galchinsky, and Susannah Heschel, 19–34. Berkeley and Los Angeles: University of California Press, 1998.

Dean, John. "Jewish Participation in Middle-Sized Communities." In *The Jews: Social Patterns of an American Group,* edited by Marshall Sklare. Glencoe, Ill.: Free Press, 1958.

Dickstein, Lore. "Southern Discomfort." *Tikkun* 5, no. 6 (Nov./Dec. 1990).

Diner, Hasia. *A Time for Gathering: The Second Migration, 1820–1880.* Baltimore: Johns Hopkins University Press, 1992.

Dinnerstein, Leonard. *Uneasy at Home: Antisemitism and the American Jewish Experience.* New York: Columbia University Press, 1987.

Dinnerstein, Leonard, and Mary Palsson. *Jews in the South.* Baton Rouge: Louisiana State University Press, 1973.

Directory of the Business and Citizens of Durham City for 1887. Raleigh: Levi Branson, 1887.

Directory of Greater Durham, 1902. Durham: Samuel Adams, 1902.

Duerr, Alvin. *Baird's Manual of American College Fraternities.* Menasha, Wis.: Collegiate Press, 1940.

Dula, W. C. *Durham and Her People.* Durham: Citizen's Press, 1951.

Durden, Arthur. *Joseph Fels and the Single Tax Movement.* Philadelphia: Temple University Press, 1971.

Durden, Robert F. *The Dukes of Durham, 1865–1929.* Durham: Duke University Press, 1975.

Durham Hadassah Yearbook. Durham: n.p., 1948–1951.

Edwards, Emma. *History of the North Carolina Association of Jewish Women.* Greensboro: NCAJW, n.d.

Ehle, John. *The Free Men.* New York: Harper and Row, 1965.

Eisenstein, Ira, and Judith Kaplan Eisenstein. *What Is Torah: A Cantata for Uni-Chorus and Piano.* New York: Jewish Reconstructionist Foundation, 1942.

Elovitz, Mark. *A Century of Jewish Life in Dixie: The Birmingham Experience.* Tuscaloosa: University of Alabama Press, 1974.

Epstein, Howard. *Jews in Small Towns: Legends and Legacies.* Santa Rosa, Calif.: Vision Books International, 1997.

Evans, Eli. *The Lonely Days Were Sundays: Reflections of a Jewish Southerner.* Jackson: University of Mississippi Press, 1993.

——. *The Provincials: A Personal History of the Jews in the South.* New York: Atheneum, 1976.

——. "Southern-Jewish History: Alive and Unfolding." In *Turn to the South: Essays on Southern Jewry,* edited by Nathan Kaganoff and Melvin Urofsky, 158–67. Charlottesville: University Press of Virginia, 1977.

Ezekiel, Herbert, and Gaston Lichtenstein. *The History of the Jews of Richmond from 1769 to 1917.* Richmond: H. T. Ezekiel, 1917.

Faber, Eli. *A Time for Planting: The First Migration, 1654–1820.* Baltimore: Johns Hopkins University Press, 1992.

Farber, Roberta Rosenberg, and Chaim Waxman. *Jews in America: A Contemporary Reader* (Hanover, N.H.: Brandeis University Press, 1999).

Fein, Issac. *The Making of an American Jewish Community: The History of Baltimore Jewry from 1773 to 1920.* Philadelphia: Jewish Publication Society, 1971.

Fein, Leonard. *Where Are We?* New York: Harper and Row, 1988.

Feingold, Henry. *Bearing Witness: How America and Its Jews Responded to the Holocaust.* Syracuse: Syracuse University Press, 1995.

———. *A Time for Searching: Entering the Mainstream, 1920–1945.* Baltimore: Johns Hopkins University Press, 1992.

Fishman, George. "Retirement Planning Survey." Durham-Chapel Hill Jewish Federation, 1991.

Fitz-Simons, Foster. *Bright Leaf.* New York: Rinehart, 1948.

Fleming, Walter. "Immigration to the Southern States." *Political Science Quarterly* 20 (1905).

Fox-Genovese, Elizabeth. "The Anxiety of History: The Southern Confrontation with Modernity." *Southern Culture* (Inaugural Issue, 1993).

Frank, Fedora Small. *Beginnings On Market Street: Nashville and her Jewry 1861–1901.* Nashville: Jewish Community of Nashville and Middle Tennessee, 1976.

Franklin, John Hope. "As for Our History. . . . " In *The Southerner as American,* edited by Charles Sellers. Chapel Hill: University of North Carolina Press, 1960.

Franklin, V. P., Nancy Grant, Harold Kletnick, and Genna McNeil, eds. *African-Americans and Jews in the Twentieth Century: Studies in Convergence and Conflict.* Columbia: University of Missouri Press, 1998.

Freedman, Molly. "Know Your House of Worship." In *Report of the Building Committee of the Beth-El Congregation.* Durham: Beth-El, 1961.

Freeze, Gary. "Roots, Barks, Berries, and Jews: The Herb Trade in Gilded-Age North Carolina." Paper presented at the Economic and Business Historical Society, April 28–30, 1994.

Friedman, John. "From the Rabbi." *Judea Reform Today* (August 1990).

Friedman, Murray. *What Went Wrong? The Creation and Collapse of the Black-Jewish Alliance.* New York: Free Press, 1995.

Galchinsky, Michael. "Scattered Seeds: A Dialogue of Diasporas." In *Insider/Outsider: American Jews and Multiculturalism,* edited by David Biale, Michael Galchinsky, and Susannah Heschel, 185–211. Berkeley and Los Angeles: University of California Press, 1998.

Gartner, Lloyd. "Jewish Migrants en Route from Europe to North America: Traditions and Realities." In *The Jews of North America,* edited by Moses Rischin. Detroit: Wayne State University Press, 1987.

Gee, Wilson. "The 'Drag' of Talent Out of the South." *Social Forces* 15 (March 1937):343–46.

Geisert, Harold Loran. "The Trend of the Interregional Migration of Talent: The Southeast, 1899–1936," *Social Forces* 18 (October 1939):41–47.

Gerber, David, ed. *Anti-Semitism in American History.* Urbana: University of Illinois Press, 1992.

Gerster, Patrick, and Nicholas Cords, eds. *Myth and Southern History.* Urbana: University of Illinois Press, 1989.

Glazer, Nathan. *American Judaism.* Chicago: University of Chicago Press, 1957.

———. "New Perspectives in American Jewish Sociology." In *American Jewish Yearbook, 1987,* edited by David Singer, 3–19. Philadelphia: Jewish Publication Society, 1987.

Glazier, Jack. *Dispersing the Ghetto: The Relocation of Jewish Immigrants across America.* Ithaca: Cornell University Press, 1998.

Goldberg, Arthur. "Report from the Campus." *American Jewish Times* (June 1944).

Goldberg, David. "An Historical Community Study of Wilmington Jewry, 1738–1925." Seminar paper for Dr. George Tindall, University of North Carolina at Chapel Hill, spring 1986.

———. "Samuel Mendelsohn." In *Dictionary of North Carolina Biography,* edited by William Powell. Vol. 5. Chapel Hill: University of North Carolina Press, 1991.

Goldberg, Herbert, and Horace Richter. "Hillel and the Jewish Fraternity." *American Jewish Times* (June 1938).

Golden, Harry. "The Golden Vertical Plan." *New South* 11, no. 11 (Nov. 1956).

———. "The Jewish People of North Carolina." *North Carolina Historical Review* 32 (April 1955):194–216.

———. *Jewish Roots in the Carolinas: A Pattern of American Philo-Semitism.* Greensboro: Deal Printing, 1955.

———. *Our Southern Landsman.* New York: G. P. Putnam, 1974.

Goldfield, David. *Promised Land: The South since 1945.* Arlington Heights, Ill.: Harlan Davidson, 1987.

Goldgar, Bernard. "Autobiographical Memoir." Unpublished typescript. Perkins Library, Duke University.

Goldscheider, Calvin. *Jewish Continuity and Change: Emerging Patterns in America.* Bloomington: Indiana University Press, 1986.

Goldscheider, Calvin, and Alan Zuckerman. *The Transformation of the Jews.* Chicago: Chicago University Press, 1984.

Goldstein, Sidney. "Profile of American Jewry: Insights from the 1990 National Jewish Population Survey." In *American Jewish Yearbook, 1992,* edited by David Singer and Ruth Selden, 77–176. Philadelphia: Jewish Publication Society, 1992.

Gordon, Milton. *Assimilation in American Life.* New York: Oxford University Press, 1964.

Goren, Arthur. "Jews." In *Harvard Encyclopedia of American Ethnic Groups,* edited by Stephan Thernstrom. Cambridge: Harvard University Press, 1980.

Grant, Daniel. *Alumni History of the University of North Carolina, 1795–1924.* Chapel Hill: University of North Carolina Press, 1924.

Grassl, Gary. "Joachim Gans of Prague: The First Jew in English America." *American Jewish History* 86, no. 2 (June 1998).

Green, Paul. *Paul Green's Wordbook: An Alphabet of Reminiscence.* Boone, N.C.: Appalachian Conservation, 1990.

Greenberg, Cheryl. "Pluralism and Its Discontents: The Case of Blacks and Jews." In *Insider/Outsider: American Jews and Multiculturalism,* edited by David Biale, Michael Galchinsky, and Susannah Heschel. Berkeley and Los Angeles: University of California Press, 1998.

——. "The Southern Jewish Community and the Struggle for Civil Rights." In *African-Americans and Jews in the Twentieth Century: Studies in Convergence and Conflict,* edited by V. P. Franklin, Nancy Grant, Harold Kletnick, and Genna McNeil. Columbia: University of Missouri Press, 1998.

Greenberg, Marilyn. *Through the Years: A Study of the Richmond Jewish Community.* Richmond: Richmond Jewish Community Council, 1955.

Greenberg, Mark. "Becoming Southern: The Jews of Savannah, Georgia, 1830–70." *American Jewish History* 86, no. 1 (March 1998):55–76.

Grossman, Lawrence. "Jewish Communal Affairs." *American Jewish Year Book, 1997.* New York: American Jewish Committee, 1997.

Gruber, Robin. "From Pine Street to Watts Street: An Oral History of the Jews of Durham, North Carolina." Oral History Seminar of Dr. Lawrence Goodwyn and Dr. Eric Meyers. Duke University Archives.

Gurock, Jeffrey. *American Jewish Orthodoxy in Historical Perspective.* Hoboken, N.J.: KTAV, 1996.

——. "The Orthodox Synagogue." In *The American Synagogue: A Sanctuary Transformed,* edited by Jack Wertheimer. New York: Cambridge University Press, 1987.

Hagedorn, Leah, ed. *Jews in the American South, 1860–1965.* Durham: Duke Office of Continuing Education and the Durham County Library, 1987.

Halkin, Hillel. "Henry Hurwitz." *Encyclopedia Judaica.* Vol. 8. New York: Macmillan, 1972.

Halperin, Edward. "Frank Porter Graham, Isaac Hall Manning, and the Jewish Quota at University of North Carolina Medical School." *North Carolina Historical Review* 67, no. 4 (October 1990):385–410.

Harris, Louis. "Kiddush at Chapel Hill." *American Jewish Times* (April 1940).

Harshav, Benjamin. *The Meaning of Yiddish.* Berkeley and Los Angeles: University of California Press, 1990.

Heilman, Samuel. "Judaism at the Turn of the Century." Judaism at the 21st Century Conference, University of North Carolina at Chapel Hill, Oct. 26, 1997.

Hero, Alfred O., Jr. *The Southerner and World Affairs.* Baton Rouge: Louisiana State University Press, 1965.

——. "Southern Jews." In *Jews in the South,* edited by Leonard Dinnerstein and Mary Palsson, 217–50. Baton Rouge: Louisiana State University Press, 1973.

——. "Southern Jews and Public Policy." In *Turn to the South: Essays on Southern Jewry*, edited by Nathan Kaganoff and Melvin Urofsky, 143–50. Charlottesville: University Press of Virginia, 1977.

Hershkowitz, Jackie. "Soviet Jews Flee Homeland for Chapel Hill Hospitality." *Daily Tar Heel*, Jan. 28, 1982.

Hertzberg, Arthur. *The Jews in America: Four Centuries of an Uneasy Encounter.* New York: Simon and Schuster, 1989.

Hertzberg, Steven. *Strangers within the Gate City: The Jews of Atlanta, 1845–1915.* Philadelphia: Jewish Publication Society, 1978.

Heschel, Susannah. "Jewish Studies as Counterhistory." In *Insider/Outsider: American Jews and Multiculturalism,* edited by David Biale, Michael Galchinsky, and Susannah Heschel, 101–15. Berkeley and Los Angeles: University of California Press, 1998.

Higham, John. *Send These to Me: Immigrants in Urban America.* Baltimore: Johns Hopkins University Press, 1984.

——. "Social Discrimination against Jews in America, 1830–1930." *American Jewish Historical Quarterly* 47 (September 1957):30–31.

——. *Strangers in the Land: Patterns of American Nativism, 1860–1925.* New Brunswick: Rutgers University Press, 1988.

"Hillel–Jewish War Board Cooperation." *American Jewish Times* (Oct. 1944).

Hill's Durham, North Carolina, Directory. Richmond: Hill Directory Co., 1903–20.

"The History Department Responds to Holocaust Ad." *Chronicle,* Nov. 13, 1992.

Hobson, Fred. "The Savage South: An Inquiry into the Origins, Endurance, and Presumed Demise of an Image." In *Myth and Southern History,* edited by Patrick Gerster and Nicholas Cords. Urbana: University of Illinois Press, 1989.

Holcomb, Brent. *Marriages of Orange County, 1779–1868.* Baltimore: Genealogical Publications, 1983.

Holland, Martha. "Sidney Rittenberg: An American Perspective of China." Master's thesis, University of North Carolina, 1986.

Hoover, Dwight. "Introduction: To be a Jew in Middletown." In *Middletown Jews: The Tenuous Survival of an American Jewish Community,* edited by Dan Rottenberg. Bloomington: Indiana University Press, 1997.

Horowitz, Sara. "The Paradox of Jewish Studies in the New Academy." In *Insider/Outsider: American Jews and Multiculturalism,* edited by David Biale, Michael Galchinsky, and Susannah Heschel, 116–30. Berkeley and Los Angeles: University of California Press, 1998.

Howe, Irving. *World of Our Fathers.* New York: Harcourt Brace Jovanovich, 1976.

Howe, Irving, and Kenneth Libo. *How We Lived: A Documentary History of Immigrant Jews in America, 1880–1930.* New York: Richard Marek, 1979.

Huggins, Leonard. *Anecdotes.* Chapel Hill: n.p., 1981.

Huhner, Leon. "The Jews of North Carolina prior to 1800." *Publications of the American Jewish Historical Society* 29 (1925):137–48.

———. "The Struggle for Religious Liberty in North Carolina, with Special Reference to the Jews." Reprint from *Publications of the American Jewish Historical Society.* November 16, 1907. North Carolina Collection, University of North Carolina at Chapel Hill.

"The Individual and the Communal Jew: Getting It All Together." June 22–24, 1973. Typescript. Judea Reform Congregation Fifth Shabbaton.

Ingalls, Robert. *Urban Vigilantes in the New South: Tampa, 1882–1936.* Knoxville: University of Tennessee Press, 1988.

Jacobson, I. H. "Hillel and the Jewish Student." *North Carolina Association of Jewish Women Yearbook, 1937–1938.* Greensboro: NCAJW, 1938.

Janiewski, Dolores E. "From Field to Factory: Race, Class Sex, and the Woman Worker in Durham, 1880–1940." Ph.D. diss., Duke University, 1979.

———. *Sisterhood Denied: Race, Gender, and Class in a New South Community.* Philadelphia: Temple University Press, 1985.

"Jewish Communities in the South: Durham, N.C." *American Jewish Times* (August 1944).

Jick, Leon. *The Americanization of the Synagogue.* Hanover, N.H.: Brandeis University Press, 1992.

———. "The Reform Synagogue." In *The American Synagogue: A Sanctuary Transformed,* edited by Jack Wertheimer. New York: Cambridge University Press, 1987.

———, ed. *The Teaching of Judaica in American Universities.* Waltham, Mass.: Association for Jewish Studies, 1970.

Johnson, Charles, ed. *Statistical Atlas of Southern Counties.* Chapel Hill: University of North Carolina Press, 1941.

Johnson, Guion Griffis. *Ante-Bellum North Carolina: A Social History.* Chapel Hill: University of North Carolina Press, 1937.

Johnson, Paul. *A History of the Jews.* New York: Harper and Row, 1987.

Johnston, Hugh B., Jr. "Oettinger's Dependable Store." 1976. Unpublished typescript. Wilson County Library, Wilson, North Carolina.

Jones, Southgate. "The Handrolled Cigarette Industry." January 22, 1945. Unpublished typescript. Duke University Manuscript Department.

Joseph, Samuel. "Jewish Immigration to the United States: From 1881 to 1910." *Studies in History, Economics and Public Law,* vol. 54. New York: Columbia University Press, 1914.

Kaganoff, Nathan, and Melvin Urofsky, eds. *Turn to the South: Essays on Southern Jewry.* Charlottesville: University Press of Virginia, 1977.

Kaplan, Alice. *French Lessons.* Chicago: University of Chicago Press, 1993.

Kaplan, Benjamin. *The Eternal Stranger: A Study of Jewish Life in the Small Community.* New York: Bookman, 1957.

Karp, Abraham J. *Haven and Home: A History of the Jews in America.* New York: Schocken Books, 1985.

———. *The Jewish Experience in America.* New York: KTAV Publishers, 1969.

———. "Overview: The Synagogue in America—A Historical Typology." In *The American Synagogue: A Sanctuary Transformed,* edited by Jack Wertheimer. New York: Cambridge University Press, 1987.

Karres, Matthew. "Alfred Mordecai." In *Dictionary of North Carolina Biography,* edited by William Powell. Vol. 4. Chapel Hill: University of North Carolina Press, 1991.

Kaufman, David. *Shul with a Pool: The "Synagogue-Center" in American Jewish History.* Hanover, N.H.: Brandeis University Press, 1999.

Kenzer, Robert Charles. *Kinship and Neighborhood in a Southern Community: Orange County, North Carolina, 1849–1881.* Knoxville: University of Tennessee Press, 1987.

———. *Portrait of a Southern Community, 1849–1881.* Ann Arbor, Mich.: University Microfilms International, 1982.

Kessel, David. "Integrate or Isolate." *Jewish Tarheel* (spring 1992).

Killian, Lewis. *White Southerners.* New York: Random House, 1985.

Knight, Douglas. *Street of Dreams.* Durham: Duke University Press, 1989.

Korn, Bertram. *American Jewry and the Civil War.* Philadelphia: Jewish Publication Society, 1951.

———. "Factors Bearing upon the Survival of Judaism in the Ante-Bellum Period." *Publications of the American Jewish Historical Society* 53 (1964):341–51.

Kosmin, Barry, Sidney Goldstein, Joseph Waksberg, Nava Lerer, Ariella Keysar, and Jeffrey Scheckner. *Highlights of the CJF 1990 National Jewish Population Survey.* New York: Council of Jewish Federations, 1991.

Kosmin, Barry, Paul Ritterband, and Jeffrey Scheckner. "Jewish Population in the United States." In *American Jewish Year Book, 1987,* edited by David Singer. Philadelphia: Jewish Publication Society, 1987.

Kostyu, Joel. *Durham: A Pictorial History.* Norfolk, Va.: Rischback and Edenton, 1978.

Landsberger, Henry, and Christoph Schweitzer, eds. *They Fled Hitler's Germany and Found Refuge in North Carolina.* Chapel Hill: Academic Affairs Library, 1996.

Lang, Berel. "Jewish Culture." *American Jewish Year Book, 1998.* New York: American Jewish Committee, 1998.

Lansburgh, Richard. "Remembering 'Pa.'" *Generations* (fall 1999).

LaPointe, Patricia. "The Prophetic Voice: Rabbi James A. Wax." In *The Quiet*

Voices: Southern Rabbis and Black Civil Rights, 1880s to 1990s, edited by Mark Bauman and Berkley Kalin. Tuscaloosa: University of Alabama Press, 1997.

Laqueur, Walter. *A History of Zionism.* New York: Holt, Rinehart, and Winston, 1972.

Lavender, Abraham. "Jewish Values in the Southern Milieu." In *Turn to the South: Essays on Southern Jewry,* edited by Nathan Kaganoff and Melvin Urofsky, 124–34. Charlottesville: University Press of Virginia, 1977.

———. "Shalom—with a Southern Accent: An Examination of Jews in the South." In *A Coat of Many Colors: Jewish Subcommunities in the United States,* edited by Abraham Lavender. Westport, Conn.: Greenwood Press, 1977.

———, ed. *A Coat of Many Colors: Jewish Subcommunities in the United States.* Westport, Conn.: Greenwood Press, 1977.

Lederhendler, Eli. "Historical Reflections on the Problem of American Jewish Culture." *Jewish Social Studies* 5, nos. 1 & 2 (fall 1998/winter 1999).

Lefler, Hugh, and Albert Newsome. *The History of a Southern State: North Carolina.* Chapel Hill: University of North Carolina Press, 1973.

Lefler, Hugh, and Paul Wagner, eds. *Orange County: 1752–1952.* Chapel Hill: Orange Print Shop, 1953.

LeMaster, Carolyn. *A Corner of the Tapestry: A History of the Jewish Experience in Arkansas, 1820s to 1990s.* Fayetteville: University of Arkansas Press, 1994.

Lestschinsky, Jacob. "The Economic Development of the Jews in the United States." In *The Jewish People: Past and Present.* Vol. 1. New York: Jewish Encyclopedia Handbooks, 1946.

Levine, Joseph. "Hillel in North Carolina." *American Jewish Times Outlook* (Dec. 1962).

Levitt, William. "The Occupational Distribution of the Jews in North Carolina." Master's thesis, University of North Carolina, 1938.

Lewis, Selma. *A Biblical People in the Bible Belt: The Jewish Community of Memphis, Tennessee, 1840s–1960s.* Macon, Ga.: Mercer University Press, 1998.

Leyburn, James. *The Way We Lived, Durham, 1900–1920.* Elliston, Va.: Northcross, 1989.

Liebman, Charles. "When Prayer Becomes Leisure." *Forward,* June 11, 1999.

Lipset, Seymour Martin, and Everett Ladd, Jr. "Jewish Academics in the United States: Their Achievements, Culture, and Politics." In *American Jewish Yearbook, 1971,* 89–128. Philadelphia: Jewish Publication Society, 1971.

Litwack, Charlotte. "The Jewish Community of Raleigh." In *The Heritage of Wake County, North Carolina, 1983,* edited by Lynne Belvin and Harriette Riggs. Winston-Salem: Hunter, 1983.

———. *Recollections: Conversations about the House of Jacob.* Raleigh: N.p., 1976.

Lowenstein, Steven. "The Shifting Boundary between Eastern and Western Jewry." *Jewish Social Studies* 4, no. 1 (fall 1997):60–78.

Lowi, Theodore. "Southern Jews: The Two Communities." In *A Coat of Many Colors: Jewish Subcommunities in the United States,* edited by Abraham Lavender. Westport, Conn.: Greenwood Press, 1977.

Luebke, Paul. *Tar Heel Politics: Myths and Realities.* Chapel Hill: University of North Carolina Press, 1990.

Mangum's Directory of Durham and Suburbs, 1897–1898. Durham: Educator Co., 1897.

Marcus, Jacob Rader. "The American Colonial Jew: A Study in Acculturation." In *The American Jewish Experience,* edited by Jonathan Sarna, 6–17. New York: Holmes and Meier, 1986.

———. *The American Jewish Woman, 1654–1980.* Cincinnati: American Jewish Archives, 1981.

———. *Early American Jewry: The Jews of Pennsylvania and the South, 1655–1790.* Vol. 2. Philadelphia: Jewish Publication Society, 1953.

———. "Light on Early Connecticut Jewry." In *Studies in American Jewish History.* Cincinnati: Hebrew Union College, 1969.

———. *Memoirs of American Jews.* Philadelphia: Jewish Publication Society, 1955.

———. *To Count a People: American Jewish Population Data, 1585–1984.* Lanham, Md.: University Press of America, 1990.

———, ed. *An Index to Scientific Articles on American Jewish History.* Cincinnati: American Jewish Archives, 1971.

McLaurin, Melton. *The Knights of Labor in the South.* Westport, Conn.: Greenwood Press, 1978.

Mebane, Mary. *Mary.* New York: Fawcett, 1981.

Medding, Peter, Gary Tobin, Sylvia Barack Fishman, and Mordechai Rimor. "Jewish Identity in Conversionary and Mixed Marriages." In *American Jewish Yearbook, 1992,* edited by David Singer and Ruth Seldan. Philadelphia: Jewish Publication Society, 1992.

Meyer, Michael. "German-Jewish Identity in Nineteenth-Century America." In *The American Jewish Experience,* edited by Jonathan Sarna. New York: Holmes and Meier, 1986.

———. *Response to Modernity: A History of the Reform Movement in Judaism.* New York: Oxford University Press, 1988.

Meyer, Sigmund. "Story of Durham Jewry." 1951. Unpublished typescript. Perkins Library, Duke University.

Miller, Randall. "The Development of the Modern Urban South: An Historical Overview." In *Shades of the Sunbelt: Essays on Ethnicity, Race and the Urban South,* edited by Randall Miller and George Pozzetta, 1–20. Westport, Conn.: Greenwood Press, 1988.

Moore, Deborah Dash. "Jewish Migration into the Sunbelt." In *Shades of the Sunbelt: Essays on Ethnicity, Race and the Urban South,* edited by Randall Miller and George Pozzetta, 41–52. Westport, Conn.: Greenwood Press, 1988.

Morawska, Ewa. *Insecure Prosperity: Small-town Jews in Industrial America, 1890–1940*. Princeton: Princeton University Press, 1996.

Moriel, Lior. "Two-tiered Temple." *Spectator,* Sept. 24, 1987.

Mostov, Stephen G. "Dun and Bradstreet Reports as a Source of Jewish Economic History: Cincinnati, 1840–1875." *American Jewish History* 72, no. 3 (March 1983):333–53.

Murray, Pauli. *Song in a Weary Throat.* New York: Harper and Row, 1987.

Nathans, Sydney, ed. *The Quest for Progress: The Way We Lived in North Carolina, 1870–1920.* Chapel Hill: University of North Carolina Press, 1983.

Newman, Samuel. "Frank Graham." *American Jewish Times* (October 1955).

———. "Frank Porter Graham: An Appreciation." *American Jewish Times Outlook* (May 1972).

North Carolina Association of Jewish Women Yearbook. Greensboro: NCAJW, 1934–1938.

North Carolina Reports. Vol. 181. Raleigh: Mitchell Printing Company, 1921.

O'Neill, Patrick. "Climb for the Summit." *Chapel Hill Newspaper,* June 7, 1992.

"An Open Letter to the *Chronicle.*" *Chronicle,* Nov. 15, 1991.

Patrick, Ben. *The Front Line: Materials for a Study of Leadership in College and After.* Durham: Duke University, 1942.

Paul, Hiram. *History of the Town of Durham, North Carolina.* Raleigh: Edwards and Broughton, 1884.

Paul Green's Wordbook: An Alphabet of Reminiscence. Vol. 1. Boone, N.C.: Appalachian Conservation, 1990.

Penslar, Derek. "The Origins of Jewish Political Economy." *Jewish Social Studies* 3, no. 3 (spring-summer 1997):26–60.

Perlman, Samuel. "Hillel at the University of North Carolina." *American Jewish Times* (Sept. 1949).

Perlmann, Joel. "Beyond New York: The Occupations of the Russian Jewish Immigrants and Providence, R.I., and Other Small Jewish Communities, 1900–1915." *American Jewish History* 72 (March 1983):369–94.

Pilch, Judith. "Education." *Encyclopedia Judaica.* Vol. 6. New York: Macmillan, 1972.

Platt, Virginia B. "Tar Staves and New England Rum: The Trade of Aaron Lopez of Newport, Rhode Island, with Colonial North Carolina." *North Carolina Historical Review* 48, no. 1 (January 1971).

Pleasants, Julian. "The Senatorial Career of Robert Rice Reynolds, 1933–1945." Ph.D. diss., University of North Carolina, 1971.

Polner, Murray. "Smalltown Rabbis: Is Anyone Listening Out There?" *National Jewish Monthly* 92, no. 1 (Sept. 1977).

Powell, William. *North Carolina through Four Centuries.* Chapel Hill: University of North Carolina Press, 1989.

——, ed. *Dictionary of North Carolina Biography*. Chapel Hill: University of North Carolina Press, 1991.

"President's Report." *North Carolina Association of Jewish Women Yearbook, 1935–1936*. Greensboro: NCAJW, 1936.

Progress: Journal of the Cigar Makers Progressive Union, 1884, 1885.

Rabinowitz, Howard. *The First New South, 1865–1920*. Arlington Heights, Ill.: Arlington Davidson, 1992.

——. *Race, Ethnicity, and Urbanization: Selected Essays*. Columbia: University of Missouri Press, 1994.

Raphael, Marc Lee. *Profiles in American Judaism: The Reform, Conservative, Orthodox, and Reconstructionist Traditions in Historical Perspective*. San Francisco: Harper and Row, 1984.

——. "The Thought of Rabbi Abram Simon, 1897–1938." *American Jewish Archives* 49, nos. 1 & 2 (1997).

Reed, John Shelton. "Ethnicity in the South: Observations on the Acculturation of Southern Jews." In *Turn to the South: Essays on Southern Jewry*, edited by Nathan Kaganoff and Melvin Urofsky, 135–42. Charlottesville: University Press of Virginia, 1977.

——. "Instant Grits and Plastic-Wrapped Crackers: Southern Culture and Regional Development." In *The American South: Portrait of a Culture*, edited by Louis D. Rubin, Jr. Baton Rouge: Louisiana State University Press, 1980.

——. *One South: An Ethnic Approach to Regional Culture*. Baton Rouge: Louisiana State University Press, 1982.

——. *My Tears Spoiled My Aim and Other Reflections on Southern Culture*. Columbia: University of Missouri Press, 1993.

——. "Shalom Y'All: Jewish Southerners." In *One South: An Ethnic Approach to Regional Culture*. Baton Rouge: Louisiana State University Press, 1982.

——. "South Polls: Where is the South?" *Southern Cultures* 5, no. 2 (summer 1999): 116–18.

——. "Whistlin' Dixie." *Spectator*, April 12, 1992.

Report of the Building Committee of the Beth-El Congregation upon the Completion of the Beth-El Synagogue. Durham: Beth-El Congregation, 1921.

Research Triangle Data Book: Raleigh-Durham-Chapel Hill, Metropolitan Statistical Area. Durham: Greater Durham Chamber of Commerce, n.d.

"The Resurgence of TEP at Chapel Hill." *American Jewish Times* (July 1947).

Reznikoff, Charles, and Uriah Engelman. *The Jews of Charleston*. Philadelphia: Jewish Publication Society, 1950.

Rischin, Moses, ed. *The Jews in North America*. Detroit: Wayne State University Press, 1987.

Rischin, Moses, and John Livingston, eds. *Jews of the American West*. Detroit: Wayne State University Press, 1991.

Ritterband, Paul, and Harold Wechsler. *Jewish Learning in American Universities: The First Century*. Bloomington: University of Indiana Press, 1994.

Robert, Joseph. *The Story of Tobacco in America.* Chapel Hill: University of North Carolina Press, 1967.

Roberts, Claudia, Diane Lea, and Robert Leary. *The Durham Architectural and Historical Inventory.* Durham: City of Durham, 1982.

Rogoff, Leonard. "Synagogue and Jewish Church: A Congregational History of North Carolina." *Southern Jewish History* 1 (1998):43–82.

Rose, Peter I. *Strangers in Their Midst: Small-town Jews and their Neighbors.* Merrick, N.Y.: Richwood Publishing, 1977.

Rosenwaike, Ira. "An Estimate and Analysis of the Jewish Population of the United States in 1790." *Publications of the American Jewish Historical Society* 50, no. 1 (Sept. 1960).

Rosenzweig, Efraim. "Dedication of New Building: Judea Reform Congregation, Durham." *American Jewish Times Outlook* (July 1971).

———. "Hillel at Chapel Hill." *American Jewish Times Outlook* (March 1955).

Rottenberg, Dan, ed. *Middletown Jews: The Tenuous Survival of an American Jewish Community.* Bloomington: University of Indiana Press, 1997.

Rountree, Moses. *Strangers in the Land: The Story of Jacob Weil's Tribe.* Philadelphia: Dorrance, 1969.

Rubin, Leonard. "On a Southern Campus: The Jewish Boy's Problem." *American Jewish Times* (April 1938).

Rubin, Louis D., Jr. *A Gallery of Southerners.* Baton Rouge: Louisiana State University Press, 1982.

———. *The Golden Weather.* New York: Atheneum, 1961.

Rypins, Frederick. "North Carolina." In *Universal Jewish Encyclopedia.* New York: Universal Jewish Encyclopedia, 1928.

Sachar, Howard M. *A History of the Jews in America.* New York: Knopf, 1992.

Salber, Eva. *The Mind Is Not the Heart: Recollections of a Woman Physician.* Durham: Duke University Press, 1989.

Sanders, Arthrell. "Former NCCU Prof Recounts Odyssey." *North Carolina Central University Newsletter* 1 (fall 1984).

Sanders, Richard. *Shores of Refuge: A Hundred Years of Jewish Emigration.* New York: Holt, 1988.

Sarna, Jonathan. "The Impact of the American Revolution on American Jews." In *The American Jewish Experience,* edited by Jonathan Sarna. New York: Holmes and Meier, 1986.

———, ed. *The American Jewish Experience.* New York: Holmes and Meier, 1986.

Scales, Junius, and Richard Nickson. *Cause at Heart.* Athens: University of Georgia Press, 1987.

Schappes, Morris, ed. *A Documentary History of the Jews in the United States, 1654–1875.* New York: Citadel, 1950.

Schewel, Steve. "Biscuits and Blintzes: Growing Up Jewish in the Fatback South." *Independent,* Oct. 7, 1992.

Schoenfeld, Eugen. "Problems and Potentials." In *A Coat of Many Colors: Jew-*

ish Subcommunities in the United States, edited by Abraham Lavender. Westport, Conn.: Greenwood, 1977.

Schwartz, David. "U.S. Senate Gains a Controversial Voice." *Carolina Alumni Review* 80, no. 2 (summer 1991).

Sedgwick, Eve Kosofsky. *The Epistemology of the Closet.* Berkeley and Los Angeles: University of California Press, 1990.

———. *Fat Art, Thin Art.* Durham: Duke University Press, 1994.

Seeman, Ernest. *American Gold.* New York: Dial Press, 1978.

Selengut, Charles. *Jewish Identity in the Postmodern Age.* St. Paul: Paragon House, 1999.

Sellers, Charles. *The Southerner as American.* Chapel Hill: University of North Carolina Press, 1960.

Shankman, Arnold. "Friend or Foe? Southern Blacks View the Jew, 1880–1935." In *Turn to the South: Essays on Southern Jewry,* edited by Nathan Kaganoff and Melvin Urofsky. Charlottesville: University Press of Virginia, 1977.

Shapiro, Edward. *A Time for Healing: American Jewry since World War II.* Baltimore: Johns Hopkins University Press, 1992.

Sharot, Steve. *Judaism: A Sociology.* New York: Holmes and Meier, 1976.

Silberman, Charles. *A Certain People: American Jews and Their Lives Today.* New York: Summit, 1985.

Simpson, Bland. "His Way from the Start." *Carolina Alumni Review* 83, no. 2 (summer 1994).

Sklare, Marshall L. *Conservative Judaism: An American Religious Movement.* Glencoe, Ill.: Free Press, 1955.

———. *Jewish Identity on the Suburban Frontier.* Chicago: University of Chicago Press, 1979.

———. *The Jews: Social Patterns of an American Group.* Glencoe, Ill.: Free Press, 1958.

———, ed. *American Jews: A Reader.* New York: Behrman House, 1983.

Snider, William. *Light on the Hill: A History of the University of North Carolina at Chapel Hill.* Chapel Hill: University of North Carolina Press, 1992.

Sollors, Werner. *The Invention of Ethnicity.* New York: Oxford University Press, 1989.

Solomon, Tandy. "Being Jewish at Duke: The Sizeable Minority." *Chronicle,* Feb. 16, 1983.

Sorin, Gerald. *A Time for Building: The Third Migration, 1880–1920.* Baltimore: Johns Hopkins University Press, 1992.

Speizman, Morris. *The Jews of Charlotte, North Carolina: A Chronicle with Commentary and Conjectures.* Charlotte: McNally and Loftin, 1978.

Spiro, Jack D. "Rabbi in the South: A Personal View." In *Turn to the South: Essays on Southern Jewry,* edited by Nathan Kaganoff and Melvin Urofsky, 41–43. Charlottesville: University Press of Virginia, 1977.

Steinberg, Stephen. *The Ethnic Myth: Race, Ethnicity and Class in America.* Boston: Beacon, 1981.

Steinreich, Otto. "For the Record." *North Carolina Medical Journal* 8, no. 53 (Aug. 1992).

Stern, Malcolm. "The Function of Genealogy in American Jewish History." In *Essays in American Jewish History to Commemorate the Tenth Anniversary of the Founding of the American Jewish Archives under the Direction of Jacob Rader Marcus.* Cincinnati: American Jewish Archives, 1958.

———. "The Role of the Rabbi in the South." In *Turn to the South: Essays on Southern Jewry,* edited by Nathan Kaganoff and Melvin Urofsky, 21–32. Charlottesville: University Press of Virginia, 1977.

Synnott, Marcia. "Anti-Semitism and American Universities: Did Quotas Follow the Jews?" In *Anti-Semitism in American History,* edited by David Gerber. Urbana: University of Illinois Press, 1992.

Tilley, Nannie May. *The Bright Tobacco Industry: 1860–1924.* Chapel Hill: University of North Carolina Press, 1948.

Tindall, George. *The Emergence of the New South, 1913–1945.* Baton Rouge: Louisiana State University Press, 1967.

———. *The Ethnic Southerners.* Baton Rouge: Louisiana State University Press, 1976.

Toll, William. *The Making of an Ethnic Middle Class: Portland Jewry over Four Generations.* Albany: SUNY Press, 1982.

Tuchman, Louis. "A Traditional Rabbi's View: The New Kesuba." *American Jewish Times Outlook* (April 1955).

Turner and Company's Durham Directory for the Years 1889 and 1890. Danville, Va.: E. F. Turner and Co., 1889.

Urofsky, Melvin. *Commonwealth and Community: The Jewish Experience in Virginia.* Richmond, Va.: Virginia Historical Society, 1997.

Viener, Saul. "Edward Calisch." *Encyclopedia Judaica.* Vol. 5. New York: Macmillan, 1971.

Walker-Lipson, Carolyn. *"Shalom Y'All: The Folklore and Culture of Southern Jews."* Ann Arbor: University Microfilms International, 1986.

Weare, Walter. *Black Business in the New South: A History of the North Carolina Mutual Life Insurance Company.* Urbana: University of Illinois Press, 1973.

Webb, Mena. *Jule Carr: General without an Army.* Chapel Hill: University of North Carolina Press, 1987.

Weiner, Deborah. "The Jews of Kingston: Life in a Multicultural Boomtown." *Southern Jewish History* 2 (1999):1–24.

Weinstein, Maurice, ed. *Zebulon Vance and "The Scattered Nation."* Charlotte: Wildacres Press, 1995.

Weissbach, Lee Shai. "Decline in an Age of Expansion: Disappearing Jewish Communities in the Era of Mass Migration." *American Jewish Archives* 49, nos. 1 & 2 (1997):39–61.

———. "East European Immigrants and the Image of Jews in the Small-Town South." *American Jewish History* 85, no. 3 (September 1997):231–62.

———. "Stability and Mobility in the Small Jewish Community: Examples from Kentucky History." *American Jewish History* 79, no. 3 (spring 1990):355–75.

Weitz, Martin, ed. *Biblio . . . Temple of Israel, Wilmington*. Wilmington: Temple of Israel, 1976.

Wenger, Beth. "Jewish Women Volunteerism: Beyond the Myth of Enablers." *American Jewish History* 79, no. 1 (autumn 1989):16–36.

Wertheimer, Jack. "The Conservative Synagogue." In *The American Synagogue: A Sanctuary Transformed,* edited by Jack Wertheimer. New York: Cambridge University Press, 1987.

———. *The American Synagogue: A Sanctuary Transformed*. New York: Cambridge University Press, 1987.

We Save Them or They Die: American Jewish Relief Committee, North Carolina Conference. Raleigh: Mitchell, 1922.

Wexler, Bonnie. "Seek a Real Cure." *Carolina Alumni Review* 86, no. 5 (Sept./ Oct. 1997).

Whitfield, Stephen. "The Braided Identity of Southern Jewry." *American Jewish History* 77, no. 3 (March 1988):363–87.

———. "Commercial Passions: The Southern Jew as Businessman." *American Jewish History* 71, no. 3 (March 1982):342–57.

———. *In Search of American Jewish Culture*. Hanover, N.H.: Brandeis University Press, 1999.

———. "Jews and Other Southerners: Counterpoint and Paradox." In *Turn to the South: Essays on Southern Jewry,* edited by Nathan Kaganoff and Melvin Urofsky, 76–104. Charlottesville: University Press of Virginia, 1977.

Wilson, Charles R., and William Ferris. *Encyclopedia of Southern Culture*. Chapel Hill: University of North Carolina Press, 1989.

Winerip, Michael. "Hot Colleges." *New York Times Magazine,* Nov. 18, 1984.

Wolf, Simon. *The American Jew as Patriot, Soldier, and Citizen*. Philadelphia: Brentano's 1895.

Wolfe, Jerome A. "The Future of Jews in the South." In *A Coat of Many Colors: Jewish Subcommunities in the United States,* edited by Abraham Lavender. Westport, Conn.: Greenwood Press, 1977.

Woocher, Jonathan. *Sacred Survival: The Civil Religion of American Jews*. Bloomington: Indiana University Press, 1986.

Woodward, C. Vann. *The Burden of Southern History*. Baton Rouge: Louisiana State University Press, 1960.

———. *Origins of the New South, 1877–1913*. Baton Rouge: Louisiana State University Press, 1971.

Wyman, David. *The Abandonment of the Jews*. New York: Pantheon, 1986.

Wynne, Francis. *Durham, North Carolina, Marriage Register, 1881–1906.* Baton Rouge: Oracle Press, 1983.

Yackety Yack. Vol. 18. Chapel Hill: Union of the University of North Carolina, 1928.

Yardley, Jonathan. "An Interview with Jonathan Yardley." *Carolina Alumni Review* 7, no. 82 (summer 1989).

Yellowitz, Irwin. "Jewish Immigrants and the American Labor Movement, 1900–1920." *American Jewish History* 71, no. 2 (December 1981):188–217.

Yeoman, Barry. "Landlord Hall of Shame." *Independent,* May 30, 1991.

———. "Strangers in a Strange Land." *Independent,* March 10–23, 1988.

Yerushalmi, Yosef Hayim. *Zakhor: Jewish History and Jewish Memory.* Seattle: University of Washington Press, 1996.

Zola, Gary. "Southern Rabbis and the Founding of the First National Association of Rabbis." *American Jewish History* 85, no. 4 (December 1997): 353–72.

Collections
Duke, J. B. Papers. Rare Book, Manuscript, and Special Collections Library, Duke University.

Duke Archives. Duke University.

Dun, R. G. & Co. Collection. Baker Library, Harvard University Graduate School of Business.

Evans Family. Papers. Rare Book, Manuscript, and Special Collections Library, Duke University.

Everett, R. O. Diary. Duke University Manuscript Department, Duke University.

Goldberg, Mattie Lehman. Papers. Rare Book, Manuscript, and Special Collections Library, Duke University.

Graham, Frank Porter. Papers. Southern Historical Collection, Wilson Library, University of North Carolina at Chapel Hill.

Manuscript Collection. North Carolina State Archives, Raleigh.

North Carolina Collection. Wilson Library, University of North Carolina at Chapel Hill.

North Carolina Room. Durham County Library, Durham.

Powderly, Terence. Papers. New York Public Library.

Southern Historical Collection. Wilson Library, University of North Carolina at Chapel Hill.

Weil, Miriam. Papers. North Carolina State Archives, Raleigh.

Newspapers
Carolina Times, 1937–
Chapel Hill Herald (daily), 1991–

Chapel Hillian (weekly), 1891
Chapel Hill Ledger (weekly), 1878–1880
Chapel Hill News (weekly), 1893–1917
Chapel Hill Newspaper (thrice weekly), 1970–
Chapel Hill Weekly, 1934–1970
Chapel Hill Weekly Gazette, 1857–1858
Columbian Repository (weekly), 1836
Daily Tar Heel, 1929–
Duke Chronicle, 1933–
Durham County Republican (weekly), 1884
Durham Daily Dispatch (daily), 1880
Durham Daily Globe, 1885–1894
Durham Daily Sun, 1899, 1904
Durham Globe (weekly), 1895–1896
Durham Herald (weekly), 1876
Durham Israelite, 1940
Durham Morning Herald (daily), 1896–
Durham Record (daily), 1898
Durham Recorder (weekly) 1879–1903, (semiweekly) 1905–1911
Durham Reporter (daily), 1885
Durham Sun, 1890–1900, 1943
Durham Tobacco Plant (daily), 1888–1889
Durham Tobacco Plant (weekly), 1872–1885, 1886–1888
Durham Truth (monthly), 1884
Durham Weekly Globe, 1889–1892
Harbinger (weekly), 1833–1834
Hillsborough Recorder, 1820–1911
Independent (weekly), 1983–
Orange County Independent (weekly), 1894
Orange County Observer, 1881–1916
Public Appeal (weekly), 1957, 1961–1963
Raleigh News and Observer (daily), 1944, 1986, 1987, 1991, 1992
Saturday Night Durham (weekly), 1893
St. Louis Dispatch, 1948
Tar Heel (weekly), 1893–1929

Public Records
Alien Naturalization and Citizenship Records, 1882–1904. Durham County, North Carolina. North Carolina State Archives, Raleigh.
Durham County, North Carolina, Enumerated District Lists. Twelfth Census of the United States, 1900. North Carolina State Archives, Raleigh.

———. Thirteenth Census of the United States, 1910. North Carolina State Archives, Raleigh.

———. Fourteenth Census of the United States, 1920. North Carolina State Archives, Raleigh.

———. Fifteenth Census of the United States, 1930. North Carolina State Archives, Raleigh.

Durham County Probate Records. Durham County Courthouse.

Durham County Real Estate Deeds. Durham County Courthouse.

Durham County Tax Rolls, 1874–1925. North Carolina State Archives, Raleigh.

Durham County Will and Testament Books. Durham County Courthouse.

Nativities of the Foreign-born Population. 57th Congress, 2d sess., 1902–1903. No. 12 Series, Doc. No. 15, Pt. 12, House Documents Vol. 42, 4390.

Naturalization Petition and Record, 1908–1922. Durham County Superior Court.

"Statistics on Population." 1900 Census Lists. North Carolina State Archives, Raleigh.

U.S. Bureau of the Census. *Population of States and Counties of the United States: 1790 to 1990,* edited by Richard Forstall. Washington, D.C., 1996.

———. *Sixteenth Census of the United States: 1940; Population, North Carolina.* Volume 2, part 5: *Characteristics of the Population.* Washington, D.C., 1943.

Interviews

Alexander, Irving. Telephone interview with author, November 3, 1988.

Anderson, Jean. Telephone interview with author, October 30, 1988.

Bane, Henry. Interview with Beth-El Confirmation Class, April 1, n.y.

———. Interview with Robin Gruber, November 19, 1985.

———. Interview with author, November 1986.

Berger, Herbert. Telephone interview with author, April 12, 1994.

Bergman, Harry. Interview with Violet Tartell, n.d.

Bernson, Ethel Mae. Interview with Robin Gruber, February 21, 1986.

Bernson, Ethel Mae, and Hazel Gladstein Wishnov. Interview with author, April 27, 1992.

Beth-El Luncheon Discussion (George and Ricky Lewin, Anna and Sigmund Meyer, May Segal, and Pat Silver). Interview with Rabbi Steven Sager and Beth-El Class, May 14, 1981.

Beth-El Presidents (Henry Bane, E. J. Evans, Gilbert Katz, Norman Letstein, Peter Ornstein, Joel Schwartz, Melvin Shimm, and Lewis Siegel. Interview with Sheldon Hanft, September 1, 1986.

Blum, Dorothy. Interview with Lori Posner, May 23, 1986.

Brady, Lehman. Interview with author, February 23, 1987.

———. Telephone interview with author, August 12, 1988.

Brandt, Yetta Sawilowsky. Interview with Robin Gruber. February 2, 1986.

Brauer, Hilde. Telephone interview with author, November 9, 1987.

Cohen, Marc, and Jo Cohen. Telephone interview with author, September 20, 1988.

Cohen, Sarah. Interview with Judith Siegel, January 1, 1987.

Dworsky, Leon. Interview with author, January 5, 1987.

Dworsky, Leon, and Phyllis Dworsky. Interview with Rabbi Steven Sager and Beth-El Confirmation Class, March 25, n.y.

Eisenberg, Ezra. Telephone interview with author, November 10, 1988.

Eliel, Ernest. Interview with author, December 11, 1986.

Elinoff, Joe, and Susan Elinoff. Telephone interview with author, September 21, 1988.

Evans, Eli. Interview with Robin Gruber, March 9, 1986.

Evans, Emanuel J. Interview with Rabbi Steven Sager and Beth-El Confirmation Class, March 25, n.y.

Evans, Sara. Interview with Rabbi Steven Sager and Beth-El Confirmation Class, March 25, n.y.

Everett, Robinson O. Interview with author, August 30, 1992.

Ezra, Rosemary. Telephone interview with author, April 15, 1994.

Fein, Ruth. Telephone interview with author, April 10, 1994.

Fink, Sam, and Jeanette Fink. Interview with Deborah Wahl, May 4, 1986.

Freedman, David. Telephone interview with author, November 10, 1988.

Freedman, Molly. Interview with Naomi Kirshner, April 1, n.y.

Friedman, John, and Efraim Rosenzweig. Interview with Sheldon Hanft and author, July 31, 1986.

Ginsberg, Brenda. Interview with author, September 3, 1992.

Gladstein, Fanny. Interview with Robin Gruber, February 5, 1986.

Gladstein, Melvin. Telephone interview with author, November 16, 1988.

Gladstein, Melvin, and Grace Gladstein. Interview with Lynne Grossman, n.d.

Glustrom, Simon. Telephone interview with author, April 12, 1994.

Goodman, Sadie, and Pat Silver. Interview with Robin Gruber, January 29, 1986.

———. Interview with author, September 1986.

———. Interview with Elyse Lazarus and Lisa Lefstein, April 1, n.y.

Gordon, Arthur. Telephone interview with author, April 10, 1994.

Greenberg, Ruth. Interview with Deborah Wahl, May 26, 1986.

Gross, Sam, and Hudi Gross. Interview with Naomi Klein, April 26, 30, 1986.

Grossman, Lynne Gladstein. Telephone interview with author, November 9, 1988.

Grunwald, Ron. Telephone interview with author, September 23, 1988.

Halperin, Edward. Telephone interview with author, November 3, 1988.

Handler, Lucille. Interview with author, September 25, 1986.

Heillig, William. Interview with author, February 9, 1989.

Hockfield, Joe. Interview with Ellie Myer, May 10, 1986.

————. Telephone interview with author, November 9, 1988.

————. Interview with Robin Gruber, n.d.

Jaffe, David. Telephone interview with author, September 10, 1987.

Jewish Experience in Durham and Chapel Hill: Conversations with Long-Time Residents (Henry Bane, Leon Dworsky, E. J. Evans, and Hazel Wishnov). Moderated by Joel Schwartz, September 27, 1987.

Judea Reform Presidents (Melvin Rashkis, Zora Rashkis, Judith Ruderman, Max Samfield, and Joel Smith). Interview with Sheldon Hanft and author, July 31, 1986.

Julian, Milton. Interview with Judith Marks, May 27, 1986.

Kaplan, Alfreda, and Jacob Kaplan. Interview with Judith Ruderman, April 23, 1986.

Katz, Gilbert. Interview with Robin Gruber, January 25, 1986.

————. Interview with author, September 23, 1986.

————. Interview with Rabbi Steven Sager and Beth-El Confirmation Class, n.d.

Keyserling, Tom. Telephone interview with author, n.d.

Lakin, Martin. Telephone interview with author, November 3, 1988.

Lefkowitz, Arna. Telephone interview with author, November 3, 1988.

Levin, Charlotte. Interview with Lori Posner, April 10, 1986.

Levitt, William. Telephone interview with author, November 10, 1988.

Lewin, George, and Ricky Rosenstein Lewin. Interview with Robin Gruber, January 29, 1986.

Lieberman, Max. Interview with David Zeiger and Nathan Siegel, n.d.

London, Edith. Interview with Ruth Blum, May 22, 1986.

Macklin, Harry. Interview with Herbert Posner, July 14, 1986.

Margolis, Jacob. Telephone interview with author, December 30, 1986.

Margolis, Mark, and Norman Margolis. Interview with author, April 30, 1992.

Margolis, Norman. Telephone interview with author, November 9, 1988.

Margolis, Sam. Interview with Robin Gruber, November 15, 1985.

————. Telephone interview with author, November 14, 1992.

————. Interview with Robert Klein and Karen Feldman, March 25, n.y.

Markham, Charlie. Interview with Robin Gruber, January 23, 1986.

Marks, Arthur. Interview with author, April 16, 1992.

Meyer, Sigmund. Interview with author, September 25, 1986.

————. Interview with Rabbi Steven Sager and Beth-El Confirmation Class, n.d.

Meyers, Eric. Interview with author, January 5, 1987.

Mintzer, Melanie. Telephone interview with author, n.d.

Morrison, Pearl. Interview with Ruth Greenberg, n.d.

Mowshowitz, Israel. Self-interview, March 1987.

Nathan, Marx. Telephone interview with author, November 2, 1988.

Ornoff, May. Interview with Mollie Fridovich, April 1, 1986.

Ornstein, Miriam. Telephone interview with author, n.d.

Patterson, Daniel. Interview with author, April 13, 1992.

Pinsky, Mark. Interview with author, May 17, 1987.

Rapoport, Amnon. Interview with author, April 18, 1987.

Rapport, Leonard. Telephone interview with author, September 9, 1987.

Rashkis, Melvin. Telephone interview with author, November 9, 1988.

Ray, Lois. Telephone interview with author, November 11, 1988.

Robbins, Jack. Telephone interview with author, November 10, 1988.

Rosenzweig, Efraim. Interview with Irene Zipper, June 22, 1986.

Sager, Steven. Interview with Sheldon Hanft and author, n.d.

Schultz, Robert. Telephone interview with author, November 10, 1988.

Schultzberg, Alvin. Telephone interview with author, November 14, 1994.

Schwartz, David. Telephone interview with author, November 8, 1988.

Schwartz, Myrna. Telephone interview with author, November 7, 1988.

Segal, May Ornoff. Interview with Molly Fridovich, April 1, 1986.

Shain, Art. Interview with Myrna Schwartz, n.d.

Shimm, Cynia, and Melvin Shimm. Telephone interview with author, January 24, 1988.

Shimm, Melvin. Interview with Robin Gruber, January 29, 1986.

———. Interview with author, December 15, 1986.

Siegel, Gladys. Telephone interview with author, November 9, 1988.

Simand, Irene. Telephone interview with author, January 8, 1988.

Slifkin, Miriam. Telephone interview with author, September 20, 1988.

Stadiem, Abe. Interview with author, April 8, 1992.

Stahl, Gerald, and Helen Stahl. Interview with Violet Tartell, n.d.

Stein, Manny. Telephone interview with author, September 20, 1988.

Stern, Kate Perlman. Interview with Melanie Roskin, n.d.

Straley, Joseph. Telephone interview with author, September 19, 1988.

Strauss, Albrecht. Telephone interview with author, n.d.

Swartz, Max. Interview with Nina Shubert and Robert Klein, April 1, 1979.

Swartz, Max, and Sara Swartz. Interview with Robin Gruber, December 4, 1985.

Tuchman, Louis. Telephone interview with author, April 12, 1994.

Wall, Monroe. Telephone interview with author, October 1, 1992.

Wishnov, Hazel Gladstein. Interview with Robin Gruber, February 12, 1986.

———. Telephone interview with author, November 9, 1987.

Yarborough, Dwight. Telephone interview with author, April 10, 1994.

Yoffie, Eric. Interview with author, July 21, 1986.

Zuckerman, Jacob. Telephone interview with author, November 10, 1987.

Letters

Daniels, Hannah Teichman. Letters to author, December 27, 1987; March 18, 1988.

Everett, Robinson O. Letter to author, December 19, 1991.

Goldgar, Harry. Letter to author, May 25, 1988.

Jaffe, David. Letter to author, September 29, 1987.

Kaufman, Gus. Letter to author, February 14, 1988.

Klein, Min. Letters to author, November 21, 1987; January 8, 1988.

Lovenstein, Meno. Letter to author, October 18, 1986.

Lurie, Morton. Letter to author, December 8, 1999.

Malis, Ruth Simand. Letter to author, n.d.

Seligson, Paul. Letter to author, January 8, 1988.

Shimm, Melvin, and Cynia Shimm. Letter to Sheldon Hanft, June 10, 1986.

Siegel, Judith. Letter to author, February 15, 1987.

Sinauer, Hannah. Letter to author, October 28, 1986.

Summerfield, Nathan. Letters to author, April 27, April 30, May 12, September 26, October 9, October 21, 1987; August 17, 1988.

Index

Abelkop, Edith, 236
Abelkopf, Harris, 61, 111, 140
Abram, Adam, 273
Abroo, Rev. Jacob, 8
Adland, Peter, 266, 302
Adler, Richard, 161, 261
African-Americans, 29, 173–76, 199,
    241, 246, 271–73, 301; business, 71–
    72; Jewish relations, 55–56, 64, 80,
    94–97, 139, 173, 191–92, 223, 257–
    58, 271–73, 312; Klan, 132; labor,
    39, 42–43, 45; politics, 219, 220–
    22, 223–31, 274
Aleph Zadik Aleph, 184, 188, 314
Alexander, Irving, 212, 293
Algranti, S., 154
Alpha Epsilon Phi, 163, 255
Alter, Robert, 257, 310
America Firsters, 150, 169
American Council for Judaism, 197
American identity, 1–2, 10, 47, 99–
    100, 116–19, 120–21, 130, 134–35,
    138, 143–44, 178, 187, 202–3, 206–
    7, 209, 217–18, 310, 314, 316
American Israel Political Action Com-
    mittee (AIPAC), 276, 282
American Jewish Committee, 116,
    165, 170
American Jewish Conference, 194–95
American Professors for Peace in the
    Middle East, 283

American Tobacco Company, 63, 72,
    153, 154, 247
Anti-Defamation League, 116, 120,
    228, 290
Anti-Semitism, 10, 11, 13, 15–16,
    18, 25–26, 85–86, 88–90; 92–93,
    130–33, 146–47, 148, 152–53, 161,
    172, 189, 225, 269, 277; in Russia,
    55–56, 132; in Germany, 11, 150;
    in employment, 153; in public
    schools, 88; in politics, 99; in aca-
    demia, 159–61, 191, 196, 213–17;
    Southern exemption, 168–70, 172.
    See also Ku Klux Klan; Philo-
    Semitism
Apsler, Alfred, 194, 199
Apsler, Mrs. Alfred, 195
Apter, Morris, 201
Aptheker, Herbert, 217
Arab immigrants, 315
Arbeiter Ring (Workmen's Circle), 52
Ariel, Yaakov, 256
Aronson, Rabbi Jacob, 142
Arson, 90–91
Asheville, 32, 67, 113, 136, 169, 178
Asian immigrants, 246, 257, 259,
    275, 315
Assimilation. See American identity;
    Jewish-American identity; social
    integration; Southern identity;
    Southern-Jewish identity

About the Author

Leonard Rogoff is Research Historian at the Rosenzweig Museum and Jewish Heritage Foundation of North Carolina and Editor of the *Rambler,* the newsletter of the Southern Jewish Historical Society.